Neighbours, Major Powers and Indian Foreign Policy

Neighbours, Major Powers and Indian Foreign Policy

Aneek Chatterjee

Orient BlackSwan

NEIGHBOURS, MAJOR POWERS AND INDIAN FOREIGN POLICY

ORIENT BLACKSWAN PRIVATE LIMITED

Registered Office
3-6-752 Himayatnagar, Hyderabad 500 029 (Telangana), INDIA
e-mail: centraloffice@orientblackswan.com

Other Offices
Bengaluru, Bhopal, Chennai, Guwahati, Hyderabad, Jaipur, Kolkata, Lucknow, Mumbai, New Delhi, Noida, Patna, Vijayawada

First published 2017

ISBN 978-81-934157-5-7

025671
07062017

Typeset in
Adobe Garamond Pro 11.5/13.5
by Shine Graphics, Delhi 110 094

Printed in India at
B. B. Press, Noida

Published by
Orient Blackswan Private Limited
3-6-752, Himayatnagar,
Hyderabad 500 029,
Telangana, INDIA
e-mail: info@orientblackswan.com

Contents

Tables and Box

Tables

Box

Abbreviations

ADD	Annual Defence Dialogue
ADF	ASEAN Development Fund
ADMM	ASEAN Defence Ministers Meeting
ADSL	Asymmetric Digital Subscriber Line
AIEPG	ASEAN–India Eminent Persons' Group
AL	Awami League
ARF	ASEAN Regional Forum
ASA	Air Services Agreement
ASLV	Augmented Satellite Launch Vehicle
ATM	Anti-Tank Missile
AWC	Army War College
BAIC	Beijing Automotive Industry Corporation
BASIC	Brazil, South Africa, India, China
BBIN	Bangladesh, Bhutan, India and Nepal
BGMEA	Bangladesh Garment Manufacturers and Exporters Association
BIMSTEC	Bay of Bengal Initiative for Multi-Sectoral Technical and Economic Cooperation
BIPA	Bilateral Investment Promotion Agreement
BIPPA	Bilateral Investment Protection and Promotion Agreement
BIS	Bureau of Indian Standards
BIT	Bilateral Investment Treaty
BJP	Bharatiya Janata Party
BLF	Business Leaders' Forum
BNP	Bangladesh Nationalist Party
BoB	Bank of Bhutan
BoP	Balance of Payment
BPDB	Bangladesh Power Development Board
BRICS	Brazil, Russia, India, China and South Africa
BRO	Border Roads Organisation
BSF	Border Security Force
BSTI	Bangladesh Standards Testing Institute
BTIA	Broad-based Trade and Investment Agreement

CA	Constituent Assembly
CAPD	Cooperation Agreement on Partnership and Development
CBI	Central Bureau of Investigation
CBM	Confidence Building Measure
CCA	Cultural Cooperation Agreement
CCP	Chinese Communist Party
CECA	Comprehensive Economic Cooperation Agreement
CELT	Centres for English Language Training
CEP	Cultural Exchange Programme
CEPA	Comprehensive Economic Partnership Agreement
CGS	Chief of General Staff
CHT	Chittagong Hill Tracts
CII	Confederation of Indian Industry
CLMV	Cambodia, Lao PDR, Myanmar and Viet Nam
CNA	Civil Nuclear Agreement
CND	Civil Nuclear Deal
COAS	Chief of the Army Staff
CPN-UML	Communist Party of Nepal-United Marxist Leninist
CPRs	Committee of Representatives
CTBT	Comprehensive Test Ban Treaty
CWC	Central Water Commission
DAE	Department of Atomic Energy
DCA	Defence Cooperation Agreement
DCGS	Deputy Chief of General Staff
DECC	Department of Energy and Climate Change
DFC	Dedicated Freight Corridor
DFTP	Duty Free Tariff Preference
DMIC	Delhi Mumbai Industrial Corridor
DPRs	Detailed Project Reports
DPT	Druk Phuensum Tshogpa
DSS	Diplomatic Security Service
DTAA	Double Taxation Avoidance Agreement
DTTI	Defence Technology and Trade Initiative
EAS	East Asian Summit
ECSC	European Coal and Steel Community
EDI	Electronic Data Interchange
EEAS	European External Action Service
EEC	European Economic Community
EEPC	Engineering Export Promotion Council

EFD	Economic and Financial Dialogue
EPA	Economic Partnership Agreement
FBI	Federal Bureau of Investigation
FDI	Foreign Direct Investment
FGFA	Fifth Generation Fighter Aircraft
FIUs	Financial Intelligence Units
FMCT	Fissile Material Cut-off Treaty
FOC	Foreign Office Consultation
FSMTC	Federal Service for Military Technical Cooperation
FTA	Free Trade Agreement
FY	Financial Year
FYP	Five-Year Plan
GAIL	Gas Authority of India Ltd
GDP	Gross Domestic Product
GNH	Gross National Happiness
GoI	Government of India
GSI	Geological Survey of India
HAL	Hindustan Aeronautics Limited
HEP	Hydroelectric Project
HLMC	High Level Monitoring Committee
HLTG	High Level Trade Group
HRD	Human Resource Development
HuJI	Harkat-ul Jihadi-al-Islami
HuM	Harkat-ul-Mujahideen
IAEA	International Atomic Energy Agency
IAF	Indian Air Force
IBF	India–Bhutan Foundation
ICCR	Indian Council for Cultural Relations
ICP	Integrated Check Post
ICT	Information and Communications Technology
ICWA	Indian Council for World Affairs
IDPs	Internally Displaced Persons
IEWON	Indian Ex-Servicemen Welfare Organisation in Nepal
IGCs	Inter-Governmental Commissions
ILAA	Independent Liberation Army of Assam
IMBL	International Maritime Boundary Line
IMCEITS	India–Myanmar Centre for Enhancement of IT Skills
IMTRAT	Indian Military Training Team
IOC	Indian Oil Corporation

IPKF	Indian Peace Keeping Force
IPPA	Investment Promotion and Protection Agreement
IPR	Intellectual Property Rights
IRFTI	India–Russia Forum on Trade and Investment
IRIGC	India-Russia Inter-Governmental Commission
IRIGC-MTC	India–Russia Inter-Governmental Commission on Military Technical Cooperation
ISI	Inter-Service Intelligence
ISLKI	India Sri Lanka Knowledge Initiative
ISRO	Indian Space Research Organisation
IT	Information Technology
ITEC	Indian Technical and Economic Cooperation
ITER	International Thermonuclear Experimental Reactor
IUFP	India–UK Financial Partnership
IWTT	Inland Water Transit and Trade
JAP	Joint Action Plan
JAXA	Japan Aerospace Exploration Agency
JBIC	Japan Bank of International Cooperation
JBWG	Joint Boundary Working Group
JC	Joint Commission
JCWR	Joint Committee on Water Resources
JD	Joint Declaration
JEC	Joint Economic Commission
JEG	Joint Economic Group
JGCOs	Joint Group of Customs Officials
JMCWR	Joint Ministerial Level Commission on Water Resources
JS	Joint Statement
JSG	Joint Study Group
JSTC	Joint Standing Technical Committee
JTC	Joint Trade Committee
JTE	Joint Training Exercise
JTECO	Joint Trade and Economic Committee
JTF	Joint Task Force
JVS	Joint Vision Statement
JWG	Joint Working Group
KKNPP	Kudankulam Nuclear Power Plant
KLO	Kamtapuri Liberation Organization
LAC	Line of Actual Control
LCS	Land Custom Station
LEP	Look East Policy

LeT	Lashkar-e-Taiba
LNG	Liquefied Natural Gas
LTTE	Liberation Tigers of the Tamil Eelam
MCF	Myanmar Computer Federation
MDA	Maritime Domain Awareness
METI	Ministry of Economy, Trade and Industry
MFN	Most Favoured Nation
MFTB	Myanmar Foreign Trade Bank
MGC	Mekong–Ganga Cooperation
MIBC	Myanmar–India Business Club
MIEDC	Myanmar–India Entrepreneurship Development Centre
MLAT	Mutual Legal Assistance Treaty
MHRD	Ministry of Human Resource Development
MoU	Memorandum of Understanding
MTA	Multirole Transport Aircraft
MTCR	Missile Technology Control Regime
MULTA	Muslim Liberation Tigers of Assam
MVA	Motor Vehicles Agreement
NAM	Non-Aligned Movement
NATO	North Atlantic Treaty Organization
NDC	National Defence College
NDFB	National Democratic Front of Bodos
NHPC	National Hydro Power Corporation
NLD	National League for Democracy
NPC	National People's Congress
NPR	Non-Proliferation Regime
NPT	Non-Proliferation Treaty
NSA	National Security Advisor
NSG	Nuclear Suppliers Group
NSS	National Security Strategy
NSSP	Next Steps in Strategic Partnership
NTPC	National Thermal Power Corporation
NWFZ	Nuclear Weapons Free Zone
ODA	Official Development Assistance
OVL	ONGC Videsh Ltd
PCC	Programme of Cultural Cooperation
PDP	People's Democratic Party
PGCIL	Power Grid Corporation of India Limited
PLA	People's Liberation Army

PMC	Post-Ministerial Conference
PoA	Plan of Action
PPP	Public-Private Partnership
PPP	Purchasing-Power Parity
PRC	People's Republic of China
PSLV	Polar Satellite Launch Vehicle
PULF	People's United Liberation Front
R&D	Research and Development
RGoB	Royal Government of Bhutan
RSA	Rail Services Agreement
RTIA	Regional Trade and Investment Area
SAARC	South Asian Association for Regional Cooperation
SAFTA	South Asian Free Trade Association
SAMs	Surface-to-Air Missiles
SCO	Shanghai Cooperation Organization
SCS	South China Sea
SDF	Self Defense Force
SDPs	Small Development Projects
SEATO	South East Asian Treaty Organization
SED	Strategic Economic Dialogue
SEWA	Self-Employed Women's Association
SLFP	Sri Lanka Freedom Party
SLORC	State Law and Order Restoration Council
SPA	Strategic Partnership Agreement
SPDC	State Peace and Development Council
SPIEF	St. Petersburg International Economic Forum
SPS	Sanitary and Phytosanitary
TAC	Treaty of Amity and Cooperation
TBT	Technical Barriers to Trade
TCIL	Telecommunications Consultants India Ltd
TCS	Technical Cooperation Scheme
TFC	Treaty of Friendship and Cooperation
TGA	Trade in Goods Agreement
TIGs	Trade in Goods
TULF	Tamil United Liberation Front
UAE	United Arab Emirates
UBI	United Bank of India
UCPN-Maoist	United Communist Party of Nepal-Maoist
UKCISA	UK Council for International Student Affairs

UKIERI	UK–India Education and Research Initiative
UKTI	UK Trade and Investment
ULFA	United Liberation Front of Assam
UMFCCI	Union of Myanmar Federation of Chambers of Commerce and Industry
UML	United Marxist Leninist (Party)
UNDP	United Nations Development Program
UNGA	United Nations General Assembly
UNHRC	UN Human Rights Council
UNP	United National Party
UPA	United Progressive Alliance
VS	Vision Statement
WTO	World Trade Organization

Acknowledgements

The present volume has many architects. Three persons associated with Orient BlackSwan have contributed immensely towards the preparation of this volume. Roopa Sharma first contacted me for this project a couple of years back. Due to heavy workload at that time, I accepted the offer a bit hesitantly. Roopa, however, stayed in touch. Her perseverance pushed me to write and complete the chapters. I take this opportunity to express my sincere thanks to her. Nilanjana Majumdar, whom I missed as a student in Kolkata's Presidency College by a year or two, worked really hard for this project. Nilanjana's meticulous copy-editing made the volume look what it is now. She set deadlines, and strictly followed those deadlines herself. And the author could not escape, but follow, happily. This volume would not have come out on time without her efforts. I offer my heartiest thanks to Nilanjana. Mimi Choudhury also took active interest in the project. I convey my thanks to her too.

Two other women back home my wife Sarbani and daughter Prerna always encouraged me for this project. They offered valuable comments on the manuscript, helped with computer work and ungrudgingly allowed me to remain glued to my study table, month after month. This book owes much to their silent support.

My thanks are also due to all the anonymous reviewers of the manuscript for their valuable suggestions which helped me improve the quality of the manuscript. People associated with typesetting, printing and other work for this volume are its real pillars. I express my gratitude to them. My students, who raised interesting issues in the class and outside, always made me rethink and shape my views. I dedicate this volume to all my students across the borders.

INTRODUCTION

After liberalisation in 1991, the Indian economy opened up to global markets, and gradually reaped benefits from this liberty. With sustained GDP (gross domestic product) growth rate, and marginal but increasing share of global trade, India, slowly but steadily, became a contender for the global economic cake. Today, after nearly three decades of economic liberalisation, the nation is poised to become a major economic force in the world. The tectonic shift in India's economic performance has attracted the attention of the world, especially its neighbours and major powers. From a sluggish growth rate, the Indian economy has changed full gear and achieved a spectacular ride, so much so that an American presidential election candidate made references to the Indian economy's upward journey while criticising low growth rates for the US economy.[1] With China, India has already emerged as the new economic powerhouse from Asia. However, this bright picture continues to offer some grey patches. Some of these (grey patches) relate to domestic socio-economic issues like poverty, healthcare, education, problems of governance and federalism. Some more refer to external issues affecting India, like energy supply, cross-border terrorism, ecological problems, including climate change, and recognition as a *de jure* nuclear power among others. But the most important question in the broader and illuminating picture of an 'Emerging India' relates to India's foreign policy. Has Indian foreign policy emerged sufficiently to shoulder the label of an economic powerhouse? In simple words, is Indian foreign policy equipped enough to sustain the glory of a Rising India?

Like the Indian economy, India's foreign policy appeared to be devoid of strength for a considerable period of time since independence. For instance, India lacked any policy for its neighbours, or a comprehensive security policy even after two decades from independence in 1947. This issue will be taken up for further analysis in the following pages with a view to know the evolutionary history of Indian foreign policy. But at this juncture, it seems pertinent to focus on the terms 'Foreign Policy' and 'Foreign Relations', and how these terms have been used in this work. Foreign policy refers to the theoretical realm of a nation's external policies, whereas foreign relations comprise the application side. Foreign Relations may be described as fruits of a

---

[1] Donald Trump, the then Republican Party nominee for the US Presidential Election in 2016, contrasted the growth of the US economy with that of India's in a debate with Hillary Clinton, the Democratic Party nominee, in Las Vegas, USA on 19 October 2016. He said, 'India was growing at 8 per cent, while our growth rate was 1 per cent as per last reports'. See in this connection, *The Wall Street Journal*, 20 October 2016, available at http://blogs.wsj.com/indiarealtime/2016/10/20/what-trump-said-about-growth-in-india-at-the-u-s-presidential-debate/, accessed on 7 December 2016.

large tree, termed as Foreign Policy. As a healthy tree produces better fruits, foreign relations, if backed by strong policy planning, are more prone to success. If foreign policy contains elements of national interest, foreign relations are efforts at securing those national interests. The two are inseparable, in practice, and in cerebral exercises, because a country's foreign policy also gets inputs from interactions among the states and other actors, and influenced by these interactions. Therefore, in foreign policy matters, theory and practice are deeply embedded. Thus, the proposition which stated that Indian foreign policy lacked strength in the past could also be understood to mean that India's foreign relations too suffered from inadequacy during that period. The terms 'Foreign Policy' and 'Foreign Relations' have not been strictly segregated and compartmentalised in this volume; they have been used interchangeably, keeping in mind their thinly separated, yet overlapping identities.

The current volume, in examining India's foreign policy vis-à-vis its neighbours and major powers, trudged along the path of history to arrive at the present. In other words, Indian foreign policy has been analysed, in every chapter of this work, in continuity, from past to the present. Conclusions and recommendations offered in each chapter are products of research in which the past and the present are intermingled to look at the future. From the foreign policy of Jawaharlal Nehru, India's first prime minister to the foreign policy of Narendra Modi, this volume also offers an evolutionary picture of Indian foreign policy while scrutinising India's relations with its neighbours and major powers. In all the chapters of this book, three major areas of foreign policy—political, economic and security—are examined, besides the cultural segment, in analysing India's relations with the neighbours and the major powers.

Jawaharlal Nehru, the first prime minister of India (1947–64) laid the theoretical foundation of his country's foreign policy. Nehru made two significant contributions to the intellectual foundation of Indian foreign policy: (i) autonomy in foreign policymaking; and, (ii) non-alignment. For a very long period, especially during the Cold War times, non-alignment remained the backbone of Indian foreign policy. After the Second World War, when international politics got entangled in superpower rivalry, Nehru's India had little options: join either of the power blocs, or stay away. Nehru preferred to stay away, not from international politics, but from the power blocs. His independent way of thinking, his desire to pursue autonomous foreign policy for India, propelled him to search for an alternative which he found in the policies of non-alignment. Although non-alignment aroused controversies within India and outside, there was little doubt that India could not have opted for a better policy after independence. However, with non-alignment as the guiding principle, Nehru's India failed to develop good relations with either of the superpowers, who suspected India's non-committed policy. Ironically for Nehru, the policy of non-alignment led him to the world stage, but the same policy distanced him and India from the superpowers, which mattered in international politics during the Cold War period.

Nehru did not have any well-defined regional policy either, which he should have developed because India had several hostile neighbours in Pakistan, China and Burma (now Myanmar) during his time. Nepal was also not a happy front for Nehru as the country gradually leaned towards China. As one expert on India's foreign policy noted, 'India's regional policy under Nehru . . . was ill-conceived and ill-defined. In fact, it was hardly conceived and hardly defined.

If anything, it was purely reactive. . . .'[2] He could not formulate a security policy for India also, a dire necessity after independence with hostile neighbours around, as he was convinced that India would not face any hostility.[3] But the ground reality was different. Immediately after independence, Nehru faced a war against Pakistan, but did not go for a comprehensive security policy or framework for India. Nehru had to pay for that in 1962 when an ill-equipped Indian military fought against China, and was convincingly defeated. Nehru's initial love for China went completely wrong, as it was not met with equal reciprocity. Moreover, the defeat in the 1962 War shattered Nehru's plans for a leading role for India in international affairs. India's relations with the two superpowers (the US and Soviet Union), China, Pakistan, and the other neighbours, as well as with the industrially developed west European countries were far from satisfactory during Nehru's tenure.

The credit for building a strong military for India as a back-up force for Indian foreign policy goes to Indira Gandhi who served two tenures as prime minister (1966–77 and 1980–84). Although the process of military build-up actually began during the premiership of Lal Bahadur Shastri (1964–66), it gained momentum and proper shape during Indira Gandhi's first tenure. Indira established India as a regional power with a quick and convincing victory against Pakistan in the 1971 War fought over the future of East Pakistan, now Bangladesh. Although she could never win the trust of the Americans, Indira Gandhi established very strong security, political and economic relations with the Soviet Union by signing the 'Treaty of Friendship' with the socialist country in 1971 prior to the war, which proved beneficial for India during the war and thereafter. The 1971 Treaty with the Soviet Union helped develop a security strategy for India to protect her national interests. Indira Gandhi's success in India's international relations were not negligible: (i) the 1971 Friendship Treaty with the Soviet Union; (ii) convincing victory against Pakistan in the 1971 War that established India as a regional power; (iii) the 1972 'Simla Agreement' with Pakistan, and (iv) India's first nuclear tests in Pokhran in 1974 which matched India's growing military status as a regional power. Whether the 1974 nuclear tests actually helped India in her international relations were never beyond controversy; the tests nevertheless propelled India's ambitions further for a regional power status. Therefore, Indira Gandhi was rewarded with more achievements in her foreign policy than her father.

Morarji Desai who replaced Indira in 1977 was the first Indian prime minister to swim against the tide with a view to establish cordial relations with the US, another superpower. The first reciprocal visits of heads of governments of India and the US in a single calendar year took place in 1978 when American President Jimmy Carter visited India in January, and Indian prime minister Desai paid a return visit to the US in June. The impact of these top-level visits on bilateral relations could be felt as India–US relations looked up after these reciprocal visits. The American Government sanctioned US $60 million to India under the USAID programme in August 1978

[2] Harish Kapur, *India's Foreign Policy: 1947–92—Shadows and Substance* (New Delhi: Sage Publications), 1994, p. 93.

[3] D. K. Palit, *War in the High Himalayas: India in Crisis* (New Delhi: Lancer), 1991, p. 20; also Kapur, *India's Foreign Policy*, n. 2, p. 22.

after the visits took place.[4] As one expert on India–US relations noted, 'In 1979, even though Tarapur remained a chronic problem, India–US relations were, nonetheless, better than they had been for more than a decade'.[5] The Desai Government (1977–79), in its short span, could also continue good relations with the Soviet Union. As the first non-Congress government in India, it was able to maintain good relations with neighbours too.

The Rajiv Gandhi Government (1984–89) had a mixed bag as far as India's international relations were concerned. While the youngest and smart Indian prime minister was able to impress Presidents Reagan of the US and Gorbachev of the Soviet Union and improve relations with the two superpowers, some of his missions next door proved futile. The failure of the Indian Peace Keeping Force (IPKF) in Sri Lanka, and escalated tensions with Pakistan and Bangladesh made Rajiv's neighbourhood policies look hollow. However, Rajiv's China visit in 1988 proved a major success as normalcy limped back to bilateral relations after the visit.[6] The most significant result of this visit was the decision to set up Joint Working Groups (JWGs) to study border problems. It was decided that the JWG would meet every year, alternately in New Delhi and Beijing. The two countries are still continuing with the JWG mechanism, initiated by Rajiv Gandhi in 1988, to solve different bilateral problems. During Rajiv's visit, the two countries also concluded agreements on cooperation in civil aviation, science and technology and cultural exchange programmes. Rajiv's visit in 1988 initiated a fresh process of top-level official visits between the two countries which is continuing till date.

The V. P. Singh and the Chandra Sekhar Governments (1989–90) could not make much impact on India's foreign relations due to more pressing domestic compulsions. However, the Narasimha Rao Government (1991–96), which initiated the 'open door' liberal economic policies, attracted the attention of the industrially developed West, probably for the first time since India's independence. For instance, India's large market potential attracted American business interests.[7] Major American corporations launched in early 1994, an 'India Interest Group'. This group included companies like AT&T, Coca-Cola, Ford, General Electric, IBM, Morgan Stanley, Raytheon and Unisys. The formation of this group was encouraged by the continuing Indian economic reforms and the increasing willingness of American business to pursue commercial activities in India. The US Commerce Department also designated India, in 1993, as one of the 10 major emerging markets in the world. The impact of economic factors on foreign policy, in a positive sense, could be realised for the first time in India during the Rao premiership. The Rao

---

[4] Dennis Kux, *Estranged Democracies: India and the United States: 1941–91* (New Delhi: Sage Publications), 1994, p. 356.

[5] Ibid., p. 364.

[6] Aneek Chatterjee, 'Post Cold War Indian Foreign Policy vis-à-vis Neighbouring States: A Security Perspective', in A. K. Basu, ed., *India's Foreign Policy and Security* (Kolkata: Orion Press International), 2001, p. 19.

[7] US House of Representatives, 103rd Congress, 'Round Table on South Asia: Testimony before the Committee on Foreign Affairs' (Washington D.C.: US Govt. Printing Press), 1994, pp. 3–7; also, Francine R. Frankel, 'Indo–U.S. Relations: The Future is Now', *The Washington Quarterly*, 19 (4), 1996.

Government's bold stance of liberalising the Indian economy, in the face of domestic resistance, certainly opened up new vistas in India's foreign relations.

The two United Front (UF) Governments (1996–98) of H. D. Deve Gowda and I. K. Gujral produced different results as far as India's foreign policy was concerned. While no significant changes took place in Indian foreign policy during the Deve Gowda period as the first UF prime minister preferred to continue the external policies of the earlier Rao Government, the Gujral premiership brought a brief but brighter period as far as Indian foreign policy was concerned. The 'Gujral Doctrine' created a feel-good factor in South Asia, and was able to do away with mistrust and schism in the Indian neighbourhood. It also helped improve relations with the US.[8] But these positives were short-lived as tension mounted in South Asia with nuclear tests, first by India and subsequently by Pakistan, in May 1998. Therefore, during the first tenure of Prime Minister Atal Behari Vajpayee in 1998–99 (excluding his earlier premiership for 13 days in 1996), India's international relations suffered as India's neighbours were apprehensive of a nuclear India, and the US, the leading protagonist of non-proliferation, was furious. The US subsequently imposed economic and military sanctions on India (as also on Pakistan) for Pokhran II and urged its friends (like Japan, Britain, Australia, Italy, etc.) to follow suit. India's foreign policy faced severe challenges during the first tenure of Vajpayee due to Pokhran II and the Kargil crisis. But there were some rays of hope in an otherwise critical situation that India's foreign policy faced during this period. The Lahore Declaration with Pakistan and the American support to India during the Kargil crisis could be identified as positive gains for India's diplomacy.[9] Although the Vajpayee Government handled the situation well, it was not before Vajpayee's second tenure (1999–2004) that India could come out of the crises successfully.

Atal Behari Vajpayee's second term as India's prime minister produced good results for Indian foreign policy objectives. The foreign relations pursued by the Vajpayee Government during its second tenure became more matured and sharp. This government was able to significantly improve relations with the US, Russia, Pakistan, the ASEAN (Association of South East Asian Nations), the European Union (EU), Nepal and Iran. It also re-established diplomatic relations with Afghanistan, which were cut off during the Taliban rule in that country. In March 2000, the US President Bill Clinton paid an official visit to India for five days. Clinton was the first American President in 22 years to visit India, after President Carter's visit in 1978. Vajpayee and Clinton signed a very comprehensive and futuristic bilateral agreement, the 'US–India Relations: A Vision for the 21st Century' on 21 March 2000 in New Delhi. This agreement came to be known as the 'Vision Document' in diplomatic circles. It outlined in detail, the scheme of close cooperation between the two countries in political, economic and security spheres. Vajpayee paid

---

[8] See in this context, J. N. Dixit, *India's Foreign Policy: 1947–2003* (New Delhi: Piens Books), 2003, p. 222.

[9] Aneek Chatterjee, *International Relations Today: Concepts and Applications* (New Delhi: Pearson), 2010, p. 222.

a reciprocal official visit to the US in September 2000, the first reciprocal visit in a single calendar year after 22 years. Other top-level dignitaries started visiting each other's nation regularly, and the institutions created by the 'Vision Document' met as per schedule after 2000. It could thus be observed that the 'Vision Document' contributed to a great extent towards the improvement of India–US relations in the recent years.[10] Russian President Vladimir Putin visited India in October 2000. During his visit, Russia and India signed defence cooperation agreements through which Russia promised to supply important arms and aircrafts to India.[11] This visit by the Russian president helped the two countries to revive close cooperation in security affairs, observed during the Soviet era. In November 2001, Vajpayee visited Russia. During his visit, Vajpayee and Putin signed the 'Moscow Declaration' to start close cooperation in trade, security and political spheres.[12]

President of Pakistan Pervez Musharraf visited India in July 2001 with a view to normalise relations between the two neighbours. Vajpayee and the Pakistani president had a summit meeting in Agra to discuss bilateral issues. But the summit did not yield any positive result due to Musharraf's uncompromising attitude on the issue of Kashmir. However, the Agra Summit did manifest the intentions of the two nations to improve relations.[13] As part of the 'Look East' policy, the Vajpayee Government established close trade and political relations with the ASEAN. India had very little connection with the ASEAN earlier; but this government was able to strengthen them, with its renewed emphasis on this policy. Prime Minister Vajpayee also visited Vietnam and Indonesia. There he signed trade and commercial agreements with both the states, giving boost to government and private investments to and from these countries. The Vajpayee Government was also the first to establish very close relations with the EU.[14] In June 2000, the first India–EU summit took place in Lisbon, the capital city of Portugal. Since then regular summits have been taking place between the two. At present, India's trade with the EU covers nearly 25 per cent of total Indian trade; but initiatives for better relations with the EU started during Vajpayee's second tenure as the prime minister of India. Therefore, Vajpayee could be credited with pursuing a more matured foreign policy in his second term as India's prime minister. India had strengthened relations with major powers, as discussed above, and sent positive signals for cordial relations with its neighbours during this period.

In his first tenure as India's prime minister, Manmohan Singh was successful in establishing close relations with the US, and some major states and regional organisations that are important in the international order today. A few bold and novel initiatives in foreign policy matters were taken up by the United Progressive Alliance (UPA) I Government headed by Manmohan Singh (2004–09). One of such initiatives was the plan expressed by India and the US in a Joint Statement issued on 18 July 2005, during Singh's official visit to the US, to enter into 'civil nuclear

---

[10] Ibid., p. 223.

[11] Ibid.

[12] Ibid.

[13] Ibid.

[14] Ibid.

energy cooperation' (CNEC). The CNEC proposed to make the two countries true partners in nuclear cooperation, rather than adversaries. The CNEC was a very bold initiative undertaken by India and the US in the background of India's refusal to sign the Non-Proliferation Treaty (NPT) and the Comprehensive Test Ban Treaty (CTBT), and India's nuclear tests only seven years ago, in 1998.[15] The Manmohan Government believed that the CNEC, which was officially signed as an 'Agreement' between India and the US later in October 2008, would help India to join the international nuclear mainstream, from which India had remained officially cut-off due to her refusal to sign the NPT and the CTBT.[16] This government was also able to establish close strategic and political partnerships with Japan, the UK, France and Russia. Manmohan's India joined other nations to launch a very important multilateral forum, known as BRIC. BRIC comprised four growing economies, namely Brazil, Russia, India and China. South Africa joined the forum later. With important regional organisations like the ASEAN and the EU, the Manmohan Singh Government continued to strengthen economic and political connections. India's relations with neighbours like Bangladesh, Myanmar and Sri Lanka showed improvement during this period. However, the 2008 Mumbai attacks and the ensuing evidence that the attackers were backed by the Pakistani military and intelligence establishment foiled any attempts at peace between the two countries.

The second tenure of Manmohan Singh as the prime minister of India began in May 2009 when he assumed office as the head of the UPA II Government (2009–14). During its second tenure, the performance of the Manmohan Singh Government in foreign affairs was not as bright as its first term. The government was more preoccupied with handling corruption charges levelled against members of the cabinet. However, a trilateral security arrangement among the US, Japan and India which began at the end of 2011 signalled India's efforts to enhance its presence in multilateral fora. The effort also manifested India's willingness to have more cooperation with Japan, a major Asian economy. But the UPA II Government could not proceed satisfactorily to provide a final shape to the Indo–US Nuclear Agreement. This created some misgivings in bilateral relations. With neighbours, and other major powers like Britain, Russia, EU or ASEAN, no significant improvement in relations took place under this government.

Narendra Modi, a BJP (Bharatiya Janata Party) leader, assumed office as prime minister of India in May 2014. Modi headed the NDA (National Democratic Alliance) coalition, although BJP on its own got majority in the 2014 parliamentary elections. From the very beginning, Prime Minister Modi put special emphasis on foreign relations. He invited heads of governments of the SAARC (South Asian Association for Regional Cooperation) nations to New Delhi for his swearing-in ceremony, with a view to send messages to the neighbouring countries that India was willing to share closer ties with them. His 'Neighbourhood First' policy was partly successful in generating positive vibes in South Asia, after many years since the 'Gujral Doctrine'. Relations with Bangladesh witnessed an upswing with ratification by India of the Land Boundary Agreement

---

[15] Ibid., p. 224.

[16] Ibid.

that had been pending for the past 40 years. Ties with Sri Lanka also got a boost, largely due to a change in domestic leadership in that country with Maithripala Sirisena replacing Mahinda Rajapaksa as President. The Indian prime minister wasted no time in improving relations with Sri Lanka, by paying an official visit to that country in March 2015, the first visit by an Indian prime minister to Sri Lanka in 30 years. With Afghanistan, relations remained friendly. Modi visited Afghanistan in June 2016. During the visit, he was conferred with the highest civilian award of Afghanistan. Modi assured the Afghan people and their leadership that India would always stand by the terror-ravaged nation. The Afghan President, Ashraf Ghani also visited India in April 2015 and in September 2016. These visits amply manifested cordial relations between India and Afghanistan.

However, India's relations with Nepal and the Maldives did not witness major improvement during Modi's first three years in office, partly because India got entangled in domestic politics of these countries. India could have adopted a more cautious approach to developments in Nepal during the adoption of the latter's Constitution, with a view to protect bilateral interests. Relations with Pakistan deteriorated due to cross-border terrorist activities. Further, flash strikes by the security forces of both the nations along the Line of Control (LoC), escalated tension between the two. On 20 September 2016, militants, backed by Pakistani forces attacked and killed Indian soldiers at Uri, in the Indian side of Kashmir. India retaliated by conducting a 'surgical strike' on 29 September 2016, destroying launch pads for pushing terrorists into India (allegedly by the Pakistani army) from the other side of the LoC. As a consequence of these strikes, tension mounted between the two neighbours, and bilateral relations deteriorated. In contrast, with Bhutan, Modi continued to pursue friendly relations. He preferred Bhutan as the country for his first foreign visit as Indian prime minister, signalling India's sincerity in forging strong relations with Bhutan. No other Indian prime minister chose Bhutan as the country of his or her first visit in 70 years of independent India's diplomatic history. This visit in June 2014 also manifested the fact that India was not taking Bhutan for granted. It was a tribute to Bhutan's continued support to India in all aspects of foreign relations, including counter-terrorism policies. Therefore, Narendra Modi's neighbourhood policy yielded mixed results during the first three years of his premiership.

As far as major powers are concerned, Modi's foreign policy proved to be more effective during this period. The Indian prime minister worked hard to strengthen the strategic partnership with the US. He visited America four times till June 2016 and established close personal rapport with Barack Obama and the US Administration. Obama also became the first American president to visit India twice during his tenure, as also the first US President to attend India's Republic Day celebrations as the chief guest. These visits by the two heads of government clearly manifested an improved relationship. However, India–US relations may be subject to closer scrutiny in the near future, because a new American president has assumed office in January 2017. President Donald Trump's policy preferences, his personal chemistry with the Indian prime minister, domestic issues in both the nations, and international events will have an impact on Indo-US relations in the near future. However, growing economic relations between the two countries, the emergence of the Indian diaspora in the US as an economic and political pressure group, India's continuing open market policies will have a positive effect in India–US relations in the coming years.

The inking of the civilian nuclear cooperation agreement with Japan in November 2016, a pending issue for a long time, was a landmark achievement for the Modi Government. The Indian prime minister also established good personal chemistry with Shinzo Abe, the Japanese prime minister. During Abe's visit to India in 2015, Japan promised to support India with an outlay of US $15 billion for constructing high-speed railway system in India. Modi was able to transform India's ties with Japan into a strategic partnership, from an earlier donor-receiver relationship. India's growing relations with the ASEAN and East Asia under Modi's 'Act East Policy' also yielded rich dividends. As observed in chapter 14 of this volume, ASEAN–India trade had grown nearly ten times from financial years (FYs) 2001–02 to 2014–15. This is a healthy trend as far as trade between the two is concerned.

Relations with Russia and Britain also improved during Modi's first three years in office. The Indian prime minister visited Moscow on 23–24 December 2015 for the Sixteenth Annual Summit meeting between the heads of government of the two nations. As observed in chapter 10 of this volume, 17 new documents covering a wide range of cooperation in civil nuclear energy, defence, hydrocarbons, satellite navigation, railways, solar energy, heavy engineering, supercomputing, visa simplification, ayurveda and media were signed by the two countries during Modi's visit to Russia. Prime Minister Modi and President Putin also adopted a Joint Statement entitled, 'Shared Trust, New Horizons' during this visit. The Russian President also visited India in October 2016 for the Seventeenth Annual Summit meeting between the two heads of government. During this meeting, the Indian prime minister reiterated that Russia would remain India's major defence and strategic partner. President Putin reaffirmed Russia's continued commitment to the Special and Privileged Strategic Partnership with India. Under the Modi Government, India's relations with Russia were energised further. As observed in chapter 13 of this book, Modi also took initiative to improve relations with Britain. He visited Britain from 12–14 November 2015. During the visit, the Indian prime minister and his counterpart endorsed a 'Vision Statement' setting out the fundamental principles on which UK–India partnership would be built, and outlined a roadmap for deepening cooperation. This is a new initiative to forge closer ties with Britain, with which India's relationship never achieved its true potentials.

However, China continued to be a tough challenge for Indian foreign policy during Modi's first three years in office. China's growing political, military and economic prowess made it increasingly assertive in areas where India's interests were concerned. Despite frequent bilateral engagements and better economic ties, China's refusal to allow India's entry into the Nuclear Suppliers Group (NSG), and increasing proximity with Pakistan, made Indo-China relations somewhat difficult. Beijing's active support for Pakistan, notably with the US $46 billion China–Pakistan Economic Corridor (CPEC) that crossed territories claimed by India, led to further strains in bilateral ties. The One Belt One Road (OBOR) policy of China, designed to make roads along the sensitive Indian border areas, also did not go down well with New Delhi. Moreover, China's aggressive political and economic presence in the neighbourhood, especially in Nepal, Myanmar, Sri Lanka and Bangladesh, besides Pakistan, continued to be irritants for Indian foreign policy. Is China a competitor or an adversary for India? Chapter 8 of the present volume discusses in detail, and offers recommendations, like other chapters do, for improving bilateral relations between two of Asia's rising powers.

What is the 'Modi Doctrine' in India's foreign policy? Is it an altogether new attempt to steer India away from the Nehruvian world-view? Is it a successful blending by Prime Minister Modi, of the country's foreign policy and domestic transformation? How the BJP leader sought to change India's foreign policy? Modi has aggressively marketed his government's landmark initiatives like 'Make in India', 'Digital India', 'Smart Cities', and 'Skill India', not only to domestic audience, but to foreign investors as well. He has successfully involved the Indian diasporas all over the world,—and not solely in the US,—to project and support his foreign and domestic policies. He energised the Indian foreign policy establishments to shrug off lethargy and bureaucratic mindset, with a view to project a new and strong India. Modi has been able to present to the world a resurgent India, with economic and digital strengths. But some grey areas in India's foreign relations may throw a spanner in the Modi Government's endeavours. Relations with China, Pakistan, Nepal and the Maldives, besides security issues like terrorism and global recognition as a mainstream nuclear state, will continue to pose as foreign policy challenges to the Narendra Modi Government.

It is hard to analyse a country's foreign policy in isolation, removed from the legacy of the past. Since independence, India's foreign policy has gone through many phases: the ideological phase of the Nehru period; the development of a security culture during Indira Gandhi's premiership; and a more realistic phases during the Rao and Vajpayee periods, backed by economic growth. Modi has made Indian foreign policy more assertive. This has been possible due to India's growing stature as a leading economy. Therefore, from ideological to pragmatic to assertive,—this has been the tale in short, of 70 years of Indian foreign policy. This volume tries to reflect this essence of Indian foreign policy. For instance, India's relations with Myanmar, analysed in chapter 7 of this book, traces the shift from ideological to pragmatic orientations in India's policies towards Myanmar. Further, chapter 10 focuses on India's efforts to rebuild closer ties with Russia keeping in view the cordial relations between India and the former Soviet Union. Relations with Pakistan, on the other hand, continue to be burdened by past legacies. Chapter 1 of this work brings out the chronology of mistrust, generated from the Partition, dominating Indo-Pakistan relations at this point of time. Although history provided points of references for this work, it aimed to go beyond history to look at the contemporary and the future. In every chapter of this volume, futuristic recommendations for fostering the growth of bilateral relations have been provided. These projections, based on pragmatic estimates, may help students, scholars and policy planners of India's international relations. India's foreign relations are passing through a crucial juncture at this point of time,—the second decade of the twenty-first century. As India aims to be a great power, its foreign policy must be equipped with greater wisdom to steer the nation through in the complex web of international politics. Occasional flickers of such wisdom are often observed now; however, these flickers need to be converted into guiding lights.

PART I

INDIA AND HER NEIGHBOURS

1

INDIA'S RELATIONS WITH PAKISTAN

Search for Multiple Dimensions

HIGHLIGHTS

- Introduction: Hostile Beginning
- The 1990s: The Missed Opportunities
- The New Century: The Old Saga Continues
- Recommendations for the Future
- Conclusion

INTRODUCTION: HOSTILE BEGINNING

India and Pakistan, the two new-born states after the Second World War, began to look at each other in a negative light due to 'unkind' historical factors. The partition of British India on religious grounds and the status of Kashmir created mistrust and hostility between these two states since their creation in 1947. Since then, these two nations have fought three full wars, one undeclared war, attempted several peace initiatives, but remained at square one. Their enmity seemed unending. After partition in 1947, both countries were dissatisfied with the status of Kashmir. India believed that the accession of Kashmir to India was full and legal and the whole of Jammu and Kashmir logically belonged to India, Pakistan, on the other hand, thought that the very accession of Kashmir to India was forcibly and fraudulently done by India, and India's action went against the very logic of Partition. Kashmir remained a contentious area,—both India and Pakistan claim Kashmir as their own. Just after attaining statehood in 1947, India and Pakistan went to war over Kashmir. Since then, schism proliferated, hostilities mounted and mistrust got deeply embedded in Indo-Pak relations.

In this perfidious situation, foreign policy took a backseat as security concerns dominated bilateral relations. When two neighbours live in distrust, national security comes to the forefront. This has actually happened in India's relations with Pakistan and vice-versa. In a sense, India and Pakistan had little policy decisions to make as far as bilateral relations were concerned. Events of the 1940s,—like the two-nation theory, Partition, status of Kashmir, the 1947 War,—had shaped the mindset of the two populations and obliterated any positive foreign policy initiative.

This mindset, ostensibly a negative perception about each other, dominated by national security concerns, has not changed in the past six decades. No ruler, no government, or regime on either side of the border, hardly dared to change this negative perception. For all these years, the key phrase in Indo-Pak relations has been like this: national security first, bilateralism next. Foreign policy has very little scope to assert itself in such a situation. Within 25 years of their existence as independent nations, India and Pakistan fought three wars. The first three prime ministers of India had to go to war against Pakistan. Though there was never a full-fledged war after 1971, war-like situations always prevailed. The call for peaceful negotiation and friendship did arise sometimes, but they were soon drowned in security concerns. As one Pakistani author correctly observes, 'Apart from the Indus Water Treaty (1960), Sallal Dam Agreement (1978) and the recent Agreement on non-striking each other's nuclear installations (1991), there are hardly any tangible achievements that have been the product of negotiation. The Tashkent Declaration and Simla Agreement were the products of special circumstances that were created by the preceding wars of 1965 and 1971, respectively. The tragedy of the region is that since 1947, India and Pakistan have not only remained consistently antagonistic towards each other, but have also fought three major wars and even during periods of peace, opted to remain closer to the brink.'[1] Due to this ubiquitous security concerns, foreign policies of both India and Pakistan did not have much scope to experiment with new ideas and new measures.

THE 1990S: THE MISSED OPPORTUNITIES

It was thought that after the end of the Cold War, when superpower patronage was diminishing in the subcontinent, India and Pakistan would search for new areas of cooperation and peaceful existence. Indeed post Cold War political environment was conducive enough for greater Indo-Pak collaborations. Internationally, superpower rivalry ended, ushering in an atmosphere of peace and amity. As elsewhere, the South Asian states, including India and Pakistan also went for economic liberalisation programmes. These programmes demand a lot of time, energy, money and above all, national determination, to succeed. Healthy trade relations with other countries are also prerequisites of such programmes. The absence of external patrons to sustain military objectives, coupled with internal economic priorities provided a greater opportunity for the South Asian neighbours to come closer during the post Cold War period.[2] But both India and Pakistan lost this opportunity. They downplayed their economic priorities, negated the prospects of bilateral trade and commerce and instead went ahead with nuclearisation. Once again, security priorities overshadowed all the other areas, including the very important economic ties.[3] The post Cold War

[1] Pervaiz Iqbal Cheema, 'Security in South Asia: An Approach', in Shelton U. Kodikara, ed., *External Compulsions of South Asian Politics* (New Delhi: Sage Publications), 1993, p. 43.

[2] Aneek Chatterjee, 'South Asia after the Cold War: Prospects and Problems for Peace in the Region', *Socialist Perspective*, 23 (2): 57–66, 1995.

[3] Ibid.

period started with a little optimism for India and Pakistan when the agreement on non-striking each other's nuclear installations was signed in 1991. But that Agreement was, perhaps, the only bright spot in an otherwise tense Indo-Pak relation in the post Cold War period. Throughout the 1990s, leaders and officials of the two countries met several times in the subcontinent and in other venues around the world to diffuse tension. But no major breakthrough in bilateralism was achieved due to a lack of willingness of the both countries to courageously put the Kashmir issue on the negotiating table. Even the much-hyped 'Gujral Doctrine',[4] known for offering substantial concessions to neighbours without demands for reciprocity, was not very successful in dealing with the Kashmir problem, and therefore, in improving relations with Pakistan. However, dialogue between India and Pakistan resumed after a long hiatus in 1997. The talks had broken down in 1994 due to Pakistan's alleged sponsorship of terrorism in India. The foreign secretary level meeting of 23 June 1997 agreed to constitute JWGs on eight 'outstanding issues of concern'. These were: (i) Peace and security, including CBMs, (ii) Jammu and Kashmir, (iii) Siachen, (iv) Wullar Barrage Project and/Tulbul Navigation Project, (v) Sir Creek, (vi) Terrorism and drug-trafficking, (vii) Economic and Commercial Cooperation (viii) Promotion of friendly exchanges in various fields. It was decided that the first two issues would be dealt with at the level of the foreign secretaries, who will also coordinate and monitor the progress of work of all the JWGs. This process is known as Composite Dialogue. But the decade (1990s) ended disastrously with the Kargil conflict. In between, there were border skirmishes, allegations about cross-border terrorism and the May 1998 nuclear explosions. The nuclear bombs did blow away early post Cold War hopes of cooperation between the two neighbours. Yet, Indian Prime Minister Atal Behari Vajpayee enthusiastically took a bus journey to Lahore. The Lahore Agreement of February 1999 had reiterated the desire of the two countries to move forward on the path of dialogue. But the Kargil conflict in May–July 1999, dashed all positive signals for bilateralism. Moreover, the failed Agra Summit in May 2000 (between Vajpayee and Musharraf), the attack on India's Parliament on 13 December 2001 and the subsequent mobilisation of troops on the border, contributed to the difficult phase in bilateral relations. These events also pointed starkly towards missed opportunities for meaningful engagement in India–Pakistan relations in the 1990s.

THE NEW CENTURY: THE OLD SAGA CONTINUES

After a gap of more than two years since the attack on the Indian parliament allegedly by Pakistan-backed terrorists, both the countries agreed to commence the process of the Composite Dialogue

---

[4] The 'Gujral Doctrine' was articulated by Gujral himself in a speech in London in August 1996. It said, 'First with neighbours ... India does not ask for reciprocity, but gives all that it can in good faith and trust. Secondly, no South Asian country will allow its territory to be used against the interest of another country in the region. Thirdly, none will interfere in the internal affairs of another. Fourthly, all South Asian countries must respect each other's territorial integrity and sovereignty. And finally, they "will settle all their disputes through peaceful bilateral negotiations".' See in this context, M. R. Biju, *India's Foreign Policy: Towards a New Millennium* (Jaipur: National Publishing House), 2000, p. 189.

in February 2004. This became possible only after General Musharraf assured Prime Minister Vajpayee that he would not allow any part of the territory under Pakistan's control to be used to support terrorism against India. Subsequently, the foreign secretaries of the two countries met on 18 February 2004, to start the process of Composite Dialogue. Trade and travel across the LoC were envisaged as key elements of the Confidence Building Measures (CBMs) between India and Pakistan among the 22 CBMs proposed by India. After several meetings between the officials of the two countries, the modalities for cross-LoC travel were finalised on 16 February 2005. The Srinagar–Muzaffarabad bus service was inaugurated on 7 April 2005 and the Poonch–Rawalakote route was opened for travel in 20 June 2006. Later, the foreign ministers of India and Pakistan met on 21 May 2008 to discuss new and existing Kashmir-specific CBMs, and agreed to increase the frequency of Srinagar–Muzaffarabad and Poonch–Rawalakote bus service and allow intra-Kashmir trade. On 18 July 2008, the India–Pakistan JWGs on cross-LoC CBMs met in Islamabad to simplify the procedure for issuing cross-LoC travel permits; to increase the frequency of the Srinagar–Muzaffarabad bus service; to launch a postal service between the two cities; and to expedite the cases of inadvertent crossings of the LoC; and discussed the list of items to be allowed for trade through the truck service. A triple-entry permit for cross-LoC travel was approved. The announcement in this regard was made on 21 July 2008, when the foreign secretaries of the two countries met in New Delhi.[5] Later on 22 September 2008, the modalities regarding the movement of trucks, code of conduct for the drivers, permits, security, timings and list of items to be traded were agreed upon between Pakistan and India to conduct cross-LoC trade.[6] Following this, cross-LoC trade on the Srinagar–Muzaffarabad and Poonch–Rawalakote routes commenced from 21 October 2008. Twenty-one items were identified for duty free entry from each side.

However, when on 26 November 2008, a group of terrorists, allegedly backed by Pakistan, attacked several key places in Mumbai, killing hundreds of people, it seemed that a war could break out between these two nuclear (weapons) capable states. Thanks to the restraint exercised by their governments as well as hectic diplomacy by major international players, including the US and the UK, a major disaster was averted. 'There can be no doubt that those who planned and carried out the attacks wanted fear and hatred between India and Pakistan to deepen. In any event, India suspended the ongoing bilateral negotiations after the Mumbai attacks and refused to revive the peace process till such time that the perpetrators of the Mumbai attacks were arrested and put on trial.'[7] For a long time, the power elite in Pakistan tried to evade responsibility for the Mumbai attacks. Finally, Pakistan conceded that the main culprit caught in Mumbai, Ajmal Kasab, was a Pakistani national. The 26/11 incidents in Mumbai caused a setback to bilateralism, and the peace process.

---

[5] Source: IDSA, New Delhi; see in this connection, idsa.in/sites/default/files/Cross-LoCCBMbetween IndiaandPakistan.pdf, accessed on 20 May 2017.

[6] Source: https://www.files.ethz.ch/isn/137394/CrossLoCCBMbetweenIndiaandPakistan.pdf, accessed on 20 May 2017.

[7] Source: www.voltairenet.org/article163897.html, accessed on 20 May 2017.

However, the leaders of the two nations continued to meet in different international fora. The first such important meeting took place when President Asif Ali Zardari of Pakistan and Indian Prime Minister Manmohan Singh met on the sidelines of the Shanghai Cooperation Organisation (SCO) meeting, held in Yekaterinburg, Russia, on 16 June 2009. Singh told Zardari that Pakistan should not let its territory be used for terrorism. A month later, Prime Minister Manmohan Singh and Pakistani Prime Minister Yousaf Raza Gilani met at the Non-Aligned Movement (NAM) summit at Sharm el Sheikh, Egypt. On 16 July 2009, they first met for three hours and together issued a Joint Communiqué. Singh reiterated the need to bring the perpetrators of the Mumbai attack to justice. Gilani assured that Pakistan would do everything within its power to do the same. They agreed that the two countries would share credible and actionable information on any future terrorist threats. Prime Minister Gilani mentioned that Pakistan had some information on such threats in Baluchistan and other areas. It was agreed, very correctly, that action on terrorism should not be linked to the Composite Dialogue process and these should not be bracketed. Prime Minister Singh said that India was ready to discuss everything frankly with Pakistan, including all outstanding issues. Both expressed the need for their countries to cooperate on issues of poverty, development and regional cooperation.[8]

The Joint Communiqué evoked opposite responses in Pakistan and India. In Pakistan, it was welcomed as a triumph of Pakistani diplomacy, especially that of Prime Minister Gilani's. The reception in India was diametrically opposite. Prime Minister Singh had to face outbursts from some opposition parties, especially from the BJP. The media also played a part in hyping up the issue. The BJP pointed out that by agreeing to Pakistan's request that he should look into the alleged unwelcome activities of Indian intelligence in Baluchistan, Singh had virtually conceded that India was involved in Baluchistan.[9] Also, objections were raised towards the delinking of the resumption of the peace process to the Mumbai terrorist attacks. Even within the ruling Congress Party in India, it seemed that some people did not like Singh's accommodation of Pakistani concerns. However, the Indian prime minister defended his decision as a friendly gesture and not an admission of guilt. He received full backing from the Congress President, Sonia Gandhi.[10] Moreover, Singh emphasised that the peace process and contact with Pakistan on other issues would remain suspended till such time that the culprits of the Mumbai attacks were brought to book. Thereafter, the uproar over Baluchistan gradually melted. The noise in India over the Sharm el Sheikh Joint Communiqué shows that 'peace diplomacy' is a very difficult task as far as India and Pakistan are concerned.

The two sides met on several occasions since then, mostly on the sidelines of international organisations' meetings. But nothing substantial could be achieved in these 'courtesy'

---

[8] See in this context, 'India, Pak issue joint statement on bilateral relations', for the full text of the joint statement issued at Sharm el Sheikh, *The Indian Express,* New Delhi, 16 July 2009.

[9] See the news item, 'Nothing Will Wash Away the Shame of Sharm-al-Sheikh: BJP', *The Indian Express,* 29 July 2009.

[10] See 'Sonia Rallies Party Behind PM Stand on Pak', *The Indian Express,* 31 July 2009.

dialogues.[11] A chronology of these meetings would reveal their nature and lesser impact on bilateral relations. On 27 September 2009, India's Foreign Secretary, Nirupama Rao and her Pakistani counterpart, Salman Bashir met on the sidelines of the United Nations General Assembly (UNGA) in New York.[12] Later, on the same day, Indian Foreign Minister, Krishna and his Pakistani counterpart, Shah Mehmood Qureshi met on the sidelines of the UNGA in New York. But the deadlock persisted with India asking Pakistan to take concrete action against the perpetrators of the 26/11 Mumbai carnage. However, there was a welcome development in bilateral relations in February 2010, when foreign secretary-level talks between India and Pakistan resumed after a considerable gap, in New Delhi.[13] But the talks ended without any meaningful breakthrough with the two diplomats only agreeing to stay in touch. In March 2010, the biannual meeting between India's Border Security Force (BSF) and Pakistan Rangers took place. In early April 2010, two Prime Ministers, Manmohan Singh and Gilani exchanged greetings at the Nuclear Security Summit in Washington D.C., but no talks took place. On 29 April 2010, Manmohan Singh and Gilani met again in the Bhutanese capital, Thimpu on the sidelines of the South Asian Association for Regional Coöperation (SAARC) summit and directed their foreign ministers and foreign secretaries to work out modalities to bridge the trust deficit. On 11 May 2010, two Foreign Ministers, Krishna and Qureshi held telephonic conversation. Qureshi invited Krishna to Islamabad in July 2010 for talks. India's Home Minister, P. Chidambaram visited Islamabad on 26 June for the meeting of home ministers of the SAARC countries. In July 2010, Indian Foreign Minister, S. M. Krishna travelled to Pakistan for talks. But the talks did not yield any results due to pressures put on the Pakistani civilian government by the Pakistani military.[14] On 30 March 2011, Singh and Gilani met during the cricket World Cup semi-finals in Mohali. No major announcements or policy decisions were made after this 'unstructured' talk. A leading Indian newspaper commented after this cricket diplomacy: '. . . not that the Singh-Yousaf Raza Gilani meeting was followed by any major announcement. It was described as not really a dialogue but informal conversations between Singh and Gilani. During the unstructured talks, Singh touched upon a large number of issues that are yet to be resolved between the two countries'.[15] On 30–31 May 2011, India and Pakistan held defence secretary-level talks on Siachen, but failed to agree on the modalities for demilitarisation of Siachen. The two countries decided to continue talks to arrive at a solution to one of the major vexed issues. Nirupama Rao and Salman Bashir met in Islamabad on

[11] Aneek Chatterjee, 'India–Pakistan Relations: A Framework for Peace in Future', in Riaz Shaikah, ed., *Back From the Brink: India–Pakistan Ties Revisited* (Karachi: Ushba Publishing International), 2012, p. 355.

[12] Ibid.

[13] Ibid.

[14] See the news item, 'To spite Zardari, Pak military foils peace talks', *Hindustan Times,* New Delhi, 18 July 2010.

[15] See, Diptosh Majumdar, 'No Breakthrough, but Singh and Gilani Have a Good Conversation', *The Times of India*, New Delhi, 31 March 2011.

23–24 June 2011. Again, nothing substantial came out of this dialogue, except the routine release of a Joint Statement.[16]

Efforts for normalisation of bilateral relations continued throughout 2012 and 2013, although such efforts were jeopardised by lack of trust and confidence. India and Pakistan signed a new visa agreement in September 2012 during the visit of Indian foreign minister to Pakistan. This agreement helped in the liberalisation of bilateral visa regime. The commerce secretaries of the two countries also met in Islamabad, showing indications of continuing resumed bilateral dialogues. Talks on conventional and non-conventional CBMs were held in December 2012 in New Delhi. A new government, led by Prime Minister Nawaz Sharif assumed office in Pakistan in May 2013. The new Pakistani prime minister showed interest in improving relations with India. This was evidenced when Sharif informed visiting British Foreign Secretary William Hague, who called on him at his office on 17 July 2013 about the 'initiatives aimed at improving relations with India, including the revival of back channel diplomacy and the resumption of the dialogue process'.[17] However, incidents in both countries betrayed hopes of the new Pakistani prime minister. Cross-border skirmishes continued throughout the year, in the Kashmir region. Other issues, such as the death of Indian soldier Sarabjit Singh in Pakistani custody, did little to improve relations. Manmohan Singh–Nawaz Sharif meeting in New York in September 2013 at the sidelines of the UN General Assembly session, produced no positives.

A new government in India, headed by Prime Minister Narendra Modi, assumed office in May 2014. The new Indian Prime Minister invited his Pakistani counterpart along with other SAARC leaders, to attend his swearing-in ceremony in New Delhi. Nawaz Sharif accepted the invitation, attended the swearing-in ceremony and had a summit meeting with the new Indian prime minister. Fresh hopes for improved bilateral relations surfaced in diplomatic circles. In 2015, at the sidelines of a regional security conference in Islamabad in December, the two countries agreed to resume the comprehensive bilateral dialogue process that had been suspended since the 2008 terrorist attacks on Mumbai. Modi also made a surprise visit to Pakistan on Christmas Day,—the first trip to Pakistan by an Indian prime minister in 11 years. However, these positive gestures were interspersed throughout 2014 and 2015 by border skirmishes, continued bitterness over the issue of Kashmir, Pakistan's opposition to India's claim for a permanent seat at the United Nations Security Council (UNSC), conventional and nuclear arms race and veiled threats to each other. In early January 2016, terrorists attacked India's Pathankot air base, located not far from the Pakistan border. Seven Indian security forces were killed in the attack. India blamed Jaish-e-Mohammed, a Pakistan-based terror group for the attack. Foreign secretary-level talks, scheduled to take place on 15 January, were postponed. New Delhi demanded that Islamabad take action against the Pathankot attackers, and insisted that dialogue would resume only if the Pakistanis did so. Bilateral relations were conditioned by mistrust again. In this context, it would be appropriate to recall Indian Prime Minister Narendra Modi's address to the UNGA on 27 September 2014 where he called for bilateral dialogues in 'a peaceful environment without the shadow of terrorism.

[16] Chatterjee, 'India-Pakistan Relations…', n. 11, p. 356.

[17] See *The Indian Express*, 18 July 2013.

On the occasion, the prime minister also underlined Pakistan's own responsibility in creating an appropriate environment for a constructive and sustainable bilateral engagement'.[18] Clearly, the shadow of mistrust and lack of confidence in the Western neighbour was reverberated in Modi's words. The new governments (in both the countries) lost to the old (schism, mistrust and unfriendly attitude) as far as India–Pakistan relations were concerned. A look into Box 1.1 below reveals a chronology of failed hopes in India–Pakistan bilateralism:

Box 1.1: How Mistrust Conditioned Relations: Chronology of Indo-Pak Bilateralism (1991–2017)

1991: Agreement on non-striking each other's nuclear installations was signed.

1992–93: Talks continued at different levels.

1994: The talks had broken down in 1994 due to Pakistan's alleged sponsorship of terrorism in India.

1994–96: No major initiative from either side to negotiate for peace.

1997: The foreign secretary-level meeting of 23 June 1997 agreed to constitute JWGs on eight 'outstanding issues of concern'.

1998: Nuclear explosions by both India and Pakistan in May increased tension between the two.

1999 (February): Vajpayee's 'Bus Diplomacy' and the Lahore Agreement. Hopes revived.

1999 (May–July): Undeclared war in Kargil took bilateral relations to a new low.

2000 (May): Agra Summit: failed due to differences over Kashmir.

2001 (December): Attack on the Indian parliament.

2002–03: Talks suspended.

2004: Composite Dialogue process resumed.

2004–08 (before 26/11): Period of relative calm. Positive initiatives like cross-LoC travel (2005); Kashmir specific CBMs (2008); intra-Kashmir trade (2008); foreign secretaries meeting (July 2008), etc.

2008 (November): Terror attacks on Mumbai, allegedly by Pakistan-based groups. Talks suspended by India.

2009: No substantial talks; the two sides interacted on the sidelines of meetings of international organisations, like the one in Sharm el Sheikh during the NAM summit in July 2009.

2010: Foreign secretary-level talks resumed in February. Nothing substantial came out of it. In March 2010, the biannual meeting between India's BSF and Pakistan Rangers took place. In July 2010, Indian Foreign Minister, S. M. Krishna travelled to Pakistan for talks. But the talks did not yield any results. On 30 March 2011, Singh and Gilani met during the cricket World Cup semifinals in Mohali. No major announcements or policy decisions were made after this 'unstructured' talk.

2011: On 30–31 May, India and Pakistan held defence secretary-level talks on Siachen, but failed to agree on the modalities for demilitarisation of Siachen. Indian Foreign Secretary, Nirupama Rao and her Pakistani counterpart, Salman Bashir met in Islamabad on 23–24 June 2011. Nothing substantial came out of this dialogue, except the routine release of a Joint Statement.

2012: A relatively better year. On 13 April 2012, India gained the most favoured nation (MFN) status in trade in Pakistan. India reciprocated by announcing the removal of restrictions on foreign direct

(*Contd.*)

[18] Ministry of External Affairs, Government of India, *Annual Report: 2014–15* (New Delhi: Government of India), 2015, p. 17.

Box 1.1 (*Contd.*)

investment (FDI) from Pakistan to India. Foreign ministers of both the nations met in September to review the progress of bilateral relations.

2013: Hopes drowned in rivalry again. Cross-border skirmishes continued throughout the year, in the Kashmir region. Other issues, such as the death of Indian soldier Sarabjit Singh in Pakistani custody, did little to improve relations. Manmohan Singh–Nawaz Sharif meeting in New York in September, at the sidelines of the UNGA session, produced no positives.

2014: The new Indian Prime Minister Narendra Modi invited his Pakistani counterpart along with other SAARC leaders, to attend his swearing-in ceremony in New Delhi. Nawaz Sharif accepted the invitation, attended the swearing-in ceremony and had a summit meeting with the new Indian prime minister. Fresh hopes for improved bilateral relations surfaced in diplomatic circles.

2015: At a regional security conference in Islamabad, the two countries agreed to resume the comprehensive bilateral dialogue process that had been suspended since the 2008 terrorist attacks on Mumbai. Indian Prime Minister Modi also made a surprise visit to Pakistan on the Christmas Day,—the first trip to Pakistan by an Indian prime minister in 11 years. Hopes continued.

2016: In January, terrorists attacked India's Pathankot air base, located not far from the Pakistan border. Seven Indian security forces were killed in the attack. India blamed Jaish-e-Mohammed, a Pakistan-based terror group, for the attack. Foreign secretary-level talks, scheduled to take place on 15 January, were postponed. New Delhi demanded that Islamabad take action against the Pathankot attackers, and insisted that dialogue be resumed only if the Pakistanis did so.

In April, the foreign secretaries met in New Delhi on the sidelines of the Afro-Asian Conference. The Pakistani foreign secretary insisted that dialogues would not be meaningful without reference to the Kashmir issue. The Indian foreign secretary insisted on speedy trial of the Pathankot attackers as a condition for meaningful talks. Due to such hard bargaining, this unscheduled meeting failed.

In September, Indian soldiers were killed in Uri, Kashmir, by Pakistan-backed militants. India retaliated 11 days later with surgical strikes on terrorist camps in Pakistan occupied Kashmir (PoK).

2017: Kulbhushan Yadav, an Indian Naval Officer, was arrested in Pakistan on charges of espionage, and sentenced to death by a military court. India took the matter to International Court of Justice (ICJ). In April 2017, ICJ stalled the death sentence, but Pakistan was not prepared to accept the ICJ ruling. Till May 2017, the issue remained unresolved as tension mounted. India cancelled maritime talks with Pakistan.

Bilateral relations were shadowed by mistrust yet again.

This chronology of mostly unproductive India–Pakistan dialogues in the new century is indicative of the fact that the peace process has been disrupted due to several factors. These factors are: mutual allegation of state-backed terrorist acts; unwillingness of the political elites in both countries to resolve disputes; stubborn attitudes by the Pakistani military and Indian right-wing parties to yield a little space to the other nation; and above all, mutual mistrust and disregard emanating from security concerns. Does bilateralism have any prospect in this seemingly bleak scenario? What is the future of India–Pakistan relations: confrontationist or peaceful? What is to be done for establishing peace in bilateral relations? The next section presents some recommendations for peace in India–Pakistan relations.[19]

[19] Chatterjee, 'India–Pakistan Relations…', n. 11, p. 357.

RECOMMENDATIONS FOR THE FUTURE

Recent initiatives like 'Aman ki Asha' (hope for peace), started by two leading media groups in India and Pakistan on 1 January 2010 for people-to-people communication are welcome efforts, but have their limitations. These can instil confidence among the cultured and literate people in both the countries but have limited access to the vastly illiterate population of the two nations. Moreover, the impact factors of such initiatives on political elites and the military, especially in Pakistan, are yet to be ascertained. Therefore, these efforts must be substantiated by continuous government-to-government dialogues and collaborations on wide-ranging issues.[20] While many dialogues failed in the past, as observed in the preceding analysis, one must not lose hopes in dialogues. After all, through bilateral dialogues, a few things like the JWG, confidence building measures (CBMs), and the 1991 Agreement on non-striking each other's nuclear installations could be achieved. But these are certainly minimums and the two nations must strive to achieve a lot more in order to normalise relations. They must collaborate on non-traditional and non-political areas to boost their relations in the future.[21] These possible areas are: (i) security and strategic collaborations; (ii) environmental engagement; (iii) increased trade; (iv) educational and cultural exchanges; (v) plans for settling the Kashmir imbroglio; and (vi) delinking 'conditions' from bilateral negotiations. Apart from items v and vi above, others are mostly non-political in nature. The potentials of these areas for the future partnership and peace are analysed further.

Security and strategic collaborations: While India and Pakistan have entered into several military CBMs, they have never tried to be security and strategic partners, because both suffer from mutual security fears. Some of the military CBMs agreed between the two at different times are: (i) agreement on the prohibition of attack against nuclear installations and facilities. This also included an informal accord of a moratorium on further testing; (ii) agreement on advance notification on military exercises, maneuvers and troop movements, brought into effect in 1991 and has an important role to play in the reduction of tensions on both sides of the LoC; (iii) the formal ceasefire along the international border as also the actual ground position line, brought into effect on 25 November 2003 and has remained in effect since; (iv) agreement on prevention of airspace violations and for permitting over flights and landings by military aircrafts, signed in 1991, has significantly reduced costs for both nations; (v) biannual meetings between the BSF and Pakistani Rangers, has been in effect since 2004, and there has been mutual agreement that local commanders should meet more frequently to resolve local problems; (vi) establishment of a communication link between Pakistan Maritime Security Agency and Indian Coast Guard, brought into effect in 2005, primarily to facilitate early exchange of information regarding fishermen apprehended for straying into each other's waters; (vii) agreement on advance notification of ballistic missile tests, brought into effect in 2005 and required both parties to inform the other 72 hours in advance before testing any ballistic missiles within a 40-km radius

---

[20] See in this context, Ashok K. Behuria, '*Aman Ki Asha* in Pakistani Media: Requiem for a Peace Process?', *Strategic Analysis,* 34 (4): 486–89, 2010.

[21] Chatterjee, 'India–Pakistan Relations...', n. 11, p. 357.

of the International Border and the LoC; (viii) a Hotline between Director General Military Operations (DGMO) of both countries had been in effect since 1965, and was most recently used in an unscheduled exchange to discuss troop movements and allay tensions, in the aftermath of the 26/11 attacks in Mumbai. Many of these CBMs had only existed in principle, but were never implemented because of the belief that dominant issues, such as those outlined in the composite dialogue, needed to be resolved before the CBM process could be initiated. The Indian military and the Pakistani military are engaged, separately, in joint exercises with many third countries (like the USA), but have never tried to collaborate between the two. Such collaborations may dilute mutual security fears, and instil confidence and belief, not only among the men in uniform, but also among the people in both the countries. But these two nations never tried to achieve military diplomacy as an instrument for peace-building in the subcontinent, although they both have substantially strong military establishments.[22] Exchange of military technology and information must be implemented and continued for peace in the future; these should not be confined only to CBM rhetoric.[23]

Environmental engagements: Possible cooperation between India and Pakistan on environmental issues has immense potential to generate trust and confidence. Collaboration on climate change science in the glaciated headwaters of the Indus basin river system, especially following the devastating floods of 2010, makes practical and political sense.[24] Climate change is a global concern and the Karakoram glaciers are a pivotal natural laboratory for understanding these dynamics. Scientists from Pakistan and India have a clear and present interest in collaborating on this matter as part of their obligations to international environmental agreements.[25] Currently, there are around 10 Indian Remote Sensing (IRS) satellites for generating information on natural resources. Data from the IRS satellites are used for a variety of applications such as drought monitoring, flood-risk zone mapping, urban planning, forestry surveys, environmental impact analysis and coastal studies. Pakistan too possesses such satellites.[26] The two countries

[22] Ali Ahmed, 'India–Pakistan Relations: Military Diplomacy vs Strategic Engagement', *Journal of Defence Studies*, 5 (1): 147–54, 2011.

[23] Chatterjee, 'India–Pakistan Relations...', n. 11, p. 359.

[24] Ibid.

[25] See in this context, Alexander Carius, 'Environmental Cooperation as an Instrument of Crisis Prevention and Peace Building: Conditions for Success and Constraints', *Study Commissioned by the German Federal Ministry for Economic Cooperation and Development* (BMZ), Berlin, Adelphi Consult GmbH, 2006, pp. 2–26.

[26] After successful launching and operation of BADR series of experimental Low Earth Observational satellites in the 1990s and early 2000s, Pakistan's Space and Upper Atmosphere Research Commission (SUPARCO) plans to launch high resolution Pakistan Remote Sensing Satellite (PRSS) to meet the national and international user requirements. The Badr satellite family has the following satellites: (i) Badr-1 (digital communication satellite); (ii) Badr-B (low earth observatory satellite); (iii) Badr-3 (communication satellite); (iv) Badr-4 (communication satellite); (v) Badr-5 (telecommunication satellite); and (vi) Badr-6 (communication satellite). PRSS is planned to be a progressive and sustainable programme. Initially, SUPARCO plans to launch an optical satellite with payload of 2.5 meter PAN in 700 km sun-synchronous orbit by the end of year 2011, which will be followed by a series of optical and SAR satellites in the future. For more on Pakistan's Remote

can share data on climate and natural resources, and collaborate closely to thwart environmental degradation in the subcontinent. A working group on sharing these resources could very well serve as a starting point for engagement. This is a vastly untapped area in bilateral relations, and needs to be used as a genuine CBM.[27]

Increased trade: India–Pakistan two-way trade is not only small, it is woefully inadequate. This particular area has huge potential to surge ahead. In an age of economic diplomacy, the two South Asian neighbours have failed to use the prospects of trade and commerce as a potential instrument for peace in the region.[28] But better be late than never. The two neighbours must concentrate on increased trade to arrest mistrust and schism. The potential gains from increased economic integration between India and Pakistan are large. Even though both the countries are members of the South Asia Free Trade Area (SAFTA) established in January 2006, trade between the two countries is alarmingly low. Total trade (exports plus imports) between India and Pakistan in 2014–15 amounted to US $2,354.40 million, down by 12.84 per cent from the previous fiscal year. Pakistan accounted for a meagre 0.31 per cent of India's total trade in 2014–15, while India accounted for a little over 1 per cent of Pakistan's trade in 2015.[29] A look at two-way trade in the recent years, presented in Table 1.1 below, would reveal that this segment requires a lot of improvement:

Table 1.1: Total Volume of India–Pakistan Trade in Recent Years (in US $ million)

Year	*Total Trade*	*Percentage Growth*	*Percentage Share (of India's Total Trade)*
2005–06	868.79	–	–
2006–07	1,673.71	92.65	–
2007–08	2,238.50	33.75	–
2008–09	1,810.05	–19.14	–
2009–10	1,849.26	2.17	0.40
2010–11	2,666.13	44.17	0.38
2011–12	1,939.21	–18.25	0.24
2012–13	2,606.66	34.42	0.33
2013–14	2,701.15	3.62	0.35
2014–15	2,354.40	–12.84	0.31

Source: Department of Commerce, Export-Import Data Bank, Government of India, available at http://commerce.nic.in/eidb/iecnt.asp, accessed on 31 January 2015.

Sensing Satellite Programme, visit SUPARCO's home page, available at http://www.suparco.gov.pk/pages.prss.asp, accessed on 16 June 2011.

27 Chatterjee, 'India–Pakistan Relations…', n. 11, p. 360.

28 Ibid.

29 Department of Commerce, Export-Import Data Bank, Government of India, available at http://commerce.nic.in/eidb/iecnt.asp, accessed on 30 January 2015.

The table above shows that the total volume of India–Pakistan trade stood at US $2,701.15 million in 2013–14, and the percentage growth in trade was 3.62 over the previous fiscal year. While the growth rate during the two fiscals (2012–13 and 2013–14) was a bit encouraging, the volume of total trade dropped again in 2014–15, as pointed out earlier. The two neighbours must try to account for at least 1 per cent of each other's total trade. This proposition sounds convincing if one looks at percentage share of India's trade with Pakistan in the backdrop of India's total foreign trade during the last six fiscals (2009–10 to 2014–15). The percentage share of India's Pakistan trade remained below 0.40 during this period. Considering the fact that India and Pakistan are the two big nations in South Asia, the trade figures, presented in Table 1.1, are not at all satisfactory. India's trade with several other South Asian countries was higher than Pakistan in 2014–15. Table 1.2 further highlights India's trade with some South Asian countries including Pakistan.

Table 1.2: India's Trade with Some South Asian Countries in 2014–15 (in US $ million)

Name of the Country	*Total Trade (Import + Export)*
Sri Lanka	6,703.72
Bangladesh	6,451.47
Nepal	4,558.77
Pakistan	2,701.15

Source: Department of Commerce, Export-Import Data Bank, Government of India, available at http://commerce.nic.in/eidb/iecnt.asp, accessed on 13 May 2016.

Table 1.2 shows that India has stronger trade relations with three other South Asian countries in comparison to Pakistan in 2014–15, although these three nations are smaller than Pakistan. The comparative data reveal a sorry state of India–Pakistan trade in the recent years. Surely politics played havoc with economics as far as India–Pakistan relations are concerned. But in the age of globalisation and economic diplomacy, it must be the other way: economics should play the pivotal role in bilateral relations.

Economic relations have immense prospects for the future of bilateralism. According to a study, the potential of formal trade between India and Pakistan is roughly 20 times greater than recorded trade. This means that at 2014–15 trade levels, the total trade between India and Pakistan could expand from its current level of US $2.35 billion to US $47 billion if adequate care is taken to improve trade. The current constraints for increased trade between the two nations are believed to be high tariff and non-tariff barriers, inadequate infrastructure, bureaucratic inertia, excessive red tape, and direct political opposition.[30] Some measures to improve trade facilitation between India and Pakistan according to the study, could include: easing restrictions on visas; opening additional road border crossings and bus routes; increasing air links between the two countries; increasing the number of customs posts; and allowing branches of Indian and Pakistani banks to operate in the other country. Some additional measures for

[30] Mohsin S. Khan, 'India–Pakistan Trade: A Roadmap for Enhancing Economic Relations', *Policy Brief* (Washington D.C.: Peterson Institute for International Economics), 2009, pp. 1–4.

augmenting trade are: Pakistan granting the MFN status to India, and in turn India significantly lowering tariff rates for goods of particular interest to Pakistan; facilitating energy trade between the two countries; allowing trade in information technology; and eliminating obstacles to FDIs by the other country.[31] However, above all these measures, the political will to implement these plans must persist.

Educational and cultural exchanges: Educational and cultural links form a major part of bilateral and multilateral diplomacy in modern times. Sadly enough, India and Pakistan have failed to seize the full potential of this vital area in their bilateral relations during the past seven decades. Governments in both the countries never indulged in educational and cultural exchanges in an organised way, backed by sound policy documents. Although sporadic cultural exchanges took place between the two countries, these lacked continuity and sustenance. Moreover, universities and research establishments in India and Pakistan have failed to engage themselves in regular faculty and student exchange programmes. Similarly, there are little initiatives to share research findings. This dismal picture must be changed, 'because through educational and cultural exchanges more and more people could be involved in the trust-building process. Both the governments must view positively, any collaborative plan between or among universities in India and Pakistan. Easing of visa restrictions is a prerequisite for such plans and the governments have a big role to play in this matter. An annual "Pakistan Week" in India, and "India Week" in Pakistan could be encouraged for cultural programmes and exchanges'.[32] India and Pakistan must move forward beyond cricket, although sporting links also face crisis often and on. Political elites in both the countries must be willing to engage their nations in meaningful educational and cutural contacts, in the lines of contemporary diplomatic ways. Strong and meaningful cultural contacts have the ability to generate mutual trust and confidence. India and Pakistan must start using this opportunity without further delay.

Plans for settling the Kashmir imbroglio: Kashmir remained the most contentious issue and the boiling point in India–Pakistan relations in the past seven decades, yet no solution was found for the Kashmir problem. Currently, both India and Pakistan control respective areas of Kashmir on either side of the LoC, although both stake claim over the whole of Kashmir. Some political parties in Kashmir also want an independent Kashmir. Therefore, solution to the Kashmir problem is difficult because any plan for solution would go against one or two stakeholders. But without a solution to the Kashmir problem, peace between India and Pakistan is very hard to establish. The two governments must work sincerely and courageously to solve the issue. It may require courageous and frank negotiations among the three main stakeholders, and if required a redefinition of the LoC to accommodate different sentiments. It is heartening to note that the Joint Statement (JS) issued in Islamabad on 24 June 2011 after the foreign secretary-level talk between the two countries, referred to a peaceful settlement of the Kashmir issue. The JS

---

[31] Ibid.

[32] Chatterjee, 'India–Pakistan Relations...', n. 11, p. 363.

stated, 'The Foreign Secretaries exchanged views on the issue of Jammu and Kashmir and agreed to continue discussions in a purposeful and forward looking manner with the view to finding a peaceful solution by narrowing divergences and building convergences.'[33] But such optimism must be implemented in reality. However, till a solution is found out, Kashmir must not always be seen as a hurdle in fruitful bilateral talks.

Delinking 'conditions' from bilateral negotiations: Both India and Pakistan must keep the process of dialogue open, and must not put any condition upon bilateral negotiations. It has been observed that both the countries usually prefer to put conditions before top-level bilateral talks; Pakistan normally raises the Kashmir issue, and India prefers to pursue the issue of alleged Pakistan-backed terror activities in India (like the 2001 attacks on the Indian parliament, and the 26/11 Mumbai attacks). As a consequence, bilateral talks ultimately lead to failed diplomacy. Both the countries must come out of this mindset, and avoid putting conditions on bilateral talks. Talks must be held between the two nations without any pre-imposed conditions. To achieve this, both the countries must first delink themselves from backing terrorist activities in the other territory.[34] The JS, cited earlier, also noted the importance of bilateral cooperation on counter-terrorism. The JS stated, 'The Foreign Secretaries noted that both countries recognize that terrorism poses a continuing threat to peace and security and they reiterated the firm and undiluted commitment of the two countries to fight and eliminate this scourge in all its forms and manifestations. They agreed on the need to strengthen cooperation on counter-terrorism.'[35] But again, little rhetoric, and more active bilateralism must be the lingering practise between these two states in South Asia. Concentration on economic diplomacy, and collaborations in educational, scientific and security areas would encourage mutual confidence, and an atmosphere for peace. State-backed terrorism may be defeated through such levels of cooperation.

CONCLUSION

South Asia has recently become a nuclear hot spot due to continuous mistrust and schism of two nuclear-capable opponents, India and Pakistan. Any future confrontation between the two may turn into a nuclear war, and would be catastrophic for the teeming millions of the region. Peace between the two is, therefore, an absolute necessity, not only for a stable South Asia, but also for the developmental efforts of these two poverty-stricken countries. Peace through economic diplomacy, and collaborative efforts in different areas must be given top priority by the two nations. The post Cold War international order demands the preference of economic diplomacy

---

[33] Ministry of External Affairs, Government of India, 'Joint Statement on Meeting between the Foreign Secretaries of India and Pakistan, Islamabad, June 24, 2011', available at http://www. http://meaindia.nic.in/mystart.php?id=530517775, accessed on 26 June 2011.

[34] Chatterjee, 'India–Pakistan Relations...', n. 11, p. 365.

[35] Ministry of External Affairs (India), n. 33.

and social collaboration over political antagonism. Pakistan and India must not remain cut-off from the acceptable trends in world politics today. They must join hands to usher in a new era in South Asian politics. Recommendations for the future, presented in this chapter, may help in establishing the peace process between the two countries. Political elites in both the countries have tremendous responsibility in guiding their nations, and establishing peace in the region. After all, political elites in Pakistan and India would have to choose how they wish to see the future: confrontationist or peaceful. They have to choose between destruction and existence,—honourable and peaceful.

2

INDIA AND SRI LANKA

Ethnic Problems and Beyond

HIGHLIGHTS

- Introduction
- Political Relations
- Economic Relations
- Security and Cultural Relations
- Recommendations for the Future

INTRODUCTION

Sri Lanka (Ceylon before 1972), an island nation which lies south of India across the Gulf of Mannar and the Palk Strait in the Indian Ocean, is one of India's closest neighbours, and toughest foreign policy challenges. Ever since the emergence of the island as an independent nation in1948, its relations with India had been uneasy due to the ethnic Tamil question. Although the Tamil issue did not assume substantial proportions to affect bilateral relations till the early 1980s, there had always been dormant tension in Sri Lankan society over this as India was viewed with suspicion by the majority Sinhalese. Despite sharing common history, culture and democratic values, India and Sri Lanka (SL) could not share a long peaceful bilateral relationship after they emerged as independent states in the late 1940s. Since both India and SL were strategically important to each other, their respective governments have always tried hard to prevent any major deterioration in their relationship. Despite that, the relationship had undergone considerable crises and setbacks due to the ethnic issue. Therefore, to understand India–SL relations, it is necessary to know the Tamil ethnic issue in SL.

Tamils in SL were traditionally categorised into two segments: the 'Indian Tamils', also known as the 'Estate Tamils', and the 'Sri Lankan Tamils'. The former was believed to be people of Indian origin who migrated to SL during the nineteenth and early twentieth centuries to work in Sri Lanka's tea and rubber estates. After independence, SL refused to grant citizenship status to these people and wanted India to take them back. India opposed the idea, and caught between the diplomatic tangles, the 'Estate Tamils' became stateless soon after. Since the early 1950s, long and arduous negotiations had taken place between India and SL over the plight of these people. In 1964, a major agreement to solve the problem was signed between the Indian and Sri Lankan heads of government (Lal Bahadur Shastri and Sirimavo Bandarnaike, respectively). However, the full implementation of the provisions of the agreement ran into rough weather. In 1974, yet another effort was made in the direction of solving this problem with the signing of an agreement between India's Prime Minister Indira Gandhi and Sirimavo Bandarnaike. More than 600,000 Indian Tamils were repatriated to India by these two agreements, and nearly 375,000 were granted Sri Lankan citizenship. Gradually, by the middle of the 1990s, nearly 400,000 'Estate Tamils' were granted citizenship status in SL.

The second category referred to the 'Sri Lankan Tamils', a minority ethnic community in SL. Since the emergence of SL as an independent state, this ethnic community has been vociferous over their rights to social and economic opportunities, which they believed, were being suppressed by the majority Sinhalese community. Their protests over equal rights gradually transformed into anti-state movements from the early 1970s. Organised Tamil militant groups, protesting against state discrimination, indulged in large-scale violent activities. The majority Sinhalese community, backed by governments empathetic towards their sentiments, began to retaliate. From the mid-1970s, SL witnessed violent conflicts between the minority Tamils (allegedly backed by governments of the Indian state of Tamil Nadu), and the majority Sinhalese community. Since then, India has been viewed with suspicion by the Sinhalese. Tamil militancy against the Sri Lankan state increased sharply from the early 1980s. Militant Tamil groups like the LTTE (Liberation Tigers of Tamil Eelam) spearheaded anti-state movements with large-scale violence. The LTTE was believed to have received initial support from India, especially from Tamil Nadu. The mistrust generated over the Tamil question affected bilateral relations for a long time. In the post-Cold War period, both India and SL concentrated on economic diplomacy to bypass their political differences. However, the Tamil question continued to bother bilateral relations. Decades later, the Sri Lankan government of Mahinda Rajapaksa finally crushed the LTTE in 2009 through military operations; but alleged to have committed violation of human rights during these operations. But this time, the Government of India (GoI) preferred to see Sri Lankan operations against the LTTE as Sri Lanka's internal affair with a view to strengthen economic diplomacy with its neighbour. With this short background, this chapter would analyse major trends in India–SL relations in the recent times, and provide some recommendations to improve bilateral relations in the future.

POLITICAL RELATIONS

India and SL achieved their independence in 1947 and 1948 respectively. The two new nations in South Asia established formal diplomatic relations in 1948. Since then India–SL relations have been witness to many happy as well as uneasy phases. From 1948 to 1956, SL was ruled by the United National Party (UNP) under three Prime Ministers: D. S. Senanayake (1948–52), his son Dudley Senanayake (1952–53) and John Kotelawala (1953–56). The Congress Party was in power in India at that time with its leader Jawaharlal Nehru as the prime minister. During this period, the foreign policies of these countries took its shape largely under Western influence. With Anglo-American victory in the Second World War, and common British colonial legacy, the ruling elites in SL and India initially preferred to stay within the Anglo-American ambit in international relations. Sri Lanka allowing British naval bases on its soil, both SL and India adopting (British-type) parliamentary democracy and membership of the British Commonwealth, are some of the early instances of this Anglo-American influence. As a consequence, divergence in policies and interests were not much pronounced during the initial phase in bilateral relations, particularly during 1948–52 when the two Senanayakes were in power in SL. Nehru also wanted to see India develop its foreign relations in accordance with Western strategic interests in international politics during this period.[1]

However, divergence of interests in India–SL ties surfaced from 1953–54 when Nehru became disenchanted with Western influences in international relations, and Cold War political calculations. The Sri Lankan political elites, led by Prime Minister John Kotalewala continued with their Western leanings. Kotalewala reportedly wanted to join the South East Asian Treaty Organization (SEATO), an American-led security pact, and cited pressures from India as the reason for his inability to join the SEATO.[2] Although internal disagreements within the ruling UNP prevented Kotalewala from joining the SEATO, he did not hesitate to put the onus on Nehru with whom he did not share good personal relations.[3] Nehru was, however, apprehensive of superpower rivalry and bloc politics dominating inter-state relations in South Asia during this period, and showed great interest in initiating the Non Aligned Movement (NAM). Kotalewala, on his part, preferred to view SL joining the SEATO, and the UK–Ceylon Defence Agreement his country concluded earlier, as strategic moves to thwart India, the giant neighbour from exerting its influence over SL.[4] Kotalewala's perception of India as a security threat put bilateral relations under substantial strain.

Normalcy was restored in India–SL relations when S. W. R. D. Bandarnaike's Sri Lanka Freedom Party (SLFP) came to power in SL in 1956. Bandarnaike supported the NAM and gradually took SL away from Western influences. His intentions in this respect became clear when he urged Britain to withdraw its naval bases from SL. The Bandarnaike government wanted to remain out of bloc politics and superpower rivalry, and pursue an independent foreign policy for SL. The new foreign policy perspectives of SL were in tune with Jawaharlal Nehru's views which India followed in international relations. Bandarnaike, unlike his predecessor, considered India as a friendly neighbour, and nurtured warm personal relations with Nehru. As a consequence, relations between the two nations improved considerably during his three-year tenure (1956–59),

---

[1] See in this context, S. D. Muni, *Pangs of Proximity: India and Sri Lanka's Ethnic Crisis* (New Delhi: Sage), 1993, pp. 32–36.

[2] Ibid.

[3] Ibid.

[4] Ibid.

and were strengthened further under the leadership of Sirimavo Bandarnaike, who came to power after the assassination of her husband (S. W. R. D.) in 1959. Sirimavo continued with the foreign policy of her husband, and viewed India as a friend and partner in the developmental process of SL. She developed good personal chemistry with Nehru, and later with Indira Gandhi, which paved ways for strong bilateral relations. Although the Sirimavo government reached out to China, such efforts did not affect Sri Lanka's proximity to India. During the Sino-Indian war of 1962, Sirimavo played an important mediatory role by setting up proposals for the resolution of border conflicts between China and India, and her role was appreciated by Nehru.[5] In this tenure, Sirimavo was in power till 1965, and she could be credited for establishing stronger ties with India during this time.

SL was ruled by a UNP government, headed by Dudley Senanayake, for the next five years (1965–70). There was no major change in relationship with India during this phase, and it continued to be normal. It must be pointed out here that during the first three decades since Sri Lankan independence in 1948, ethnic issues did not become explicitly prominent to derail India–SL relations, although it constituted sources of tension in Sri Lankan society and politics. After Sri Lankan independence, different Sinhala-dominated governments were engaged in arousing Sinhala nationalism, and pursued policies to discriminate against the minority Tamil community in the areas of land, language, educational and economic opportunities. The first three UNP governments in SL (1948–56), pursued land colonisation policies aimed at habitating Sinhalese population in Tamil-majority provinces of the northeastern and eastern parts of SL. These policies were aimed at altering the demographic character of a multi-ethnic SL. Moreover, S. W. R. D. Bandarnaike had come to power in the 1956 elections on the slogan of 'Sinhala only'. Although the policy behind this slogan was primarily aimed at reducing the influences of English language in Sri Lankan education and culture, it nevertheless encouraged the majority Sinhalese community to exert its own influence in Sri Lankan society and culture. This policy of the SLFP also encouraged the other Sinhala-dominated political parties in SL to try and win elections by pandering to the sentiments of the majority Sinhalas. As a consequence, the minority Tamil community felt neglected and got increasingly alienated within that country. The 'Sinhala only' sentiment gradually reached all spheres of socio-economic life, with tacit approval of all subsequent Sinhala-dominated governments led by either the SLFP or UNP. The Tamils found it increasingly difficult to protect their language and culture in a multi-ethnic SL, and were placed in a disadvantageous position, in comparison to the Sinhalese, as far as jobs, land-holding, education and business were concerned. Driven to desperation, they began to protest, and by the mid-1970s, the Tamil United Liberation Front (TULF), the party spearheading the protest movements at that time, raised the demand for a separate state. By the time Sirimavo Bandarnaike returned to power in SL in 1970, Tamil dissent started to manifest, and by the end of her second tenure (in 1977) as HoG in SL, demands for a separate Tamil state had been raised.

---

[5] See in this context, H. S. S. Nissanka, *Foreign Policy of Sri Lanka under Bandarnaikes* (New Delhi: Vikas), 1984, pp. 146–53.

The UNP came back to power in 1977 and its leader J. R. Jayewardene enjoyed office as HoG till 1988. During Jayewardene's tenure, the control over the Tamil movement went to the LTTE, as the ultra extremist stance taken by the organisation attracted the attention of the Tamil population in SL. The LTTE sought to create an independent Tamil state out of SL by force, carried through militant activities. The rise in Tamil militancy could be attributed to the failure of the UNP to fulfil its promises for the Tamils as envisaged in the Election Manifesto (1977) of that party. The manifesto vowed to resolve the Tamil problems without much loss of time.[6] However, after coming to power, the UNP government showed little interest to solve the problems, and went on appeasing the Sinhalese community, like all previous governments. Within a month of the UNP's electoral victory in 1977, ethnic riots took place in the Northern provinces which witnessed large-scale Tamil casualties.[7] A desperate and frustrated Tamil community turned to armed militancy thereafter, and the popularity of the LTTE, the hard-core advocates of armed rebellion, started to increase among the Tamils. However, ethnic problems in SL did not rupture India–SL relations till the end of the 1970s, although India expressed its concern over the Tamil problems in SL. After the 1977 riots, India's Prime Minister Morarji Desai, yielding to the view that these riots were anti-Indian in nature, sent his emissary, S. A. Chidambaram to SL to study the situation. Chidambaram's visit did not raise many eyebrows in SL, and he was received well by the Sri Lankan government,[8] which indicated that ethnic issues had not affected bilateral relations till that time. Chidambaram reported to Prime Minister Desai that the riots were not against India, and that they were caused by domestic events.

Bilateral relations came under considerable strain since the early 1980s due to rising ethnic problems in SL, and after 1983, the relationship deteriorated in the aftermath of severe ethnic riots that continued for weeks in the north and northeastern parts of the island. India's Prime Minister Indira Gandhi spoke to Jayewardene over phone and proposed to send her External Affairs Minister Narasimha Rao to SL to assess the situation. Although the Sri Lankan President agreed, probably for diplomatic reasons, Rao was not received well in SL. Rao's visit only aroused suspicion and mistrust. Later, G. Parthasarathy, another emissary of prime minister, was also given cold shoulders by the Sri Lankan government, indicating its displeasure over Indian 'interference' in its internal matters. As one Sri Lankan author writes, 'Unlike the visit of Chidambaram, the visit of Narasimha Rao and Parthasarathy were received suspiciously by Sri Lanka which felt that unlike under Desai, under Mrs. Gandhi, India was turning to be hegemonistic.'[9] The twin visits drew sharp criticism from different sections of people throughout the island. By the middle of the 1980s, bilateral relations reached very low as SL began to accuse India of giving all possible

---

[6] See, Muni, *Pangs of Proximity*, n. 1, pp. 43–44.

[7] Ibid.

[8] See in this context, Bertram E. S. J. Bastiampillai, 'Ethnic Conflicts in South Asia and Inter-state Relations Especially in Relation to Sri Lanka', in Shelton U. Kodikara, ed., *South Asian Strategic Issues: Sri Lankan Perspectives* (New Delhi: Sage), 1990, p. 91.

[9] Ibid.

support to Tamil militants with a view to fomenting trouble in SL. Huge amount of schism dominated bilateral relations as India also viewed with caution Sri Lanka's growing contacts with China, Pakistan and Israel.

In 1987, the Sri Lankan government started fresh military offensive against the Tamil militant organisations in the Jaffna province. A parallel embargo on the movement of fuel and other necessities caused severe hardship to the people of the Jaffna and its adjacent regions. India protested against the military offensive and declared its intention to send relief and food supplies to the Tamils of Jaffna. An Indian relief vessel was subsequently stopped in mid-sea by the Sri Lankan navy. India decided to airdrop relief materials in Jaffna. All these events caused severe damage to bilateral relations which reached its nadir in 1987. In order to prevent further strains in bilateral relations, and to find a solution to the Tamil problem, President J. R. Jayewardene of SL and Prime Minister Rajiv Gandhi of India entered into an agreement on 29 July 1987. The agreement, known as the India–Sri Lanka Peace Accord, made India an active partner, along with SL, in the process of establishing peace and normalcy in the island. Among the salient features of the agreement, the Sri Lankan government made a number of concessions to the demands of the Tamils. These demands included devolution of power to the provinces, merger, which is subject to a referendum later, of the northern and eastern provinces, and the official status for the Tamil language. More immediately, the anti-insurgency operation by the Sri Lankan forces in the Northern peninsula would come to an end. The Sri Lankan troops were to withdraw to their barracks in the north, and the Tamil rebels were to disarm. The agreement proposed that India would send a peace-keeping force, on an invitation from the Sri Lankan President, to curb separatist and militant activities in SL.

As per the provisions of the Accord, an Indian Peace Keeping Force (IPKF) was invited to SL to maintain peace and normalcy in the island. But the LTTE refused to disarm, and declared its intention to continue arm struggle for an independent Tamil state. Therefore, the Peace Accord ran into rough weather, and ethnic troubles continued in the island despite the presence of the IPKF. In fact, the IPKF experience proved embarrassing as well as disastrous for India. The IPKF had to confront the LTTE in different parts of the island, and suffered huge loss of lives. With a high casualty figure, the IPKF gradually got demoralised to fight militants in a foreign land. Moreover, with escalating costs to maintain the IPKF in SL, and mounting casualties, the rationale behind sending the IPKF was questioned in India by the opposition parties. The IPKF failed to maintain peace in the strife-torn island, and was finally withdrawn in early 1990 by India. The IPKF mission, contrary to expectations outlined in the Peace Accord, was unable to restore peace in the island. It also failed to salvage a downslide in bilateral relationship.

Ethnic violence continued in SL throughout the 1990s, and the next decade of the new century. But the IPKF experiment made Indian diplomacy cautious with regard to ethnic problems in SL. After the withdrawal of the IPKF, and particularly after the assassination of Rajiv Gandhi by the LTTE, India treaded cautiously and preferred to maintain distance from ethnic troubles in SL. Instead, India chose to follow the path of economic diplomacy with regard to SL. All Indian governments since 1990 have preferred to push the Tamil issue to the background and concentrate more on economic issues in Indo–SL relations. The economic diplomacy proved beneficial for India during the 1990s and after in several ways:

(i) It helped to wipe out the memories of the IPKF mission;
(ii) It gradually restored India's falling image in SL;
(iii) It was in tune with India's economic liberalisation;
(iv) It went well with the changing world order after the Cold War; and
(v) It provided a new 'economic' dimension to bilateral relations, which remained focused on ethnic issues earlier.

By the middle of the 1990s, India and SL were engaged in important commercial activities. For instance, at the end of 1995, 13 joint ventures were under operation in SL, while 17 others were waiting to start. Most significantly, about 50 per cent of these joint ventures were in manufacturing and service sectors, considered to be growth-oriented industries.[10] Further, a very significant step was taken on 28 December 1998, when the visiting Sri Lankan President Chandrika Kumartunga and the Indian Prime Minister A. B. Vajpayee signed the India–SL Free Trade Agreement (FTA). The Indian High Commissioner to SL, S. Menon sounded optimistic about the FTA when he said, '. . . for several years now, the political relations between the two countries have been reduced to just one issue (Tamil problem) . . . the FTA is one important instrument which will broadbase the ties by creating mutual stakes'.[11] The FTA became fully operational from March 2000, and contributed positively in promoting bilateral relations. An India–SL Foundation was created in November 1999 to foster relations in non-political areas. This Rs 400 million Foundation was set up to promote ties in the field of education and culture, archaeological studies, agriculture, technical training, development studies and women's development. Clearly, the focus was on non-political areas, a trend observed throughout the 1990s.

India's self-imposed distance from ethnic troubles in SL continued in the first decade of the new century as well, although the island was tormented by ethnic violence till 2009. The Sri Lankan government led by Mahinda Rajapaksa began a major military offensive against the LTTE in January 2008. The initial resistance of the LTTE gradually crumbled as the Sri Lankan military captured several LTTE bastions in the north and the east of the island. In May 2009, the Rajapaksa government finally declared victory over the LTTE. The end of the military offensive resulted in nearly 300,000 internally displaced persons (IDP) and allegations of violations of human rights and international humanitarian law by both the sides in the final stages of the conflict. The Indian government led by Manmohan Singh also distanced itself from ethnic conflicts in SL, and kept silent on the military offensive on the LTTE till 2011. However, in March 2012, India voted in favour of a United Nations Human Rights Council

---

[10] Aneek Chatterjee, 'Missed Opportunities for Regional Cooperation in South Asia', *Politics India*, 3 (6), 1998.

[11] Quoted in *The Statesman*, Kolkata, 14 February 2000; parenthesis by the author.

(UNHRC) resolution, initiated by the United States, condemning the Sri Lanka government for human rights violations and war crimes against the Tamils. The Manmohan Singh Government had to vote in favour of the resolution for domestic political compulsions, when the Tamil Nadu (India) based Dravida Munnetra Kazhagam (DMK) party, which supported the Singh Government, put pressure on the government to vote in favour of the UNHRC resolution. India's vote against Sri Lanka at the UNHRC did not go well with the Lankan government, which called India's action unfortunate. But India reiterated that Indo-Lanka relations would continue to be cordial. While India preferred to remain silent initially on the military offensive and alleged violation of human rights by the Rajapaksa government with a view to safeguard normalcy in bilateral relations, it tried to console Tamil sensibilities as well by announcing a massive rehabilitation programme for the IDP. Finally, to redress growing Tamil opinion against military offensive and war crimes by the SL government, and to appease the DMK, the Singh Government voted in favour of the UNHRC resolution in March 2012.

Political relations between the two neighbours improved a bit with the installation of new governments, in India in 2014 and in Sri Lanka in 2015. Rajapaksa travelled to New Delhi in May 2014 to attend the swearing-in ceremony of the new Prime Minister of India, Narendra Modi. The visit marked a positive gesture by Rajapaksa to renew contacts with the new Indian government. However, Rajapaksa was voted out of power in the next presidential election held on 8 January 2015, and Maithripala Sirisena was elected as the new President of Sri Lanka. The new President showed his willingness to put India on his priority list when he visited India on a four-day trip starting 15 February 2015. India took this opportunity to forge a refurbished relationship with SL. India signed a civil nuclear cooperation agreement with SL during the visit. This is Lanka's first nuclear agreement with any country. This agreement would boost strategic partnership between India and SL. The new Indian government also reciprocated its desire to establish close contacts with SL. Prime Minister Narendra Modi visited Sri Lanka on 13 and 14 March 2015. Modi's visit to SL underlined India's quest for a cooperative maritime security approach in the Indian Ocean Region (IOR) and its willingness to play a critical role in ensuring peace and prosperity in the IOR countries. Sri Lanka is an important maritime neighbour and an integral element in India's maritime strategy in the Indian Ocean. Modi's visit was also significant in the context of India's engagement in infrastructure development in SL. Since 2015, political relations between the two countries have been marked by high-level exchanges of visits at regular intervals. However, a sense of mistrust persisted between the two neighbours. The Rajapaksa government's strategic engagement with China and its decision to allow the Chinese navy to berth nuclear submarines in Sri Lankan ports disregarding Indian sensitivities, had led to setbacks in the bilateral relationship. However, the new governments in both the countries are trying hard to put their relations back on track.

ECONOMIC RELATIONS

In the economic segment, India and SL enjoy a better chemistry. Since the operationalisation of the FTA in 2000, trade between the two countries has been growing at a rapid pace. Bilateral trade multiplied nearly five times from 2000 to 2015.[12] Sri Lanka is India's largest trade partner in South Asian Association for Regional Cooperation (SAARC). India in turn is one of SL's largest trade partners in the world. Bilateral trade achieved significant progress since the financial year 2010–11 compared to the preceding years. Table 2.1 below shows India–SL trade in the recent years.

Table 2.1: India–Sri Lanka Trade in Recent Years (in US $ million)

Year	*India's Export*	*India's Import*	*Total Trade*	*Trade Balance*
2006–07	2,258.30	470.33	2,728.63	1,787.96
2007–08	2,830.43	634.96	3,465.39	2,195.47
2008–09	2,425.92	356.57	2,782.49	2,069.35
2009–10	2,188.01	392.19	2,580.20	1,795.81
2010–11	4,039.90	501.73	4,541.62	3,538.17
2011–12	4,378.79	637.43	5,016.22	3,741.36
2012–13	3,983.87	625.81	4,609.68	3,358.06
2013–14	4,534.35	666.93	5,201.28	3,867.42
2014–15	6,703.76	756.17	7,459.23	5,947.59

Source: Department of Commerce, Export-Import Data Bank, Government of India, available at http://commerce.nic.in/eidb/iecnt.asp, accessed on 20 November 2015.

Table 2.1 above shows significant growth in bilateral trade in 2010–11. India–SL total trade reached US $4,541.62 million in 2010–11, a 76 per cent increase from the previous year. India's export to SL almost doubled from the previous year to US $4,039.90 million. There was notable increase in India's import from SL as well in 2010–11. Bilateral trade witnessed an overall increase of 66 per cent, from 2006–07 to 2010–11. As evident from the table, trade in 2009–10 dipped to the lowest in the last five years since 2006 due to world-wide economic recession. However, with sincere efforts from both the governments, bilateral trade recorded an impressive growth in 2010–11. Again in the 2014–15 fiscal, India–SL trade recorded impressive growth. Bilateral trade rose to US $7,459.23 million in 2014–15, an all time high since 2006–07. But trade balance between India and SL has also been increasing since 2006–07 an area which might create concerns for both the nations in the future.

Indian direct investment to SL has been steadily rising, particularly since 2000. By the end of 2007, India became one of the top-five countries investing in SL accounting for 6.5 per cent of the total foreign direct investment (FDI) inflow to the island. Over 50 per cent of Indian investments in the SAARC region are located in SL. The period after 2000 was even more significant because investment from India grew at an average of US $33 million per annum,

[12] Ministry of External Affairs, Government of India, 'India–Sri Lanka Relations', available at http://mea.gov.in/mystart.php?id=50044525, accessed on 5 December 2014.

accounting for 16 per cent of the total FDI flows to the country. The increase in Indian FDI to SL may be partially attributed to the FTA. It increased the scope for the expansion of trade in goods between the two countries, and broadened the scope for investment expansion. India and SL signed an Investment Promotion and Protection Agreement (IPPA) in 1997. The IPPA has also contributed significantly to the growth of Indian investment in the island. At 2012, India has nearly a 100 projects in SL, compared to 13 in the 1990s. The sectoral distribution of Indian FDI to SL changed remarkably after 2000. Indian FDI to SL is now mostly in the service sector, which consumes nearly 63 per cent of total Indian FDI inflow to SL. In 2000, the service-sector share of FDI was only 30 per cent; and there was no service-sector investment from India in 1990. This change was due to the fast growth of Indian investments in services such as fuel distribution, hotel industry, tourism, health, education, Information Technology (IT) training, computer software and professional services. Among the big Indian companies which are present in SL are Indian Oil Corporation (IOC), Tatas, Bharti Airtel, Piramal Glass, Life Insurance Corporation (LIC), Ashok Leyland and the Aditya Birla Group. The growth of Indian investment to SL could be assessed from the fact that India became the largest FDI contributor to SL in 2010, contributing US $110 million out of total US $516 million received by SL. The two nations are on the verge of concluding a Comprehensive Economic Partnership Agreement (CEPA) soon, and the CEPA is expected to strengthen their economic relationship further.

Tourism has also flourished between the two countries, adding vigour to their economic relations. More than 125,000 Indian tourists visited SL in 2010, making up nearly 20 per cent of the total tourist inflow into the island. Due to prolonged ethnic troubles in SL, tourists from the Western world visiting the island dwindled over the years. As a consequence, Indian tourists constituted a major chunk of foreign tourist inflow to the island, which added strength to the Sri Lankan economy. Tourists from SL too are among the top five sources for the Indian tourism market. In 2013, nearly 300,000 visas were issued by the High Commission in Colombo to facilitate travel between India and SL.[13] The percentage share of Sri Lankan tourists to total foreign tourists to India was 3.93 in 2014–15, up from 3.77 in the previous year. Table 2.2 reveals top 10 sources for foreign tourists to India.

It is evident from Table 2.2 that tourists from only two SAARC countries, Bangladesh and SL, come within the top five source countries of FTA. However, Indian tourist outflow to Bangladesh is lesser compared to Indian tourists visiting SL. Therefore, tourism constitutes a strong area in India–SL economic relations. According to a Government of India (GoI) report compiled by the Ministry of External Affairs (MEA), two-way tourism and connectivity between India and SL would get further fillip with the commencement of ferry services between Colombo and Tuticorin, and Talaimannar and Rameswaram, an agreement for which has been signed in June 2010 between the two countries.[14] Therefore, tourism is a potential bright spot in India–SL economic relations in the future.

[13] Ibid.

[14] Ibid.

Table 2.2: Top Ten Source Countries for Foreign Tourist Arrivals (FTA) in India in 2014–15

Serial No.	*Source Country*	*FTA in Million*	*Per cent Share of Total FTA*
1	USA	1,118,983	14.57
2	Bangladesh	942,562	12.27
3	UK	838,860	10.92
4	Sri Lanka	301,601	3.93
5	Russian Federation	269,832	3.51
6	Canada	268,485	3.50
7	Malaysia	262,026	3.41
8	France	246,101	3.20
9	Australia	239,762	3.12
10	Germany	239,106	3.11

Source: Ministry of Toursim, Government of India, available at http://tourism.gov.in/writereaddata/CMSPagePicture/file/marketresearch/New/2010.pdf, accessed on 20 July 2015.

SL is one of the major recipients of development credit given by the GoI. As per reports of the MEA, GoI, a line of credit of US $167.4 million for repair and upgradation of the tsunami-damaged Colombo–Matara rail link is already fully operational. The upgraded coastal railway track between Galle and Matara was inaugurated on 16 February 2011. Another line of credit of US $800 million for construction of railway tracks and supply of rolling stock for the northern railway line in SL was announced during the visit of the President of SL to India in June 2010. Of this amount, an agreement for a credit line of US $416.39 million was signed in November 2010 to support construction of Medawachchiya to Madhu, Madhu to Talaimannar and Omanthai to Pallai railway lines in northern Sri Lanka. India also continues to assist a larger number of development projects through its grant funding. These include setting up e-learning centres, provision of fishing equipment to cooperatives, supply of buses for assisting transportation in hilly and remote locations and a variety of small development projects in areas such as education, health and training in many parts of the island. Other important infrastructure-related projects under consideration by both the governments include the 500 MW coal-based power plant in Trincomalee and inter-connectivity of the Indian and SL electricity grids. Work is expected to start soon for setting up of a cultural centre in Jaffna and renovating the famous Duraiappah Stadium. Moreover, with a view to boost domestic and regional travel and commerce, India is also assisting with the restoration of the Kankesanthurai Harbour and the development of the Palaly airfield as a civil airport. An agreement to formalise Indian assistance for the rehabilitation of the Kankesanthurai Harbour was signed in July 2011.[15]

[15] Ibid.

SECURITY AND CULTURAL RELATIONS

Sri Lanka's important strategic location in the Indian Ocean is crucial for India's security and trade. Indian Ocean accommodates half the world's containerised freight, one-third of its bulk cargo, and two-thirds of its oil shipments. Many international shipping routes go by SL's southern coast. Therefore, India can hardly ignore its security relations with SL. Influence of important powers or terrorist outfits on the politics of the island may prove to be inimical for India's security and commercial interests. In fact, India has important strategic and economic reasons for ensuring a stable security situation in and around the Indian Ocean. Sea trade dominates India's overall transnational trade, and nearly 89 per cent of oil imports to India arrive by sea.[16] In this respect, SL plays a particularly important role in India's security and maritime trade. Over 70 per cent of Indian imports arrive through the port of Colombo before they are shipped on local carriers to Indian ports.[17] Securing the Indian Ocean is crucial to India's continued engagement with the international market, and SL assumes special significance in these security arrangements.

With increasing competition among major powers for gaining economic and military footholds in the island, SL always remained vulnerable to major power penetration. In the past, Portugese, Dutch and British had gained control over the island nation. After SL's independence, major powers endeavoured to exert their influences over it. America, China and Pakistan have established strong security and economic links with the island with a view to make their presence strong in the IOR. While it is practically impossible for India to prevent other powers from wooing the Sri Lankan governments, India can try to minimise their influence by forging strong security and economic relations with SL. India has started to move in this direction, and currently the two countries enjoy a growing defence relationship built on extensive training and service-to-service linkages. The two neighbours have decided to hold an Annual Defence Dialogue (ADD) starting from 2011. The ADD would be an additional mechanism as Staff Talks between the two armies, navies and air forces are already in place. Bilateral exchanges of visits for strengthening security relations take place on a regular basis. The Indian Defence Secretary as well as the Chiefs of Staff of the Indian navy and Indian army visited SL in 2010. Gotabaya Rajapaksa, the defence secretary of SL, visited India in 2010. The Sri Lankan Navy Commander participated in the Golden Jubilee celebrations of the National Defence College in New Delhi in 2010. A major area of concern for the two countries is the illegal straying and poaching of fishermen due to the proximity of the territorial waters of both countries, especially in the Palk Straits and the Gulf of Mannar. Detention of fishermen for illegal poaching may cause damage to bilateral relations. Therefore, both the governments have agreed on certain practical arrangements to deal with the issue of bonafide fishermen on either side crossing the International Maritime Boundary Line (IMBL).

---

[16] Brian Orland, 'India's Sri Lanka Policy: Towards Economic Engagement' (New Delhi: Institute of Peace and Conflict Studies), 2008, p. 8.

[17] Ibid.

Through these arrangements, it has been possible to deal with the issue of detention of fishermen in a more pragmatic and decent manner in recent times. But it should be kept in mind that India–SL security relationship is still not very strong, and needs to be augmented further as there is vast scope for increasing cooperation between the two in this area.

India and SL signed a Cultural Cooperation Agreement (CPA) on 29 November 1977 in New Delhi. The CPA, over the years, has remained as the foundation for various Cultural Exchange Programmes between the two countries. A Programme of Cultural Cooperation (PCC) for 2010–13 was signed during the official visit of President Mahinda Rajapaksa to India in June 2010. According to MEA, GoI, '... the PCC seeks to enhance the level of cooperation in a wide variety of fields such as performing arts, visual arts, libraries, museums, archives and cultural documentation, archaeology, handicrafts, sports and youth affairs, publications and professional exchanges and mass media'.[18] Further, the Indian Cultural Centre in Colombo acts as a cultural link between the two nations. Besides promoting awareness of Indian culture, the Centre draws artists and performers from different parts of the island to its own cultural events which take place throughout the year.

Cultural troupes from both the countries exchange visits every year. India is also helping SL in the restoration of important icons of cultural heritage in the island. India is currently working on the restoration of the Thirukeeteswaram Temple in Mannar, and is setting up an Indian Gallery at the International Buddhist Museum in Kandy. Education is another significant area of cooperation between the two neighbours. Both the countries agreed to launch an India Sri Lanka Knowledge Initiative (ISLKI). This was done during President Rajapaksa's visit to India. Under the ISLKI, India proposes to double its scholarships for Sri Lankan students for studies in Indian universities. According to MEA sources, '... a significant number of scholarships are also offered by India in Sri Lanka itself to support needy and deserving students pursue "A" Level as well as university education. In addition to that, under the Indian Technical and Economic Cooperation Scheme and the Colombo Plan, India offers nearly 200 slots annually to Sri Lankan nationals for short- and medium-term training courses in a wide variety of technical and professional disciplines'.[19] Strong cultural ties between the two countries have added a new dimension to bilateral relations in the recent times.

RECOMMENDATIONS FOR THE FUTURE

India's relations with SL are age-old and deep. The ethnic problem in SL did create some misunderstandings; but both the countries have learnt many lessons from these troubles, and these experiences would help them overcome future hurdles in bilateral relations. For instance, India's experiences with the IPKF led it to follow the course of economic diplomacy with regard

[18] Ministry of External Affairs (India), n. 12.

[19] Ibid.

to SL in the 1990s and after, a course that suited India's interests during the period. Economic diplomacy continues to be the best bet for Indian foreign policy in SL, as India prefers not to get involved in Sri Lankan politics. After India's vote in favour of the UNHRC resolution, India must walk extra miles to strengthen relations with SL. India's economic relations with SL should be strengthened within a rule-based liberalised trade regime which can provide policy environment conducive for strengthened economic relations with clearly defined rules. This would avoid the frictions associated with *ad hoc* problem solving. This is especially important for services, where there are no tariffs to reduce, only non-tariff barriers to remove.

Further, it would be unwise for both the countries to delay the already negotiated CEPA. A commitment should be given to set up a time-bound mechanism to examine and resolve any problems goods exporters may have experienced in the first years of the FTA. The Report of the Joint Study Group on the CEPA made detailed recommendations of trust-building actions that could be taken prior to and in parallel with the implementation of CEPA. In addition, the GoI should encourage more Indian private companies to set up business in SL. With normalcy and political stability back in the island, Indian private business must look forward to SL for increased investment. This will not only generate more FDI for the island, but will also strengthen bilateral economic relations.

Defence cooperation between the two neighbours is a vastly untapped area which can be augmented in the future. Indian and Sri Lankan navies can cooperate closely to stave off the problems of illegal poaching by fishermen of both the countries, as well as illegal migration to India. The two air forces may also be jointly used for this purpose. The two nations can sign memoranda of understanding (MoUs) for exchange of security information and defence technology. These steps may work as counterbalancing forces to terrorism in the Gulf of Mannar and the Palk Strait. A Defence Cooperation Agreement (DCA) proposed between the two nations should be concluded as early as possible. The DCA may prove to be helpful for India in countering the growing influence of China over SL in security matters like supply of arms, information and technology. While it would be imprudent for India to show any knee-jerk reaction over the growing Chinese contacts with SL on defence matters, India must chart its own course to increase defence cooperation with the island with a view to generate trust in SL over its willingness to cooperate on important security issues. An early conclusion of the long-awaited DCA may help in this regard.

3

INDIA AND BANGLADESH

Close or a Distant Neighbour?

HIGHLIGHTS

- Introduction
- Political Relations
- Economic Relations
- Security and Cultural Relations
- Recommendations for the Future

INTRODUCTION

India's relations with Bangladesh have always been full of ups and downs since the time Bangladesh was born in 1971. Initially, after the creation of Bangladesh, the relationship was cordial. The first head of government (HoG) of independent Bangladesh, Sheikh Mujibar Rahman (1972–75) acknowledged India's positive role in the liberation of Bangladesh and perceived India as a friend of the new country in South Asia. India offered helps for the state-building process of Bangladesh and the two neighbours appeared set for a booming relationship. However, the bonhomie was cut short by the assassination of Mujibar Rahman in an army coup in August 1975, allegedly masterminded by the anti-Indian segment of the Bangladeshi army. Khondakar Mushtaq Ahmad formed a new government in August 1975 and ruled the country till November 1975. But another army coup, led by Major General Ziaur Rahman brought him to power in late 1975. After Mujib's assassination, Indo–Bangla relations went through rough phases. Anti-India sentiments ran high in Bangladesh during the period of two military rules, one of Ziaur Rahman (1975–81), and the other under H. M. Ershad (1982–90). Civilian rules returned to Bangladesh during the 1990s, but relations with India were not always warm. Domestic politics in Bangladesh was largely polarised under the dominance of two political parties,—the Bangladesh Nationalist Party (BNP) currently headed by Khaleda Zia (widow of Ziaur Rahman), and the Awami League (AL), currently headed by Sheikh Hasina (daughter of Mujibar Rahman). Under two BNP governments headed by Khaleda Zia (1991–96 and 2001–06), relations with India suffered. However, during two AL governments headed by Sheikh Hasina (1996–2001 and 2009–present), relations with India progressed. During 2006–08, Bangladesh had two 'caretaker governments', which attempted to maintain formal good relations with India. With this historical background, the present chapter wishes to analyse the major trends of India–Bangladesh relations, and propose a future course for stronger bilateral relationship.

POLITICAL RELATIONS

For the last four decades, India's relations with Bangladesh have been broadly determined by a few factors. These are:

(i) Bangladeshi domestic politics and the perception of the Bangladeshi political elites about India;
(ii) Border and water disputes;
(iii) Trade and transit issues;
(iv) Illegal migration; and
(v) Insurgency and security concerns.

While factors (iii) and (v) above would be analysed separately under 'economic' and 'security' relations, the other three issues would be taken up for discussion under this section. To begin with domestic politics in Bangladesh, the country's relations with India were always determined by the twists and turns of internal political courses, and the perceptions of the ruling elites in Bangladesh about India. From 1971 till Mujib's death in 1975, Indo–Bangla relations were friendly and cordial because Mujib had a good perception about India and its role in the creation of Bangladesh. The Mujib-led AL government wanted to be a friend of India, and extended all possible cooperation to strengthen bilateral relations. In March 1972, the two nations signed a 'Treaty of Peace and Friendship', which stipulated, among other issues, that the two countries would not enter into or participate in military alliances directed against each other, or give assistance to a third party engaged in an armed conflict against the other party. Article 6 of the Treaty pledged to make joint studies and take action in the fields of flood control, river basin development and the development of hydro-electric power and irrigation. In May 1974, the two countries signed an agreement concerning the demarcation of land boundary between India and Bangladesh and related matters. The agreement proposed to demarcate land borders along the Mizoram-Bangladesh Sector, Tripura-Sylhet Sector, Muhuri River (Belonia) Sector, Fenny River, Rest of Tripura-Chittagong Hill Tract Sector, Beanibazar-Karimganj Sector, Enclaves, Hilli, Berubari, and Lathitilla-Dumabari areas. The two governments agreed that any dispute concerning the interpretation or implementation of this agreement shall be settled peacefully through mutual consultations. The 1974 Agreement on border demarcation is still considered a major guideline to settle border-related problems between the two countries.

The excellent beginning of bilateral relationship due to Mujib's positive attitude could not be sustained later due to negative perceptions about India nurtured by the subsequent ruling elites in Bangladesh. Under the military rule of Ziaur Rahman, Bangladesh began to move away from India, and search for extra-regional 'friends' in the pan-Islamic movement, and in China. Ziaur came to power with anti-India sentiments, and he was determined to foster this feeling, and erase Mujib's legacy from Bangladeshi politics. Ziaur also wanted to create a 'Bangladeshi' identity in world politics without much dependence on India. Bangladesh was declared an Islamic republic by Ziaur, desperate to alter the secular foundation of the nation initiated by Mujib. His policies frightened minority Hindus and Buddhists as fundamentalism received a fillip in Bangladesh.[1] For Ziaur, a Muslim identity for Bangladesh served a few purposes: (i) of moving away from Mujib's legacy; (ii) of appeasing the Muslim fraternity throughout the world including Pakistan; and (iii) of creating a sense of religious nationalism for Bangladesh. To fulfil these interests, Ziaur was prepared to antagonise India. As a consequence, Indo–Bangla relations dipped to a new low between the late 1970s and early 1980s.

Bangladesh also suffered from security fears. The army rulers, Ziaur and later, H. M. Ershad, some religious leaders, and a section of the intelligentsia, believed that India nurtured plans to destabilise military governments in Bangladesh. This fear was one of the reasons for Ziaur to take cover under the pan-Islamic umbrella, and establish a Muslim, and 'Bangladeshi' identity for his country. To arouse nationalism and self-esteem among the people, Ziaur made clear distinctions between a 'Bengali' and a 'Bangladeshi'. Citizens of Bangladesh are not Bengalis, like citizens of some parts of India are; they are a separate and distinct nationality. They are Bangladeshis. Ziaur mixed ethno-nationalism with religious nationalism in a subtle but clever manner. Thus, it was during Ziaur's rule that Bangladesh found a new national identity, self-esteem, and a theocratic state. Ziaur revived the issue of sharing the Ganga river water and made it a very passionate national issue. In March 1976, India declared that it would increase the flow of water from the Ganga to Bangladesh, but Ziaur was not satisfied. In November 1976, he took the issue to the United Nations General Assembly (UNGA). However, he finally reached an agreement with India in 1977 and signed the Farakka Accord with the then prime minister of India, Morarji Desai. The 1977 Farakka Accord was entered upon for a period of five years. On its expiry in 1982, a further two-year agreement was signed by Bangladesh and India; but the issue remained contentious and unresolved till 1996, when a new agreement was signed.

Ziaur's successor H. M. Ershad, another military ruler, continued with the legacy left behind by Ziaur. Bangladesh under Ershad, became a staunch Muslim state, much to the dislike of the secular-minded people in the country. In foreign affairs, Bangladesh sought to align itself with the Muslim countries, especially Saudi Arabia and Pakistan. Like Ziaur, Ershad also nurtured close diplomatic ties with China. All these policies did not go well with New Delhi. During Ershad's tenure, problems surrounding the Chakma tribes in the Chittagong Hill Tracts (CHT) exacerbated, and India became hugely concerned due to heavy influx of the Buddhist tribes

[1] See, in this context, Shelton U. Kodikara, 'Bangladesh', in Shelton U. Kodikara, ed., *External Compulsions of South Asian Politics* (New Delhi: Sage), 1993, p. 136.

(mainly Chakmas) to the northeastern states of India. A 'UN Human Rights Commission Working Group on Indigenous Peoples' was told by a representative of the Chakma tribe in July 1985 that violation of human rights by the Bangladeshi armed forces was increasing and that the Buddhist tribe faced virtual genocide unless they converted to Islam.[2] Since the inflow of refugees created internal problems in the northeastern states, India was keen to have a settlement of the Chakma issue. India also raised the issue of illegal migration of Bangladeshi people to India. But the military regime in Bangladesh was not interested in a political solution. It continued with army repression in the CHT. India was not amused. Ershad's domestic and foreign policies were causes for irritation in India, and as a consequence, bilateral relations suffered immensely throughout the 1980s.

Ershad's fall from power in December 1990 almost coincided with the beginning of the post-Cold War era in international politics. After Ershad, civilian rule returned to Bangladesh, though normalcy did not return to Indo–Bangla relations. The BNP won the February 1991 elections in Bangladesh, and Khaleda Zia took over as the prime minister in September 1991 after an amendment of the constitution that made way for a parliamentary system of government, a shift from the presidential form of government. In domestic and foreign affairs, Khaleda reinforced most of the policies of her late husband. Bangladesh vigorously emphasised upon its Islamic identity in domestic and foreign policies. She also continued with the policy of weaning Bangladesh away from India. Khaleda accused India of trying to starve Bangladesh by blocking the Ganga water at Farakka. The Chakma problem also remained unresolved. Religious nationalism continued to grow in Bangladesh during Khaleda's tenure. The new civilian ruler of Bangladesh offered olive branches to Pakistan and China, and sought to strengthen further security relations with these two countries with a view to counterbalance India's influence in the region. Negative perception (about India) of the Bangladeshi prime minister again came in the way of improving bilateral relations, and kept Bangladesh away from India. Till the end of 1995, the two countries remained where they were in 1975,—geographically close, yet politically distant neighbours. For 20 years (1975–95), perceptional problems of the Bangladeshi political elite remained a stumbling block in Indo–Bangla relations.

Relations between the two countries took a positive turn when the AL won parliamentary elections in 1996, and the party's leader Sheikh Hasina Wajed assumed office of the prime minister. Hasina's government worked hard to improve relations with India. The new prime minister was able to solve, with India's cooperation, many contentious issues like sharing of the Ganga waters, repatriation of Chakma refugees and cross-border terrorism. In December 1996, Hasina signed a comprehensive bilateral treaty with her Indian counterpart, H. D. Deve Gowda for sharing the Ganga river water. This treaty provided for a 30-year water sharing arrangement with guaranteed minimum quantities of water supply for Bangladesh, whose rights as a lower riparian country was recognised. It marked a genuine breakthrough in the Ganga water sharing dispute, considered to be the most crucial issue in Indo–Bangla relations for over two decades. Another problematic

[2] Ibid., p. 142.

issue solved during Hasina's premiership was the Chakma refugees' repatriation to Bangladesh. After an agreement was signed between the two neighbours in 1997, Bangladesh agreed to take back CHT refugees from the northeastern states of India. By the end of the year 2000, more than 50,000 CHT refugees returned to Bangladesh. An agreement on cross-border terrorism was also signed in 1997. It was decided that both the countries would not allow terrorist activities to proliferate from across the border. From India's security perspective, this agreement was important because Bangladesh, since the mid-1970s, was a safe haven for anti-India activities. Due to the Hasina government's positive attitude, cross-border crimes were substantially reduced. Bilateral relations were also bolstered by the introduction of the Kolkata–Dhaka bus service from 1999. The High Commissioner of Bangladesh to India, C. S. Shafi Sami described the bus service as 'an incremental development to the spirit of cooperation'.[3] Further, the moderate reaction of the Bangladesh government over the May 1998 nuclear tests by India brought the two countries closer. According to Sami, 'Hasina felt that India has a right to have her own security perceptions and decide on measures to address these perceptions.'[4] Change of attitudes by the Bangladeshi political elites towards India helped to improve bilateral relations substantially during 1996–2001.

But perceptional problems returned again to haunt bilateral relations when the BNP-led coalition headed by Khaleda Zia came back to power in Bangladesh in October 2001. Khaleda's second tenure as the prime minister of Bangladesh was not very different from her first as far as relations with India were concerned. Bilateral relations suffered heavily during Khaleda's second term (2001–06) because unlike the previous AL government, Khaleda was not interested in addressing India's security concerns. Anti-India activities on Bangladeshi soil increased after the BNP came to power. The United Liberation Front for Assam (ULFA) leader, Anup Chetia, and All-Tripura Tiger Force (ATTF) leader, Sanjeev Deb Barman, who were arrested by the previous government, were allowed to seek political asylum in Bangladesh. There were reports of the growing presence of Taliban and Al Qaeda activists in Bangladesh. Links between terrorist outfits in India and Bangladesh also came to light. Bangladesh witnessed a spurt in terrorist attacks against minority groups, secular institutions and prominent personalities during this period (2001–06).[5] A few high-level visits during this period undertaken by the Indian Ministers for External Affairs, Yashwant Sinha (2002) and Jaswant Singh (2005), and the Bangladeshi Foreign Minister, Morshed Khan (2003), could not repair the overall damage in bilateral relations. Even Prime Minister Khaleda Zia's visit to India in March 2006, just months before she left office, failed to make any significant impact. During the tenures of the two 'caretaker governments' in Bangladesh (2006–08), bilateral relations gradually limped back to normalcy, although no major contentious issue was resolved during this time. The caretaker governments encouraged close contacts with India through high-level bilateral visits, and talks surrounding these visits. This period (2006–08) may be termed as formal and peaceful in Indo–Bangla relations without any notable upswing.

[3] See, *The Times of India*, New Delhi, 9 November, 1999.

[4] Ibid.

[5] Sreeradha Datta, *Bangladesh: A Fragile Democracy* (New Delhi: Shipra), 2004, pp. 149–51.

A significant and mature phase in bilateral relations began in January 2009, when the AL-led coalition returned to power in Bangladesh after electoral victories in the December 2008 polls. Sheikh Hasina Wajed took charge as the prime minister of Bangladesh for a second term. Hasina showed her eagerness to improve relations with India, and the Manmohan Singh government (in India) reciprocated positively. The two countries embarked upon a series of unprecedented bilateral visits and talks which helped ease tensions and strengthen relations. Soon after the Hasina government assumed office, India's External Affairs Minister (EAM), Pranab Mukherjee paid an official visit to Dhaka on 9 February 2009. Two agreements on trade and bilateral investment promotion and protection were signed during the Indian EAM's visit.[6] Somnath Chatterjee, the then Speaker of the Lok Sabha, visited Dhaka between 21 and 23 February, 2009 to address the Members of Bangladesh Parliament at the opening ceremony of 'Parliamentary Orientation Program' in Bangladesh. The Indian Prime Minister, Manmohan Singh had a bilateral meeting with his Bangladeshi counterpart on 15 July 2009 at Sharm el Sheikh (Egypt) on the sidelines of the NAM Summit. The two leaders met again on 29 April 2010 at Thimphu during the 16th SAARC Summit and discussed issues of mutual concern. The Bangladeshi Foreign Minister, Dipu Moni met Indian EAM and finance minister on 9 July 2009 during a stop-over in New Delhi and discussed a range of bilateral issues. This was followed by her official visit to India between 7 and 10 September 2009. During Moni's visit, several key decisions in areas of water sharing, connectivity, power, trade, infrastructure development, security and land boundary were made.[7] The foreign ministers of the two nations met on the sidelines of various regional and multilateral conferences and summits during 2009–10. Other bilateral visits included Indian Minister of Agriculture and Consumer Affairs, Sharad Pawar (January 2010), Minister of Youth Affairs and Sports, M. S. Gill (January 2010) and Minister for Health and Family Welfare, Ghulam Nabi Azad (February 2010) to Bangladesh and visit of Bangladesh Minister for Water Resources to India in March 2010. Indian Foreign Secretary, Nirupama Rao visited Dhaka on 14 and 15 November 2009 and held discussions with her Bangladeshi counterpart.[8]

The Prime Minister of Bangladesh paid an official visit to India between 10 and 13 January 2010 with a 123-member delegation that included her ministers of foreign affairs and water resources, advisers and a 50-member strong business contingent. The large accompanying delegation was an indicator of the importance the Bangladeshi prime minister attached to her visit. A Joint Communique (JC) was issued on 12 January on the occasion of the visit. The 50 sections in the JC touched upon almost all aspects of bilateral relations. Among other issues, the JC contained an announcement of the Indian prime minister about a line of credit of US $1 billion for Bangladesh for a range of projects, including railway infrastructure, supply of locomotives and passenger coaches, rehabilitation of Saidpur workshop, procurement of buses

---

[6] Ministry of External Affairs, Government of India, *India-Bangladesh Relations*, available at http://meaindia.nic.in/mystart.php?id=50042439, accessed on 18 October 2011.

[7] Ibid.

[8] Ibid.

including articulate buses and dredging projects.[9] The JC also declared that '... with a view to encouraging imports from Bangladesh, both countries agreed to address removal of tariff and non-tariff barriers and port restrictions and facilitate movement of containerised cargo by rail and water'.[10] Both the prime ministers agreed to comprehensively address all outstanding land boundary issues keeping in view the spirit of the 1974 Land Boundary Agreement. In this context, they agreed to convene the Joint Boundary Working Group to take this process forward. India agreed to supply to Bangladesh 250 MW electricity from its grid. In this context, both the prime ministers emphasised the need to expedite inter-grid connectivity. They also agreed that the two countries need to cooperate in development and exchange of electricity, including generation from renewable sources, and may set up joint projects or corporate entities for that purpose. It was agreed that Bangladesh will allow use of Mongla and Chittagong sea ports for movement of goods to and from India through road and rail. It was further agreed that the construction of the proposed Akhaura–Agartala railway link be financed by grant from India. A joint team of the railway authorities of the two countries would identify the alignment for connectivity. According to the JC, 'Both Prime Ministers condemned terrorism in all its forms and manifestations. They noted that security remained a priority for both the countries, as terrorists, insurgents and criminals respect no boundaries. They underscored the need for both countries to actively cooperate on security issues. Both leaders reiterated the assurance that the territory of either would not be allowed for activities inimical to the other and resolved not to allow their respective territory to be used for training, sanctuary and other operations by domestic or foreign terrorist/militant and insurgent organizations and their operatives.'[11] During Hasina's visit, the following accords were signed: (i) Agreement on Mutual Legal Assistance on Criminal Matters; (ii) Agreement on the Transfer of Sentenced Persons; (iii) Agreement on Combating International Terrorism, Organised Crime and Illicit Drug Trafficking; and (iv) Memorandum of Understanding on Cooperation in Power Sector and Cultural Exchange Programme. Hasina's January 2010 visit to India, and the desire shown by both the nations to cooperate closely on regular basis on outstanding bilateral issues, provided tremendous boost to India–Bangladesh relations. With a view to operationalise promises made in the JC, Indian Finance Minister, Pranab Mukherjee visited Dhaka on 7 August 2010 to witness the signing of the $1 billion Line of Credit Agreement between EXIM Bank of India and Government of Bangladesh. Both the countries have initiated actions to fulfil other pledges in the JC.[12]

---

[9] Ministry of External Affairs, Government of India, available at http://www.mea.gov.in/mystart.php?id=100515482, accessed on 18 October 2011.

[10] See in this context, Ministry of External Affairs, Government of India, *Joint Communiqué issued on the occasion of the visit to India of Her Excellency Sheikh Hasina, Prime Minister of Bangladesh*, available at http://www.mea.gov.in/ mystart.php?id=100515482, accessed on 18 October 2011.

[11] Ibid.

[12] For details on steps taken on the Joint Communique, see Institute for Defence Studies and Analyses, *India–Bangladesh Relations: Towards Convergence: An IDSA Task Force Report* (New Delhi: IDSA), 2010, pp. 89–93.

Prime Minister Manmohan Singh paid an official visit to Bangladesh in September 2011. During the visit, the Indian prime minister and his Bangladeshi counterpart noted that India and Bangladesh have entered a new phase in bilateral relations with a pragmatic and practical approach based on sovereignty, equality, friendship, trust and understanding. They also recalled, according to Indian Ministry of External Affairs (MEA) sources, '. . . the landmark visit of Sheikh Hasina to India in January 2010 and noted that, during the visit, the two sides had reached an agreement on a set of initiatives that had elevated the bilateral relations to new heights. The two Prime Ministers noted with satisfaction the recent exchange of high-level visits and agreed that these exchanges had helped reach an understanding on many of the issues under discussion. They agreed to encourage more such high level interactions between the two sides.'[13] The two neighbours also welcomed various institutional mechanisms for promoting bilateral relations, such as Foreign Office Consultations, Commerce Secretary level talks, Joint River Commission meetings, Home Secretary level talks, Border Conferences between paramilitary forces of the two nations, as well as meetings of other Joint Working Groups (JWGs) on various issues. During Singh's visit, the two sides signed important agreements such as (i) Framework Agreement on Cooperation for Development; and (ii) Protocol to the Agreement Concerning the Demarcation of the Land Boundary between India and Bangladesh and Related Matters. In the 'Framework Agreement', both nations pledged to continue cooperation for development through reducing trade imbalance; sharing of river waters; promoting scientific, educational and cultural exchanges; developing mechanisms for technical cooperation and exchange of advance information with respect to natural disasters; and harnessing the advantages of sub-regional cooperation in the power sector, water resources management, physical connectivity, environment and sustainable development for mutual advantage, including jointly developing and financing projects. By the agreement on demarcation of land boundary, both nations agreed to demarcate boundary as per the provisions of the 1974 Agreement. They agreed to implement demarcation provisions decided upon in the 1974 Agreement in the Assam, Meghalaya, Tripura and West Bengal sectors. This agreement was a landmark achievement in bilateral relations as it successfully addressed the land boundary problem, which remained a source of mistrust between the two neighbours for a long time.

A few other important bilateral documents were also signed during Manmohan Singh's visit to Bangladesh. These were: (i) Addendum to the MoU between India and Bangladesh to Facilitate Overland Transit Traffic between Bangladesh and Nepal; (ii) Memorandum of Understanding on Renewable Energy Cooperation; (iii) Memorandum of Understanding on Conservation of the Sundarban; (iv) Protocol on Conservation of the Royal Bengal Tiger of the Sunderban; (v) Memorandum of Understanding on Cooperation in the Field of Fisheries; (vi) Memorandum of Understanding on Mutual Broadcast of Television Programmes; (vii) Memorandum of Understanding between Jawaharlal Nehru University and Dhaka University;

---

[13] Ministry of External Affairs, Government of India, *Joint Statement on the Occasion of the visit of the PM of India to Bangladesh*, available at http://www.mea.gov.in/mystart.php?id=510118210&flg=1, accessed on 19 October 2011.

and (viii) Memorandum of Understanding on Academic Cooperation between National Institute of Fashion Technology (NIFT), India and Bangladesh Garment Manufacturers and Exporters Association (BGMEA) University of Fashion and Technology (BUFT), Bangladesh. The nature and diversity of these documents revealed the fact that the two nations were very keen to engage in sincere cooperation with a view to build a strong relationship. The Indian prime minister also announced grants for Bangladesh for several developmental projects and initiatives. These grants would be detailed in the next section under 'Economic Relations'. Although the Teesta river water sharing accord and the Transit Treaty could not be reached during Singh's visit, the two sides pledged to implement these important bilateral accords soon.[14] Singh's September 2011 visit to Bangladesh and Hasina's January 2011 visit to India gave a tremendous and unprecedented fillip to India–Bangladesh relations, which witnessed positive upswing in bilateral relations, for the first time since 1975.

In keeping with the promises, the Indian prime minister made during his official visit to Bangladesh (in September 2011), India opened the 'Tin Bigha Corridor' for 24 hours for Bangladeshi citizens. The Tin Bigha Corridor in the Coochbehar district in West Bengal (India) links the Bangladeshi enclaves of Angarpota and Dahagram with the Bangladesh mainland. India's decision to give Bangladeshis 24-hour-access to the Tin Bigha instead of the 12 hours access earlier, has come as a major boost to the 1.5 lakh people residing in the 51 Bangladeshi enclaves in Indian territory (all in Coochbehar). They could now connect to Bangladeshi mainland through the day and year. Prime Minister Sheikh Hasisna, who visited Tin Bigha on 19 October 2011 to mark the opening of the corridor said, 'Residents of these enclaves have been waiting for 64 years to get unrestricted connection with the Bangladesh mainland. We are grateful to the Indian government. It only validates the firm relations between the two countries.'[15] In Tin Bigha, Hasina also reiterated her belief that the Teesta Water Accord and the Transit Treaty with India would be concluded very soon.[16] The continuous opening of the Tin Bigha Corridor for Bangladeshi citizens also pointed towards noteworthy improvement in bilateral political relations. However, illegal migration to India is continuing, and the issue still remains an irritant, although during Hasina's latest tenure as prime minister, the issue has not cast any negative impact on Indo–Bangla relations. But the issue may pose challenges to Indian foreign policy in the future.

The ratification of the four-decade-old Land Boundary Agreement was the centrepiece of Indian Prime Minister Narendra Modi's visit to Bangladesh on 6 and 7 June 2015. During the visit, the Indian prime minister and his Bangladeshi counterpart, Sheikh Hasina Wajed witnessed the ratification and exchange of documents to implement the 1974 Land Boundary Agreement that will allow the two sides to swap more than 160 small enclaves whose residents were virtually stateless people living in uncertainty and despair. The historic agreement provided definite states to

---

[14] See *The Times of India*, 8 September 2011.

[15] See *The Times of India*, 20 October 2011.

[16] Ibid.

these people. Beside this Agreement, the two sides signed a few more treaties to foster connectivity, trade and security cooperation. India and Bangladesh signed 20 more pacts and MoUs in diverse areas of mutual interest. The two sides renewed a bilateral trade agreement and signed two separate pacts on coastal shipping with the use of Bangladesh's Chittagong and Mongla ports. Indian merchant vessels can now use the two ports to directly ship cargo to Bangladesh, instead of routing goods through ports such as Singapore. This will bring shipping time down to a week or even less. India and Bangladesh also renewed a protocol on inland water transit and trade, and signed two agreements for starting trans-border bus services on the Dhaka-Shillong-Guwahati and Kolkata-Dhaka-Agartala routes. In the field of security, the two sides signed MoUs between their Coast Guards on preventing human trafficking and smuggling and circulation of illegal currency. There was also a 'string of trade and investment agreements, with a $2 billion credit facility for Bangladesh to use for infrastructure, power, health and education projects. Another MoU on economic zones marked the first time a neighbouring country was allowed such zones exclusively for Indian firms. The move was aimed at encouraging Indian investments in Bangladesh'.[17]

Surely Modi's visit to Bangladesh boosted bilateral relations. The signing of the Land Boundary Agreement and other important pacts, bore testimony to this proposition. The land boundary issue remained a bone of contention between the two neighbours for a long time, and created mistrust in bilateral relations. Finally, with this visit, the issue was settled and the all-important feel-good factor returned to Indo–Bangla relations. In this 'feel-good' atmosphere, the prime minister of Bangladesh visited India again during 7–10 April 2017. During this visit, the two countries signed a total of 22 agreements. Special emphasis was given on energy cooperation and connectivity between the two neighbours. Prime Minister Narendra Modi assured Sheikh Hasina, his Bangladeshi counterpart, that the Teesta water issue would be resolved soon. This promise was important for the Bangladeshi prime minister and Leader of the AL, because her party would face parliamentary election in 2018. In the election, water from Teesta river will be a major issue in Bangladesh. The two nations also signed an MoU on a framework for defence cooperation. India's announcement of further lines of credit (LoC) of US $5 billion dollars, including US $500 million for defence purchases, was another important commitment made during the visit of Sheikh Hasina. It was one of the largest LoC India extended to any country so far. This gesture amply manifests cordial Indo–Bangladesh relations in the recent times.

ECONOMIC RELATIONS

Historically, economic relations between the two neighbours have not always been hassle-free. Bangladesh has been vocal about the issue of tariff and non-tariff barriers from the Indian side as a major irritant. Unfavourable balance of trade also remained a concern for Bangladesh.

[17] *Hindustan Times*, 7 June 2015.

Political discontentment in Bangladesh often stemmed from the huge trade gap, supported by the fact that India has a lot of non-trade barriers for Bangladeshi exports. Even though exports from Bangladesh to India are growing, the trade gap continues to exist. Table 3.1 shows trends in India–Bangladesh trade in recent times.

Table 3.1: India–Bangladesh Trade in Recent Years

(in US $ million)

Year	*India's Export*	*India's Import*	*Total Trade*	*Balance*
2006–07	1,629.57	228.00	1,857.57	1,401.57
2007–08	2,923.72	257.02	3,180.74	2,666.70
2008–09	2,497.87	313.11	2,810.98	2,184.76
2009–10	2,433.77	254.66	2,688.44	2,179.11
2010–11	3,606.39	446.75	4,053.15	3,159.64
2011–12	3,789.20	585.73	4,374.93	3,203.47
2012–13	5,144.99	639.33	5,784.31	4,505.66
2013–14	6,166.93	484.34	6,651.27	5,682.59
2014–15	6,464.49	609.90	7,074.39	5,854.59

Source: Department of Commerce, Export-Import Data Bank, Government of India, available at http://commerce.nic.in/eidb/ecnt.asp, accessed on 20 July 2015.

As the table above reveals, Bangladeshi export to India (that is India's import, column 3 of the table) has more than doubled from US $228.00 million in 2006–07 to US $609.90 million in 2014–15, yet the trade balance continues to remain large. In 2006–07, trade balance in India's favour was US $1,401.57 million, but it increased to US $5,854.59 million in 2014–15. Trade deficit was reduced in fiscal year 2008–09 when India's export to Bangladesh fell, and import from the country rose. Trade deficit was also reduced in 2009–10 due to a fall in India's export. Although India's import from Bangladesh also fell in the same fiscal year, trade deficit remained the lowest in 2009–10 among the nine fiscals shown in the table, due to reduced Indian export. However, with increase in the total volume of trade during the last nine fiscal years, trade deficit with Bangladesh is also increasing. Bangladesh is not too happy with the growing trade deficit. A former foreign secretary of Bangladesh commented, 'The trade gap has been another major issue and here, again, perceptions are important. The perception in Dhaka has been that while Bangladesh has been, both on the official and unofficial account, a major market for Indian products, India has devised a number of non-tariff barriers that have stood in the way of mutually beneficial trade'.[18] India is aware of such concerns and wishes to address these. During his September 2011 visit to Bangladesh, the Indian prime minister assured the Bangladeshis that India would look into these matters with a view to improve bilateral relations. Addressing the

[18] See in this context, Farooq Sobhan, 'India-Bangladesh Relations: Past, Present and Future', Observer Research Foundation (ORF) Discourse, 3 (3) (New Delhi: ORF), 2008, p. 2.

students and faculty at Dhaka University, Manmohan Singh said, 'We recognize the sensitivity of our Bangladeshi friends over the large bilateral trade deficit. We will work sincerely to address this issue. I commit the Government of India to providing greater market access to Bangladeshi products in India by removing both tariff and non-tariff barriers to trade.'[19]

With a view to strengthen economic relations, India and Bangladesh have agreed to address the issue of the removal of tariff and non-tariff barriers and port restrictions and facilitate movement of cargo by rail and water. India provided duty-free access to SAARC countries to the Indian market and reduced the number of items on India's negative list. In January 2008, under the South Asian Free Trade Area (SAFTA) provisions, India had permitted duty-free entry of Bangladeshi products into Indian markets. The negative list was also reduced from over 700 products to about 400. The tariff free quota system has been applied for where duty-free entry was not possible. Bangladesh was given access to 8 million pieces of readymade garments in 2007, which was subsequently raised to 10 million pieces in July 2011.[20]

India–Bangladesh economic relations have been augmented through several agreements and MoUs in the recent times. These are: (i) Protocol on Inland Water Transit and Trade (IWTT); (ii) Bilateral Air Services Agreement between India and Bangladesh; (iii) Bilateral Agreement on the Establishment of Joint Economic Commission (JEC); (iv) India–Bangladesh Convention for the Avoidance of Double Taxation; (v) India–Bangladesh Agreement for the Regulation of motor vehicle passenger traffic; (vi) Agreement on Revised Travel Arrangements between India and Bangladesh; (vii) Rules for Interchange of Traffic between India and Bangladesh; (viii) MoU between Bureau of Indian Standards (BIS) and Bangladesh Standards Testing Institute (BSTI) for cooperation in the area of standards; (ix) MoU for cooperation in the field of agriculture; (x) MoU for cooperation in the field of science and technology; (xi) Protocols for operation of passenger bus service between Dhaka and Kolkata, and Dhaka and Agartala; (xii) Bilateral Investment Protection and Promotion Agreement (BIPPA). Discussions are also underway for concluding agreement on regulation of passenger and cargo vehicular traffic; (xiii) Agreement on Bulk Power Transmission between Power Grid Corporation of India Limited (PGCIL) and Bangladesh Power Development Board.[21] Many of these agreements and MoUs were signed during the Indian prime minister's visit to Bangladesh in September 2011. During this visit, both sides agreed to examine the establishment of new land ports, Land Custom Stations (LCS) and immigration points to facilitate trade and movement of people. In this context, it may be mentioned that the two countries took initiatives to open the Banglabandha-Fulbari Land Port as well as seven Integrated Check Posts (ICPs), for facilitating bilateral trade. Border *haats* (markets) have also been opened in Baliamari (Kurigram)-Kalaichar (West Garo Hills,

---

[19] See in this connection, Ministry of External Affairs, Government of India, *PM's address at Dhaka University*, 7 September 2011, available at http://meaindia.nic.in/mystart.php?id=510118208&flg=1, accessed on 20 October 2011.

[20] *IDSA Task Force Report*, n. 12, p. 48.

[21] Ministry of External Affairs, *India–Bangladesh Relations*, n. 16.

Meghalaya) and in Balat (East Khasi Hills, Meghalaya)-Dalora (Sunamganj) as a fulfilment of the long-standing demand of the local people of the area. Others such haats have been proposed in Sonarhat-Lyngkhat border (Sylhet-East Khasi Hills), and Narayantala-Balat border (Sunamganj-East Khasi Hills). The haats will provide the locals with a platform to sell indigenously produced goods and crops.

Moreover, under the bilateral Inland Water Transit and Trade Protocol, the operationalisation of Ashuganj and Silghat as additional Ports of Call was a welcome development. The successful commencement of trial run of the bulk cargo for Tripura (India) using multi-modal facilities through Ashuganj river port in Bangladesh would certainly help in augmenting trade between the two neighbours. The two nations have agreed to construct an Inland Container Terminal at Ashuganj. Till its completions, the port could be used for movement of bulk cargo. Other than the use of the Ashugunj port, Bangladesh has also allowed India the use of Mongla and Chittagong sea ports for movement of goods to and from India through road and railway network. Both India and Bangladesh are aware that road, rail and waterways are essential for an interdependent and mutually beneficial economic relationship. Therefore, establishment of physical infrastructures would promote not only exchange of goods and traffic, but would also lead to the connectivity of services, information, ideas, and people.

Cooperation in the renewable energy sector between the two countries has also begun. Bangladesh Power Development Board (BPDB) and the PGCIL have signed a 35-year power transmission agreement on 26 July 2010. Under this agreement, Bangladesh will import 250 MW of electricity in the first year from India from late 2012, gradually going up to 500 MW. The 250 MW grid interconnection requires an investment of Rs 869.21 crore, of which Rs 160.33 crore would be used for building infrastructure on the Indian side.[22] The BPDB and National Thermal Power Corporation (NTPC) of India are working towards concluding a Joint Venture Agreement for setting up of 1,320 MW coal-based power plant in Bagerhat in Bangladesh. A similar 1,320 MW coal-based power plant at a suitable location in Chittagong has also been proposed. India has also offered to set up a liquefied natural gas (LNG) terminal as a joint venture in Bangladesh to create a power generation capacity of around 1,000 MW. As demands for energy are rising in South Asia, and particularly in Bangladesh where energy sources are scarce, such joint ventures would help the people of Bangladesh, besides promoting trade as well as trust between the two nations.

As per reports of the MEA, technical cooperation between the two neighbours continues unabated. Bangladesh is an important Indian Technical and Economic Cooperation Programme (ITEC) partner country, and a number of participants from Bangladesh have availed of training courses under the ITEC programme. An MEA Report states that India offers 100 slots under ITEC and 35 slots under Technical Cooperation Scheme of Colombo Plan every year to Bangladesh. In the last three years (2006–07 to 2009–10), 414 participants from Bangladesh

---

[22] *IDSA Task Force Report*, n. 12, p. 51.

have undergone training in India under ITEC Programme and Technical Cooperation Scheme of Colombo Plan.[23] During his official visit to Bangladesh in September 2011, the Indian prime minister announced grants to Bangladesh for several cooperative and developmental projects and other initiatives. These included:

(i) Construction of state-of-the-art India–Bangladesh Culture Centre in Dhaka;
(ii) Undertaking feasibility study for upgradation of Dhaka–Chittagong railway line;
(iii) Construction of railway line between Akhaura and Agartala;
(iv) New Indian Scholarship to 100 students at graduate, post-graduate and doctoral/ research level;
(v) Setting up of an IT Lab in a model school in each of the 64 districts in Bangladesh;
(vi) Setting up of IT centres in Bangladesh Public Administration Training Centre, Military Institute of Science and Technology and Bangladesh Police Academy;
(vii) Provision of solar lanterns to 2,800 families affected by the Sidr Cyclone.[24] These developmental projects, if implemented as planned, would help chart a new course of trust and friendship between India and Bangladesh.

SECURITY AND CULTURAL RELATIONS

India and Bangladesh share more than 4,000 kms of land border, maximum of which is porous. Apart from illegal migration, the porous land border causes security concerns in both nations. Terrorist activities, drug, arms, human trafficking and other crimes are connected with long, mostly open India–Bangladesh borders. India has vital security concerns in Bangladesh because Indian terrorist organisations have formed bases in Bangladesh, and these organisations use land and sea borders for movement of terrorists, arms and money. Cadres of the United Liberation Front of Assam (ULFA), trans-border Islamic terrorist groups like Muslim Liberation Tigers of Assam (MULTA), the Independent Liberation Army of Assam (ILAA) and the People United Liberation Front (PULF) have made Bangladesh their bases, and they frequently carry out terrorist activities in different parts of India from these bases. Pro-Al Qaeda organisations of Pakistani origin such as the Lashkar-e-Taiba (LeT), Harkat-ul Jihadi-al-Islami (HuJI) and Harkat-ul-Mujahideen (HuM) operating from Bangladeshi territory pose grave security concerns for India. Arms trafficking in India's North-east from and through Bangladesh, illegal migration into Assam and West Bengal, transfer of funds from West Asia to fundamentalist groups in the Bangladesh–India region, money laundering through India–Nepal and India–Bangladesh border are regular features and constant sources of security concern for India.

---

[23] Ministry of External Affairs, *India–Bangladesh Relations*, n. 16.

[24] Ministry of External Affairs, *Joint Statement on the Occasion of the Visit of the PM of India to Bangladesh*, n. 13.

After assuming office in January 2009, the AL-led coalition government began to pay heed to India's security concerns. During Bangladeshi Prime Minister Hasina's official visit to India in January 2010, both the sides noted the need to actively cooperate on security issues. The two prime ministers had also assured each other that their territories would not be allowed for activities inimical to the other. During Hasina's visit, three MoUs relating to security issues were signed. These were: (i) Agreement on mutual legal assistance on criminal matters; (ii) Agreement on the transfer of sentenced persons; and (iii) Agreement on combating international terrorism, organised crime and illicit drug trafficking. Discussions on a bilateral extradition treaty between the two countries are currently underway. Security cooperation by Bangladesh had been above par between 2007 and 2010. In this context, it should be noted that Bangladesh initiated the process to hand over ULFA leader Anup Chetia (arrested in Dhaka and kept in custody since 1997) to India before Indian Prime Minister Manmohan Singh's visit to Bangladesh in September 2011.

The investigation into the Mumbai terrorist attacks (on 26 November 2008 and earlier) revealed links between terrorist outfits in Pakistan and HuJI of Bangladesh. India conveyed its security concerns to Bangladesh over such links. It was heartening to note that the Bangladesh government took prompt action over India's concerns. On 27 May 2009, Abdul Rouf Daud Merchant, a member of the mafia gang headed by Dawood Ibrahim, was arrested with his accomplices from the Chitttagong area. Arif Hossain, another Indian fugitive and accomplice of Daud, was also arrested from Dhaka in June 2009. On 20 July 2009, Moulana Mohammad Mansur Ali, a notorious terrorist and an Indian national linked to Pakistan-based LeT was arrested from a madrassa in Dhaka on 20 July 2009. Ali was an organiser of Asif Reza commando force, the terrorist outfit responsible for the attack on American Center in Kolkata on 22 January 2002. Ali's arrest came a day after another LeT activist, Mufti Obaidullah, linked to the Dawood gang was apprehended from Dhaka. In November 2009, Dhaka facilitated the arrest and handover of five top ULFA leaders, including its 'chairman' Arabinda Rajkhowa. In February 2011, Indian Home Minster P. Chidambaram, during his visit to Bangladesh, submitted a list of 50 'wanted' terrorists (all Indian nationals), who were believed to be either hiding in Bangladesh or have been kept under detention. Dhaka also submitted to Delhi a list of 100 criminals hiding in India, which included two convicted killers of Mujibar Rahman and a few accused of being involved in a grenade attack on the AL office in 2004. This issue was also discussed during Indian Foreign Minister S. M. Krishna's visit to Dhaka between 6 and 8 July 2011. Both the countries once again expressed their determination to jointly combat the menace of terrorism and insurgency, and reiterated their position to not allow their territories to be used by elements detrimental for each other.

The two neighbours have formed several institutional mechanisms for security purposes. These are: annual consultations at the level of home ministers; JWGs on Security; Joint Boundary Working Group (JBWG); regular Border Coordination Conferences between the Directors General of Indian Border Security Force (BSF) and Bangladesh Rifles (BDR); and Joint Group of Customs Officials (JGC). In the Joint Statement (JS) issued during Manmohan Singh's visit to Bangladesh (in September 2011), the two prime ministers expressed satisfaction at the level of cooperation between the two countries on security-related issues and reaffirmed their uncompromising position against terrorism in all its forms and manifestations, which also included insurgency. They also noted with satisfaction the signing of the Coordinated Border Management Plan during the visit of the home minister of India to Bangladesh in July 2011. They expressed confidence that it would enhance cooperation between the border guarding forces of the two countries, and enable them to manage the identified vulnerable areas with a view to preventing criminal activities, illegal movement, acts of violence and loss of lives along the border areas. The prime ministers directed the agencies concerned to implement the Plan immediately.[25] The JS further stated, 'The two Prime Ministers also underscored the need to conclude an Extradition Treaty between the two countries expeditiously to complete the legal framework for bilateral security cooperation while expressing satisfaction that the Agreement on Mutual Legal Assistance on Criminal Matters, Agreement on the Transfer of Sentenced Persons and Agreement on Combating International Terrorism, Organised Crime and Illicit Drug Trafficking, signed in January 2010, were now in force following their ratification.'[26]

Apart from cooperation in security-related areas, India and Bangladesh also share close cultural links. Due to a long history of common language, food and culture, it was natural that the two neighbours would like to develop close cultural links. The Government of India (GoI) has laid special emphasis on promotion of exchanges in the fields of music, theatre, literature, art, and painting, According to an MEA report, the 'Indian Council for Cultural Relations (ICCR) has been playing a prominent role by sponsoring visits of artists from and to India. A bilateral Cultural Exchange Programme (CEP) 2009–2012 provides the framework for such exchanges. To promote bilateral cultural exchanges, the Indira Gandhi Cultural Centre (IGCC) of Indian Council for Cultural Relations was inaugurated at Dhaka on March 11, 2010 by President, ICCR Dr. Karan Singh.'[27] With a view to promote people to people exchanges, 100 scholarships are provided by ICCR every year to students from Bangladesh for pursuing general courses in arts, sciences, engineering, and also specialised courses for culture, drama, music, fine arts and sports. During Sheikh Hasina's visit to India in January 2010, India has offered to provide 300 more such scholarships annually for five years to students from Bangladesh for studying and training in universities and training institutions in India.[28]

During Manmohan Singh's Bangladesh visit (September 2011), both the countries agreed to promote and support joint research projects and exchange of scientific personnel. India offered to invite eminent scientists and researchers from Bangladesh to participate in the Indian National Science Congress, and school children to participate in the Annual National Children Science Congress. The two nations have agreed to organise joint celebrations to commemorate the 150th birth anniversary of Rabindranath Tagore. The two prime ministers noted in the JS referred to

---

[25] Ibid.

[26] Ibid.

[27] Ministry of External Affairs, *India–Bangladesh Relations*, n. 16.

[28] Ibid.

earlier that the '. . . joint celebration had enthused the people on both sides to explore the common cultural heritage and linkages and had promoted exchanges not only among Tagore experts, but also a whole range of artists, singers, dancers, dramatists, poets, writers, actors, etc. which had led to greater understanding among the two sides'.[29] It was also agreed during Manmohan Singh's visit that the 90th anniversary of the publication of 'Bidrohi' by poet Nazrul Islam would be jointly celebrated. During these talks, the Bangladesh prime minister conveyed her intention to set up a 'Bangladesh Bhaban' in Shantiniketan as a resource centre for the use of the visiting academicians and researchers from Bangladesh.[30] Recognising the value of television channels as a means to promote cultural exchange and dissemination of information, the two countries welcomed the signing of an MoU on mutual broadcast of television programmes between Doordarshan and Bangladesh Television. The two neighbours also proposed to encourage private channels to explore opportunities to expand the viewership in each other's territories. The two nations also underscored the need to preserve the memory of freedom fighters by undertaking various initiatives, including observance of anniversaries of their martyrdom. India announced that it would enhance scholarships to the heirs of the Muktijjoddhas from Bangladesh to pursue higher secondary and graduate studies in India. Bangladesh requested India to facilitate setting up of memorial plaques and visits of family members to the identified graves of freedom fighters buried along the borders of India.[31] However, it should be noted here that despite enhanced security and cultural links in the recent times, there are huge uncovered grounds in these areas, as well as in economic and political segments of Indo–Bangla relations. The two countries need to work hard and engage in continuous cooperation to improve and strengthen bilateral relations in the future.

RECOMMENDATIONS FOR THE FUTURE

India–Bangladesh relations traversed through ups and downs during the last few decades, but followed a unique pattern. Bilateral relations tended to improve whenever an AL-led government assumed office in Bangladesh, and, deteriorate whenever other governments came to power. This uniqueness dominated Indo–Bangla relations in the past; and as a consequence downward trend in bilateral relations could be observed more than upward movement because AL-led governments assumed office for lesser times compared to other governments in Bangladesh during 1971–2012. As the preceding analysis indicated, the military and BNP-led governments in Bangladesh did not view India as a friend and, therefore, were not interested to strengthen bilateral relations. India also viewed the non-AL governments in Bangladesh with suspicion, and never wanted to walk extra miles to improve relations. As a result, relations mostly suffered.

---

[29] Ministry of External Affairs, *Joint Statement on the occasion of the visit of the PM of India to Bangladesh*, n. 13.

[30] Ibid.

[31] Ibid.

In order to strengthen relations in the future, the **first** recommendation would be to change the perceptional problems in bilateral relations. Both the countries must come out of perceptional problems and view each other as potential friends, not adversaries. It is heartening to note that bilateral relations witnessed upswing since 2009. But subsequent governments in both the countries must be ready to keep up the momentum. This upswing must not be confined to certain periods, as observed in the past, but must be continuous, and political elites in both nations must be ready to adjust small issues for better relations. In an era of globalisation, when economic interests prevail over other interests, such adjustments are necessary, and not impossible to make. With good economic growth rates in the recent times, both India and Bangladesh should be willing to sacrifice minor problems for greater benefits.

The **second** recommendation emerges out of the first. Both the countries must try to amicably solve outstanding issues. As the biggest country in the region, India must come forward in settling problems first and set examples for others to follow. India showed positive intentions by agreeing to sign the historic Land Boundary Agreement in 2015, during Prime Minister Narendra Modi's visit to Bangladesh. More such adjustments are necessary in the future. Sharing of river water, a constant irritant in Indo–Bangla relations, must also be solved through negotiations. India has agreed to Bangladeshi proposals for sharing of Teesta, Feni and three other river waters. Formal Agreements on these are awaiting final conclusion. Similarly, India's assurance to Bangladesh, given during Manmohan Singh's visit, that India would not take steps on the Tipaimukh project[32] (on Barak river) that might adversely impact Bangladesh, would help in the generation of trust. In order to strengthen relations, the subsequent governments in the two nations must offer such cooperation in many other areas in the future.

It is time for India to think in terms of reducing tariff and non-tariff barriers for trade. The reduction would not affect India's interests adversely; instead it would foster trust and goodwill for India. The Bangladeshi High Commissioner to India recently said, '... if India were to facilitate Bangladesh's exports to India by completely removing all tariff and non-tariff barriers, then the loss in revenues to India from duties and levies would be insignificant while in return, huge goodwill will be created...'.[33] As tariff and non-tariff barriers in trade form problem areas in bilateral relations, the **third** recommendation would refer to removing these barriers to facilitate enhanced trade between the two nations. A related issue to this is unfavourable trade balance for Bangladesh. India must take steps to overcome this problem. The **fourth** recommendation, therefore, suggests that India could propose a Free Trade Agreement (FTA) to Bangladesh as a long-term measure. Till the completion of the FTA, the GoI can think of

---

[32] 'The Tipaimukh project is a proposed dam on the river Barak in Manipur state in India. It was planned in 1984 for flood control and hydroelectric generation. But Bangladesh was opposed to the project for fear of scarcity of water from the Barak river during the dry seasons. The project has not been implemented till date.'

[33] See in this context, Institute of Peace and Conflict Studies (IPCS), 'India–Bangladesh Relations', *Seminar Report,* no. 313 (New Delhi: IPCS), 17 February 2010.

making unilateral concessions as a short-term option. It can also consider pruning the negative list, and make it as small as possible. Further, both the governments must encourage private business to invest more in the neighbouring country. The **fifth** recommendation, therefore, suggests more involvement of private sectors in bilateral trade and commerce. Congenial socio-political atmosphere should be created to attract investment from the other country. Both the governments must ease restrictions for private business and investment, and must develop proper environment for trade and commercial activities.

India and Bangladesh are now engaged in enhanced security cooperation with several institutional mechanisms to oversee security issues. The **sixth** recommendation pertains to additional institutional mechanisms for strengthening security relations further. The annual bilateral dialogue at the level of the defence ministers may be initiated by the two neighbours. Further, regular visits by army, navy and air force chiefs of both countries to the other territory are strongly recommended. Joint military exercises to combat terrorism, joint patrolling in the Bay of Bengal to check piracy, enhanced military connectivity to share information, joint patrolling of the border regions by paramilitary forces on a regular basis, and aerial patrolling of remote and difficult border terrains by joint groups of air force personnel on a regular basis could be initiated. These measures would not only strengthen security, but would also create trust and goodwill between the two neighbours.

Scientific and technological cooperation are the need of the hour for India and Bangladesh for many reasons. Both India and Bangladesh deal with common issues such climate change, endemic diseases, contamination of water, food security, agricultural research, natural disasters, connectivity and information sharing. Some of the issues noted above are common problems for both the countries. Therefore, the **seventh** recommendation refers to increasing scientific and technological cooperation between the two neighbours. Problems like environmental degradation, climate change, diseases and natural disasters can be tackled better with joint efforts. Government and private organisations in both the countries can collaborate to fight these problems. Appropriate agencies in India and Bangladesh can also collaborate in areas like agricultural research, connectivity and information technology. Scientific and technological cooperation between these two nations remains a vastly untapped area with huge collaborative potential.

Similarly, educational links between universities and research organisations of both the countries must be strengthened. The **eighth** recommendation puts emphasis on this area. Leading universities and research institutions in both the countries should establish links through student and faculty exchange programmes, and collaborative research projects. Currently, students and faculty in both the countries look towards the Western world for educational opportunities. To change this mindset, Governments in India and Bangladesh must widely publicise about educational opportunities available in their countries. Private universities should also be allowed to reach out to students in both the countries. Fruitful cooperation in the field of educational would dispel mistrust and foster friendship.

A related issue is the necessity for easing visa restrictions. The **ninth** recommendation is a pointer to this necessity. Increased collaboration and exchange require increased movement of people across borders. Both the governments must make entry to the other territory flexible, and ease visa restriction. A gradual waiving of visa requirements, as followed by several nations, can be planned for the future. Apart from efforts to strengthen bilateral relations, the **tenth** recommendation suggests that both Bangladesh and India must work closely to energise their cooperation in regional fora like the SAARC and Bay of Bengal Initiative for Multi-Sectoral Technical and Economic Cooperation (BIMSTEC). As these multilateral fora aim to augment regional peace, harmony and economic development, both Bangladesh and India must try to fulfil the aims and objectives of these fora, and work in close tandem to achieve regional development.

Despite satisfactory improvement in bilateral relations in the recent times, Bangladesh and India could not fully overcome the problem of trust deficit. The two countries need to work hard in future to remove this trust deficit. Current Indo-Bangla relations could be compared to India–US relations during the 1980s and early 1990s. Mutual mistrust hindered the progress of India–US relations during that period. It was believed by many in both the countries that during the Democratic Party rule in the US relations with India improved, but relations deteriorated under the Republican Party rule, much like the present AL-BNP factors in Indo–Bangla relations. But since the late 1990s, both the countries (India and the US) worked hard to do away with this perception, and increased links in almost all areas of bilateral relationship which resulted in closer cooperation. As a consequence, relations got strengthened irrespective of party colours of governments in both the countries. Both India and the US showed maturity to overcome minor problems for bigger gains. The Indo-US Nuclear agreement is a case in point here. The two countries had to overcome many hurdles to achieve the agreement. Further, they gave preference to economic diplomacy over political problems. Gradually trust was generated, and strong relations could be established. Bangladesh and India must also bring back trust in their relations. The neighbours should also give priority to economic diplomacy, and cultural and scientific collaboration over political differences. They must be ready to sacrifice smaller issues for larger benefits. All future governments in both the nations must try to achieve closer cooperation in all areas of bilateral relationship. The turnaround has started, but it should not be confined to any specific period or government. All future governments in Bangladesh and India have the responsibility to sustain cordiality in bilateral relations observed since 2009.

4

INDIA AND NEPAL

Emerging Issues

HIGHLIGHTS

- Introduction
- Political Relations
- Economic Relations
- Security Relations
- Recommendations for the Future

INTRODUCTION

Nepal situated in the northeastern side of India, shares more than 1,800 km of long open borders with India. Five Indian states, West Bengal, Bihar, Uttar Pradesh, Sikkim and Uttarakhand have borders with Nepal. A landlocked country, Nepal is situated between India and China, two big states, and emerging economies of the world. Nepal has more than 1,400 km long borders with China on the north, mostly in uninhabited terrains of the upper Himalayas. With India, Nepal shares borders on three sides: west, south and the east. Nepal's location makes it very important, along with another Himalayan state Bhutan, for India's foreign policy. Nepal is a buffer state between India and China, and both these emerging powers consider Nepal as geo-strategically crucial for their national interests. After China's control over Tibet, Nepal has become more important for China because of Nepal's geographical proximity to Tibet.

Traditionally, the British who controlled India, made close connections between India and Nepal, and kept the long borders open, because the British required Nepalese men for the British–Indian army. Another important factor for maintaining open border by the British was to have easy and free access of British and Indian manufactured goods into Nepal. The British signed several treaties with the monarchs in Nepal for location of boundaries, and also for open migration of Indian and Nepalese people across the borders. For instance, the Treaty of 1 November 1860 signed between India and Nepal restored the territory ceded to India under the 1816 Treaty of Suguali. The Treaty of 1860 controlled relations between British India and Nepal till India's independence in 1947. Thereafter, India–Nepal relations were largely influenced by the 'Treaty of Peace and Friendship' signed between the two nations in 1950. But gradually, a section of the Nepalese political elite, and intelligentsia raised their voices against the 1950 treaty, which was viewed as 'unequal' by them. They also called for a review of the treaty. With this brief background, this chapter proposes to analyse India–Nepal relationship by examining all the major segments of bilateral relations in the recent times.

POLITICAL RELATIONS

Since the early 1950s, Indo–Nepal relations were largely influenced by three issues: the Friendship Treaty (of 1950), Nepal's domestic political events, and Nepal's overtures towards India and China. These three issues still exert considerable impact on bilateral relations. The Nepal–India Peace and Friendship Treaty which was signed on 31 July 1950 agreed to grant on a reciprocal basis, to the nationals of one country in the territory of the other the same privileges on matters of residence, ownership of property, participation in trade and commerce, movement and other opportunities of a similar nature. It became a major turning point in the movement of the Indians and the Nepalese, and was further reinforced by the Nepal–India open border. The treaty also stated that neither government shall tolerate any threat to the security of the other by a foreign aggressor, and obligated both sides to inform each other of any serious friction or misunderstanding with any neighbouring state likely to cause any breach in the friendly relations between the two governments. The treaty established a 'special relationship' between the two countries, and enabled Nepal to overcome the disadvantages of being a land-locked country. However, the treaty did not materialise until the installation of democracy in Nepal in February 1951, which replaced the oligarchic Rana regime within three and a half months of its signing.

Nepal was not uncomfortable with the Friendship Treaty during the 1950s. However during the 1960s, India–Nepal relations faced considerable tests due to Nepal's domestic political events, and also due to China's active involvement in Nepal. B. P. Koirala became the first prime minister of Nepal after elections were held for the Nepalese parliament in 1958. However, King Mahendra dismissed Koirala in December 1960 and assumed all powers. The King also started the 'Panchayat System' in 1962 under which powers were concentrated in the monarchy and all political parties in Nepal were banned. India was unhappy and considered the step as a setback for democracy. Anti-monarch forces protesting against this step launched movements inside Nepal and India. While the movement gathered momentum, Sino-Indian border conflicts started which escalated into a war in 1962. Sino-Indian hostility was to have a profound impact on relations between Nepal and India as well. When the anti-monarchy movement continued in India, the Chinese Defence Minister Chen Yi, in a statement on 5 October 1962 said that the Chinese people would help Nepal if it were to be attacked.[1] The Chinese signed an agreement to

[1] See, *New China News Agency Report*, 6 October 1962.

construct a road linking Kathmandu with the Chinese border and assisted Nepal in constructing a ring road around the capital city of Nepal, and in setting up some industries. The Indians were unhappy but were unable to prevent the construction of the road to the border. Therefore, during the 1960s, under active patronage of King Mahendra, Nepal began to lean towards China, and reduce Nepal's dependence on India.

King Mahendra proved a shrewd statesman as he slowly but steadily steered Nepal out of India's periphery of influence. But he did not wish to antagonise India altogether, and played the Chinese card to balance Indian influence in Nepal. When he offered the Chinese to construct parts of East–West Highway along the Terai region in the southern part of Nepal, India raised objections as it did not want the Chinese working too close to the Indian borders. King Mahendra respected Indian sensitivity in this regard and parts of the highway in the far eastern and the far western sectors were built with Indian assistance. Under the King, Nepal had established diplomatic relations with many countries and had exchanged residential diplomatic missions too. But relations with India did not suffer much, and continued to be close throughout the 1960s. King Birendra Bir Bikram Shah Dev succeeded his father in 1972, and he attempted to gather international support to declare Nepal as a 'Zone of Peace'. In 1975, King Birendra proposed that Nepal be recognised internationally as a Zone of Peace. He received support from China, Pakistan and many other countries. The King also opposed Sikkim's accession to India in 1975, causing considerable damage to bilateral relations. The Zone of Peace proposal was quite irritating for India, which viewed the proposal as a contradiction to the 1950 Peace Treaty, and as a threat to India's security from anti-India forces operating from Nepal. However, Nepal persisted with the proposal since then, risking friendly relations with India.

In 1978, India agreed to separate trade and transit treaties, respecting Nepalese sentiments over the issue. However, in the late 1980s, relations deteriorated over the issue of Nepal's purchase of arms from China. In 1988, Nepal had purchased anti-aircraft guns, medium-range Surface-to-Surface Missiles (SSMs), and assault rifles from China. India perceived the arms purchase as an indication of Nepal's intention to build a military relationship with China in violation of the 1950 Peace Treaty. Further, in 1988, when the separated trade and transit treaties were up for renewal, Nepal's refusal to accommodate India's wishes on the transit treaty caused India to call again for a single trade and transit treaty. After two extensions, the two treaties finally expired on 23 March 1989. After the expiry of the two treaties, there was a virtual Indian economic blockade of Nepal that lasted till the end of April 1990. The Indian economic blockade might also have been a fall-out of India's displeasure over Nepal's arms haul from China.

In 1990, the popular movement against the 'Panchayat System' gathered momentum in Nepal, and the King had to dismantle the party-less system to restore a multi-party system. But multi-party democracy faced testing times in Nepal as the King usurped power many times thereafter through 'palace coups', a term that indicated the monarch's suzerainty over party governments. Uncertainty in Nepal's domestic politics continued throughout the 1990s. In mid-1994, Parliament was dissolved due to dissension within the Nepali Congress Party. The subsequent general elections resulted in a hung parliament. A minority government led by the

Communist Party of Nepal-United Marxist Leninist (CPN-UML) with Man Mohan Adhikari as prime minister assumed power. The next five years saw five successive unstable coalition governments and the beginning of a Maoist insurgency. Meanwhile, India made the trade treaty with Nepal separate from transit treaty and guaranteed Nepal's access to the sea through the Kolkata port for all times, without provisions for periodic renewal. The hijacking of an Indian Airlines aircraft from Kathmandu airport on 24 December 1999 and its landing in Kandahar airport in Taliban-ruled Afghanistan had an adverse impact on Indo–Nepal relations at the end of the decade. India expressed serious concern about threat to its security by foreign forces operating from Nepalese soil.

The growing Maoist movement in Nepal from 1996, and its spillover effects into India was also a matter of grave concern for New Delhi. India was worried about the linkages between Maoists in Nepal and similar outfits in India and emphasised better coordination between security and intelligence agencies of the two nations. Nepal's domestic political events again impacted Indo-Nepal relations from the middle of the 1990s. In February 1996, the leaders of the Maoist United People's Front began a violent insurgency in more than 50 of the country's 75 districts, which ultimately led to a civil war in Nepal. The 10-year-long civil war (1996–2006) tormented Nepal, and its relations with India, because India was accused of fomenting pro-democracy movements in Nepal. Between 2002 and 2005, King Gyanendra changed five prime ministers, before assuming direct power for 15 months. Country-wide agitation and violence continued to restore democracy in Nepal. Under pressure, King Gyanendra announced the reinstatement of Parliament in April 2006. The Maoists declared a three-month unilateral cease-fire immediately (in April 2006), which the new seven-party alliance (SPA)-government reciprocated on 3 May 2006. The SPA and the Maoists signed five agreements, culminating in the comprehensive peace agreement of 21 November 2006, effectively ending the Maoist insurgency.

However, turmoil in Nepalese politics continued after 2006. The main agenda of the SPA and the Maoists was to hold a Constituent Assembly (CA) election, with the primary responsibility of drafting and promulgating a new constitution defining the future political system in Nepal. The interim constitution, adopted on 15 January 2007, expressed full commitment to parliamentary democracy, including competitive multi-party system, adult franchise, periodic elections, human rights, independent judiciary, and the rule of law. Freedom of the press and civil liberties were also guaranteed in the interim constitution. Nepal's historic CA election was finally held, after two abortive attempts earlier, on 10 April 2008. None of the parties succeeded in getting a simple majority in the CA. The United Communist Party of Nepal-Maoist (UCPN-Maoist) won 218 out of 575 elected seats, and emerged as the single largest party. In August 2008, Prime Minister Pushpa Kamal Dahal, popularly known as 'Prachanda', supreme leader of the UCPN-Maoist, was sworn in as prime minister. But within eight months into his term, Prime Minister Dahal resigned on 4 May 2009 following a dispute over his plan to dismiss the Chief of the Army Staff. On 23 May, members from 22 political parties represented in the CA elected United Marxist Leninist (UML) leader Madhav Kumar Nepal as the new prime minister. Madhav was sworn in on 25 May 2009. However, the UCPN-Maoist, the largest political party in the CA, started a strong campaign for Madhav's removal. The UCPN-Maoist wanted to reinstate Dahal as the prime minister. Following months of Maoist protests, on 30 June 2010, Prime Minister Nepal resigned with a view to end the country's political turmoil. But for months, the parliament was unable to select a new prime minister, and Nepal continued as caretaker prime minister of the Himalayan nation.

In February 2011, Jhala Nath Khanal took over as the new prime minister of Nepal. But Khanal submitted his resignation to the President of Nepal, Ram Baran Yadav on 14 August 2011 after days of vacillation and mounting pressure from political allies and opponents. The Khanal government was the third to fall in three years, as Nepal headed for another political crisis. In his short tenure as country's prime minister, Khanal was unable to bring peace after Nepal's decade-long civil war (1996–2006). He failed to integrate the Maoist People's Liberation Army (PLA) into mainstream politics; and he also could not make much progress in framing the new constitution. As the Maoists lacked majority to form a government in Nepal, despite it being the single largest party in the CA, the deadlock continued. Political parties close to the monarchy, refrained from supporting the Maoists, as they accused them of perpetuating violence, and illegal practices such as forcible land acquisition.

Nepal's continuous political instability affected Indo–Nepal relations to a great extent. India was accused of showing initial softness to the Maoists, and sheltering them when they were fighting against the monarch for the restoration of democracy in Nepal.[2] But when the Maoists' links with Indian insurgent groups came to the open, India deserted the Maoists, and backed the conservative political parties in Nepal. Therefore, India was accused of meddling into Nepal's internal politics, mainly by a section of the Nepalese intelligentsia.[3] After his resignation in May 2009, Prime Minister Dahal cited 'foreign hands' as the reason behind his quitting, thereby indicating India's involvement in the political turmoil of Nepal.[4] Indian Ambassador to Nepal, Rakesh Sood was attacked, allegedly by a group led by a former Maoist minister of Nepal in October 2010 in Kathmandu. This incident put further strains on India–Nepal relations in recent times. India summoned the Nepalese envoy to New Delhi and lodged strong protests against the attack.[5] During his official visit to Nepal between 20 and 22 April 2011, Indian Foreign Minister S. M. Krishna also raised the issue with the Nepalese leaders and expressed India's concern and displeasure over the attack.[6] It appeared that India enjoyed less credibility among Nepal's political elite and the intelligentsia during the last few years. Anti-India sentiments remained high in Nepal in the recent times.[7]

---

[2] Surendra K.C., 'Maoist Insurgency in Nepal and Its Implications to India', *TelegraphNepal.com*, available at http://www.telegraphnepal.com/national/2011-07-08/maoist-insurgency-in-nepal-its-implications-to-india, accessed on 22 August 2011.

[3] Ibid.

[4] Ibid.

[5] See in this context, *The Times of India*, 23 October 2010.

[6] See *The Times of India*, 23 April 2011.

[7] See, in this context, Indrani Bagchi, 'Anti-India Sentiment in Nepal', *The Times of India*, 15 May 2009.

However, India continued its efforts to engage Nepal in collaborative projects and to support the Himalayan state in finding a settlement that would end the nation's long political crisis. During his April 2011 visit to Nepal, the Indian Foreign Minister S. M. Krishna gave special emphasis on economic engagement and expanding infrastructure in the Terai region for trade. This would be done by construction of an integrated check-post at Birgunj built with Indian assistance of Rs 86.9 crore. The Birgunj–Thori 53 km road for which the foundation stone was laid is one of the 19 roads totaling 605 kms being built under Phase I of the Terai Roads project with Indian assistance. The long-term India–Nepal Cooperation Programme has over 400 projects with a total outlay of NRs 5,800 crore in the sectors of education, health, agriculture, roads and bridges and infrastructure. Krishna requested Nepal for speedy formalisation of the Bilateral Investment Protection and Promotion Agreement (BIPPA) and Double Taxation Avoidance Agreement (DTAA) for promoting further investments by India in Nepal.

The Indian foreign minister also discussed with Nepalese leaders issues like cross-border terrorism, preventing circulation of fake Indian currency notes through Nepal, a proposed Extradition Treaty and the Mutual Legal Assistance Treaty (MLAT). These would facilitate coordination and cooperation between security agencies and put a check on elements which have cross-border bases to evade detection and prosecution by the security agencies. The Indian foreign minister requested the Nepali authorities to formalise boundary maps so that the management of the border areas could be implemented more effectively. However, the Indian foreign minister treaded a murky zone when he put emphasis on maintaining 'the professional integrity and apolitical nature of the Nepal Army'. This Indian position indicated that India would not support wholesale merger of the PLA with the Nepal Army, a proposal mooted by the Maoists. The third force option would be the most likely way ahead for India,—one in which there would be a mix of the Army, Armed Police Force and PLA cadres with a primary role for the PLA in disaster management. The stance taken by Krishna on PLA was indicative that India would remain engaged in the peace process in Nepal, directly or indirectly, because an amicable solution of the political stalemate in Nepal would be crucial for India's strategic interests.

Bilateral relations continued to witness ups and downs in the recent years. Prime Minister Narendra Modi's visit to Nepal in August 2015, the first Indian prime minister to visit Nepal in 17 years, raised hopes of improvement in bilateral ties. Modi provided Nepal with US $1 billion as concessional line of credit for various development purposes, and another US $1 billion for rebuilding Nepal after the devastating earthquake of April 2015. Modi also aroused confidence in the Nepalese mind when he insisted that open borders between Nepal and India should be seen as a bridge and not as a barrier. He promised that India would always stand for the sovereignty and integrity of Nepal. Earlier, Nepal and India signed an important deal on 25 November 2014 according to which India will build a 900 MW hydropower plant at a cost of another US $1 billion. If these were positive signs of bilateralism, India's stance on the 135-day long Madhesi Movement in Nepal that started in September 2015, aroused Nepalese suspicion. The movement was precipitated as Nepal's CA passed a new constitution in September. 'People in the Madhesi region—the country's southernmost plains—began agitating against the boundaries of the provinces demarcated in the new constitution, reasoning that their voices would be marginalised if they are clubbed with people from the hills and higher slopes. The Madhesis blockaded the border points with India cutting off supply chains from India.'[8] The Nepalese government accused India of providing indirect support to the Madhesis and deliberately worsening the embargo by not allowing vehicles to pass from check-points where no protests were held. The Indian government denied such allegations. The Madhesi movement did cause suspicion and mistrust in bilateral relations during 2015–16. In this atmosphere of schism, the new Nepalese Prime Minister K. P. S. Oli began his six-day official visit to India on 19 February 2016 with a view to strengthen ties with India. He met his Indian counterpart in New Delhi on 20 February. Both leaders agreed that an atmosphere of trust and confidence must prevail in bilateral relations. The Indian prime minister reiterated that Nepal's stability is dependent on India's security.[9] During the visit, the two sides agreed to continue closer engagements in different areas of bilateral relations. Despite such rhetoric, there was no denial of the fact that India–Nepal relations went low during 2015–16.

ECONOMIC RELATIONS

India was a premier donor country that played an important role in mobilising aid to Nepal since 1951. India's economic relations with Nepal covered areas such as bilateral trade, investment and transfer of technology. India's cooperation has been noteworthy in accelerating the pace of economic development in Nepal in the recent years and it continues to be Nepal's largest trade partner, source of foreign investment and tourist arrivals. Table 4.1 highlights India–Nepal trade in recent years:

Table 4.1: India–Nepal Trade in Recent Years

(in US $ million)

Year	*Total Trade*	*Growth (%)*
2005–06	1,239.82	–
2006–07	1,233.42	–0.52
2007–08	2,135.98	73.18
2008–09	2,066.19	–3.27
2009–10	1,985.93	–3.88
2010–11	2,717.80	36.85
2011–12	3,271.54	22.01
2012–13	3,631.94	11.02
2013–14	4,122.23	13.50
2014–15	5,196.39	26.06

Source: Export-Import Data Bank, Department of Commerce, Government of India, available at http://commerce.nic.in/eidb/iecnt.asp, accessed on 24 November 2015.

As Table 4.1 shows, the total volume of bilateral trade has decreased in both 2008–09 and 2009–10 fiscal years. Perhaps political instability in Nepal had an adverse impact on bilateral trade in the recent years. However, it is heartening to note that bilateral trade registered a 36.85 per

[8] https://scroll.in/.../its-a-coincidence-that-on-the-day-baburao-bhattarai-resigned-they-t..., accessed on 10 May 2017.

[9] See *The Indian Express*, 20 February 2016.

cent growth rate in 2010–11 and 26.06 per cent growth in 2014–15. India accounted for nearly 60 per cent of Nepal's total external trade in 2014–15. This data reveals Nepal's dependence on India as far as external trade is concerned. In 2009, India and Nepal revised their Trade Treaty for another seven years. The revised trade treaty would help in facilitating intense bilateral trade. Article II of the revised treaty says, 'The Contracting Parties shall endeavour to grant maximum facilities and to undertake all necessary measures for the free and unhampered flow of goods, needed by one country from the other, to and from their respective territories'.[10] As per the revised Treaty, several items of import would be exempt from customs duty and quantitative restrictions. In this context, Article IV of the treaty states, '. . . the Contracting Parties agree, on a reciprocal basis, to exempt from basic customs duty as well as from quantitative restrictions the import of such primary products as may be mutually agreed upon, from each other'.[11] The 2009 Treaty, lists 15 types of primary products eligible for preferential treatment. These are: (i) agriculture, horticulture, floriculture and forest produce; (ii) minerals which have not undergone any processing; (iii) rice, pulses, flour, *atta*, bran and husk; (iv) timber; (v) jaggery (*gur* and *shakkar*); (vi) livestock, poultry birds and fish; (vii) bees, bee-wax and honey; (viii) raw wool, goat hair, bristles and bones as are used in the manufacture of bone-meal; (ix) milk, home-made products of milk and eggs; (x) *ghani*-produced oil and oilcakes; (xi) herbs, ayurvedic and herbal medicines, including essential oils and its extracts; (xii) articles produced by village artisans as are mainly used in villages; (xiii) *akara*; (xiv) yak tail; (xv) stone aggregate, boulder, sand and gravel. Apart from these items, the revised Trade Treaty agreed to provide preferential treatment to any other primary products, which may be mutually agreed upon from time to time. It may be hoped that through such mutual preferential imports, bilateral trade would get additional boost in the future. Currently, India and Nepal have a separate Transit Treaty, which confers transit rights through mutually agreed routes and modalities in both countries. The treaty was last renewed in March 2006 for a period of seven years.

India is also the largest foreign investor in Nepal. According to the Indian Ministry of External Affairs (MEA), Indian investments in Nepal amounted to Rs 1,586 crore in 2010 with 462 foreign direct investments (FDIs) projects. India accounted for 44 per cent of the total foreign investments in Nepal in the same year.[12] Indian investors have identified advantages offered by Nepal such as attractive incentives, government's positive attitude towards investors, low cost locations and cheap labour as some of the factors favourable for investment. Indian companies such as Dabur, Hindustan Lever, Oberoi Hotels, Manipal Education and Medical Group have invested in Nepal. However, due to persistent political instability, Indian investment flow to

[10] Ministry of Commerce and Industry, Government of India, 'Revised Treaty of Trade between the Government of India and the Government of Nepal (New Delhi: Government of India), October 2009, p. 3.

[11] Ibid.

[12] Ministry of External Affairs, Government of India, 'India–Nepal Relations', available at http://www.mea.gov.in/mystart.php?id=50044504, accessed on 31 August 2011.

Nepal was restricted to some extent, despite Nepal's positive attitude for FDIs. Tourism and hydropower development are two sectors in which Nepal enjoys comparative advantage and could prove to be attractive for Indian investors. Nepal is an attractive destination for Indian tourists who visit the country for pilgrimage and sightseeing. There are also prospects of developing health tourism. There is scope for cooperation in hotel management between India and Nepal. For India, there are opportunities for more investment in information technology (IT) services and software, areas in which India has gained considerable strength in the recent times.

Nepal has one of the highest potential for development of hydroelectric power. As demands for consumption of electric power in the adjoining Indian provinces like Bihar, Uttar Pradesh and Uttarakhand have increased tremendously in the recent years, there are prospects for cooperation between Nepal and India in this sector. Bilateral and multilateral donor agencies are interested in funding hydroelectric power development projects in Nepal when they are assured that India can be a potential buyer. Nepal and India should undertake feasibility projects to cultivate this vastly untapped source for electricity. It is heartening to note that both the countries have recognised the importance of cooperation in this field and have decided to establish a three-tier bilateral mechanism at the ministerial, secretary and technical levels to oversee cooperation in water-related issues. The two countries have set up in 2008, Joint Ministerial Level Commission on Water Resources (JMCWR), Joint Committee on Water Resources (JCWR) and Joint Standing Technical Committee (JSTC) at the three levels respectively. The last meeting of the JCWR was held in November 2009 in Pokhra in Nepal. As demand for electricity is likely to increase in both the countries, this area offers huge prospects for cooperation in the future.

The two countries have concluded a Rail Services Agreement (RSA) and a revised Air Services Agreement (ASA) to enhance bilateral cooperation in rail and air communication. A Motor Vehicles Agreement (MVA) for passenger vehicles is also awaiting formal approval from the two governments.[13] India regularly contributes to the development efforts of Nepal by undertaking various development projects in areas of infrastructure, rural and community development, agriculture, health and education. A report issued by the Indian MEA states, '... the grant assistance extended to Nepal during 2009–10 under "Aid to Nepal" budget was [Rs] 161 crores. In addition, GoI (Government of India) has extended considerable economic assistance to the ongoing peace process in Nepal. The overall quantum of India's assistance to Nepal is approx. [Rs] 3,600 crores which include the Small Development Projects (SDPs) scheme offered by the Embassy of India ... at [the] grass-roots level in sectors identified with the local population.'[14] The SDP scheme now covers over 370 projects with an outlay of nearly Rs 402 crore. In the education sector, over 1,500 scholarships are offered annually for Nepalese students to pursue different courses in India and Nepal.[15] Therefore, India is integrally connected to the development

[13] Ibid.

[14] Ibid., parentheses by the author.

[15] Ibid.

programmes of Nepal. But the two countries must augment bilateral trade in the future with a view to achieve more healthy and bright economic relations.

SECURITY RELATIONS

India–Nepal security relations always remained important for both the countries due to a few reasons. These are: (i) Nepal's strategic importance for India; (ii) long open borders between the two countries; (iii) the China factor in India–Nepal relations; and (iv) problems of drug trafficking and terrorism. All these issues are closely related to one another. For instance, China's growing influence in Nepal in all spheres, political, economic and security, makes the Himalayan state strategically very important for India. Further, long open borders are believed to be crucial reasons for drug trafficking and insurgency-related problems. Again, the use of Nepalese territory by drug traffickers and terrorists makes Nepal strategically significant for India. Therefore, the two neighbours have tried to maintain close security relations between them. Nepal's military consists of nearly 100,000-strong Nepalese Army (NA), which is organised into six divisions, namely, Far-Western, Mid-Western, Western, Central, Eastern, and Valley Divisions, with separate Aviation, Parachute, and Security Brigades as well as brigade-sized directorates encompassing air defence, artillery, engineers, logistics, and signals. India had played a leading role in helping the NA in its modernisation through provisions of equipment and training. According to the Indian MEA Report, 'More than 180 training slots are provided every year for training of NA personnel in various Indian Army training institutions. In 2009, India had agreed to resume the military aid package to Nepal, suspended earlier due to an Indian embargo imposed in February 2005 following the seizure of power by King Gyanendra. Before 2005, India had been regularly providing Nepal with military weapons free of cost. The Chief of Army Staff of the Indian Army is given the honorary rank of a General in the Nepal Army and a reciprocal honour is conferred on the Chief of the Nepal Army.'[16]

For a long time, since the days of British control over India, the Nepalese people have been working in the Indian army. After India's independence, the Indian army continued to be a major source of employment for the Nepalese youth. As per reports, there are more than 1.23 lakhs of former Indian servicemen residing in Nepal at present. In 2010–11, the payments of pensions to the Indian ex-service men in Nepal amounted to Rs 1,100 crore. The GoI has tried to ensure that these ex-servicemen, their families and dependents are looked after well, while residing in Nepal. To ensure this, the GoI has established the Indian Ex-Servicemen Welfare Organisation in Nepal (IEWON).[17] But these are a few positives of India–Nepal security relations. However, India faces security challenges from the territory of Nepal due to Maoist connections with Indian insurgent groups (as observed earlier), drug trafficking, and growing Nepal–China

---

[16] Ibid.

[17] Ibid.

economic and security ties. It is mainly the responsibility of India, due to its national interests and strong paramilitary forces, to build security mechanisms with Nepal only to curb and curtail trans-border organised crime.

From the middle of the 1990s, the Chinese governments have been providing grant assistance to Nepal under the economic and technical cooperation programme. The volume of such assistance is to the tune of US $12.50 million every year. In 2005, China supplied huge quantity of arms to Nepal. In the same year, Nepal supported the inclusion of China into SAARC despite India's reservations on this issue. In September 2008, China announced a military aid package of US $1.3 million to Nepal. In December 2008, Lieutenant General Ma Xiaotan of the Peoples' Liberation army (of China) pledged US $2.6 million in military aid to Nepal during his visit to the country. China was involved in the reconstruction of China–Nepal highway during 2010–11. Built at a cost of more than US $100 million, the highway would become the 'golden gateway', connecting Lhasa in Tibet to Kathmandu, and would serve as China's gateway to South Asia. Along with the Qinghai–Tibet railroad, this highway would be China's alternative trade and military route to reach out to Nepal. China has been wooing Nepal with a view to increase its sphere of influence in South Asia, as well as to reduce India's preeminent position in Nepal. India's biggest challenge would be to neutralise China's increasing economic and security clout in Nepal.

RECOMMENDATIONS FOR THE FUTURE

Since the signing of the Treaty of Peace and Friendship in 1950, India has been deeply engaged in Nepal. However, the Nepalese people have nurtured mixed and contradictory feelings towards India. Currently, India does not enjoy a favourable image in Nepal. From the middle of the 1990s, India was focused on the politics of the peace process in Nepal, without much dividend. Therefore, India needs to refrain from its attempts to influence the political process in Nepal, and reorient its approach towards her. One better way of engaging Nepal and build confidence among the Nepalese people is to pursue long-term economic relations with the Himalayan state. Long-term economic engagement between the two countries could be pursued through the following measures:

(1) By increasing the number of joint ventures (JVs), and identify new areas for JVs. Increased and new JVs could be undertaken in the following sectors:

   (a) hydropower,
   (b) tourism, especially travel-trek and hotels,
   (c) infrastructure,
   (d) banking, insurance and financing,
   (e) health services,
   (f) education,

(g) IT and software,
(h) biodiversity, especially forest and herbal products, and
(i) food processing.

(2) By taking initiatives to appraise the Indian private sector about JVs in Nepal and encourage them to participate in them. The private sector in India is not fully aware of the existing rules and regulations about JVs in Nepal. Hence, this should be done in tandem by the governments of the respective countries.

(3) By increasing interaction with the private sector in India through chambers' of commerce and industries in India and Nepalese chamber of commerce;

(4) By initiating joint study on foreign investment by the private sector, government and academicians of both countries; and

(5) By further liberalisation of foreign investment policies and foreign exchange regime. Most importantly, India should try to depoliticise its economic relationship with Nepal.

Issues like open borders between the two countries, hydro-electric power, and Nepal's increasing reliance on China are some of the irritants in India–Nepal relations at this juncture. Both the countries need to handle these issues carefully. The long, unregulated and open borders have generated cross-border crime, smuggling and infiltration of fake currency, terrorists and arms. As a consequence, open borders have always remained as security concerns for the two nations. India and Nepal need to cooperate intensely on effective border management. Forces guarding the borders from the two sides need to meet frequently and chalk out both short and long-term plans with a view to effectively prevent crimes across the borders. This is easier said than done, especially in the backdrop of Nepal's political instability. India, being the more resourceful country, must go the extra mile to safeguard the border by allocating more money and security personnel along the border. But India must always consult Nepal on this matter and seek Nepal's opinion and cooperation in this area. India must see that Nepal's sensitivities should not be disturbed on the issue of border management.

Many in Nepal believe that Nepal's potential for hydro-electricity has not been fully utilised due to India's negative attitude. As one Nepalese journalist wrote, 'Nepal's vast hydropower sector has remained untapped. Some blame for this rests on New Delhi. Whenever an investor proposes to invest in Nepal's hydropower, India finds that this threatens its national interest and blocks the development—thanks to the 1950 Treaty, which allows it to do that.'[18] In the context of such adverse feelings, India should reorient its policies for hydro-electric power in Nepal. As an Indian observer correctly pointed out, 'India should engage the Nepali government and Nepali businessmen as well as environmentalists to understand Nepal's concerns and then chalk out a new policy. Many Nepali experts believe that the India–Bhutan hydro-electricity model is not

[18] Bhumika Ghimire, 'Time to Redefine India–Nepal Relations', *Los Angeles Times*, 7 December 2009.

suitable for India–Nepal water cooperation. Nepali experts want India to pay peak-hour price for electricity generated in Nepal. They also want India to pay for the storage dams in Nepal for their considerable benefits downstream.'[19] India should pay heed to Nepalese sensibilities in this regard and show a soft attitude with a view to win the confidence of the Nepalese people. After all, Indian foreign policy in Nepal has been trying to achieve this 'confidence' over the last decade. The issue of hydro-electric power is a good opportunity for Indian diplomacy to win over the trust of the Nepalese people in the future.

India must not be overawed by Chinese presence in Nepal, and must handle the China factor with well-designed and long-term plans. Culturally, Nepalese people are more close to India than China. Religious and linguistic similarities (Nepali is one of the official languages of India), scope for higher education and employment in India for the Nepalese youth, and marriages across borders have brought these two nations closer. From an economic point of view, India is still the largest trade partner of Nepal. The total volume of India–Nepal trade is higher than China–Nepal trade in 2009–10. India–Nepal bilateral trade reached US $1,985.93 million in 2009–10 (see Table 4.1), while China–Nepal trade amounted to US $440 million during the same period.[20] China outpaced India in the number of JVs in Nepal in 2010. While China entered into 58 JVs with Nepal, India was engaged in 27 JVs in Nepal in 2010. But the amount of investment by India in JVs in Nepal was much higher than China's total investment in JVs in Nepal. In 2010, China invested US $731.25 million in 58 JVs in Nepal. Indian investment in 27 JVs in Nepal reached a staggering US $7,078 million in the same year.[21] In 2015–16 FY, India's total trade with Nepal was US $4,400.68 million. In contrast, China's trade with Nepal was US $971.3 million in FY 2015–16.[22] Therefore, India still holds an edge over China as far as economic relations with Nepal are concerned. But India must not be complacent also. China is trying to economically engage Nepal in a big way. The total number of China–Nepal JVs in 2010 is a case in point here. But India should not be unduly worried about being outpaced by China in Nepal. Instead India should also enhance its own pace. India must view China as an economic competitor in Nepal, not as an adversary. A strong competitor like China would help India to be engaged more in Nepal economically in the future, and that would help India in the long run. India must be ready and willing to give China a very tough economic competition in Nepal. In doing so, India must take Nepal into confidence, and always seek Nepalese cooperation. Nepal must not feel alienated to witness India–China economic race on its soil. In the future India–Nepal–China trilateral economic initiatives might even be launched. This analysis, therefore,

---

[19] Arvind Gupta, 'India Needs a New Paradigm in its Nepal Policy', *IDSA Comment*, available at http://www.idsa.in/idsacomments/IndianeedsanewparadigminitsNepalpolicy_agupta_180810, accessed on 1 September 2011.

[20] Ministry of Commerce, People's Republic of China, available at http://english.mofcom.gov.cn//statistic/BriefStatistics/201109/20110907724032.html, accessed on 4 September 2011.

[21] Ibid.

[22] Source: http:www.atlas.media.mit/edu/em/.

puts emphasis on the recommendation that India must lessen its political engagements in Nepal, and increase its economic engagements. Due to cultural proximity, India gets tempted occasionally to involve itself in the political process in Nepal. Sometimes it becomes difficult also for India to remain aloof, like China, from the currents of Nepalese politics. But India should learn to disassociate itself from Nepalese politics and concentrate more on economic diplomacy. This attitude may help India win back the trust of the Nepalese people, a vital factor for improving bilateral relations in the future.

5

INDIA'S RELATIONS WITH BHUTAN

Trusted Proximity

HIGHLIGHTS

- Introduction
- Political Relations
- Economic Relations
- Security Relations
- Cultural Relations
- Recommendations for the Future

INTRODUCTION

India's relations with Bhutan, the small Himalayan state, may be viewed as a perfect example of friendship and cordiality in South Asia. In the last six decades, India–Bhutan relations had been guided mainly by the 1949 Treaty of Friendship and Cooperation (TFC), which was ratified in 2007 to suit the needs of the changing times. The TFC was almost an extension of a 1910 Treaty that Bhutan signed with the British rulers. Bhutan became a protectorate of British India after signing the treaty in 1910, allowing the British to 'guide' its foreign affairs and defence. A protectorate in international law is an autonomous territory that is protected diplomatically or militarily against third parties by a stronger state or entity. The TFC between India and Bhutan was signed on 8 August 1949. For long, this treaty governed the basic framework of bilateral relations between the two countries. The treaty provided for, among other things, peace and friendship, free trade and commerce and equal justice to each other's citizens. The TFC also established extradition protocols.

Events in China and Tibet were at the core of India's policy towards Bhutan in the late 1940s. In 1949, when the treaty was signed, China had begun to assert its control over Tibet. This was viewed with concern by both India and Bhutan. India needed to ensure that Bhutan would not fall under Chinese influence and Bhutan wanted India's protection. The TFC was signed under these circumstances. It served the interests of both the countries at that time. Under the TFC,

India used to play a significant role in Bhutan's external relations. Article 2 of the treaty required Bhutan to be guided by the advice of India in the conduct of its external relations, and Article 6 allowed Bhutan to import arms, ammunition, machines, and other warlike materials for its 'strength and welfare', but with India's assistance and approval. Unlike the Nepalese political elite, who were never at ease with the 1950 Indo–Nepal Treaty, the Bhutanese rulers and people never felt uncomfortable with the TFC, and accepted India's 'guidance provision' in the TFC very cordially. For long, Bhutan shut its doors for the outside world, and remained comfortable with India, its neighbour next-door, who never interfered in Bhutan's internal issues and respected the identity of the Bhutanese people. Therefore, an atmosphere of mutual respect and restrain, a rare phenomenon in South Asian international relations, developed in India–Bhutan relations from the very beginning. It was in conformity with this mutual respect that Bhutan and India embarked on a new epoch of friendship on 8 February 2007, by revising the 1949 TFC. The new treaty removed the clause that India would 'guide' Bhutan's foreign policy and allow Bhutan to purchase military equipment from other countries. The new Treaty was signed in New Delhi in an atmosphere of mutual trust, friendship and confidence.

Traditionally, a decentralised theocracy, Bhutan turned into a full-fledged practising monarchy since 1907. However, Bhutan completed its successful transition to a constitutional monarchy in 2008 when parliamentary democracy was introduced in the country. Bhutanese officials began preparations for the first-ever elections in 2006, shortly before King Jigme Singye Wangchuck abdicated in December 2006. The National Council (Upper House) of the new bicameral parliament was elected in December 2007, and National Assembly (Lower House) elections followed in March 2008. Two political parties contested in the first parliamentary elections. These parties were: the People's Democratic Party (PDP), founded on 24 March 2007 and Druk Phuensum Tshogpa (DPT), formed on 25 July 2007. The DPT won 44 out of 47 seats in the parliamentary elections, and the leader of the party, Jigmy Y. Thinley became the first democratically elected prime minister of Bhutan. Mr Tshering Tobgay of the PDP became the first Leader of the Opposition in the Bhutanese parliament. Therefore, the year 2008 marked a crucial period for Bhutan which had made a smooth transition to parliamentary democracy following its first historic parliamentary elections. What is unique about the transition to democracy in Bhutan is that unlike many other countries where democracy was introduced through revolution or even bloodshed, it was gifted to the people from the monarch. The establishment of a democratic political system in Bhutan would strengthen further its future relations with India, South Asia's most vibrant, and world's largest democracy. But before delving into the future, it would be appropriate to look into the traditionally strong bilateral relations between these two South Asian neighbours. This chapter would cover major segments of bilateral relations. It begins with political relations between India and Bhutan.

POLITICAL RELATIONS

Indo-Bhutan relations began to mature following state visits made by the Third King of the Himalayan state, Jigme Dorji Wangchuck to India, and by Indian Prime Minister Jawaharlal Nehru to Bhutan during the 1950s. Besides emphasising India's recognition of Bhutan's independence and sovereignty in his public statement in Paro, Nehru's visit in 1958 was also significant with discussions initiated for development cooperation between the two countries. Formal relations between India and the small Himalayan nation started with the appointment of a special officer of the Government of India (GoI) to Bhutan. The Embassy of India in Thimpu, known as the 'India House' began operating from 14 May 1968. Resident representatives of both the countries were exchanged in 1971. In 1978, ambassadorial-level contacts between the two neighbours began when Residents were upgraded to embassies. Bhutan's formal ties with the world began when India sponsored in 1971 Bhutan's application for UN membership. In 1972, Bhutan established diplomatic relations with Bangladesh. Thereafter, the small Himalayan nation established diplomatic ties with many countries, although Bhutan had not yet entered into diplomatic relations with five permanent members of the UN Security Council (UNSC). Bhutan's diplomatic relations with the rest of the world demonstrate that Article 2 of the Indo-Bhutan TFC was not a restricting factor in Bhutan's foreign policy.

These countries contribute extensively for Bhutan's social development. As already observed, Bhutan currently enjoys diplomatic relations with many countries; but with India, it has a special relationship of friendship and bonhomie. This special relationship is manifested through a rich tradition of bilateral visits and regular exchange of views by leaders of the two countries. This special relationship is further sustained by the tradition of regular visits and extensive exchange of views at the highest levels between the two countries. 'After the very successful visit of Jawaharlal Nehru in 1958, Indian prime minister Indira Gandhi visited Bhutan in 1968, and the President of India, V. V. Giri undertook an official trip to Bhutan in April 1970.'[1] Indira Gandhi again visited Bhutan as the prime minister of India in October 1972, and Indian President V. V. Giri went to the Himalayan Kingdom in June 1974. Prime Minister Rajiv Gandhi went to Bhutan in 1985. In the year 1988, both the Indian president and the prime minister paid official visits to Bhutan. While Prime Minister Rajiv Gandhi visited Bhutan in September, President R. Venkataraman went there in October 1988. Such close visits of two very high dignitaries pointed towards the importance India provided to Bhutan, and the proximity in bilateral relations. Indian Prime Minister P. V. Narasimha Rao made an official visit to Bhutan in August 1993. High-level visits from the Bhutanese side continued since the early 1950s symbolising close connections between the two friendly neighbours of South Asia. In recent times, the fourth king of Bhutan, Jigme Singye Wangchuk was the Chief Guest at the Republic Day celebrations in January 2005 and visited India for bilateral discussions in August 2005 and July 2006. The next King of Bhutan, Jigme Khesar Namgyel Wangchuk also visited India in February 2007. These visits provided an opportunity to discuss bilateral political, economic and other issues of mutual interest. The King's visit was followed by a state visit to India by the first democratically elected prime minister of Bhutan Lyonchen Jigmi Y. Thinley in July 2008. Indian President Pratibha Patil visited Bhutan from 5 to 8 November 2008 and was the Guest of Honour at the coronation

[1] Source: https://2001-2009.state.gov › … › Background Notes, accessed on 21 May 2017.

celebrations of His Majesty Jigme Khesar Namgyel Wangchuk, the King of Bhutan. The Fifth King of Bhutan, Jigme Khesar Namgyel Wangchuk, paid a State Visit to India between 21 and 26 December 2009 at the invitation of the President of India. The King again visited India in October 2010, during which the University of Calcutta conferred upon him the Honorary Doctorate Degree of Law. The King visited India again from 20 to 29 October 2010 as a Special Guest of Honour to the golden jubilee celebrations of the National Defence College. Bhutan's new Prime Minister Lyonchen Jigmi Y. Thinley visited India from 28 June to 3 July 2009 to felicitate the new Indian government headed by Prime Minister Manmohan Singh, which assumed office for a second term. The prime minister of Bhutan was the first head of government to visit India during the second term of the Singh Government. Bhutan also opened a Consulate in Kolkata in December 2009. The Indian Prime Minister, Manmohan Singh visited Bhutan from 28 to 30 April 2010 for the 16th SAARC Summit. Bhutanese Prime Minister Thinley again visited Delhi from 30 October to 3 November 2010. This was also the first of his visits to SAARC capitals in the capacity of the Chairman of SAARC. Apart from the heads of state and government, many other ministers, parliamentarians, and top officials from both countries visited India and Bhutan during the last six decades.[2] In fact, the lengthy list of visits by top-level leaders and officials from the two nations provides an unambiguous indication of very close relations between India and Bhutan, because heavy flow of reciprocal visits always signals (in international relations) a strong, matured and trustworthy relationship. These high-level visits manifest the fact that India and Bhutan indeed enjoy a very strong bond between them.

The harmonious nature of India–Bhutan relations could be further identified by several Agreements and Memoranda of Understanding (MoUs) signed by the two nations during the last six decades. These agreements and MoUs were targeted mostly at socio-economic development projects of Bhutan with the help from India. Notable among such projects were:

(i) Project 'Dantak' of the Indian Border Roads Organisation started in May 1961. It was headquartered at Simtokha, near Thimphu under a Chief Engineer. Project Dantak has constructed over 1,500 km of roads through very difficult and mountainous terrain in Bhutan. Project Dantak has built all the major highways such as the East–West highway (548 km) and Thimphu–Phuentsholing Highway (181 km), airfields at Paro and Yangphula and airport terminal at Paro, a number of helipads, the Indo-Bhutan microwave link, Bhutan Broadcasting Station, India House Complex, Chukha Hydroelectric Housing Complex, power sub-stations, river-training works, and several important buildings, including the SAARC Convention Centre. Project Dantak would be taking up Pasakha–Manitar road, double laning of Thimphu–Phuentsholing road, Gyelpozhing–Nanglam road, extension of runway at Paro airfield under funding from the Indian government in the Ninth Plan of Bhutan.

[2] Ministry of External Affairs, Government of India, 'India–Bhutan Relations', available at http://meaindia.nic.in/mystart.php?id=50042442, accessed on 24 July 2011.

(ii) The Geological Survey of India (GSI) initiated exploration of Bhutan's mineral resources in 1960. It prepared the first geo-scientific database of Bhutan, which was presented to the World Scientific Community at the 22nd International Geological Congress held in New Delhi in 1964. This database helped in identifying several cement-grade limestone, dolomite, coal, and gypsum deposits in Bhutan. GSI, Bhutan Unit, had its headquarters at Samtse and it had made major contributions to the development of cement industry in Bhutan. The GSI Bhutan Unit, however, has closed down operations since March 2003.

(iii) The Central Water Commission (CWC), an Indian organisation, established its Bhutan Investigation Division in Phuentsholing in 1961 for examining hydro power potentials in Bhutan. The CWC has been closely associated with the investigation of Chukha Hydroelectric Project on river Wangchu. Its activities have expanded, over the years, to meet the demands of mutually beneficial cooperation between India and Bhutan.[3]

In the recent years also, India and Bhutan have signed many agreements and MoUs. During the visit of the Fourth King of Bhutan in July 2006, an agreement laying down the framework for cooperation in the field of hydropower, Protocol to the Inter-Governmental Agreement on the Tala Hydroelectric Project, and laying down commercial arrangements for purchase of power from the project were signed. Further, an Agreement on Trade, Commerce and Transit was also signed. Before these, an MoU on Air Services Agreement was signed in June 2005 providing for an increase in the flight frequencies between two nations from 12 to 49 per week. Institutional cooperation between the Indian Union Public Service Commission (UPSC) and Royal Civil Service Commission of Bhutan was formalised through signing of an MoU in November 2005. Another MoU for cooperation between the two election commissions was signed in May 2006. The MoU on Nehru–Wangchuk Scholarship was signed during the Indian Foreign Minister's visit to Bhutan in June 2009.

In December 2009, 12 agreements and MoUs were signed between the two nations during the visit of King Jigme Khesar Namgyel Wangchuk to India. These covered closer cooperation in areas like IT, hydropower, health and medicine, agriculture, civil aviation and narcotics. Out of these 12 agreements and MoUs, four were signed for preparation and updation of Detailed Project Reports (DPRs) of the Amochhu Reservoir Hydroelectric Project (HEP), the Kuri Gongri HEP, the Chamkharchhu-I HEP and the Kholongchhu HEP. Other notable MoUs were: Establishment of the Bhutan Institute of Medical Sciences; MoU on Drug Demand Reduction and Prevention of Illicit Trafficking in Narcotic Drugs, Psychotropic Substances and Precursor Chemicals and Related Matters; Air Services Agreement; Agreement for Search and Rescue Operation Services; MoU on Technical Assistance to the National Environment Commission of Bhutan; and MoU for Consultancy Services for the Preparation of the National Transmission Grid Master Plan

[3] Ibid.

of Bhutan. During Prime Minister Manmohan Singh's visit to Bhutan in April 2010 for the 16th SAARC Summit, Implementation Agreements for the Punatsangchhu–II and Mangdechhu HEPs were signed by the Minister of Economic Affairs of Bhutan Lyonpo Khandu Wangchuk and the External Affairs Minister of India, S. M. Krishna, in the presence of the prime ministers of India and Bhutan.[4] All these agreements and MoUs, signed during the last six decades, manifest mutual trust, understanding and goodwill between Bhutan and India. In continuation of this goodwill and trust, Narendra Modi chose Bhutan as his first foreign visit after becoming the Prime Minister of India. Modi's official trip to Bhutan on 15–16 June 2014 signalled India's emphasis on neighbourhood relations, including priorities to Bhutan, a traditional friend and a new democracy. Prime Minister Modi took a high-level delegation to Bhutan, which included the foreign secretary, the national security advisor and other senior officials. The new Indian prime minister addressed the Joint Session of the Bhutanese Parliament on 16 June 2014. During the visit, Narendra Modi laid the foundation stone of 600 MW Kholongchu HEP and inaugurated the Supreme Court building, which was constructed with India's assistance. Besides exchanging views and discussing bilateral relations and economic cooperation, Prime Minister Modi announced doubling of Nehru Wangchuck Scholarship to Rs 2 crore per year. He also announced that the GoI's assistance for establishment of e-library in the National Library of Bhutan and in all the 20 districts of Bhutan. The two sides agreed to continue close coordination and cooperation in areas relating to their national interests and not allow each other's territory to be used for interests inimical to the other.[5] At the invitation of the King of Bhutan, the President of India, Pranab Mukherjee, paid a State Visit to Bhutan on 7–8 November 2014. During the visit, he held wide-ranging discussions with His Majesty the King of Bhutan, including on bilateral and regional issues. He also met His Majesty the Fourth Druk Gyalpo and Prime Minister Lyonchhen Tshering Tobgay.[6] India's Minister of Road Transport, Highways and Shipping, Nitin Gadkari visited Bhutan on 15–16 June 2015. The BBIN (Bangladesh, Bhutan, India and Nepal) Motor Vehicle Agreement was signed in Thimphu by the Transport Ministers of the four countries on 15 June 2015. The high-level bilateral visits continued and amply demonstrated the strength in India–Bhutan relations.

ECONOMIC RELATIONS

India has been closely linked to Bhutan's economic development programmes. As already observed, many of Bhutan's development projects have been fully financed by India over the decades. Planned development in Bhutan began in 1961, with the first two Five-Year Plans (FYPs) wholly financed by the GoI. Indian assistance has increased steadily from Rs 107 million in the

---

[4] Ibid.

[5] Ministry of External Affairs, Government of India, 'India-Bhutan Relations', available at http://www.mea.gov.in/Portal/ForeignRelation/Bhutan_2015_07_20.pdf, accessed on 25 February 2016.

[6] Ibid.

First FYP (1962–66) to Rs 9,000 million in the Eighth FYP (1997–2002). While Bhutan's source of foreign aid has diversified significantly since it became a member of the UN, India continues to be the major donor of external aid to Bhutan. India accounted for about 41 per cent of total external outlay during Bhutan's Eighth FYP. India's contribution went into Bhutanese social sectors like education, health, hydropower, agriculture, roads and human resources.

India's assistance to Bhutan's Ninth FYP (2002–08) was Rs 2,610.14 crore. This included, according to the Indian Embassy in Thimpu, Rs 907 crore for project-tied assistance, Rs 820 crore as programme grant and rest as various refunds and subsidies.[7] Major India-assisted projects completed in the Ninth Plan included 350-bed JDWNR Hospital in Thimphu, Regional Referral Hospital in Mongar, Phase I of double-laning of Thimphu-Phuentsholing road, double laning of Paro-Chuzom road, construction of 10 new schools, 306 low-income housing units, renovation of Semtokha Dzong, two youth centres, human resource development, telecommunications and projects in agriculture and allied sectors.[8] India also funded feasibility studies for establishing rail linkages between a few towns located along the border of India and Bhutan. The GoI committed assistance worth Rs 3,400 crore during the Tenth FYP (2008–13): This includes project-tied assistance (Rs 2,000 crore for about 70 projects in key socio-economic sectors such as agriculture, information and communications technology (ICT), media, health/hospitals, education/schools, capacity-building, energy, culture and infrastructure, etc.), programme grant (Rs 700 crore) and the small development projects (Rs 700 crore). Some of the important projects being executed under the Tenth Plan include construction of the Supreme Court, strengthening of constitutional officers such as the Royal Audit Authority, Election Commission, anti-Corruption Commission and Attorney General, renovation of major Dzongs, preparation of DPRs for major power projects, widening of major roads, scholarships and expansion of tertiary educational institutions.[9]

Bhutan and India also share very close trade links. Currently, India is Bhutan's leading trade partner. A free trade regime exists between India and Bhutan. The India–Bhutan Trade and Commerce Agreement which expired in March 2005, has been renewed for a period of 10 years. Table 5.1 below shows total volume of India–Bhutan trade in the recent years:

As Table 5.1 shows, India's total trade with Bhutan increased from US $187.94 million in 2005–06 to US $487.52 million in 2014–15, a growth rate of more than 100 per cent. Earlier, India's imports from Bhutan used to remain higher than India's exports to Bhutan, creating a negative trade balance for India. But recently (since 2011–12), India's exports have surpassed India's imports. This trend is not uncommon in trade between a relatively strong economy and a weak economy. Although a trade growth rate of more than 100 per cent is satisfactory, there is much scope for improvement in this sector.

---

[7] Ibid.

[8] Ibid.

[9] Ibid.

Table 5.1: Total Volume of India–Bhutan Trade in Recent Years (in US $ million)

Year	*India's Exports to Bhutan*	*India's Imports from Bhutan*	*Total Trade*
2005–06	99.17	88.17	187.94
2006–07	57.66	142.05	199.71
2007–08	86.74	194.72	281.46
2008–09	111.15	151.79	262.94
2009–10	118.86	153.11	271.98
2010–11	176.00	201.57	377.57
2011–12	229.86	202.55	432.41
2012–13	233.22	164.00	397.22
2013–14	355.60	152.17	507.77
2014–15	337.69	149.83	487.52

Source: Department of Commerce, Export-Import Data Bank, Government of India, available at http://commerce.nic.in/eidb/iecnt.asp, accessed on 15 July 2015.

Indian exports to Bhutan mainly comprise the following items: Machinery and mechanical appliances, mineral products, base metal and base metal products, cereals, fruits, nuts, coffee, prepared food stuffs, transport equipment, chemical products, animal products, vegetable oil, plastic and rubber products, textiles, wood and wood products. Besides these, high speed diesel oil, polyester motor spirit, including aviation spirit, mineral products, machinery and mechanical appliances and transport vehicles formed major part of Indian exports over the years. Indian vehicles dominate the automobile market and have captured more than 80 per cent of the market in Bhutan. Indian imports from Bhutan mainly consists of electricity, calcium carbide, gypsum, ferro-silicon, particle board and Portland cement. Over the period of 1981–2001, Bhutan's exports to India accounted for an average of 86.5 per cent of its exports, and imports from India accounted for an average 79 per cent of the total imports.[10] The Bank of Bhutan (BoB) and the State Bank of India (SBI) have become partners in management and share-holding. The SBI provides expert services in managing share-holding of BoB and training of personnel of Bhutan's leading bank. Moreover, Indian nationals operate a range of small-scale trading and service activities on licenses issued by the Ministry of Trade and Industry in Bhutan. Such ventures include small shops trading in a variety of products like grocery, auto parts and furniture, as well as scrap dealers, distribution and dealership agencies. Indians in Bhutan also run hotels and restaurants, saloons, tailoring and cobbler services. On a larger scale, Indian investment in Bhutan exists in the manufacturing and processing industries, construction, service, engineering, steel and electronic industries and consultancy. Since Bhutan still pursues a conservative policy with regard to FDI, India mainly invests in Bhutan through its public and private sector enterprises which participate in the social and economic development projects in Bhutan.

[10] Source: https://books.google.co.in/books?isbn=1405100621, accessed on 21 May 2017.

SECURITY RELATIONS

Bhutan's location between India and China has added to its geo-political significance, and made the country very crucial for India's strategic interests. Therefore, India always maintained close security relations with Bhutan. The TFC of 1949 stated that Bhutan's security would be ensured by India. After the TFC was ratified in 2007, Bhutan continued to enjoy Indian support for its security. Indian defence forces provided training and equipments to the Royal Bhutan army to make it a potent force. The training has been provided by the Indian Military Training Team (IMTRAT), which has also set up hospitals, not only for the military personnel of Bhutan, but for the civilians as well. The Bhutan government continues to send Bhutan's military cadets to the National Defence Academy in Pune, and the Indian Military Academy in Dehra Dun (both in India). The Border Roads Organisation (BRO) of India has constructed extensive and important road links in Bhutan which helped Bhutan to implement its security policies more effectively. Bhutan also supported India's position on the Comprehensive Test Ban Treaty (CTBT), the establishment of a Nuclear Weapons Free Zone (NWFZ) in South Asia, and India's claim for a permanent seat in the UNSC. Bhutan also backed India strongly after the 1998 Indian nuclear tests.

The security relations between India and Bhutan were put to severe tests when Indian insurgent groups like the United Liberation Front of Assam (ULFA), National Democratic Front of Bodos (NDFB) and the Kamtapuri Liberation Organization (KLO) set up camps in the jungles of south-east Bhutan for carrying out militant activities against the Indian state. Apart from disrupting normal life, businesses and development activities in Bhutan, the presence of these militants was a potential threat to the friendly relations between India and Bhutan. Their presence also posed security threats for the small Himalayan state. The Bhutanese government repeatedly urged the militants to leave the country peacefully. Finally, in December 2003, when the Bhutan government's talks with the ULFA and NDFB failed, and the KLO did not respond, the Bhutanese army launched military operations to flush out militants. It quickly took control of more than 30 of the militants' camps, and was successful in crushing the militants. Bhutan's timely actions against the militants not only manifested its strong resolve to prevent anti-India activities on its soil, it also brought to focus the desire of Bhutan to work for India's peace. The Bhutanese army clearly demonstrated that it has the ability to restore peace on its soil, and in the neighbourhood. Bhutan's positive attitude in flushing out anti-India elements and activities, also added strengths to India–Bhutan security relations.

CULTURAL RELATIONS

The two South Asian neighbours share close bilateral contacts in the educational and cultural areas. India provides technical expertise and services of specialists to Bhutan in various educational fields. Earlier, the GoI scholarships were granted to 50 Bhutanese students both at under-graduate and post-graduate level every year in Indian institutions of higher learning. Under Bhutan's Tenth Plan (2008–13), the under-graduate scholarships have been increased to 85 per year and the post-graduate, to 77. These GoI scholarships are in addition to the Indian Technical and Economic Cooperation (ITEC) and the Technical Cooperation Scheme (TCS) for the neighbouring countries (in accordance with the Colombo Plan) in which 80 training slots have been allocated to Bhutan every year. Participants under both ITEC and TCS are provided with air ticket, book allowance, and accommodation and living allowance by the GoI. Further, the Indian ambassador (to Bhutan)'s scholarships are granted to meritorious and deserving students for studies in India. Ten Bhutanese school students are admitted to Sainik schools in India every year, and all expenditure is borne by the GoI. Sherbutse College situated in east Bhutan, has developed into a premier institution in Bhutan with its affiliation to the Delhi University in India. About 30 India-based lecturers are posted to this college under the TCS of the Colombo Plan.

An India–Bhutan Foundation (IBF) was established in August 2003 with the aim to enhance people to people exchanges in the focus areas of education, culture and environment preservation. The ambassadors of Bhutan and India are the co-chairpersons of IBF. The GoI has contributed Rs 5 crore as main corpus amount for IBF with a matching contribution from the Royal Government of Bhutan (RGoB).[11] The last meeting of IBF was held in India in January 2011. It supported the first ever seminar between India and Bhutan on Gross National Happiness (GNH) in March 2011 in Thimphu. The IBF also sponsored a Literary Festival 'Mountain Echoes', in May 2010. This was the first ever India–Bhutan Literary Festival, in which leading authors and publishers from India and Bhutan participated. In 2010, India instituted the Nehru-Wangchuk Scholarship to encourage students from Bhutan to study in the leading Indian universities and institutions.[12] The GoI and RGoB also jointly founded the 'Nehru-Wangchuck Cultural Centre' at Thimphu in September 2010. Cultural exchanges between the two nations take place on a regular basis with supports from government and non-government agencies in India and Bhutan.

RECOMMENDATIONS FOR THE FUTURE

Bhutan almost enjoyed a protectorate status in security and trade with India till 2007, when the TFC was finally ratified. The Himalayan state, sandwiched between India and China, needed Indian security and trade protections for its development programmes, as well as for India's strategic interests. However, with sweeping changes in the Indian economy, brought about by strong liberalisation policies, Bhutan may in the future, lose out on its economic benefits from India. Bhutanese industries would have to acquire a competitive edge soon to sustain their market shares in the increasingly open market economy in India. Bhutan is already under the impact of (economic) reforms in India and its subsidy policies, with decreasing budget assistance for Bhutan. Bhutan may also face the effects with India gradually moving towards privatisation of

[11] Source: https://www.mea.gov.in/Portal/ForeignRelation/Bhutan-February-2012.pdf, accessed on 21 May 2017.

[12] Ibid.

its power, mining and other traditional public sectors. This would mean lesser GoI budgetary assistance for Bhutan. Bhutan must modernise its traditional industrial bases with helps from India and other friendly countries to remain competitive in the age of economic diplomacy. It must be economically self-reliant in the future. With relatively modern and additional industrial infrastructure, Bhutan's trade with India could be augmented as well.

At this point of time, Bhutan's security relations with India are strong, and the recent actions by the Bhutanese army against secessionist groups from India are commendable. However, Bhutan needs to develop and modernise its military further to combat increasing terrorist activities in the South Asian region. It would be most beneficial for her to establish a few paramilitary forces which can effectively guard its long borders with China and India, and combat insurgent activities within Bhutan and its border areas. In that case, the Bhutanese army can concentrate only on national security. Traditionally, Bhutan receives military assistance, expertise and technologies from India. The time has come to develop paramilitary forces in the country by using these potentials. These forces would be increasingly in demand with increasing subversive and terrorist activities in and around Bhutan.

Bhutan's transition to democracy has been very peaceful, and a welcome development in South Asia. But so far, this transition had taken place mainly under the guidance of the monarchy. With gradual strengthening of democracy in Bhutan, the Bhutanese society is likely to become more pluralistic. On the flip side, proliferation of antagonistic groups and associations may take place. In that scenario, articulation of variegated demands and interests may not be easy in the future. Bhutan must concentrate on developing adequate democratic infrastructure to sustain the demands for democracy in the country. Here, Bhutan can seek crucial guidance from India, which is a matured democracy in the region. In simple words, going forward, Bhutan and India must cooperate more closely for the proper development of a democratic political setup in Bhutan. Further, a democracy must be self-sufficient economically and also, militarily, to sustain its objectives. Bhutan must proceed on this road to economic and military self-sufficiency. Cooperation and guidance from India would be very significant for Bhutan in the future for its economic development, and for the sustenance of democracy in the small Himalayan state.

6

INDIA AND AFGHANISTAN

The Democratic Formula

HIGHLIGHTS

- Introduction
- Political Relations
- Economic Relations
- Security and Cultural Relations
- Recommendations for the Future

INTRODUCTION

The geographical location of Afghanistan holds significant strategic importance for India. Flanked by Iran on the west, Pakistan on the east and the Central Asian Republics of Turkmenistan, Uzbekistan and Tajikistan on the north, Afghanistan's geo-strategic position is of crucial importance to India. The country also shares a very small stretch of the border with China in the northeast. For many South Asian nations, including India, Afghanistan is considered as a gateway to oil and mineral rich Central and West Asia. The important strategic location of Afghanistan attracted several rulers from different parts of the globe who invaded the land since ancient times. Culture and economy had flourished in the northern and eastern parts of the region before Persian King Darius I conquered these areas around 500 BC. Later, the land was conquered by Alexander the Great during 329–327 BC. After Alexander's death in 323 BC, the area became part of the Seleucid Empire. Bactria, in the north became independent, while the southern part of the land was acquired by the Maurya dynasty. In its long history of nearly 2,500 years, different parts of Afghanistan were ruled by Persians, Russians, Indians, and various Central Asian and Afghan tribes. Afghanistan also came under British influence during the long British rule in the Indian subcontinent.

The Anglo-Russian agreement of 1907 guaranteed the independence of Afghanistan under British influence in foreign affairs. Despite British pressure, Afghanistan was able to remain neutral in the First World War. Habibullah was the ruler of the land at that time. After his assassination in 1919, his successor, Amanullah assumed power and became the Emir of Afghanistan. Amanullah attempted to free himself of British influence, and therefore invaded British India in 1919. This led to the Third Afghan War which lasted from 6 May 1919 to 8 August 1919. The British won a tactical victory in the war. As per British designs, the Durand Line, first conceived in 1893, was reaffirmed as the political boundary between the Emirate of Afghanistan and British India. The Afghans also agreed not to foment trouble on the British side of the border. Thereafter, the Treaty of Rawalpindi was signed between Afghanistan and the British which gave Afghanistan full control over its foreign relations. Amanullah (who, after 1926 styled himself 'King') was deposed in 1929 for his attempts at reducing the power of the religious leaders. A tribal leader, Bacha-i Saqao, held Kabul for a few months until defeated by Amanullah's cousin, Muhammad Nadir Khan, who became King Nadir Shah. Nadir Shah pursued cautious modernisation efforts until he was assassinated in 1933. His son Muhammad Zahir Shah succeeded him. Afghanistan was able to remain neutral in the Second World War as well, and it joined the United Nations (UN) in 1946. Afghanistan remained neutral in the Second World War as well. After the War, it joined the UN in 1946. When British India was partitioned in 1947, Afghanistan began to maintain cordial relations with India. Until the late 1970s, Afghanistan was able to remain neutral of superpower politics, and it got aid from both Soviet Union and the United States (US). However, from the late 1970s, Afghanistan began to align with the Soviet Union under the leadership of Noor Mohammed Taraki. When Taraki was killed in September 1979, allegedly by anti-Soviet elements in Afghanistan, Hafizullah Amin assumed power. In December 1979, Soviet Union sent troops to Afghanistan, Amin was deposed, and a new Soviet-backed government under Babrak Karmal was installed. The Karmal government lasted till 1986.

Historically, India has enjoyed good cultural and economic relations with Afghanistan, a land where civilisation flourished in ancient times. During the long rule of King Zahir Shah (1933–73), India cultivated strong relations with Afghanistan. Even after Zahir Shah's overthrow in 1973, India maintained close ties with the subsequent Soviet-backed regimes in Afghanistan. Except for the five years of Taliban rule from 1996 to 2001 (a government India did not recognise), India's relations with Afghanistan had been cordial. After the fall of the Taliban regime, India engaged itself with the reconstruction of the democratic process in Afghanistan, and also in the process of development of the Afghan economy and society, devastated due to the inefficient and adventurous Taliban rule. In the post-Taliban Afghanistan, India has played a constructive role in the development of its neighbour with a view to prepare bases for a socially and economically stable Afghanistan that would be able to contribute to regional peace and harmony. India has already pledged a US $1.3 billion package till December 2011 for the reconstruction process of Afghanistan. The new government, which came to power in 2014 in Afghanistan, also showed its intentions to maintain close contacts with India for the reconstruction of the democratic process, and for the revival of the Afghan economy. As a consequence, the relationship between the two countries is warm at this moment (early 2017). The two countries need each other. India has political and strategic interests in Afghanistan—a resurgence of fundamental forces would be inimical to India's interests as it would encourage divisive forces within India. Afghanistan needs

India for its economic development and stability.[1] With this background, this chapter now proceeds to examine the political, economic and security relations between India and Afghanistan.

POLITICAL RELATIONS

After India's independence in 1947, India–Afghanistan relations began to flourish with renewed emphasis for closer ties from both the countries. The two neighbours signed a Peace and Friendship Treaty in 1950, which among other issues, placed importance to closer cooperation in trade, culture and securing peace in the region as priority areas. As noted earlier, during King Zahir Shah's tenure in Afghanistan which lasted till 1973, India and Afghanistan shared a very warm relationship. The King visited India in February 1958 and signed a joint communiqué with India in which the two nations resolved to strengthen their 'good relations'. In 1959, Afghan Prime Minister Sardar Daud paid an official visit to India. Welcoming Daud to India, Jawaharlal Nehru said, 'Ever since India's independence, we have grown closer to each other, for a variety of reasons. The long memory of our past contacts was there, and the moment it was possible to renew them, we renewed them. And then came mutual interest, which is a powerful factor. There has also been a very great community of interests between our two countries in the many important matters which affect the world.'[2] Indian President S. Radhakrishnan visited Kabul in May 1963 and reiterated that India–Afghan friendship was on a strong ground. In fact, regular bilateral visits by important leaders of the two countries helped strengthen relations. This could be ascertained from the official visit of Indian Prime Minister Indira Gandhi to Afghanistan in June 1969. During the visit, the two countries agreed to set up a Joint Commission (JC) for economic, trade and technical cooperation. The JC was entrusted with the responsibility to chalk out programmes of cooperation in the fields of agriculture, irrigation and power, industry and health. India promised Afghanistan to assist in the setting up of agricultural research centres in Bamiyan, Kandahar, and Kabul, and an 'Industrial State' in the capital region of Kabul. The Indian Prime Minister also offered help to set up irrigation projects in different parts of Afghanistan. Indira Gandhi and Afghan Prime Minister Etemadi declared that the two nations would steer clear of controversial issues like Kashmir and Pushtunistan, showing respect to the sovereignty of both the countries.

The 1970s witnessed further spurt in bilateral relations. A new trade agreement was signed between the two countries in February 1972. The agreement provided for the setting up of a joint venture for the production of extracts of medicinal herbs and plants in Afghanistan which India agreed to use in its pharmaceutical industry. The agreement also chalked out measures to strengthen trade on 'healthy lines'. Indian Foreign Minister Swaran Singh visited Afghanistan in

---

[1] Aneek Chatterjee, 'Will Democracy Survive? Afghanistan and the International Community Post-2014', *Journal of South Asian and Middle Eastern Studies*, 38 (4): 37, 2015.

[2] See in this context, A. Appadorai, *Select Documents in India's Foreign Policy and Relations: 1947–1972*, vol. II (New Delhi: Oxford University Press), 1985, pp. 3–4.

April. During his visit, Swaran Singh reviewed with Afghan leaders areas of cooperation between the two neighbours with special emphasis on economic and technical cooperation. The two countries agreed to set up an isotope dispensing unit in Kabul. India offered to send technical experts for assistance in the restoration of the Bamiyan monuments in Afghanistan. India also agreed to dispatch 60 additional teachers for schools in Afghanistan. In July 1972, Indian President V. V. Giri visited Kabul. President Giri stressed on the need for closer bilateral ties for peace and stability in the region. The Indian president expressed the view that India–Afghan relations were crucial for peace and prosperity in South Asia. The Afghan crown prince visited India towards the end of 1972, and reviewed bilateral relations with the Indian leaders. On the occasion of the visit of the crown prince, it was noted by the two sides that bilateral trade and economic cooperation was growing rapidly.

New governments in Afghanistan in 1973 and in India in 1977 did not hinder progress in bilateral relations as both the countries continued to repose faith in each other. Bilateral visits of the top leaders continued showing signs of strong relations. Indian Foreign Minister A. B. Vajpayee visited Afghanistan in September 1977. Vajpayee was accorded a warm welcome in Kabul, where he proclaimed India's commitment towards improved ties between the two states. Relations with Afghanistan were cordial during the premiership of Morarji Desai (1977–79) in India. However, the caretaker government of Charan Singh in India faced a major foreign policy challenge when Soviet troops entered Afghanistan in December 1979. Due to India's proximity with both Afghanistan and Soviet Union, the Singh Government was in a dilemma, and tried a balancing act when the Western world, led by the US wanted immediate withdrawal of Soviet troops from Afghanistan. India's permanent representative told the UN on 12 January 1980 that India had no reason to disbelieve the Soviet assurance to withdraw its troops when asked to do so by the Afghan government. India also expressed its concern over the response of the US, China and Pakistan on this issue, and also, over the supply of arms to Afghan rebels and the expansion of naval activities in the Indian Ocean, which India conceived as threats to India's security.[3] New Delhi, however, tried to maintain good relations with two Soviet-backed governments in Afghanistan under Babrak Karmal (1979–86) and Mohammed Najibullah (1986–92), due to security perceptions resulting from the external forces' support to Afghan rebels.

After the withdrawal of Soviet troops in 1989, Afghanistan faced a political crisis. Different ethnic groups were trying to oust the Najibullah Government, which became weak sans the Soviet support. India remained concerned with the continuous arming of the Afghan rebels by Pakistan and China and the deteriorating social conditions in Afghanistan. New Delhi did try to provide political support and material assistance to the Najibullah Government. In a Joint Communique (JC) issued in New Delhi in August 1990 during the Afghan President's visit, India's support to Najibullah's policy of national reconciliation in Afghanistan was endorsed.[4] New Delhi also sent medicines and food supplies to Afghanistan immediately after the visit.

---

[3] See in this context, M. H. Ansari, 'Afghanistan', in J. N. Dixit, ed., *External Affairs: Cross-Border Relations* (New Delhi: Roli Books), 2003, p. 175.

[4] Ibid., p. 180.

However, the Najibullah Government could not survive for long and fell in April 1992. After Najibullah's exit, the control of Kabul went into the hands of the rebels loyal to Ahmad Shah Masood, who was considered as close to Pakistan. On 26 October 1992, the Mujahideen factions of Afghanistan met in Peshawar, Pakistan and concluded the Peshawar Accord which settled for a rotational arrangement of governments in Afghanistan, and proclaimed the establishment of the Islamic Republic of Afghanistan. This post-Najibullah government, headed by Mujaddidi, was recognised by many countries including India, with whom the new government wished to have warm and cordial relations.[5] Mujaddidi relinquished presidency as per the terms of the Peshawar Accord after two months, and was replaced by Burhanuddin Rabbani, who in turn declined to quit, and continued to rule Afghanistan till 1996 amid widespread resentment of the rival ethnic factions, including the Talibans. Afghanistan plunged into ethnic conflicts, with Rabbani facing challenges from his Prime Minister Gulbuddin Hekmatyar, who was supported by Pakistan's Inter-Services Intelligence (ISI). Pakistan was against the Rabbani government as it violated the ISI-sponsored Peshawar accord. India, on its part, remained in touch with leaders of all groups in Afghanistan during this period (1992–96).

In September 1996, the Taliban captured Kabul and declared it the legitimate government of the Islamic Emirate of Afghanistan. Taliban imposed puritanical form of Islamic law in the areas they controlled. In August 1998, as the Taliban appeared on the verge of taking over the whole country, US missiles destroyed extensive terrorist training complex near Kabul run by Osama bin Laden, a Saudi-born militant accused of masterminding the 1998 bombings of the American embassies in Kenya and Tanzania. However, the Taliban effectively controlled the country by 2000, but its government was not generally recognised by the international community (the United Nations recognised President Burhanuddin Rabbani and the Northern Alliance), which also included India. In early 2001, the Taliban militia destroyed all statues in the nation, including two ancient giant Buddhas in Bamian, outside Kabul. The destruction was ordered by the religious leaders, who regarded the figures as un-Islamic. This action incurred condemnation from across the world, which also included many Islamic nations. In September, Ahmad Shah Massoud, the leader of the Northern Alliance, was killed by the Taliban in a suicide bomb attack. Two days after that attack, on 11 September, devastating terrorist assaults on the World Trade Center and the Pentagon, which Laden masterminded, prompted US President George Bush to demand for his arrest. When the Taliban refused to hand over Bin Laden, the US launched attacks, in October 2001, against Taliban and Al Qaeda's (Bin Laden's organisation) positions and forces.

India did not recognise the Taliban government in Afghanistan, and India–Afghan relations touched an all-time low during 1996–2001 when the Taliban ruled Afghanistan. India was apathetic to the Taliban government for many reasons. Taliban pronouncements on Kashmir, the training of Kashmiri, Pakistani and other Central Asian militants in Taliban camps (in Afghanistan) and their induction into Jammu and Kashmir for the 'liberation' of Kashmir,

[5] Ibid.

Taliban's proximity with the ISI, and the hijacking of an Indian Airlines plane to Kandahar by terrorists linked to the Taliban angered the Indians. However, India kept a close watch on the developments in Afghanistan during this period, and supported the Northern Alliance, which was fighting the Taliban forces.

After the fall of the Taliban regime in late November 2001, a pan-Afghan conference in Bonn, Germany, appointed Hamid Karzai as the nation's interim leader in December the same year. Muhammad Zahir Shah, the former king of Afghanistan, returned to the country from exile. In June 2002, the king convened a 'loya jirga' (a traditional Afghan Grand Council) to form a transitional government. Karzai was elected President of Afghanistan for a two-year term, and the king was declared the father of the nation. But sporadic violence continued. Soon after the formation of the government, one of Karzai's vice presidents was assassinated, and an attempt was also made on the president's life. However, by the end of 2002, some measure of stability could be observed in the country. However, sporadic fighting continued, particularly in the southeast, with the Taliban regaining some strength and even control in certain districts. In August 2003, the North Atlantic Treaty Organization (NATO) troops assumed command of the international security force in the Kabul area. In January 2004, a new constitution for the nation was approved by a loya jirga. The new constitution provided for a strong presidency. It also gave some concessions to the minorities; but tension among different ethnic groups was felt in the loya jirga. In early 2004, the US and NATO announced increases in the number of troops deployed in the country. Karzai was elected president in October 2004, in the country's first democratic elections. The Spring of 2005 was marked by an increase in attacks by the Taliban and their allies. National and provincial legislative elections were held in September 2005 amid allegations of rigging and fraud. The supporters of Karzai won a substantial number of seats in the lower house (Wolesi Jirga). Religious conservatives, former mujahidins, Taliban, women and Pashtuns, which are overlapping groups, were all elected in significant numbers to the body.

India stood by the government of Hamid Karzai from the very beginning. India actively participated in the development process of Afghanistan, as well as in the process of restoration of democracy in the country. According to a report released by India's foreign ministry, 'India has played an active role in the development of Afghanistan based on the understanding that social and economic development is key to Afghanistan becoming a source of regional stability. India's pledged assistance to Afghanistan stands at US $1.3 billion and is the sixth largest bilateral donor in Afghanistan.'[6] Assistance from the Election Commission of India was sought by the Afghan government to help conduct democratic elections in the country. Indian poll observers, as part of the international monitoring team, were present during the Afghan elections. After the ouster of the Taliban regime, India's relations with Afghanistan became normal and healthy, reminiscent of the traditionally closer ties between the two neighbours. India also supported Afghanistan's

[6] See in this context, Ministry of External Affairs, Government of India, *India–Afghanistan Relations*, available at, http://meaindia.nic.in/meaxpsite/pressrelease/2011/01/bilateralafganistan.pdf, accessed on 10 March 2012.

membership of South Asian Association for Regional Cooperation (SAARC) with a view to achieve increased regional cooperation. Afghanistan joined the SAARC at the 14th SAARC Summit held in New Delhi in April 2007. This opened up possibilities for Afghanistan to become a trade, transportation and energy hub linking together the countries of the region from Central to South Asia.

India is currently stepping up its engagement with Afghanistan because any change in power equations in Afghanistan may greatly affect India's interests. In January 2011, India's Foreign Minister S. M. Krishna visited Kabul, during which several MoUs of cooperation were signed. Afghan President Hamid Karzai and Indian Prime Minister Manmohan Singh signed a historic Strategic Partnership Agreement (SPA) in New Delhi on 4 October 2011 during the Afghan president's visit to India. The SPA will greatly enhance security cooperation between the two countries. It will help generate closer security ties between the two nations, and may prove to be beneficial for Afghanistan after the withdrawal of international forces from the country in 2014. Apart from security cooperation, the two leaders agreed during talks that Afghanistan's economic integration with the Indian economy and South Asia as a whole was in the national interest of the people of Afghanistan, and one of the ways to achieve this is to promote closer trade, investment and transit links. India–Afghanistan relations are quite strong at this moment (early 2017). Frequent high-level bilateral visits provide indications of this strong relationship. The report of the Indian Foreign Ministry also supports this proposition as it points out, 'The India–Afghanistan close bilateral relationship is marked by frequent high level bilateral visits and their strong commitment to combat terrorism and build a united, democratic and pluralist Afghanistan.'[7] As observed, the two countries need each other. India has strategic interests in Afghanistan,—a resurgence of fundamental forces would be inimical to India's interests. Afghanistan needs India for its development and stability.

In 2014, two new governments assumed office in New Delhi and Kabul respectively. Close cooperation in different areas of bilateral interests continued between the new governments. India continued to extend its support towards the development programme of Afghanistan. In his meeting with the Afghan president on 27 May 2014, the new Indian Prime Minister, Narendra Modi thanked Afghanistan for the 'assistance provided by the Afghan National Security Forces in repelling the attack on our consulate in Herat. He also indicated India's commitment to the development and reconstruction of Afghanistan and India's interest in seeing a prosperous, independent and sovereign Afghanistan where the reconciliation process would be Afghan-led, Afghan-owned and Afghan-controlled. India continues to assist Afghanistan's reconstruction through a comprehensive bilateral assistance program of US $2 billion.'[8] Therefore, convergence of interests and the urge to establish closer links have encouraged the two nations to establish intimate political ties in recent times.

---

[7] Ibid.

[8] Ministry of External Affairs, Government of India, 'Annual Report: 2014–15' (New Delhi: Government of India), p. i.

ECONOMIC RELATIONS

After the ouster of the Taliban government from Afghanistan, India has engaged itself with the process of economic reconstruction of Afghanistan and restoration of democracy in the country. For this purpose, India has pledged assistance to the level of US $1.3 billion to Afghanistan. India has been involved in the civil and infrastructural reconstruction process in Afghanistan since 2001. According to India's Ministry of External Affairs (MEA) sources, India's development assistance programme in Afghanistan covers four broad areas: infrastructure projects, humanitarian assistance, small and community-based development projects, and education and capacity development.[9] India constructed 202 km of the 220 KV DC transmission line from Pul-e-Khumri to Kabul and a 220/110/20 KV substation at Chimtala, which would facilitate bringing Uzbek electricity and lightening up the city of Kabul throughout the year. India was also engaged in the construction of the Afghan Parliament in Kabul and the Salma Dam power project in Herat province. Further, India pledged to support, along with other international agencies, the construction of the 218 km road project from Zaranj to Delaram in south-western Afghanistan. This road would facilitate movement of goods and services to the Iranian border and, onward, to the Chahbahar Port.

In humanitarian assistance, according to MEA sources, India supplies 100 gm of fortified, high-protein biscuits to nearly two million school children in 33 of the 34 provinces of Afghanistan every day under a School Feeding Programme administered through the World Food Programme. During the visit of Afghan President Hamid Karzai to India in January 2009, India announced a package of 250,000 metric tonnes of wheat to assist Afghanistan overcome its food shortage.[10] The Indian Medical Missions are providing free medical consultations and medicines to over 30,000 Afghans every month. A scheme focusing on small and community-based development projects having a direct impact on community life was inaugurated during Indian Prime Minister Manmohan Singh's visit to Afghanistan in August 2005. So far, 101 such projects with emphasis on local ownership and management in the field of agriculture, health, education, rural development, vocational training and solar energy have been initiated.[11] According to MEA sources, capacity-building programmes are also underway in the fields of diplomacy, media and information, civil aviation, agriculture research, healthcare and medicinal science, tourism, education, standardisation, rural development, public administration, electoral management and administration and local governance. Besides these, India is also involved in the reconstruction of Indira Gandhi Institute of Child Health and Habibia School in Kabul. India has assisted in the expansion of Afghan National TV network by providing an uplink from Kabul and downlinks in all 34 provincial capitals for promoting greater connectivity.

---

[9] Ministry of External Affairs, Government of India, 'India–Afghanistan Relations' (New Delhi: Government of India), February 2016.

[10] Ibid.

[11] Ibid.

It has also gifted around 1,000 vehicles including buses, utility vehicles and ambulances to Afghanistan.[12]

Further, the Confederation of Indian Industry (CII) built an India–Afghanistan Vocational Training Centre for training Afghan youth in carpentry, plumbing, welding, masonry and tailoring. Another programme was completed by SEWA (Self-Employed Women's Association), a well-known Indian non-governmental organisation (NGO), which built a Women's Vocational Training Centre in *Bagh-e-Zanana* in Kabul for training of Afghan women, mainly war-widows and orphans, in garment-making, nursery plantation, food processing and marketing.[13] In education and institution development, India has provided 675 annual long-term university scholarships sponsored by the Indian Council for Cultural Relations (ICCR) for under-graduate and post-graduate studies for Afghan students in India. Similarly, another 675 annual short-term Indian Technical and Educational Cooperation (ITEC) training scholarships for Afghan public servants have been provided in Indian technical and professional institutions. More than 20 Indian civil servants served as instructors and mentors for Afghan public administration programme supported by the United Nations Development Program (UNDP) and the governments of Afghanistan and India.[14]

India's bilateral trade with Afghanistan has attained considerable progress during the last five financial years. Table 6.1 highlights India's trade with Afghanistan from 2006–07 to 2014–15:

Table 6.1: India's Bilateral Trade with Afghanistan, 2006–07 to 2014–15 (in US $ million)

Year	*India's Export*	*India's Import*	*Total Trade*
2006–07	182.11	34.37	216.48
2007–08	249.21	109.97	359.18
2008–09	394.23	126.24	520.47
2009–10	463.55	125.19	588.74
2010–11	411.78	146.03	557.81
2011–12	510.90	132.50	643.41
2012–13	472.63	159.55	632.18
2013–14	474.34	208.77	683.10
2014–15	422.57	261.91	684.48

Source: Export-Import Data Bank, Department of Commerce, Government of India, available at http://commerce.nic.in/eidb/iecnt.asp, accessed on 19 July 2015.

Table 6.1 shows substantial progress in India–Afghanistan trade in the recent years. In the 2006–07 fiscal year, bilateral trade volume was US $216.48 million. In the 2014–15 fiscal year,

[12] Ibid.

[13] Ibid.

[14] Ibid.

total trade volume rose to US $684.48, more than three-fold increase in eight years. While India's export to Afghanistan rose nearly 2.3 times since 2006–07, India's import from the country increased more than seven times in the last eight years. This trend shows that in the recent years India is giving more importance to Afghanistan in its trade. It is evident from the table that there was a slight dip in total trade volume in 2010–11 and 2012–13 compared to the preceding years, but the decrease was marginal. Such ups and downs are common factors in any bilateral trade, and do not call for much anxiety. However, an issue of concern in India–Afghanistan trade is that India's total trade volume with Afghanistan in 2014–15 constituted only 0.09 per cent of India's total trade. In 2006–07, the percentage share of India's trade with Afghanistan, compared to India's total trade, was 0.07. This percentage rose marginally to 0.09 in 2014–15[15] as noted above. The two governments must take note of this issue and try to augment bilateral trade volume in the future.

Significantly, India–Afghanistan SPA, noted earlier, has taken due cognizance of this issue and pledged to strengthen bilateral trade and economic relations. The text of the SPA placed special emphasis on 'Trade and Economic Cooperation' in a separate section. Part 1 of this section of SPA says, 'The Sides (India and Afghanistan) commit to strengthening trade, economic, scientific and technological cooperation, as well as cooperation between other bodies of business and industry representatives, with a view to expanding trade and economic relations.'[16] Both the countries agreed to take effective measures to promote bilateral trade and investment. These measures would include:

(i) Enhancing investment protection;

(ii) Simplifying customs and other procedures and promoting the removal of non-tariff barriers, and gradually lowering tariff barriers;

(iii) Working towards the creation of air-cargo facilities for promotion of commercial exchanges;

(iv) Cooperating in the areas of banking and finance, and improving credit and insurance facilities and;

(v) Enhancing cooperation and coordination at international trade, economic and financial bodies.

It was agreed, in part 4 of the SPA, that the two nations would establish effective mechanisms for interaction between Indian and Afghan entities with a view to achieve a sustained expansion of bilateral trade and economic ties with a long-term perspective.[17] The conclusion of the SPA

---

[15] Ibid.

[16] See Ministry of External Affairs, Government of India, 'Text of Agreement on Strategic Partnership between the Republic of India and the Islamic Republic of Afghanistan', New Delhi, 4 October 2011, available at http://www.mea.gov.in/mystart.php?id=510218343&flg=1, accessed on 11 March 2012, parenthesis by the author.

[17] Ibid.

was a welcome development in India–Afghan relations in recent years. It may be hoped that the plans for closer economic cooperation, outlined in the SPA, would give a significant boost to India–Afghan trade and commercial relations in the near future.

SECURITY AND CULTURAL RELATIONS

Afghanistan and India are important to each other as far as security issues are concerned. The political elites of the two countries realised this factor as early as in the 1950s, when the two nations signed the 'Treaty of Friendship', which provided for, among others, security cooperation between the two neighbours. Subsequently, both India and Afghanistan engaged in security cooperation. However, with deterioration in political relations during the 1990s, the two nations drifted apart from close security engagements. After the exit of the Taliban regime from Afghanistan, normalcy was restored in bilateral relations and the two neighbours started to develop closer cooperation in all areas including the security segment. The SPA, signed during Afghan President Karzai's visit to India in early October 2011, provided a satisfactory framework for security cooperation between the two countries.

In a section of the SPA entitled 'Political and Security Cooperation', it was noted that 'The Sides (India and Afghanistan) agree to establish a Strategic Dialogue to provide a framework for cooperation in the area of national security. The dialogue will be led by NSAs (National Security Agencies) and involve regular consultations with the aim of intensifying mutual efforts towards strengthening regional peace and security.'[18] Such dialogues were missing from bilateral relations since the 1990s, and therefore, aroused hopes for a strong security partnership. The SPA further noted that security cooperation between the two states is '... intended to help enhance their respective and mutual efforts in the fight against international terrorism, organized crime, illegal trafficking in narcotics, money laundering and so on.'[19] India also agreed, as per terms of the SPA, to assist in the training, equipping and capacity-building programmes for Afghan National Security Forces. The strategic partnership between India and Afghanistan is based upon the principles of sovereignty, equality and territorial integrity of the two states, non-interference in their internal affairs, mutual respect and mutual benefit, and it is not directed against any other state or group of states.

India and Afghanistan share age-old cultural bonds between them. 'Kabuliwala', the short story written by Nobel laureate Rabindranath Tagore, narrates the story of an Afghan national selling spices in the streets of Kolkata and how he became a close friend of a little girl, and endeavoured to integrate himself with Indian culture. This short story by Tagore is only a reflection of closer contact between the people of the two countries. Such contacts have been maintained throughout ages. The two countries have officially agreed to expand such contacts in the recent times. The SPA

[18] Ibid.
[19] Ibid.

mentioned before, has pledged to enhance these contacts. In a section of the SPA devoted to 'Social, Cultural, Civil Society and People-To-People Relations', it was noted that in pursuit of further expanding the existing people-to-people bonds between the two countries, the two nations envisage greater exchanges between parliament, media, women, youth, sports, academic, cultural, intellectual and religious figures and bodies.[20] Mechanisms for these exchanges have also been outlined in the document. The India–Afghanistan Foundation would promote social and cultural ties, with a focus on arts, literature, poetry, music and related areas.

Enhanced people-to-people contacts call for free movement of citizens of both countries into the other territory. With a view to promote such movements, the two countries agreed, as per the provisions laid out in the SPA, to simplify rules and procedures for legitimate travel by citizens of both the countries. For this purpose, the two nations would promote tourist exchanges and cooperation between tourist organisations in both the countries; and encourage sister-city agreements between the cities, provinces and states of the two countries.[21] The SPA further provided that to facilitate legal cases involving nationals of one country in the other, the two nations will work towards agreements on mutual legal assistance in civil and criminal matters. Moreover, to promote relations between civil societies and, enable intellectual exchanges, India and Afghanistan intend to establish India–Afghanistan Round Table consisting of eminent persons representing different fields. Both countries also agreed to promote cooperation and exchanges in the field of sports.[22]

Afghanistan and India put special emphasis on sharing of democratic values and ideals, and knowledge about parliamentary proceedings and democratic devolution of power. As per terms of the SPA, both sides agreed to share and learn from each other's experience of the values and institutions of democracy, including the sharing, distribution and devolution of powers, relations between the Centre and Provinces, and procedures for electoral reforms.[23] India's contribution in this regard would be immensely vital because India has remained a stable democracy and a successful federal system for over six decades. Indian electoral processes and institutions are time-tested, and may also prove to be helpful for Afghanistan in its quest for a democratic political system. The sides also agreed in the SPA to establish parliament-to-parliament exchanges between the two countries by organising visits of parliamentary delegations and establishing parliamentary friendship groups in the two countries. These exchanges would further strengthen the democratic bond between Afghanistan and India.

RECOMMENDATIONS FOR THE FUTURE

American President Barak Obama's Af-Pak Policy, and the international military engagement in Afghanistan under the auspices of the US, has made this country more important for India.

20 Ibid.
21 Ibid.
22 Ibid.
23 Ibid.

While the new government in Afghanistan is trying to restore peace and democracy in the country, the process may be jeopardised with the increasing prospect of a Taliban comeback, and its participation in future governments in Afghanistan. The possibility of Afghanistan returning to civil wars after the withdrawal of international forces from its territory could not be ruled out. What are India's policy options in Afghanistan under these circumstances? India has been engaged in the reconstruction process in Afghanistan, mainly in the civilian, infrastructural and social sectors. India should continue to do the same in the near future, and must not engage in any military activity in the country. In the recent times, India's military adventurism in Sri Lanka did not yield expected results. Since there is still trust deficit among the South Asian countries, India must refrain from engaging itself militarily in Afghanistan, even if requested by the government of Afghanistan.

However, India must not disengage itself politically from Afghanistan. While it must continue to maintain good relations with the new government with which it has established good rapport, it must cultivate cordial relations with other ethno-political groups in Afghanistan because any congregation of such groups may control Afghanistan in the future. Politically, India should try to ensure that anti-India groups in Afghanistan do not become dominant in the strife-torn nation, but at the same time India must not hesitate to go for improved relations with any group including the Taliban. Diplomatically, India should try to reduce the influence of other regional actors in Afghanistan. To achieve these objectives, it must continue to send signals to all the Afghan governments, present and future, that India would provide all kinds of civilian, economic, security and technological help to Afghanistan in times of crises.

India and Afghanistan must also see that the provisions outlined in the recently-signed SPA are implemented quickly. In the post-Taliban Afghanistan, the SPA may be cited as a diplomatic achievement for both India and Afghanistan. But the two countries must ensure that the agreement does not remain as another diplomatic rhetoric, and gets implemented. The SPA has outlined almost every detail for improvement in bilateral relations. From political and security to trade and economic cooperation, to capacity development and education, to social, cultural, civil society and people-to-people relations, the agreement provides every aspect of bilateral engagement. It also contains details about implementation mechanism. The need of the hour is to go for its actual implementation. If the SPA is properly respected, and if its implementation mechanisms are maintained, it would help the two countries to cement their relationship in the future.

As already observed, India–Afghanistan bilateral trade is not very healthy at this moment. India's trade with Afghanistan constituted only 0.09 per cent of India's total trade in 2014–15. This picture needs to be altered towards significant development in bilateral trade and commerce. Without overlooking the issue of expansion of exports to Afghanistan, India must also give due importance to its imports from Afghanistan. Although India's imports from Afghanistan increased in the recent years, but this increase is far from satisfactory as Table 6.1 reveals. In this connection, measures identified in the SPA for the promotion of trade and economic relations between the two countries could be followed to give a boost to bilateral trade. The two neighbours must strive to increase the total volume of bilateral trade to US $1.5 billion from the current US $684.48 million (see Table 6.1) within the next five years. Alongside, non-formal aspects of relations like cultural, civil society and people-to-people engagements must be emphasised in the future.

7

INDIA–MYANMAR RELATIONS

Trapped between Realism and Idealism

HIGHLIGHTS

- Introduction
- Political Relations
- Economic Relations
- Security Relations
- Recommendations for the Future

INTRODUCTION

The state of Myanmar (formerly known as Burma), situated in the south-eastern side of India, bears immense strategic significance for India because it shares more than 1,600 km of land borders, and also, maritime boundaries with India in the Bay of Bengal. Myanmar has borders with four Indian provinces: Arunachal Pradesh, Mizoram, Manipur and Nagaland, and is geographically close to China. Therefore, Myanmar's geo-strategic location is of crucial significance for India, and India needs to cultivate good friendly relations with Myanmar. But history reveals that relations between Myanmar and India have not always been cordial. Myanmar became an independent country after a long British rule on 4 January 1948, and adopted the name of 'Union of Burma'. It became the 'Socialist Republic of the Union of Burma' in 1974, before reverting to the 'Union of Burma' status in 1988. On 18 June 1989, the State Law and Order Restoration Council (SLORC) adopted the name 'Union of Myanmar', which is currently the official name of the country. It may be mentioned here that both India and Burma were under British rule till their independence in the late 1940s. India was one of the leading supporters of Burmese independence and established diplomatic relations after Burma's independence in 1948. Initially, Indo-Burmese relations were strong due to common cultural links, flourishing commerce, common interests in regional affairs and the presence of a significantly large Indian community in Burma. India also provided considerable support when the Burmese state was struggling with regional insurgencies. Personal chemistry between the two new prime ministers,

Jawaharlal Nehru of India and U Nu of Burma was excellent and the two shared many common views on international politics, and the Non-Aligned Movement (NAM). India and Burma also signed the Treaty of Friendship in 1951.

However, the overthrow of the democratic government led by U Nu by a military coup in 1962 began to generate strains in ties. The new military regime, led by General Ne Win, started massive nationalisation programme after capturing power. The nationalisation drive evicted thousands of Indian businessmen, professionals, workers and labourers from Burma. India, along with many other nations of the world, criticised the suppression of democracy in Burma. However, the military regime did not pay heed to such criticisms, and ordered the expulsion of the Indian community from Burma. Thereafter, General Ne Win's Government chose to isolate Burma from the rest of the world for nearly three decades. Although India signed the Land Boundary Agreement (in 1967) and the Maritime Boundary Agreement (in 1986) with Burma, India, in effect, neglected Burma during this period (1962–88), due to India's idealistic commitment for democracy, and its foreign policy obsession for another neighbour, Pakistan. China, however, maintained close links with Burma during this period. With this brief historical background, this chapter proposes to analyse important segments of India–Myanmar relations, and offers a future course of actions to improve bilateral relations.

POLITICAL RELATIONS

India's relations with Myanmar were characterised by ups and downs. As already observed, the two neighbours shared cordial relations from 1948 to 1962, when India helped Burma in its state-building process, and also, to curb insurgencies. Burma supported the NAM, and endorsed India's position on international issues. The two countries also signed the Treaty of Friendship in 1951. However, after the military takeover in Burma in 1962, relations with India deteriorated. For the next three decades, Burma isolated itself from India (and almost from the rest of the world), because India was not in favour of the military rule, and wanted democracy to be restored in Burma. India on its part showed little interest in Burma, and did not pursue any comprehensive policy to work closely with the Burmese military government. As a consequence, the two neighbours maintained distance from each other. As the two countries did not apprehend any security threat from each other, they were not dissatisfied with this estranged relationship. This estrangement also resulted due to the existence of two different types of government: democratic in India, and military in Myanmar. Although, Indian Prime Ministers Indira Gandhi and Rajiv Gandhi paid official visits to Burma in 1967 and 1987 respectively, relations did not improve much, and the two neighbours continued with their policies of staying away from the other.

Movements for democracy created stirs in Burma in 1988, 26 years after the establishment of the military rule, as hundreds of students, monks and pro-democracy activists demanded the restoration of a civilian government. The movement was strengthened by the return of Aung San Suu Kyi and her followers to Burma. The movement reached its peak in July–August 1988.

After some initial hesitation, the Burmese army cracked down on the protesters killing many and arresting several pro-democracy activists. A new 'Military Junta' assumed power in Burma in September 1988 through another coup-de-tat which replaced General Ne Win's military regime. The new Military Junta continued its repression on the pro-democracy activists. India strongly condemned the violent attitude of the Burmese military rulers against pro-democracy movements, and openly sympathised with the protesters through the Indian Ambassador, P. M. S. Malik. The Indian government also provided shelter to Burmese 'rebels' who fled to India. There were appeals from the pro-democracy activists for Indian military intervention to restore democracy in Burma. But the Indian government resisted, perhaps correctly, from interfering in Burma's internal affairs. In May 1990, the Military Junta openly defied the General Election results in Burma, which declared the National League for Democracy (NLD) led by Aung San Suu Kyi and other ethnic leaders as winners. It arrested several newly elected Members of Parliament (MP) and put them behind bars. Suu Kyi was also arrested, and put under house arrest. India condemned these incidents, and practically detached itself from the Military Junta. Therefore, from 1962 to 1990, India–Myanmar relations were mostly down, as the two nations chose to ignore the other. From 1988 to 1990, during movements for democracy in Myanmar, bilateral relations touched an all-time low.

After the end of the Cold War, with changed international political and economic order, both India and Myanmar showed eagerness to redefine their relationship. The Narasimha Rao Government in India launched the 'Look East' Policy in 1991 with a view to strengthen India's relations with South-East Asian nations, due to increasing economic clout of these countries, and, to overcome India's long estrangement with these states. Myanmar was also focused in India's 'Look East' Policy. There were two more unstated reasons for the shift in India's policy towards Myanmar after the Cold War: first, to counter China's growing influence over Myanmar; and second, to control insurgency, drug trafficking, and smuggling in India's northeastern states. With these objectives, India started to cultivate friendly relationship with Myanmar, and the Military Junta in Myanmar also responded positively. India's Foreign Secretary J. N. Dixit visited Myanmar in March 1993 and a bilateral agreement to control drug trafficking and border trade was signed between the two nations. India and Myanmar again held talks in Yangon, Myanmar's capital, in 1994 and a Memorandum of Understanding (MoU) to maintain peace along the border was signed. India assured Myanmar that it would not interfere in Myanmar's internal affairs and Yangon assured New Delhi that Myanmar's proximity with China would not be directed against India.

However, India–Myanmar relations deteriorated a bit in 1995, when New Delhi conferred the Jawaharlal Nehru Award for promoting international understanding on Aung San Suu Kyi. Myanmar's military government protested New Delhi's move, and bitterness resurfaced in bilateral relations for some time. Despite such irritants, India kept open the doors of diplomacy with Myanmar. During the tenure of I. K. Gujral as India's prime minister (1997–98), India went back to its ideological stance of supporting the pro-democracy movement in Myanmar. The United Front government led by Gujral put emphasis on human rights issues, and restoration of democracy in Myanmar as prerequisites for improving India–Myanmar relations. As a consequence, bilateral relations suffered again.

A new momentum was infused in the otherwise dormant Indo–Myanmar relations in 1998 under the leadership of A. B. Vajpayee, India's new prime minister. Fresh diplomatic engagements with Myanmar began with a view to realise the full potential of the 'Look East Policy' initiated in 1991, but not effectively implemented since then. India's Foreign Secretary, K. Ragunath, visited Myanmar in 1998. He discussed issues like strategic cooperation on internal security, border management and modalities to enhance border trade. To keep the momentum high, India–Myanmar Foreign Secretary-level meeting was held in Yangon in August 2000. Discussions were held primarily on effective border management, which included steps to curb drug trafficking and smuggling. The two countries agreed to strengthen infrastructure and step up security to promote border trade. Jaswant Singh, Vajpayee's foreign minister, also visited Myanmar and signed a number of agreements. In fact, regular visits by high dignitaries from both the sides started from the year 2000, signalling improvement in Indo-Myanmar relations. Myanmar's Vice Senior General Maung Aye, Vice Chairman of the State Peace and Development Council (SPDC) came to India in January 2000. This was followed by General Maung Aye's week-long visit to India in November 2000 at the invitation of the Indian Vice President.

The Indian Vice President, B. S. Shekhawat himself visited Myanmar between 2 and 6 November 2003. This was the first visit by a top Indian statesman since 1987 when Prime Minister Rajiv Gandhi had visited Myanmar. Seven MoUs and agreements were signed during this visit. Myanmar's Foreign Minister Win Aung visited India in January 2003. During Aung's visit, the two countries signed a protocol to establish regular bilateral ministerial consultations and agreed cooperation in projects related to infrastructure, energy and information technology.

India–Myanmar relations took a positive turn with the official visit of General Than Shwe to India in October 2004. General Shwe's visit was the first by a head of state of Myanmar to India in 24 years. General Than Shwe was accompanied by eight Cabinet ministers during his historic state visit to India from 24 to 29 October 2004 at the invitation of the Indian president. The presence of so many senior ministers in Than Shwe's delegation manifested the factor of high importance that Myanmar attached to this visit. During this visit, two MoUs for Cooperation in the field of Non-traditional Security issues and the Tamanthi Hydroelectric Project on Chindwin River in Myanmar were signed between the two countries. Both the sides also expressed interest in furthering cooperation in the field of infrastructure and energy. Other agreements on the setting up of cultural exchanges between the two nations were also signed. The two sides also explored cooperation in areas like industry, energy, rail transportation, communications, science and technology, and health. India raised the issue of insurgency in its North-east region with support bases in Myanmar. General Shwe assured India that his country would take necessary steps to oust insurgent groups from its soil.

India also provided help to Myanmar in its developmental activities. During the official visit of the Indian President, A. P. J. Abdul Kalam to Myanmar in March 2006, India announced a grant of US $1.3 million for upgrading the remote sensing Ground Receiving Station in Yangon, a grant of US $3 million for assistance with delineation of Myanmar's continental shelf, a line of credit for US $10 million to cover Myanmar's contribution to the Kaladan multi-modal transport project and another line of credit for US $20 million for purchase of heavy duty water pumps.[1] Kalam's was the first ever visit by an Indian president to Myanmar since India's independence in 1947. During President Kalam's visit, new vistas of cooperation in information technology (IT), automobile, textiles, agro-based industries, river- and land-based transportation system were explored. The Indian president promised all help to Myanmar in the institution-building process and also in restoring the democratic system of governance. The SPDC chief and Myanmar's head of state, General Than Shwe assured the Indian president that he would take India's help in implementing his proposed seven-point plan for democracy and may give a sympathetic consideration to India's request for the release of Suu Kyi.

India's Foreign Secretary Shyam Saran followed up President Kalam's trip by visiting Yangon in June 2006. This was for the seventh round of Foreign Office Consultations between the two countries. The two sides held talks on issues like common security challenges, reconstruction of the Settwe port in Myanmar, and Tamu–Kalewa–Kalemyo road project. The India–Myanmar gas pipeline project, an important area in bilateral cooperation was also discussed during Saran's visit. Vice Senior General Maung Aye, Vice Chairman of the SPDC of Myanmar visited India in April 2008. Three agreements were signed during the visit. These were:

1. Framework Agreement for construction and operation of a Multi-Modal Transit Transport Facility on Kaladan River,
2. Intelligence Exchange Cooperation, and
3. Avoidance of Double Taxation[2]. Indian Vice President Hamid Ansari visited Myanmar in February 2009. Two agreements on setting up of Myanmar–India Industrial Training Centre at Pakokku and setting up of Myanmar–India Centre for English Languages Training were signed during the visit.[3] Senior General Than Shwe, Chairman of the SPDC of the Union of Myanmar, paid another official visit to India from 25 to 29 July 2010. During the visit, the following agreements and MoUs were signed:
   - (i) Treaty on Mutual Assistance in criminal matters,
   - (ii) MoU regarding Indian Grant Assistance for Implementation of small developmental projects,

[1] Ministry of External Affairs, Government of India, 'India–Myanmar Relations', available at http:// meaindia.nic.in/mystart.php?id=50044503, accessed on 8 August 2011.

[2] Ibid.

[3] Ibid.

(iii) MoU on information cooperation,
(iv) Agreement on cooperation in the fields of science and technology,
(v) MoU on conservation and restoration of Ananda Temple in Bagan, Myanmar. New projects in telecom, railways, roads, health and agriculture, among others, were announced during the visit. Following discussions in Delhi, the delegation also went to Hyderabad and Jamshedpur, where they visited biotech, information technology and automobile industries.[4]

Apart from intense bilateral exchanges, the two countries also used multilateral fora like the Association of South East Asian Nations (ASEAN), the Bay of Bengal Initiative for Multi-Sectoral Technical and Economic Cooperation (BIMSTEC) and the Mekong–Ganga Cooperation (MGC) to get closer. Prime Minister of India Manmohan Singh held talks with his counterpart, Soe Win on the sidelines of the 11th ASEAN Summit in Kuala Lumpur in December 2005. Manmohan requested his Myanmarese counterpart to initiate a process of national reconciliation, and work for the restoration of democracy in Myanmar. The Indian prime minister also raised the issue of insurgency in the northeast region of the country. The ASEAN and BIMSTEC provided good opportunities to both the countries to be politically engaged on a regular basis and exchange views on different matters, on the sidelines of the meetings of these multilateral fora. A few important initiatives in this regard could be mentioned here. The Prime Minister of Myanmar, General Thein Sein visited India in November 2008 to attend the 2nd BIMSTEC Summit meeting in New Delhi. He also held talks with the Indian leaders on important issues during his visit for the BIMSTEC summit. India's Foreign Minister S. M. Krishna led the Indian delegation to the 12th BIMSTEC Ministerial Meeting held in Nay Pyi Taw on 11 December 2010. Krishna also used the opportunity to meet the Myanmarese leaders and exchange views. Preneet Kaur, India's Minister of State for External Affairs, led the Indian delegation to the 13th BIMSTEC Ministerial Meeting, also held in Nay Pyi Taw on 20–22 January 2011, and held talks with the leaders of Myanmar. These visits, along with regular bilateral exchanges, helped in easing tensions between the two nations, and improve relations. These also helped in joint initiatives to solve problems. For instance, India's pressure on Myanmar to curb insurgency bore results in 2006 when India and Myanmar jointly conducted military operations in January to flush out the rebels operating from the territory of Myanmar.

Manmohan Singh visited Myanmar in March 2014 to attend the 3rd BIMSTEC Summit. On the sidelines of the Summit, the Indian prime minister had discussions with the President of Myanmar, U Thein Sein and Chairperson of National League of Democracy (NLD) and Opposition Leader Aung San Suu Kyi. The new Indian Prime Minister, Narendra Modi, who assumed office in May 2014, visited Myanmar from 11–13 November 2014 to attend the ASEAN–India Summit and the 9th East Asia Summit (EAS). During the visit, he met President U Thein Sein and Aung San Suu Kyi. Indian External Affairs Minister Sushma Swaraj visited

[4] Ibid.

Myanmar from 8–11 August 2014 to attend the 4th EAS Foreign Ministers' Meeting and the 21st ASEAN Regional Forum, which was followed by official bilateral visit. Sushma Swaraj discussed the entire gamut of bilateral relations with the Foreign Minister of Myanmar, U. Wunna Maung Lwin and called on President U Thein Sein and Speaker of the Union Parliament of Myanmar, Thura U. Shwe Mann. The Vice President of Myanmar, Sai Mauk Kham led a 35-member delegation on an official visit to India from 19–23 January 2015. The vice president was accompanied by Minister of Construction, Deputy Minister of Foreign Affairs, Deputy Minister for Health, Deputy Minister for Culture, Minister of Transport, Minister for Social Affairs, Sagaing Region, besides other high ranking officials. During his visit, he called on the Indian President, Pranab Mukherjee and Prime Minister Narendra Modi and held discussions with the Indian Vice President M. Hamid Ansari.[5]

It could be observed from the spate of mutual visits and exchanges in multilateral fora that the political relations between India and Myanmar began to take concrete shape since the beginning of the twenty-first century. However, the groundwork for a close relationship was started during the premiership of A. B. Vajpayee in 1998, through effective implementation of the 'Look East Policy' adopted immediately after the Cold War, in 1991. Before 1998, this tie witnessed many ups and downs, with a long period of estrangement when both states preferred to ignore each other. Myanmar became close to China during this period (1962–92). Indian policy-makers were late to implement a realistic policy framework for Myanmar, which was finally used by the Vajpayee Government. This realistic framework suggested closer cooperation with Myanmar for its important geo-strategic significance for India. It also marked a shift from the earlier ideology-based policy of distance from Myanmar for its anti-democratic activities. This stand started to yield results from the beginning of the twenty-first century, as the two nations inched closer to each other, and started serious bilateral engagements, as the analyses presented before revealed. With the installation of an NLD-led democratic government in Myanmar after the 2015 General Elections, and with Aung San Suu Kyi at the helm of power, it is expected that India–Myanmar relations will flourish in the future; because India always backed Suu Kyi (during her long period of detention) and restoration of democracy in Myanmar.

ECONOMIC RELATIONS

Improvement in political relations also influenced bilateral economic relations, which witnessed significant progress in the new century. For instance, in 1980–81, the total volume of India–Myanmar bilateral trade amounted to US $12.4 million; this rose to US $1,497.77 million in 2009–10. Currently, India is the fourth largest trading partner of Myanmar after Thailand, China and Singapore. India also constitutes the second largest export market for Myanmar, absorbing 25 per cent of Myanmar's total exports; and the seventh largest import source of Myanmar.

---

[5] Ministry of External Affairs, Government of India, 'Annual Report: 2014–15' (Delhi: Government of India), 2015, pp. 11–14.

Agricultural products make 90 per cent of Myanmar's total exports to India. Myanmar's imports from India are mainly semi-finished steel and pharmaceuticals. As the statistics reveals, the two countries currently enjoy a healthy trade relationship, which got a boost since the beginning of the twenty-first century due to improvement in political relations. Table 7.1 highlights the growth in bilateral trade during the first decade of the twenty-first century.

Table 7.1: India–Myanmar Bilateral Trade in Recent Years (in US $ million)

Year	*India's Export*	*India's Import*	*Total Trade*	*Growth (%)*
2005–06	110.70	525.96	636.66	–
2006–07	140.44	782.65	923.09	44.99
2007–08	185.82	808.63	994.45	7.73
2008–09	221.64	928.97	1,150.61	15.70
2009–10	207.97	1,289.80	1,497.77	30.17
2010–11	334.42	1,017.67	1,352.09	–9.73
2011–12	545.38	1,381.15	1,926.53	43.95
2012–13	544.66	1,412.69	1,957.35	1.60
2013–14	787.01	1,395.67	2,182.68	11.51
2014–15	773.74	1,231.54	2,005.28	–8.13

Source: Export-Import Data Bank, Ministry of Commerce, Government of India, available at http://commerce.nic.in/eidb/iecnt.asp, accessed on 20 July 2015.

As the table above shows, India–Myanmar trade registered noteworthy growth during the last 10 fiscal years. In the fiscal year 2006–07, the total volume of bilateral trade recorded 44.99 per cent growth over the previous financial year. In 2009–10 and 2011–12, significant growths in bilateral trade were registered. Two-way trade crossed US $2 billion for the first time in the fiscal year 2013–14. Although there was a slight dip in growth in bilateral trade in 2014–15, it registered more than US $2 billion again in the 2014–15 financial year (FY). As observed earlier, India–Myanmar total trade was only US $12.4 million in 1980–81. Clearly, political indifference had an adverse impact on bilateral trade for a long time since the early 1960s. Economic relations began to look up when both India and Myanmar endeavoured to come close politically, since the year 2000, as the table above reveals. Further, it could be also ascertained from the table that percentage growth in total trade was satisfactory all along, except for a few years. In the fiscal year 2009–10, growth rate in total trade was 30.17 per cent from the previous fiscal year (2008–09). However, there was a slight fall in total trade in the 2010–11 fiscal due to a dip in India's import from Myanmar. As a consequence, growth rate in bilateral rate remained negative (–9.73 per cent) in 2010–11. But after a long time, Indian export to Myanmar increased substantially in 2010–11 as is evident from Table 7.1. Therefore, the fall in total trade is not too worrisome because growth in either export or import would arrest this trend in the future. However, both the countries must work hard to improve bilateral trade in the future, and take it to substantial proportions.

India and Myanmar signed a border trade agreement in 1994 and have two border trade points at Moreh-Tamu and Zowkhatar–Rhi on the 1,664 km-long border. The agreement has also been reached on setting up a third border trade point at Avakhung-Pansat or Somra. During the Third India–Myanmar Joint Trade Committee (JTC) in October 2008, it was agreed that border trade at the existing points would be upgraded to normal trade to promote overall bilateral trade between the two countries.[6] It was hoped that greater border trade with Myanmar, on the basis of the agreement signed in 1994, would help revitalise the economy of the northeastern states of India and help quell narcotic and arms trafficking. But the hope has not been fulfilled. Trade traffic along the border remained thin, and India's share among Myanmar's border trade partners has been low, much behind China, Thailand and Bangladesh. The volume of border trade between India's four northeastern states and Myanmar has not been encouraging, with only 7 per cent growth in export in 2008–09. Limited number of items on the trade list and problems of cross-border insurgency are factors behind low volume of border trade. Only one of the two proposed border posts is open. The road on the Indian side to Moreh is in a very bad shape. Two-way trade is further constrained by excessive regulation and restrictions. The Third India–Myanmar JTC decided to increase items on the trade list to 40 from the current 22, and operationalise the banking system in the border areas through signing of MoUs. These measures may help strengthen border trade in the future.

India is currently involved in over a dozen projects in Myanmar, both in infrastructural and non-infrastructural areas through governmental initiatives. Notable among these projects are upgradation and resurfacing of the 160 km-long Tamu-Kalewa-Kalemyo road; construction and upgradation of the Rhi-Tidim and Rhi-Falam roads in Myanmar; and the Kaladan Multimodal Transport Project. An Asymmetric Digital Subscriber Line (ADSL) project for high speed data link in 32 Myanmar cities has been completed by the Telecommunications Consultants India Ltd (TCIL). ONGC Videsh Ltd (OVL), and Gas Authority of India Ltd (GAIL), two of India's leading public sector companies, and Essar Oil, a prominent Indian private company are major participants in the energy sector in Myanmar. RITES, a Government of India (GoI) enterprise, is actively involved in development of the rail transportation system and in supply of railway coaches, locomotives and parts. In September 2008, Ministry of Electric Power-1 (MoEP-1) of Myanmar and National Hydro Power Corporation (NHPC) of India signed an agreement for the development of the Tamanthi and Shwezaye hydro-electric power project in Chindwin River Valley and NHPC is working on the preparation of updated Detailed Project Reports. A heavy turbo-truck assembly plant set up in Myanmar by TATA Motors, a leading private company in India, with GoI financial assistance was inaugurated on 31 December 2010. An India–Myanmar Industrial Training Centre has been set up by HMT(I) in Myanmar with the assistance of GoI. A Myanmar–India Entrepreneurship Development Centre (MIEDC) and an India–Myanmar Centre for Enhancement of IT Skills (IMCEITS) are also operating currently.

---

[6] https://www.mea.gov.in/Portal/ForeignRelation/myanmar-july-2012.pdf, accessed on 12 May 2017.

The Confederation of Indian Industry (CII) and the Union of Myanmar Federation of Chambers of Commerce and Industry (UMFCCI) signed an MoU in February 2000. Another MoU was signed between CII and the Myanmar Computer Federation (MCF) in 2001. In 2004, a new MoU was signed between the Myanmar–India Business Club (MIBC) and Federation of Industries and Commerce of North-Eastern Region for the promotion of border trade and business. In addition to these, a Bilateral Investment Promotion Agreement (BIPA) and a Double Taxation Avoidance Agreement (DTAA) were also signed in 2008. India and Myanmar are both signatories to the India–ASEAN Trade in Goods Agreement, which was signed in August 2009. Myanmar is also a beneficiary country under India's Duty Free Tariff Preference (DFTP) scheme for Less Developed Countries (LDCs).[7]

India and Myanmar signed four more economic cooperation agreements in June 2008 when Indian Minister of State for Commerce, Jairam Ramesh visited Myanmar. These agreements related to bilateral investment promotion, a US $20-million credit line between the Exim Bank of India and the Myanmar Foreign Trade Bank (MFTB) for the establishment of a manufacturing facility; another US $64-million credit line for three 230 KV transmission lines; and for establishing banking arrangement between the Myanmar Investment and Trade Bank and the United Bank of India (UBI). However, most of the economic engagements have so far been between the two governments, in areas like agriculture, telecommunications, aviation and gas exploration.

Myanmar has been trying to entice Indian companies to invest in sectors like pharmaceuticals, cement, fertiliser, steel, information technology (IT) and food processing. But according to one source, 'Indian firms are not very keen to invest in Myanmar for fear of a repetition of the nationalisation drive carried out by the military rulers'.[8] In spite of such fears, India's contracted investments in Myanmar reached nearly US $320 million as of January 2011, of which US $157 million was in the oil and gas sector. India has given US $100 million credit for Myanmar's infrastructure, while US $57 million has been offered to upgrade the railway system. A further US $27 million in grants has been pledged for road and rail projects.[9]

Myanmar possesses one of the largest natural gas reserves of the world. India has shown keen interest to procure gas from Myanmar to meet its energy needs. However, India is currently facing the problem of transportation of gas from Myanmar. A tri-nation pipeline project involving Myanmar, Bangladesh and India was proposed by Bangladesh in 1997. Under this proposal, the 290-km pipeline would run through the Arakan state in Myanmar, via the Indian state of Mizoram and Tripura to cross over to Bangladesh, before entering back into the Indian state of West Bengal.[10] The three countries signed an agreement on this project, estimated to be more than

---

[7] www.insightsonindia.com/2014/01/18/insights-daily-current-events-january-18-2014/, accessed on 13 May 2017.

[8] www.c3sindia.org/india/1012, accessed on 13 May 2017.

[9] For sources to all economic data, see Ministry of External Affairs, 'India–Myanmar Relations', n. 1.

[10] www.indolink.com/displayArticleS.php?id=082706104219, accessed on 13 May 2017.

US $1 billion in Yangon on February 2005. The construction of the India–Myanmar pipeline was scheduled to start in 2006 and the delivery of gas was to commence from 2009. However, this project got entangled in a political row after Bangladesh wanted many concessions from India to allow the passage of the pipeline through its territory. India rejected Bangladesh's demands that bilateral issues cannot become part of a trilateral agreement and decided for an alternative route to bypass Bangladesh. A technical consultant company from Belgium was engaged by India to prepare a detailed feasibility report for an alternative pipeline route to Myanmar. But the pipeline project is still in its finalisation stage. However, India has offered to buy Myanmar gas and import it through the Bay of Bengal.[11] For this purpose, India has invited bids for long-term chartering service of a compressed natural gas (CNG) ship for the transportation of the Myanmar gas. Such arrangements are necessary for a few reasons. First, India is short of natural gas, and demands are high within India; second, China is eyeing the lucrative energy trade with Myanmar, and trying to outsmart India in this endeavour; and finally, Myanmar is getting anxious due to the delay in the pipeline project, and is proposing to sell gas to other parties, including China. As India's energy diplomacy has not been very successful in the recent times compared to China's drive for procuring energy resources, India is determined not to waste this opportunity to import natural gas from Myanmar.

SECURITY RELATIONS

India's security relations with Myanmar have not been strong due to a long period of mutual negligence. However, security relations began to consolidate since the year 2000. High-level military-to-military contacts began in that year. In January, Indian Army Chief, General V. P. Malik paid a two-day visit to Myanmar. This was reciprocated by Myanmarese General Maung Aye's visit to India. After these visits, India started providing military support to Myanmar troops along the border. India also provided combat gears to Myanmarese soldiers. It also provided military helicopters on lease to Myanmar, required to counter the ethnic insurgents operating along both sides of the border. Since the initial exchange of visits, there has been a steady flow of high-level visits from both the sides. General Thura Shwe Mann, the third highest ranking officer in Myanmar's military, visited India in 2006. The General visited the National Defence Academy (NDA) of India, and the Tata Motors plant in Pune, which makes military vehicles. High-level visits to enhance security collaborations between the two countries continued, and these have become quite regular now. The desire for military cooperation also resulted in the joint military operation against the insurgents working along the borders, in January 2006.

The two countries are now seriously engaged in naval cooperation in the Bay of Bengal, and also in the Indian Ocean. The strategic importance of Myanmar in the Indian Ocean Region (IOR) has made India initiate naval cooperation with Myanmar. A non-declared objective of

---

[11] www.indolink.com/displayArticleS.php?id=082706104219, accessed on 13 May 2017.

India was also to neutralise increasing Chinese strategic relations with Myanmar. For enhancing naval cooperation, Indian Navy Chief, Admiral Arun Prakash first visited Myanmar in 2003 and then again in January 2006, where he presented a consignment of communication equipment to his Myanmarese counterparts. Two Indian warships, *INS Ranjit* and *ISN Kuthar* were engaged in joint exercises with Myanmar's navy in December 2005. These were not the only instances of naval cooperation between the two neighbours. Earlier, in December 2002, an Indian naval fleet, comprising a submarine and two destroyers, went to Myanmar as part of defence cooperation exercise. Further, in September 2003, two more Indian warships carried out four-day joint exercises with the Myanmar navy. In exchange, a Myanmarese corvette came to Port Blair in India to take part in 'Milan' naval exercises in 2006. This was for the first time in four decades that a Myanmar ship visited a foreign port. India has also been providing training to military officers of Myanmar since 2007.

The Indian military also provided critical material support to Myanmar when cyclone 'Nargis' devastated Myanmar in May 2008, killing 80,000 people and rendering thousands homeless. The Indian military launched operation 'sahayata' (help) to provide manual and material support to the cyclone ravaged people of Myanmar. Two Indian naval ships transported more than 100 tons of relief materials to the cyclone affected people. Further, two Indian Air Force (IAF) aircrafts supplied 4 tons of relief materials. India was the first country to provide relief materials to Myanmar after cyclone 'Nargis', and India's gestures certainly helped to strengthen relations between the two countries. The third annual staff talk between the two navies was held in September 2014 in New Delhi. Issues relating to further cooperation in the field of operational sea training and maritime security were discussed. Contract between Myanmar army and Tata Motors was signed for supply of 400 more TATA Xenon vehicles in addition to 600 Xenon vehicles which the Myanmar army had purchased in February 2014.[12]

RECOMMENDATIONS FOR THE FUTURE

For a long time, Indian foreign policy was caught between idealism and realism as far as dealing with Myanmar was concerned. From the early 1960s to the middle of 1990s, India was less interested to forge close relations with Myanmar, due to the existence of military regimes which suppressed democratic and human rights in Myanmar. Idealism dominated Indian foreign policy during this period. From 1998 onwards, Indian policy-makers started to pay sincere attention to Myanmar due to its geo-strategic importance, China's increasing clout in the country, and insurgency in India's northeastern states. Realism began to take roots in India's policies towards Myanmar from this time. Bilateral relations have become much stronger since the late 1990s, as the discussion above pointed out. But the two countries need to work hard to achieve more intensity and dynamism in their relations. The following recommendations, which cover all major

---

[12] Ministry of External Affairs, 'Annual Report: 2014–15', p. 14.

areas of bilateral relations, may help the two nations to go for closer cooperation and friendship in the future:

Indian foreign policy must be guided by realism as far as Myanmar is concerned: The realist phase of India's foreign policy for Myanmar started with the 'Look East Policy' in which Myanmar was considered an important bridge in India's diplomatic connections with Southeast and East Asia. Through the 'Look East Policy', India shed its idealism, and began to nurture close cooperation with the Military Junta in Myanmar. India's national interests demand the continuation of this realist policy for Myanmar in the future. India must not be obsessed, like it was in the past, with the restoration of democracy and human rights in Myanmar; but continue to pursue issue-based diplomacy with the military regime in that country. This does not, however, indicate that Indian foreign policy would be devoid of idealism altogether. India must put continuous pressure on Myanmar for achieving democracy, but must not limit its relations with Myanmar to the 'ideals' of democracy only. For instance, India had chosen the right path of supporting the pro-democracy movements in Myanmar in 2007, but unlike earlier times, had not shown total apathy to military rulers in that country, and went ahead with closer cooperation in various fields. In simple words, India must not push for democracy in Myanmar, or in any part of the world, if it does not serve India's national interests. India must learn to adjust with military and totalitarian regimes for the sake of India's national interests, and effective diplomacy. After all, military regimes are not eternal in any country, as Myanmar's return to democracy has proved.

Two-way trade must be augmented in future: India's bilateral trade with Myanmar, although on the rise in the recent times, has the potential to surge ahead further in the future. In 2014–15, India's total trade with Myanmar stood at US $2.05 billion. However, the volume of total trade with Myanmar is one of India's lowest with neighbouring countries. In 2014–15, the total volume of India's trade with Myanmar was lower compared to India's trade with China, Bangladesh, Sri Lanka, Nepal, and Pakistan. Table 7.2 highlights India's trade with some neighbouring countries in 2014–15:

As evident from Table 7.2, India–Myanmar trade volume is the lowest in 2014–15 among many of India's neighbours. Leaving China aside, India–Myanmar total trade stood low in comparison with India's smaller and economically weaker neighbours in 2014–15, as shown in Table 7.2. A main reason behind this low trade was political estrangement between the two countries for a long time. With improvement in political relations, India and Myanmar must concentrate on increasing bilateral trade now. India must not hesitate to include more items like pharmaceuticals, cement,

Table 7.2: India's Trade with Some Neighbouring Countries in 2014–15 (in US $ billion*)

Name of the Country	*Total Trade*
China	72.34
Sri Lanka	7.45
Bangladesh	7.07
Nepal	5.19
Pakistan	2.36
Myanmar	2.05

Note: * Converted to US $ billion by the author from the original US $ million.

Source: Export-Import Data Bank, available at http://commerce.nic.in/eidb/iecnt.asp, accessed on 20 July 2015.

fertiliser, steel, and food processing in its 'export list' to Myanmar. Another largely ignored item in export to Myanmar is software and IT, an industry where India is relatively strong, and demands for which are increasing in Myanmar. It is heartening to note that India has started to export IT-related items to Myanmar, but the volume is still very low, and needs massive augmentation. Although the volume of Indian imports from Myanmar are higher compared to exports to that country, India has been completely outsmarted by China in importing precious oil and natural gas from Myanmar,[13] demands for which are very high in India. India must give adequate attention to this area, and try to increase the volume of imports of oil and natural gas from Myanmar. Overall, the two countries need to sit together and fix a time-bound growth of bilateral trade. By 2020, the total volume of two-way trade should reach US $10 billion or more. This target proposes only five times growth in trade from the current volume, and is not impossible to achieve.

India must compete with China for Myanmar: India must not hesitate to compete with China for proximity with Myanmar, because India has many interests in Myanmar. Close political and security relations with Myanmar are necessary for India to control insurgency-related problems in India's Northeast, to improve peace in India's neighbourhood, and to strengthen India's position in multilateral fora like the BIMSTEC, MGC, and the ASEAN. From an economic point of view, India must get adequate access to Myanmar's oil and natural gas fields, and other commercial sectors. There is little doubt that China currently holds a huge advantage over India in its relations with Myanmar. India's long estrangement with Myanmar was gradually but surely compensated by China, which extended an olive branch to the military rulers of Myanmar in the mid-1970s, and continued to nurture good relations with the country since then. China's diplomacy was more successful than India's with regard to Myanmar. China's very successful 'oil diplomacy' in Myanmar in recent years is a case in point here.[14] Another indicator of China's successful diplomacy was the volume of China–Myanmar two-way trade, which surpassed US $10 billion in 2015–16.[15] It should be mentioned here that China is currently the largest trading partner of Myanmar. Therefore, China is way ahead of India at present with regard to relations with Myanmar. But this factor must not deter India from forging stronger relations with Myanmar, for the fulfilment of India's national interests. Myanmar's Military Junta is also seeking to change the country's over-dependence on China, and, looking for new partners to strengthen Myanmar's position in international politics. According to one report, 'Myanmar regards China's growing influence with suspicion and sees India as the only viable means to balance China's increasing encroachment, especially in the Kachin and Shan states.

[13] R. Swaminathan, *India–Myanmar Relations: A Review,* Paper No. 3480 (New Delhi: South Asia Analysis Group), 30 October 2009.

[14] Ibid.

[15] *China Daily,* available at http://www.chinadaily.com.cm/business/2016-02/16/content_23499905.htm, accessed on 14 May 2017.

For this and other reasons, Myanmar is keen to have good relations with India.'[16] India should not waste this opportunity to entice Myanmar away from its Chinese fold with a view to secure its national interests.

Promote cultural relations and tourism: From a cultural point of view, India shares a historic relationship with Myanmar. The presence of a large Indian diaspora in Myanmar helped in promoting cultural links between the two countries for centuries. The origin of the Indian people in Myanmar could be traced back to 1852, with the advent of British rule in Burma.[17] But of late, cultural links between the two nations have become weak, and require adequate boosts. Although government-sponsored cultural programmes are regularly held currently in two countries, but these are not enough. Very few Indian students go to universities in Myanmar for higher studies, as there is dearth of mutual agreements for student exchange programmes among universities in India and Myanmar. Some Myanmar students come to India for higher studies, mainly on government-sponsored stipends and scholarships, but many prefer to go to China and the West for higher studies. Indian and Myanmarese universities need to collaborate more intensely in this regard, and enter into MoUs for this purpose. Such engagements would foster people-to-people contacts and may help dispel misunderstanding among the common men in both countries. Tourism and cultural fairs should be frequently organised by government and non-government agencies with a view to promoting cultural bonds between the two peoples. Tourism may particularly help Myanmar because many Indian tourists go to Thailand, Malaysia, Singapore and the far east, but ignore Myanmar, partly due to lack of interest in that country. Tourism fairs may help to generate valuable interests in Myanmar. The government in Myanmar should pay due attention to bring back the interest of the outside world in Myanmar. Cultural exchanges may also help in bringing people of the two neighbouring countries close.

---

[16] Swaminathan, *India–Myanmar Relations*, n. 13.

[17] Ministry of External Affairs, 'India–Myanmar Relations', n. 1.

PART II

INDIA AND MAJOR POWERS

8

INDIA AND THE UNITED STATES

Evolving Partnership

HIGHLIGHTS

- Introduction: Bilateral Relations during the Cold War
- India–US Relations after the Cold War
- Recommendations for the Future

INTRODUCTION: BILATERAL RELATIONS DURING THE COLD WAR

The warmth and maturity observed in India–United States (US) relations in recent times were missing during the Cold War period. India's relations with the US were not close during the Cold War years. Mutual disbelief and misunderstanding dominated bilateral relations from 1947 to 1990. Since India's independence in 1947, India–US relations had never achieved the kind of harmony and cordiality that many in both countries had anticipated. India and the US shared a mutually suspicious relationship. A few reasons for this distant relationship were different foreign policy goals, ambitions and perspectives of the two nations during this period. The US, despite sharing a common ideology of liberal democracy, followed a different course of pulls and pressures with India during the Cold War. The main objective was to fulfil its national interests. Despite democratic commonality with India, the US had no hesitation in aligning with Pakistan, which for intermittent periods, was ruled by military dictatorships, and later China, a communist state. The main foreign policy objective of the US during the Cold War was to contain the Soviet Union. India, on its part pursued the policy of non-alignment, which the Americans viewed with suspicion. The US, for the most part, remained aloof from India, which it considered as a Soviet 'stooge' during the Cold War period. From Jawaharlal Nehru to Chandra Sekhar, no Indian prime minister (during the Cold War era) had been successful in establishing intimate relations with the US due to attitudinal and perceptional differences, with Cold War political calculations accentuating these differences on the American side. The Pakistan factor, from the Indian point of view, and the Soviet factor, from the American perspective, put severe strains on India–US relations in this period.

The relationship was, however, not one of sustained animosity either. During the Cold War years, the relationship was not strictly controlled by bilateral issues. As observed earlier, the Soviet factor and the Pakistan factor had tended to dominate Indo–US relations during the Cold War years. Despite India's proclaimed policy of non-alignment, the US viewed India with suspicion that it was a Soviet partner trying to thwart American interests, particularly in Asia. India, on the other hand, resented America's patronage of Pakistan in security and economic matters, especially because arms supplied by the US had been used by Pakistan against India in the 1965 as well as the 1971 wars between the two countries, and the US policy of equating a smaller undemocratic Pakistan with a big democratic India. For more than 40 years since India's independence, the Soviet and the Pakistan factor had loomed large in Indo–US relations.

On almost all major international issues during the Cold War, American and Indian policies had differed. The main areas of difference were:

(i) The US zeal to contain communism, in which India was not interested.
(ii) India had rejected America's desire to create blocs of allies to thwart the advancement of communism, and had remained officially non-aligned, which only strengthened US suspicions.
(iii) The US branded India as a Soviet supporter, while America was considered to be hegemonic by India.
(iv) American funding of Pakistan as an important frontline US ally in South Asia further alienated India from the US.
(v) The US called for non-proliferation of nuclear weapons, while India viewed this non-proliferation regime as detrimental to its national interests. Moreover, it condemned the Nuclear Non-Proliferation Treaty (NPT) to be unfair and unequal, and refused to sign it.
(vi) Although economic and cultural spheres were considered as brighter spots in an otherwise indifferent relationship, economic relations were dependent on political relations during the Cold War. Further, India's economic policies, which were based on the principles of 'socialism', were very different from America's market-driven economy.

Despite these differences, India–US relations had never been uniformly hostile during the Cold War years, probably because India was not a party to the Cold War. There were times when the leaders of both countries tried sincerely to forge friendship between the two nations. The tenure of India's Prime Minister Morarji Desai (1977–79) who was considered 'soft' on the US witnessed brighter patches in bilateral relationship. The American President Jimmy Carter's official visit to India in 1978, the first American President to visit India in 25 years after President Eisenhower's visit in 1953, brought the two countries closer. However, this proximity could not be sustained for long. Further, Prime Minister Rajiv Gandhi (1984–89) developed a very cordial relationship with President Ronald Reagan of the US and their good personal chemistry helped to improve bilateral relations. But different foreign policy perspectives again drove the two nations away from each other after Rajiv's premiership came to an end. In fact, during most of the Cold War period, India–US relations were marked not so much by animosity as indifference. For the US, India had a lesser priority compared to many other states in Asia. India too, never worked hard to change this attitude due to opposing national interests and foreign policy objectives.

INDIA–US RELATIONS AFTER THE COLD WAR

The end of the Cold War in 1991 provided unique opportunities for a close Indo–US relations because of several reasons. These were:

(i) The collapse of the Soviet Union led to subsequent changes in the international political and strategic environment.
(ii) As the only surviving super power, the US became very important to India as well as to most other countries in the world.
(iii) America showed an increased zeal for non-proliferation after the Cold War and this led to a further growth of its interest in South Asia, where both India and Pakistan were known to have developed nuclear capability.
(iv) India's shift from a Nehruvian socialist-type economy to a market-oriented American-type liberal economy improved its status as an investment destination in an increasingly globalised economy, particularly because India had a rapidly growing middle class with an enhanced buying power.
(v) A stable democratic Indian polity had the potential to best serve the US post Cold War interests in South Asia.
(vi) The increasing economic and political clout of Americans of Indian origin.
(vii) There were changes in the geo-strategic scenario which may have led to a rethinking in the American foreign policy-making circles: instability in the region resulting from the eclipse of the Soviet Union as a factor in the balance of power game; the rise of various kinds of nationalistic challenges as well as Islamic militancy in Pakistan and its neighbouring states; the rise of China as an economic giant which had increasing political clout.

All these and more might have led to a reassessment of American foreign policy interests in the region, in which India appeared in a better light than earlier. The emerging post Cold War world order, therefore, offered the best possible environment for both India and the US to forge a stronger relationship. The two nations tried to work positively to improve relations at all levels during this period.

Some of the opportunities noted above were used significantly by both governments after the Cold War to strengthen US–India relations. For instance, India's economic liberalisation in 1991 helped to initiate close economic ties between the two nations. The US welcomed India's economic reforms and American investment in Indian markets enhanced to a great extent. US–India two-way trade also registered significant growth. In 1991, the total volume of US–India bilateral trade was US $5,070 million. The volume of bilateral trade rose to US $14,353.80 million in the year 2000. This amount grew further to US $45,599.12 million in the fiscal year 2010–11.[1] In 1991, the total American investment to India was US $97 million. American investment to India grew to US $900 million in 2000. It further enhanced to US $1,802.0 million in 2008–09 (April 2008–March 2009).[2] These data indicated that India's economic reforms gave a boost to US–India trade and American investment in India.

However, opposing foreign policy objectives and national interests continued to keep the two democracies apart even after the end of the Cold War. The US placed great emphasis on the non-proliferation of weapons of mass destruction in this period, and followed a policy of economic diplomacy. India's foreign policy objectives, on the other hand, mainly centred on its national security interests. The presence of a nuclear China and Pakistan, a potential nuclear power (it ultimately tested nuclear weapons in May 1998) in India's neighbourhood, made India rethink its security and nuclear policies, and provided an explanation of Narasimha Rao government's attempt at nuclear testing. The Vajpayee Government finally tested nuclear weapons in May 1998. India also could not be persuaded to sign the NPT or the Comprehensive Test Ban Treaty (CTBT) due to its national security concerns. India's security policies were in tune with its national interests, which, however, contradicted the foreign policy objectives of the US after the Cold War. India's refusal to sign the CTBT and the May 1998 nuclear tests were viewed by the US as a violation of the non-proliferation regime and a challenge to US foreign policy. As a consequence, relations after the Cold War suffered to a certain extent. The mistrust of the Cold War era continued till the middle of 1999, when the Kargil crisis[3] between India and Pakistan began. The US support to India during the Kargil crisis and the pressure it apparently exerted on Pakistan, went a long way in creating the all-important factor of faith in India–US bilateral relationship. It almost appeared that the US began to understand and appreciate India's security concerns from that time. The Kargil crisis was followed by reciprocal visits of President Clinton and Prime Minister Atal Behari Vajpayee to each other's countries and bilateral relations reached a new high after these visits in 2000. Therefore, a strong India–US relationship seems to be a comparatively recent phenomenon that is, from around the middle of 1999. Prior to that, India–US

---

[1] Department of Commerce, Government of India, Export-Import Data Bank, Department of Commerce, Government of India, available at http://www.commerce.nic.in/eidb/iecnt/asp, accessed on 10 April 2011.

[2] Ibid.

[3] Kargil is a small town in the high altitudes of the Himalayas on the Indian side of the Line of Control (LoC). On 6 May 1999, the Indian army first detected intruders in the Kargil area. In the next few weeks, groups of militants clashed with the Indian army patrols throughout an area ranging from the Muskoh Valley to Batalik. By 26 May, army efforts to flush out the infiltrators through ground action failed, and air strikes were carried out for this purpose. On 27 May, an Indian Air Force MIG fighter was shot down by Pakistan, a Squadron Leader of the Indian Air Force (IAF) died, and the heaviest fighting since the 1971 India–Pakistan war was under way.

relations, despite incrementally closer economic ties, had remained indifferent. If we consider India–US relations according to the tenures of Indian prime ministers since the end of the Cold War in 1991, we would observe that bilateral relations did not become strong immediately after the end of the Cold War. It was not before the middle of 1999 that relationship between the two nations started to improve significantly. In the following pages, the post Cold War course of India–US relations has been analysed as per the tenures of Indian prime ministers.

From Rao to Vajpayee's Second Term (1991–99): Ups and Downs in Relations

Bilateral relations during the premiership of Narasimha Rao, the first post Cold War prime minister of India (1991–96) did not meet the post Cold War expectations. Rao faced two major obstacles in his efforts to improve relations with the US. These were: non-proliferation issues and the American concern for human rights in India. India, which had not signed the NPT, had a missile technology programme which was making major advances during the Rao period. In 1992, India successfully tested the Augmented Satellite Launch Vehicle (ASLV) and the Polar Satellite Launch Vehicle (PSLV). India test fired intermediate range missiles *Agni* and *Prithvi* in 1994; and announced the launch of *Trishul*, a surface-to-air missile and *Akash*, an anti-tank ballistic missile. The US viewed these Indian missile programmes as a destabilising factor in the military balance of South Asia, while India perceived these as necessary for national security.

This was in the background of the Clinton administration's efforts to effectively install an international non-proliferation regime through the passage and acceptance of the CTBT, the Fissile Material Cut-off Treaty (FMCT), and the Missile Technology Control Regime (MTCR). India's missile technology programme was viewed as a destabilising factor in the regional context, for the non-proliferation regime (NPR), which the Clinton administration hoped to achieve. India's opposition to the CTBT in the Conference on Disarmament in the summer of 1996 also went against American interests. The US viewed India's opposition to the CTBT as an infringement of the NPR. Since the NPR was a major focus of US foreign policy during the Clinton presidency, India's missile programme put Indo–US relations under strain during the Rao premiership.

Human rights constituted another disturbing area in India–US relations during the Rao period. Human rights had been used as a foreign policy tool by earlier American Presidents like Jimmy Carter and George Bush (Sr), but it had assumed greater importance in US foreign policymaking during the Clinton presidency.[4] The US Congress and the Clinton administration openly accused India of human rights violation during the Rao period. Throughout the first term of the Clinton presidency (1992–96), the US government used human rights issues to embarrass India. India, on its part, rejected US charges of human rights violations in Kashmir and the North-east and

---

[4] Aneek Chatterjee, 'From Uncertainty to Solidarity: An Anatomy of Post Cold War India–U.S. Relations', *Jadavpur Journal of International Relations*, 14 (1): 22, 2010.

declared that Pakistan-backed foreign terrorists were responsible for the violation of human rights in Kashmir and other parts of India. Human rights and non-proliferation issues, therefore, remained obstacles to stronger Indo–US relations during the Rao period.[5]

On the other hand, economic relations began to improve from the early 1990s and this was the result of the launching of India's economic reforms programme in 1991. India–US trade which was a little less than US $6 billion in 1989, reached nearly US $9.5 billion in 1996.[6] In 1991, at the beginning of Rao's premiership, actual investment in India by American institutional investors was US $97 million. This reached US $1,166 million at the end of Rao's term in 1996. Less than 100 American companies were doing business in India in 1990, but by 1996, their numbers rose to 147.[7] These figures indicate that the economic segment of India–US bilateral relationship improved considerably during the Rao period. However, improvement in only one sector does not indicate an overall improvement in relationship. Even in the economic sphere, the progress was not spectacular. For example, India–US trade did not comprise even 1 per cent of the total US trade in 1996.[8] Compared to America's trade with China in 1996, India–US trade remained quite small.[9] The Clinton administration gave a Most Favoured Nation (MFN) status in trade to China in 1993. The same status was denied to India, because of differences over non-proliferation and human rights issues. There were also other problem areas in India–US economic relations during the Rao period over matters like Intellectual Property Rights (IPR) and Balance of Payment (BoP). Economic relations only started to look up after the Indian economic reforms were initiated. Therefore, it may be said that during Narasimha Rao's tenure as prime minister (1991–96), there was only marginal improvement in India–US relations, and this was primarily in the field of bilateral trade. Cold War indifference, in fact, continued into the Rao premiership.

Following Narasimha Rao, the two United Front (UF) governments of H. D. Deve Gowda and I. K. Gujral endeavoured to improve relations with the US. During the first UF government of Deve Gowda (1996–97), economic relations between India and the US continued to grow. India's export to the US increased at 7.5 per cent in 1996 and 18.7 per cent in 1997. Indian imports from the US grew at 0.7 per cent in 1996 and 9.1 per cent in 1997. The substantial increase of exports and imports in 1997 contributed significantly to improved economic relations. Increased imports also reduced the trade deficit in 1997. During Deve Gowda's tenure, the actual inflow of foreign direct investment (FDI) also increased. In 1996, the actual FDI inflow

---

5 See in this context, Aneek Chatterjee, 'Human Rights and India–US Relations during the Rao Premiership', *Jadavpur Journal of International Relations*, 9: 151–63, 2005.

6 Embassy of India, Washington D.C., available at http://www.indianembassy.org/indoustrade.asp, accessed on 10 September 2002.

7 Tata Services Ltd, *Statistical Outline of India: 1997–98* (Mumbai: Tata Services), 1998, p. 147.

8 See in this context, Thomas A. Timberg, 'The Impact of Indian Economic Liberalization on US–India Relations', *SAIS Review* Winter–Spring, 1998, p. 125.

9 Ibid.

to India was US $2,383 million, which constituted 21.4 per cent of the FDI approval to India. In 1997, the actual FDI inflow was US $3,330 million, and it constituted 21.1 per cent of the total FDI approval to India. It must be mentioned in this context that in 1995, the actual FDI inflow into India was only 18.7 per cent of the total FDI approvals. Most of the FDI to India came from the US during this period.[10]

Despite the growth in bilateral trade and American investment, it should be noted that non-proliferation issues continued as irritants in India–US relations even during Deve Gowda's premiership. The CTBT draft was brought to the United Nations General Assembly (UNGA), despite India's opposition, and India voted against it at the UNGA.[11] India's action earned US displeasure. As a consequence, bilateral relations went through considerable tension during Deve Gowda's premiership. Between June 1996 and April 1997 (the Deve Gowda period), India–US relations continued to largely follow the pattern observed during the early post-Cold War period (the Rao premiership): improvement in the economic segment, but a perceptible setback in the overall relationship.

I. K. Gujral took charge as prime minister of the second UF Government on 21 April 1997. There was a degree of improvement in bilateral relations during the Gujral premiership (1997–98), and several factors were responsible for this. First, the 'Gujral Doctrine'[12] was successful in India's international relations, and it helped to improve India's ties with her neighbours.[13] The American administration welcomed the easing of tension in South Asia, which was considered a nuclear-active zone. Second, the CTBT issue, which proved to be disturbing for bilateral relations since the Rao period, lost its importance during Gujral's premiership. It was sent for the approval of the US Senate after President Clinton had signed it. The US Senate kept the CTBT under prolonged consideration with strong indications that it might not approve the Treaty. As a result, the significance of the CTBT became less important in India–US bilateral relations, and this helped in the gradual improvement of relations. Third, politically important reciprocal visits took place during Gujral's tenure. These visits not only indicated improvement in relations, but helped foster better understanding between the two nations. The Indian prime minister made an official visit to the US. Shortly thereafter, the Indian industry minister also visited the US to discuss investment and tourism prospects in both the countries. American Secretary of State, Madeleine Albright paid an official visit (the first by a US Secretary of State in 14 years) to India. Other prominent visits from the American side were made by the secretary of commerce, and under secretary of state for South Asian affairs. As a consequence, several important agreements and memoranda of Understanding (MoUs) were signed between the two countries. For instance,

---

[10] Embassy of India, Washington D.C., available at http://www.indianembassy.org/indoustrade.asp, accessed on 6 October 2002.

[11] See *The Times of India*, 11 September 1996.

[12] For more on the 'Gujral Doctrine', refer n. 4 in chapter on India–Pakistan Relations.

[13] See in this context, J. N. Dixit, *India's Foreign Policy: 1947–2003* (New Delhi: Piens Books), 2003, p. 222.

Pickering and India's Foreign Secretary K. Raghunath signed an 'Agreement to Combat Terrorism' in New Delhi during the former's visit to India.[14] This agreement preceded the 9/11 events and signalled the growing concern of the two nations regarding terrorist activities, an area where there was an emerging convergence of opinion. The two countries also signed an important 'Extradition Treaty' in June 1997 to facilitate the reciprocal deportation of criminals and terrorists from their respective territories. These important reciprocal visits and the signing of significant agreements and MoUs indicate a departure from the earlier stances of both the countries. The fruits of this improvement were later enjoyed by the Vajpayee Government, which was elected in May 1998, but the seeds were sown during this time.

Two-way trade and commerce also increased during this period. Indian exports to the US registered an 18.7 per cent increase in 1997, while Indian imports from the US recorded a healthy growth of 9.1 per cent. The total turnover of bilateral trade (in 1997) was US $10,931 million, which was a record since 1991.[15] Though disturbing issues concerning the IPR and the BoP persisted, they never became important enough to affect bilateral relations, which improved considerably during the Gujral period.[16]

During Atal Behari Vajpayee's second term as prime minister of India (from 19 March 1998 to 13 October 1999), including a 13-day stay in office earlier in 1996, India–US relations once again reached a new low due to India's nuclear tests. Pokhran II (the 1998 Indian nuclear tests) had a negative impact on the Clinton administration which viewed India's nuclear tests as a challenge to the American-led attempts to impose a world-wide NPR. As a punishment for the violation of the NPR, the US imposed economic sanctions on India under the US Arms Export Control Act. The sanctions regime dealt a blow to the trust and confidence which had been building up over the past few years, but interestingly it had little impact on the Indian economy, which was its primary target.

The effect of the sanctions regime on India was negligible. A resilient Indian economy and the pressure from American business lobby on its government to relax sanctions provisions reduced the effects of sanctions on India. But a significant development occurred from June 1998, within a month from India's nuclear explosions. India and the US engaged themselves in diplomatic dialogues that continued for two and a half years. The dialogues between the Deputy Chairman of India's Planning Commission (later, India's External Affairs Minister), Jaswant Singh and Strobe Talbott, the US Deputy Secretary of State for South Asian Affairs, who represented the two nations, acted as confidence-building measure (CBM) between the two countries. The talks which were the longest ever diplomatic dialogues between India and the US spanning two and

---

[14] Chatterjee, n. 4, p. 26.

[15] Embassy of India, Washington, D.C., *India–US Economic Relations*, available at http://www.indianembassy.org/economyrelations.asp, accessed on 26 December 2003.

[16] See in this context, Aneek Chatterjee, 'Beyond Expectations: Remarkable Development in India–U.S. Relations during the Gujral Premiership', *Jadavpur Journal of International Relations*, 11–12: 25–46, 2008.

half years from June 1998, helped to restore mutual trust and confidence in bilateral relations. Partial lifting of the economic sanctions by the US began within a year of their imposition, partly because of the satisfactory progress of the Singh–Talbott talks, and partly because the sanctions also hurt US exports to India and Pakistan (and thus impacted American economic interests, which was a prime focus of US national interests). By the middle of 1999, the relations began to limp back to normalcy. The mutual trust built up by the Singh–Talbott talks might have partly been responsible for the American support to India during the Kargil crisis in May–July 1999, because for the first time since the Second World War, the US openly sided with India, or there might have been other reasons involving American foreign policy interests, but American actions heralded the beginning of an engaged relationship that further flourished in the year 2000 and beyond.[17]

The Kargil Crisis and Beyond: Engagement Begins

At this point, it is important to analyse the reasons behind the US support to India during the Kargil crisis. While India–US bilateral dialogues might have acted as catalysts behind America's support, these were certainly not the sole factors. Without lessening the significance of these talks, it should be noted that the US was also holding similar talks with Pakistan to diffuse tension after the nuclear tests in the South Asian region. Therefore, there was little rationale to suggest that America's diplomatic talks with India constituted the sole factor behind the US support. One reason could be America's dissatisfaction with Pakistan's reciprocal nuclear tests. After India's nuclear tests, the US made all possible efforts to stop Pakistan from going nuclear but failed, causing much embarrassment to the Clinton administration. What was of greater significance perhaps was the Pakistani support for the Taliban regime in Afghanistan, which gave tacit approval and territorial space to Osama bin Laden, whose Al-Qaeda outfit had already bombed US embassies in Kenya and Tanzania. Pakistan, being one of the very few countries which recognised the Taliban regime, was obviously the subject of US suspicion and disapproval. It should be remembered that a US missile attack had been launched against Bin Laden over Pakistan's airspace without prior intimation or information. Further, the instability in Pakistani politics with the army castigating the Nawaz Sharif Government for its soft handling of the Kargil crisis, and the fragile nature of Pakistan's democracy, might have also encouraged the US to side with India. Pakistan's instability and its connections with Talibani Afghanistan would have gone against US security interests in the region at that point of time. Moreover, destabilisation of the region as a result of Pakistan's adventurism in Kargil, which could have resulted in a nuclear war between India and Pakistan, was something that would have been negative to US interests. On the other hand, India's long-standing democratic culture and its economic potential and big emerging market, when compared to Pakistan's problems would have appeared more stable and, therefore, attractive to the US policymakers. America's support for India in the Kargil crisis, acted as a motivating factor in the improvement of India–US bilateral relations, as it had the effect in

[17] Chatterjee, n. 4, p. 27.

India of restoring confidence in US policies, and the ball was set rolling for further cooperation between the two countries.

It is in this background that reciprocal visits of President Clinton and Prime Minister Vajpayee to each other's countries took place in the year 2000. Clinton visited India in March 2000. This signalled America's wish to cooperate more with India, as it marked the beginning of a new era in Indo–US relations. Clinton was the first American President to visit India in 22 years. The 'Vision Statement' signed by President Clinton and Prime Minister Vajpayee in New Delhi during the visit was the first ever comprehensive document between the two countries which outlined closer cooperation in the future. Its importance should be underlined because it acted as a guideline for subsequent governments in both countries. Similarly, Vajpayee's reciprocal visit to the US in September 2000 brought the two nations closer.

From a low and mutually suspicious relationship after the Cold War, India and the US embarked on a friendlier relationship from the middle of 1999. It should, however, be mentioned that from 1991 to 1999, there were ups and downs in the relationship, but it never fell too low. While there was not much improvement during the Rao and Deve Gowda periods, relations began to improve from the Gujral period. There was a new low during the initial years of Vajpayee's second premiership, due to Pokhran II and the subsequent American sanctions, but from July 1999, there was a marked improvement in bilateral relations, partly because doors were left open for dialogue and largely due to America's support to India in the Kargil crisis. During Vajpayee's third term as India's Prime Minister (October 1999 to March 2004), India–US relations reached a substantial high. This trend continued thereafter with the two nations scaling new heights in their relations, including the signing of the Civil Nuclear Agreement (CNA).

Closer Cooperation and Evolving Partnership in the New Century

In the new century, the defining moment in bilateral as well as international relations was marked by the 9/11 incidents[18] when US foreign policy took a new turn with the introduction of its 'war on terrorism'. However, India–US relations had been improving even before the 9/11 incidents. George W. Bush, who had been elected to the American presidency in 2000, placed due importance on relations with India and decided to include India in his strategic plans. The Republican Party, which Bush represented, was less obsessed with non-proliferation than the Democrats. As one Indian foreign policy expert has correctly observed, 'The Republican Administration under President Bush is less didactic and intrusive on non-proliferation issues compared to the Clinton administration. This has also helped reduce mutual tensions...'.[19] President Bush signalled his good intentions to India when he lifted the last remnants of the economic sanctions imposed by the

---

[18] On 11 September 2001, in an unprecedented terrorist attacks against the US, planes hijacked by Al-Qaeda terrorists crashed into the World Trade Center in New York killing nearly 10,000 people. Planes flown by the terrorists also hit the Pentagon and the US Defence Headquarters, and a car bomb exploded outside the State Department office in Washington, D.C. For further details, see *The Telegraph*, 12 September 2001.

[19] See Dixit, *India's Foreign Policy*, n. 13, p. 40.

earlier administration without any reference to the CTBT. The sanctions were lifted unconditionally in late 2001 and this act sent signals that the new president was willing to work closely with India. The Deputy Secretary of State of the new administration, Richard Armitage, visited India soon after President Bush took charge. India's Foreign Minister Jaswant Singh was one of the first few statesmen to visit Washington, D.C. after President Bush assumed office. These visits created a 'feel-good' factor in India–US relations that was nurtured by both the countries.

The 11 September 2001 terrorist attacks on the US strengthened the desire of the US to work with India (and also Pakistan) in its strategic plans. There was a transformation in America's geo-strategic thinking as Afghanistan, the base of the Al Qaeda, the prime accused in the 9/11 terrorist attacks, became the central focus of its war against terror. While Pakistan shares a border with Afghanistan, it was one of the three countries which recognised the Taliban regime. India, on the other hand, had never recognised it. While the US needed Pakistan's logistic support, India might have been seen as a second line of defence. India was very quick to condemn the 9/11 attacks, and offered to side with the US in its fight against terrorism.[20] The US took India's help during 'Operation Enduring Freedom' in Afghanistan. The Indian navy escorted and protected high-value American shipping through the Straits of Malacca. India also allowed US flights across its territory, and provided refuelling facilities for American aircraft. American naval ships used Indian ports for rest and refuelling. India's friendly gestures provided the American navy the logistical support required to conduct its trans-oceanic operations. More importantly, India's support to the US in its fight against terrorism had a far-reaching impact on bilateral relations. As one official American document aptly puts it, India's response to the 9/11 attacks galvanised the change in military ties.[21] Close cooperation between the two countries in the defence sector and counter-terrorism areas increased to a great extent after the 9/11 incidents. Regular joint exercises between the army, navy and air force of the two countries took place after 9/11. In 2001, India and the US restarted the Defence Policy Group Dialogues after a lapse of five years. The US administration appeared to understand, for the first time, India's concern for terrorism. This could be ascertained from the measures taken by the Bush administration. The new administration sent positive signals to India by banning terrorist groups like the Lashkar-e-Toiba, condemning the underworld mafia don Dawood Ibrahim who was a suspected mastermind behind terrorist attacks in Mumbai. In 2002, the Bush administration released the National Security Strategy (NSS), a

---

[20] Within hours of the 9/11 attacks, India's Foreign Minister Jaswant Singh issued the following statement: '... the events of the last couple of hours are shocking beyond words.... The present is the moment for all mankind to condemn, in unequivocal terms, this dastardly crime, for the victims are all innocent, and this crime of "terrorism" is against all humanity. India offers to the US its deepest sympathy. We stand with the US, and the rest of the international community in our commitment to defeat terrorism.' See, Ministry of External Affairs, Government of India, 'India condemns terrorist attacks on the US', available at http://www.mea.gov.in.pr110901.html, accessed on 29 December 2003. See, in this context, Embassy of the United States of America, *People, Progress, Partnership: The Transformation of US–India Relations* (New Delhi: Public Affairs Section of the U.S. Embassy), 2004, p. 41.

[21] See in this context, Embassy of the United States of America, *People, Progress, Partnership*, p. 41.

guiding document that focused on the transformation of India–US relations. The NSS noted, 'The United States has undertaken a transformation in its bilateral relationship with India based on a conviction that U.S. interests require a strong relationship with India.'[22] However, it must be noted that in spite of an atmosphere of close cooperation between the two countries, the US was unwilling to include India's fight against terrorism in its own war on terrorism. Due to the geo-strategic advantages of Pakistan, the US relied more on that country to fight the Al-Qaeda in Afghanistan during this period (2001–02). Since the US required Pakistan for its counter-terrorism activities in Afghanistan, it did not wish to antagonise Pakistan by inducting India's fight against terrorism into the American war on terrorism. America, therefore, was following a kind of issue-based diplomacy at the beginning of the new century. For counter-terrorism, it developed closer links with Pakistan; for economic, as also counter-terrorism (because the US requires both Pakistan and India for this purpose), the US endeared India.

The other spheres where India–US bilateral relations gained momentum after 2000 were those of intelligence and law enforcement, science and technology, and healthcare and environment, the guidelines for which had been laid in the 'Vision Statement'. The two countries worked closely on common areas of intelligence and law enforcement like cyber crime, narcotics smuggling, terrorist cells, trafficking in persons, trade fraud, etc. The Diplomatic Security Service (DSS) of the US and Indian law enforcement agencies are currently working together to fight terrorism. The Federal Bureau of Investigation (FBI) of the US and the Central Bureau of Investigation (CBI) of India are also working together to provide intelligence services to each other. The extradition from Dubai of Aftab Ansari, the mastermind of the attack on the American Center in Calcutta, was a success story of the FBI-CBI collaboration since 2001.[23]

In 2004, India and the US announced the 'Next Steps in Strategic Partnership' (NSSP) between the two countries. Under NSSP, India and the US agreed to expand cooperation in three specific areas: civilian nuclear activities, civilian space programmes and high-technology trade. In addition, the two countries agreed to expand their dialogue on missile defence. These areas of cooperation were designed to progress through a series of reciprocal endeavours. Under NSSP, the two countries have worked closely to implement measures to address proliferation concerns and ensure compliance with US export controls. Under NSSP, the US made modifications to American export licensing policies that would encourage cooperation in commercial space programmes and permit exports to power plants at safeguarded nuclear facilities.

---

[22] See, Embassy of the United States of America, 'The National Security Strategy', *Official Text* of the US Government (New Delhi: Public Affairs Section of the Embassy of the United States of America), 2002, p. 3.

[23] In January 2002, terrorists on motorbikes sprayed bullets at the American Center in Kolkata, killing four policemen who were guarding the building, and injuring 14 others. Investigations carried out by the CBI, in collaboration with the FBI, revealed that underworld gangster Aftab Ansari, based in the United Arab Emirates (UAE), had masterminded the attack. The FBI took up the matter with the government of the UAE and arranged Ansari's deportation to India. See, n. 21, p. 51.

India and the US have set up a joint implementation group for achieving the objectives outlined in the NSSP.

Manmohan Singh, the Civil Nuclear Agreement and Beyond

Manmohan Singh, who succeeded Vajpayee as the prime minister of India in June 2004, showed his eagerness to continue close cooperation with the US, which had been heralded by his predecessor, Atal Behari Vajpayee, in the areas of nuclear energy, economic and security issues. In his first meeting with President Bush on 21 September 2004 in New York (during the annual General Assembly Conference), Prime Minister Singh expressed his desire to fully implement the NSSP. He also promised to strengthen all bilateral efforts including the US–India Economic Dialogue and the High Technology Cooperation Group.[24] During his official visit to the US in July 2005, Prime Minister Singh and the American President discussed an 'India–US Civilian Nuclear Cooperation' Deal that would make the two countries true partners in nuclear cooperation, rather than adversaries. It would also bring India into the international non-proliferation mainstream, from which India had remained cut-off due to her refusal to sign the NPT and the CTBT. During the discussion on Civilian Nuclear Cooperation, India agreed to adhere to the following:

(i) identify and separate civilian and military nuclear facilities and programmes and file an IAEA (International Atomic Energy Agency) declaration regarding its civilian facilities;
(ii) place its civilian nuclear facilities under IAEA safeguards voluntarily;
(iii) sign and adhere to an Additional Protocol with respect to civilian nuclear facilities;
(iv) continue its unilateral moratorium on nuclear testing;
(v) work with the US for the conclusion of a multilateral Fissile Material Cut Off Treaty;
(vi) refrain from transfer of nuclear-related technologies; and
(vii) secure nuclear materials and technology through comprehensive export control legislation.

The US assured India that the Bush administration would consult the US Congress to adjust American laws and policies with a view to implement the deal. The US would also consult its friends to adjust norms of international regimes to accommodate India's participation in global nuclear research and trade. It was discussed that the deal would be signed during President Bush's India visit in 2006. The Joint Statement (JS) issued during the Manmohan Singh visit pledged to continue close cooperation in the areas of economy, energy and environment, technology and space, democracy and development, non-proliferation and

[24] See in this connection, US Department of State, 'Joint Statement between the United States of America and India', a *White House Press Release*, New York, 21 September, available at http:// www.us.state.gov/usindiajs/ html, accessed on 30 December 2004.

security, counter-terrorism and health. The JS also promised to strengthen the NSSP between India and the US.

President George W. Bush (Jr) of the US visited India from 1 to 3 March 2006. On 2 March 2006, President Bush and Prime Minister Manmohan Singh signed the Civil Nuclear Deal (CND) in New Delhi, as planned during Singh's US visit in July 2005. According to the deal, India would open up 14 of its 22 (that is 65 per cent) nuclear reactors to IAEA safeguards. India would also decide the status of all future reactors, whether civilian or military. This separation plan, that is, civilian or military reactors would have to be completed by the year 2014. It also stated that India must adhere to the IAEA safeguards agreement as a nuclear weapons state. According to this deal, any new Indian civilian breeder reactors must be placed under IAEA safeguards. In return, India would be given recognition as a *de facto* nuclear weapons state; and nuclear-related supplies to and from India would be accepted by the Nuclear Suppliers Group (NSG). India would also be given access to high technology in space and dual-use technologies which had been denied to India thus far. The CND was converted into a CNA in October 2008 after Parliaments of the two countries approved the deal separately after heated debates. In the long run, the conclusion of the India–US CNA in October 2008 was a remarkable event in the diplomatic history of the two nations. In the final analysis, the Singh Government in India and the Bush (Jr.) Government in the US showed commendable courage in the face of domestic and international criticisms to sign the CNA. This effort also brought out the sincere urge of the two nations to strengthen relationship despite odds. The two governments had to overcome seemingly insurmountable problems to sign the CNA. But both New Delhi and Washington D.C. worked very hard with utmost sincerity to overcome these problems. The two governments, it appeared, did not want to make the nuclear deal a source of embarrassment in their history of bilateralism. The CNA was also the outcome of mutual trust and confidence, missing for a long time in India–US relations, but generated steadily in bilateral relations after the Kargil crisis. The CNA is a big step forward in the strategic partnership between the two nations.

President Barak Obama, who succeeded George W. Bush as the US president in January 2009, has shown keen interest to continue engaged relations with India. He invited Prime Minister Manmohan Singh to the US for bilateral talks in November 2009. During Manmohan Singh's visit to the US, President Obama called India 'indispensable' for the US and assured that close links with India in economic and strategic areas would continue. Earlier, the American president hinted that he was committed to take the CNA to fruition.[25] Singh opined during the visit that US–India relations rested on 'five E's' at the concluding stages of the first decade of the twenty-first century. The 'five E's' that Manmohan Singh highlighted were: economy, energy, environment, education and empowerment. He believed that these five Es would guide future US–India relations along with defence, security and counter-terrorism. Further, President Obama's official

---

[25] Aneek Chatterjee, *International Relations Today: Concepts and Applications* (New Delhi: Pearson Education), 2010, p. 235.

visit to India in November 2010 underscored India's importance to the Obama administration. During his stay in India, the US President reiterated once again America's commitment towards building an economic and strategic partnership with India. In the recent past, the two nations have overcome many crucial hurdles (like India's nuclear tests; American sanctions on India), yet their relationship never remained hostage to these seemingly insurmountable hurdles, but surged forward. The relationship between these two countries has attained considerable strength by this time. Since 2000, American presidential visits to India have tremendously boosted bilateral relationship. In that context, President Obama's visit to India has further strengthened relations between the two nations.

Prime Minister Modi and India's Relations with the US

The momentum in bilateral relations continued after Narendra Modi assumed office as India's prime minister in May 2014. Under the stewardship of Prime Minister Modi and American President Obama, India–US bilateral relations have developed into a 'global strategic partnership', based on shared values and convergence of interests. 'Regular exchange of high-level political visits has provided sustained momentum to bilateral cooperation, while the wide-ranging and ever-expanding dialogue architecture has established a long-term framework for India–US engagement.'[26] The frequency of high-level visits and exchanges between India and the US has gone up significantly in recent times. Prime Minister Modi visited the US from 26 to 30 September 2014. During this visit, the Indian prime minister held meetings with American President Obama, members of the US Congress and political leaders, and interacted with members of President Obama's Cabinet. Modi also reached out to American commerce and industry, the American civil society and think-tanks, and the Indian American community. During this visit, the two sides set up a contact group for advancing the full and timely implementation of the Civil Nuclear Cooperation Agreement, and to resolve pending issues. The group has held many meetings so far, and reached an agreement on the compatibility of India's nuclear liability law with relevant international conventions and creation of an insurance pool drawing experience from best practices to take care of nuclear liability risk.[27] This visit also facilitated the creation of an India–US investment initiative, with a special focus on augmenting FDI, portfolio investment, capital market development and financing of infrastructure. A US–India Infrastructure Collaboration Platform to deploy cutting-edge American technologies to meet India's infrastructure needs was also established during Modi's visit.[28] According to India's MEA, 'The visit also succeeded in reaffirming India's strategic priorities in critical spheres of

---

[26] Ministry of External Affairs, Government of India, 2016, 'India–United States Relations', available at https://www.mea.gov.in/Portal/ForeignRelation/USA_15_01_2016.pdf, accessed on 13 September 2016.

[27] Ibid.

[28] Ibid.

high technology, security, counter-terrorism and defence'.[29] A 'Vision Statement' and a Joint Statement were issued during the visit.

American President Barack Obama visited India from 25 to 27 January 2015 as the Chief Guest at India's Republic Day. During the visit, the two sides issued a 'Delhi Declaration of Friendship' and adopted a Joint Strategic Vision for Asia-Pacific and the Indian Ocean Region (IOR). Both sides elevated the Strategic Dialogue between their foreign ministers to Strategic and Commercial Dialogue of Foreign and Commerce Ministers. The 'Delhi Declaration' announced making '... tangible and enduring the commitment of our two countries to harness the inherent potential of our two democracies, and upgrade the unique nature of our relationship, committing our Governments to work through areas of difference.'[30] Indian Prime Minister Narendra Modi visited the US again from 23 to 28 September 2015. During this visit, he held a bilateral meeting with President Obama, interacted with leaders of business, media, academia, the provincial leaders and the Indian diaspora in the US.

The economic segment of bilateral relationship also witnessed healthy progress in the recent years. According to the MEA sources, direct American investment in India was estimated at about US $28 billion in 2014. Cumulative FDI inflows from the US from April 2000 to September 2014 amounted to about US $13.19 billion constituting nearly 6 per cent of the total FDI into India, making the US the sixth largest source of foreign direct investments into India.[31] In the recent years, growing Indian investments into the US, has been a bright feature of bilateral ties. More than 65 large Indian corporations, including Reliance Industries Limited, Essar, Tata Consultancy Services, Wipro and Piramal have together invested about US $17 billion in the US[32] Indo–US bilateral trade has grown over the years, although this growth rate could have accelerated more. From a modest US $5.6 billion trade in 1990, India–US bilateral trade reached US $62.11 billion in the FY 2015–16. Although this rate of growth appears healthy, bilateral trade has not

Table 8.1: India–US Trade from 2011–12 to 2015–16 (in US $ billion)

Year	*India's Export*	*India's Import*	*Total Trade*
2011–12	34.74	23.45	58.19
2012–13	36.15	25.20	61.35
2013–14	39.14	22.50	61.64
2014–15	42.44	21.82	64.26
2015–16	40.33	21.78	62.11

Source: Export-Import Data Bank, Department of Commerce, Government of India, available at http://www.commerce.nic.in/eidb/iecnt.asp, accessed on 17 September 2016.

[29] Ministry of External Affairs, Government of India, *Annual Report: 2014–15* (New Delhi: Government of India), 2015, p. 114.

[30] Office of the Press Secretary, The White House, *India–U.S. Delhi Declaration of Friendship*, available at https://www.whitehouse.gov/the-press-office/2015/01/25/india-us-delhi-declaration-friendship, accessed on 18 September 2016.

[31] Ministry of External Affairs, 'India–United States Relations', n. 26.

[32] Ibid.

progressed much during the last five fiscals. Table 8.1 presented above, shows bilateral trade figures during the last five financial years.

Table 8.1 shows that bilateral trade has gone down from $ 64.26 billion in the FY 2014–15 to $62.11 billion in 2015–16. Although bilateral trade in FY 2015–16 was higher than FYs 2011–12, 2012–13 and 2013–14, it fell short compared to the previous FY (2014–15). Marginal rise and fall in trade figures are routine in bilateral relations. But both India and the US must give due priority to this sector in order to achieve a strong and healthy relationship.

RECOMMENDATIONS FOR THE FUTURE

India–US relations, which got strengthened from the middle of 1999, have immense potential to get augmented further in the future. The following recommendations may help both the countries to take their relations to further heights to take up the challenges of the future. To begin with economy, the two-way trade volume is not very high at this moment. Therefore, the first course of action would be to enhance bilateral trade to US $200 billion by 2025. Allow more American and Indian private business to operate in the other land. This could see a significant rise in FDI in both the countries. Settle the issue of 'outsourcing' with mutual dialogue and consent, rather than harsh unilateral actions. Outsourcing has the potential to generate two-way benefits, and should be seen by the US in that context.[33] Currently, India is among the 20 largest trade partner of the US. In the near future, India must be among the 10 largest trade partners of the US, and plan meticulously to move into the group of top five trade partners of the US within a targeted period of say, 2025. India is pressing the US to start negotiations for a bilateral investment treaty (BIT). A BIT is frequently seen as the first step in the possible progress towards a free trade agreement (FTA). In addition, a BIT between India and the US might foster greater FDI flows between the two nations. At present 6 per cent of the total FDI inflow to India comes from the US.[34] This is not a very satisfactory figure for India which has the second largest market (in terms of population) in the world and the presence of a strong and growing middle class. A BIT may help augment American FDI inflow to India. It will also brighten the possibility of Indian investments in the American market, an area not well addressed in the past, but very crucial for India to fulfil its big power ambitions. After BIT, the two countries must try to achieve the FTA as quickly as possible. Talks for a BIT and FTA have been going on for a considerable period of time, without concrete results. America's cautious approach in this regard deferred the signing of the BIT. Further delays in achieving these mechanisms (BIT, FTA) will only manifest lack of trust and schism in bilateral relations.

---

[33] See, William S. Cohen, 'Obama and the Politics of Outsourcing', *The Wall Street Journal*, New York, 12 October 2010.

[34] Ministry of Commerce, Govt. of India (2016), source of Table 8.1.

The recommendations for strengthening bilateral security relations are as follows:

(i) achieve the CNA in its totality;

(ii) engage more in knowledge sharing for counter terrorism purposes;

(iii) bring trust in bilateralism to augment technology transfers; and

(iv) implement fully earlier security instruments like the NSSP. In this context, it is heartening to note that India and the US have completed a few good defence deals recently. In 2008, Washington D.C. and New Delhi finalised a deal to send to India six C-130J Hercules military transport aircraft (along with related equipment, training, and services). The deal, which represented the largest-ever US defense sale to India to date, is worth nearly US $1 billion to the manufacturer, Maryland-based Lockheed Martin. In 2009, New Delhi signed a US $2.1 billion deal to purchase eight P-8I maritime surveillance aircraft from Illinois-based Boeing. These aircraft, slated for delivery in 2013, also provide anti-submarine warfare capabilities, and their sale set a new record as the largest-ever US arms transfer to India. Such deals, which demonstrate mutual trust and confidence, should be concluded more in the future for a strong strategic partnership. Another mega defence deal, the US $4.1 billion contract (with the US) for 10 C-17 Globemaster-III giant strategic airlift aircraft was signed in May 2011.[35] By 2015, the aggregate worth of defence acquisition from the US has crossed over US $13 billion.[36] India and the US have launched a Defence Technology and Trade Initiative (DTTI) aimed at simplifying technology transfer policies and exploring possibilities of co-development and co-production. During President Obama's visit to India in January 2015, the two sides agreed to start cooperation on four DTTI pathfinder projects and two pathfinder initiatives, which are currently at various stages of execution.[37] The Defence Framework Agreement between India and the US was updated and renewed for another 10 years in June 2015. Such initiatives in the defence area manifest confidence and mutual trust in bilateral relations.

With converging national interests, political relations will be closer. An indication of this increasingly closer political relationship has been provided through President Obama's support for India's inclusion into the Security Council as a permanent member, a stand the Americans hesitated to openly announce for long. After the American president, the French president also supported India's demand for a permanent membership in the SC.[38] Although the reform of the United Nations Organization (UNO) is not an easy task, and will make many headaches and

---

[35] See, *The Times of India*, 'India Ready to Clear $4.1 bn US Def Deal', 13 May 2011.

[36] Ministry of External Affairs, 'India–United States Relations', n. 26.

[37] Ibid.

[38] See *The Indian Express*, 'Sarkozy Backs India's Bid for Permanent UNSC Seat', 5 December 2010.

heart burns, besides complex procedures for the revision of the UN Charter[39], India seems to be getting the support of some present permanent members, with America taking the lead. After American and French support, British or Russian endorsements of India's demand may not be unexpected. A reluctant China may still veto the proposal, but that may help bring India and the US further closer on the issue. The two nations may also join hands to promote democracy in the world, if their national interests require. With the erosion of anti-Americanism in India, Indian foreign policy must not hesitate to strongly support America on different international issues, not directly affecting India's national interests. This would not only bring the two countries closer, but would also instil trust and confidence in each other. If the two countries show sincerity and eagerness to follow these not so difficult but important steps, bilateral relationship has the potential to turn into a meaningful partnership.

Donald John Trump of the Republican Party was elected as the 45th President of America. He assumed office of the President of the United States on 20 January 2017. With a new president in office in the US, bilateral relations with India provides many possibilities. Although the Trump administration is not yet (as of May 2017) explicit about its policies on India, there are hopes and apprehensions among policy analysts in India. During his election campaign, Trump had called himself a 'big fan of India and promised to stand shoulder to shoulder with India in sharing intelligence and keeping our people safe mutually'.[40] He also praised Indian Prime Minister Narendra Modi for his decisive leadership and ability to move fast, bypassing the lethargic bureaucracy.[41] Further, the new US Defense Secretary, James Mattis stressed on the need for closer strategic partnership with India.[42] If all these words raised hopes in India about a positive and cordial US administration under President Donald Trump, a few other moves of the new administration generated apprehensions in India. Trump's plan to curb the 'misuse' of H1B visa, the most sought-after entry permit (to the US) by Indian professionals, has already aroused negative vibes in India. The plan was aimed at providing more jobs to the Americans, a promise Trump had made during his election campaign. If implemented, it might reduce the chances of many Indians getting jobs in the US. Further, the new American president's desire to mediate in the Kashmir problem goes against official Indian position of no third party mediation in Kashmir. This 'desire' would not go well with New Delhi. With Trump as president, a new balance of power might also emerge in the South Asian region, where the US, India, Pakistan, Russia and China are already major actors. Trump's diplomacy might make this balance favourable to either India or Pakistan.

---

[39] See in this context, Aneek Chatterjee, 'The UN at Sixty Three: Problems and Prospects of Reforming a Veteran', *Journal of Management and Social Sciences*, 5 (1): 2009, pp. 22–29.

[40] See in this connection, *First Post*, 12 May 2017, [on line web] http://www.firstpost.com/politics/donald-trump-is-americas-problem-but-indias-opportunity-3239172.html; accessed on 13 May 2017).

[41] Ibid.

[42] Ibid.

Currently, the US shares a strong strategic relationship with India. It would not be possible for the new American president to undermine this strategic partnership, keeping in view America's national interests. An economically strong India provides good opportunities for American business. Politically, India might be of help to the US to counterbalance China in Asia. US–Russia friendship would not harm Indian interests in the long run. The Trump administration has already blamed Pakistan for '... the deterioration of bilateral relations between New Delhi and Islamabad'.[43] Daniel Coats, Director of National Intelligence of the US, in a Report titled 'World Wide Threat Assessment of the U.S. Intelligence Community', has put the blame on Pakistan. The report was presented to the US Senate by Coats and his team.[44] This report manifests Trump administration's intention to take India into confidence. However, these are only early signs. A strong India–US relationship would require mutual trust, adjustment and respect for each other's sensibilities. It appears that the US and India are keen to forge closer relations. President Donald Trump and Prime Minister Narendra Modi are willing to take bilateral relations to new heights.

---

[43] See in this connection, *India Today News*, 12 May 2017, available at http://indiatoday.intoday.in/story/united-states-blames-pakistan-for-deteriorating-indo-pak-ties/1/951855.html, accessed on 13 May 2017.

[44] Ibid.

9

INDIA AND CHINA

Competitors or Adversaries?

HIGHLIGHTS

- Introduction: Early Warmth to Animosity
- Quest for Normalcy in Relations (1988–2000)
- Political Relations in the New Century
- Economic Relations
- Security and Cultural Relations
- Conclusion: Perception Problems

INTRODUCTION: EARLY WARMTH TO ANIMOSITY

The Indian state and the new socialist state of China began their journey almost simultaneously,— India as an independent nation in 1947, and China as the first socialist country in Asia in 1949. Although these two neighbours cherish age-old civilisations, their journey to modern statehood began after the Second World War, almost at the same time. Initially the two big Asian neighbours shared a cordial relationship between them. Jawaharlal Nehru, the first prime minister of India, welcomed the creation of a socialist China as a victory in the struggle against imperialism and colonialism. Nehru's socialist leanings encouraged him to establish close connections with China. China reciprocated by sending its leader Zhou Enlai to India, and the two countries declared that their friendship would be guided by the 'Panchsheel' (five principles), which essentially called for mutual respect to each other's sovereignty, territorial integrity and the policy of non-interference.[1] In 1955, China joined the conference of Afro–Asian nations in Bandung, and supported the endeavour of these Afro–Asian nations for non-alignment, in a sharply divided bipolar world perpetuated by the Cold War. India also hailed the Chinese stance in Bandung.

---

[1] Aneek Chatterjee, *International Relations Today: Concepts and Applications* (New Delhi: Pearson), 2010, p. 243.

However, the warmth did not last long. By the late 1950s, differences between the two nations emerged over border issues, and Tibet's accession to China. Both China and India accused each other of illegal occupation of territory. China further alleged that India was instigating the separatist Tibetans by giving shelter to the Dalai Lama, the Tibetan religious leader. From 1957, border skirmishes between the armies of the two nations began. The two nations went to a war in 1962 in which China won convincingly. China's victory in the 1962 War with India helped to fulfil, to some extent, a few political designs of China. These were:

(i) To teach India a lesson on the issue of Tibet
(ii) To nullify the Indian position on the border issue
(iii) To scuttle India's desire for leadership of the Third World and
(iv) To harm Nehru's image as a global leader.[2]

After the 1962 War, diplomatic relations were cut off, and the two nations distanced themselves from each other. As a consequence, during the 1960s and the 1970s, Sino–Indian relations remained very low. Although ambassadorial relations between the two nations were restored in 1979 after the visit of the Indian foreign minister, Atal Behari Vajpayee to China in that year, bilateral relations did not improve much after Vajpayee's visit to China, the first top-level visit by any leader of the two countries since the 1962 War.

However, Vajpayee's 1979 visit did help to break some ice. In 1981, China's Foreign Minister Huang Hua visited India. It was decided during Hua's visit that China and India would resume talks to resolve border problems. Accordingly, seven rounds of talks were held between the two countries from 1981 to 1987 in New Delhi and Beijing. But due to the inflexible attitude of both nations the talks failed. As a consequence, Sino–Indian relations did not improve till the late 1980s. After the Indian Prime Minister Rajiv Gandhi's China visit in 1988, bilateral relations started to get back to normalcy. It was decided during Rajiv's visit to China that the two nations would form 'Joint Working Groups' (JWG) to continue dialogues to resolve outstanding border issues. The annual meeting of the JWG would take place alternately in the capital cities of the two nations.

QUEST FOR NORMALCY IN RELATIONS (1988–2000)

The JWG were successful in reducing tensions in the border areas. For instance, after an agreement reached in the JWG meeting in 1993, the two countries reduced troops in the border areas. As a result, tensions subsided along the 4,000-km border between the two countries. After the JWG meeting in 1996, China and India announced a series of Confidence Building Measures (CBMs) to restore peace in the border areas. Further in the Eleventh JWG meeting in 1999, the two

[2] Ibid.

nations agreed to work for regional peace and security, and reduction of nuclear weapons, alongside border problems. The JWG met 14 times in Beijing and New Delhi till 2002, and this proved to be a very useful and successful mechanism for bilateral talks. Apart from the creation of the JWG, the two nations signed important agreements on cooperation in civil aviation, exchange of technology and cultural delegations.[3] Rajiv's visit to China helped to normalise relations between the two Asian giants. It also paved the way for further top-level reciprocal visits by the leaders of the two countries.

Chinese Premier Li Peng visited New Delhi in December 1991. Peng was the first Chinese prime minister to visit India in 37 years after Zhou Enlai visited India in 1954. It was also the first top-level visit from China after the Cold War. Three important agreements were signed during Peng's visit: resuming border trade; cooperation in space research; and opening of consulate offices in Mumbai and Shanghai. Peng's visit was hailed as a success by the media in the two countries.[4] Indian Prime Minister Narasimha Rao visited China in 1993. During his visit, Rao and the Chinese leaders agreed to reduce tension and restore peace along the Line of Actual Control (LAC). An expert committee comprising diplomats and military personnel from the two countries was also formed to assist the JWG in bilateral talks. In 1992, the President of India, R. Venkataraman visited China, while Indian Vice President, K. R. Narayanan paid an official visit to China in 1994.[5] From the Chinese side, Li Ruihan, a top leader of the Chinese Communist Party (CCP) visited India in 1993, and the Chairman of the National Peoples' Congress (NPC), Qiao Shi visited India in 1995. All these reciprocal visits helped improve Sino–Indian relations after the Cold War.[6]

Chinese President Jiang Zemin paid a very successful visit to India in 1996. Zemin's was the first-ever visit to India by a Chinese President. Four important agreements were signed between the two countries during Zemin's visit. These were:

(i) Agreement on CBMs in the military along the LAC
(ii) Agreement concerning the maintenance of the consulate office of India in the Hong Kong Special Administrative Region in the People's Republic of China (PRC)
(iii) Agreement on cooperation for combating illicit trafficking in narcotic drugs and psychotropic substances and other crimes; and
(iv) Agreement between the two countries on maritime support.

The visit initiated a process of cooperation between the two countries in new and newer areas. In April 1998, General Fu Quanyon, Chief of the Chinese army, came to India and met

[3] Ibid., p. 244.
[4] Ibid.
[5] Ibid.
[6] Ibid.

senior Indian leaders, which included Prime Minister Vajpayee to discuss defence and security issues concerning the two nations. India's Foreign Minister Jaswant Singh visited China in June 1999 to discuss bilateral issues.[7] So there was a spurt of high-level visits between India and China throughout the 1990s. The two neighbours shed many of their differences in this decade, and endeavoured to forge an amicable relationship between them. The effort continued into the new century with Indian President K. R. Narayanan's official visit to China in May 2000, and Chairman of the Standing Committee of the National People's Congress (NPC), Li Peng's visit to India in January 2001.[8]

POLITICAL RELATIONS IN THE NEW CENTURY

Two-way high-level visits continued showing improvements in bilateral relations, and Zhu Rongji, the Chinese premier came to India in January 2002. Agreements on trade, science and technology and environment were signed during Rongji's visit. In June 2003, Vajpayee visited China again, this time as the prime minister of India. Vajpayee met President Hu Jintao, Premier Wen Jiabao and other Chinese leaders during his stay in China. The two nations agreed to strengthen mechanisms for bilateral cooperation and decided to create the Joint Study Group (JSG) consisting of experts from the two nations to explore trade and business opportunities. It was also decided during Vajpayee's visit that the defence ministers of China and India would exchange regular visits to monitor security issues including border problems.

Wen Jiabao paid a reciprocal visit to India in April 2005 and met Prime Minister Manmohan Singh and other Indian leaders. During Wen's visit, the two sides issued a Joint Statement (JS) establishing a Strategic and Cooperative Partnership for Peace and Prosperity. Chinese President Hu Jintao visited India in November 2006. India and China issued a joint declaration outlining a ten-point strategy to intensify cooperation in all areas and to give greater strength to India–China Strategic and Cooperative Partnership. Indian Prime Minister Manmohan Singh visited China in January 2008. A joint document entitled 'A Shared Vision for the 21st Century of the Republic of India and the People's Republic of China' was issued during the visit, highlighting common positions on various international and bilateral issues. Prime Minister Singh visited China again in October 2008 to participate in the 7th Asia–Europe Summit held in Beijing on 24–25 October. India and China have stepped up functional cooperation in all areas. The two foreign ministries have instituted dialogue mechanisms on issues relating to counter-terrorism, policy planning and security, besides strategic dialogue and regular consultations. There are also close cooperation in areas as diverse as water resources, judiciary, science and technology, audit, personnel, finance, labour, etc.[9] India and China are now also parts of important multilateral groupings like the

---

[7] Ibid.

[8] Ibid.

[9] Ministry of External Affairs, Government of India, available at http://www.meaindia.nic.in/, accessed on 9 March 2009.

BRICS (Brazil, Russia, India, China and South Africa) and BASIC (Brazil, South Africa, India, China), which try to protect the interests of group members in other international political, economic, environmental or trade fora. This reflects the desire of the two nations to work more closely in bilateral and multilateral mechanisms.

The President of India, Pratibha Patil paid a state visit to China from 26–31 May 2010. In Beijing, she held talks with Chinese President Hu Jintao and met with National Peoples' Congress Chairman Wu Bangguo and Premier Wen Jiabao. The Indian President, along with Chinese Vice President Xi Jinping, attended the reception to mark the 60th anniversary of diplomatic relations between the two nations. She visited Luoyang to inaugurate the Indian-style Buddhist Temple which was dedicated as a gift from India to the people of China. In Shanghai, she visited the Indian and the Chinese pavilion at the Shanghai EXPO and also had a meeting with Shanghai Communist Party Secretary, Yu Zhengsheng. A bust of Nobel laureate Rabindranath Tagore was also inaugurated by the Indian president.

Chinese Premier Wen Jiabao visited India between 15 and 17 December 2010. During his visit, Premier Wen met Indian President Patil, Prime Minister Manmohan Singh, Vice President Hamid Ansari, Sonia Gandhi, Chairperson of the United Progressive Alliance (UPA) and the Leader of the Opposition, Sushma Swaraj. Premier Wen also interacted with children at the Tagore International School; addressed India–China business cooperation summit; delivered a lecture at the Indian Council of World Affairs (ICWA); and attended the closing ceremony of the Festival of China in India along with the Indian prime minister. Six agreements were signed during the visit of Wen Jiabao. These agreements covered areas like cultural exchange, green technologies, media exchanges, hydrological data and banking. During the visit, a bilateral trade target of US $100 billion was set to be reached by 2015. A Strategic Economic Dialogue and a CEO Forum were established; and 2011 was declared as 'Year of India-China Exchange'. The establishment of hotline between the Indian prime minister and the Chinese premier, a mechanism of annual foreign ministers meeting and a regular high-level exchange mechanism were also announced.

In the year 2011, bilateral relations continued to remain steady. This was manifested through several top-level visits by leaders of the two countries. Indian Prime Minister Manmohan Singh visited Sanya from 12–15 April to participate in the BRICS Summit. On the sidelines, the prime minister also had a bilateral meeting with Chinese President Hu Jintao. The chief ministers of Bihar, Madhya Pradesh and Gujarat visited China in June, September and November respectively. Similarly, chairman of Xinjiang Autonomous Region and Party Secretary of Gansu also visited India as part of the 'MEA-ILD Exchange' and 'Distinguished Visitors Programme of MEA'. One of the highlights of the 'Year of Exchanges' was the visit of a youth delegation to China, which was increased from 100 to 500. Premier Wen Jiabao met and addressed the Indian youth. Several ministerial and official visits to China were made to participate in the activities of the BRICS. For the first time, India–China consultations on issues pertaining to the UNSC were held in March 2011. The leaders of the two countries have maintained regular contacts and have met frequently during international gatherings and meetings of multilateral fora in the recent past.[10]

The year 2012 was declared as the 'Year of India–China Friendship and Cooperation'. In this year, high-level official visits between India and China continued unabated. In early February 2012, the Indian Foreign Minister, Salman Khurshid visited China. He met with important Chinese leaders and discussed bilateral issues. About his trip, Khurshid told the media: 'On the bilateral front, we have discussed our growing trade relationship. We are confident in our reaching the goal of US $100 billion by 2015. I have highlighted the need for initiating measures to balance our trade relations. The prowess of Indian companies in software and pharmaceuticals is well known. I expressed the hope that market access will be provided for them to grow in China. Similarly, investment from China in the infrastructure sector in India would be welcome. We also reviewed the "outstanding" issues in our bilateral relations and agreed that while we work to resolve them, we should not let them adversely affect our growing cooperation in other areas. Specifically, we have agreed that the newly established working mechanism for consultation and coordination in border affairs will have its first meeting at an early date.'[11] Chinese Foreign Minister, Yang Jiechi visited New Delhi in late February 2012 on an official trip and met with top Indian leaders. After his talks with Prime Minister Manmohan Singh, Jiechi told the media: '... Under the current international and regional situation, China and India enjoy broad prospects for growth of bilateral ties. 2012 is an important year for the two countries to build on the past progress and usher in a better future. The two sides have agreed on programmes of exchanges and cooperation, which will increase friendship between the two peoples, advance exchanges and cooperation in various fields and send a positive signal about the growth of the relationship. The two sides have agreed to maintain high-level exchanges and contacts, strengthen diplomatic consultation and dialogue as well as exchanges between parties, legislatures and the militaries to enhance strategic and political mutual trust...'.[12] Singh sounded very optimistic about bilateral relations. After his meeting with the visiting Chinese Foreign Minister, Singh said, 'India–China relationship is one of the most important bilateral ties in the world. There is enough space in the world for India and China to grow and work together. The relationship has tremendous potential. The Indian government is firmly committed to its strategic and cooperative partnership with China and stands ready to make every effort to advance cooperation in all fields.'[13]

---

[10] Ministry of External Affairs, Government of India, 'India–China Bilateral Relations', available at http://www.mea.gov.in/Portal/ForeignRelation/China-January-2012.pdf, accessed on 3 May 2013.

[11] Ministry of External Affairs, Government of India, 'Opening Remarks by EAM at Media Interaction in Beijing', available at http://mea.gov.in/outoging-visit-, detail.htm?18282/Opening+remarks+by+EAM+at+media+interaction+in+Beijing, accessed on 5 May 2013.

[12] Ministry of Foreign Affairs of the People's Republic of China, 'Indian Prime Minister Manmohan Singh Meets with Visiting Chinese Foreign Minister Yang Jiechi', available at http://www.fmprc.gov.cn/eng/zxxx/t910469.htm, accessed on 5 May 2013.

[13] Ibid.

Chinese President Hu Jintao visited New Delhi for the BRICS Summit in late March 2012. On the sidelines of the BRICS Summit, the Chinese president met senior Indian leaders and discussed bilateral issues. During his meeting with the Indian prime minister, the two leaders discussed about enhancing economic, cultural and people-to-people exchanges. The Indian prime minister raised the issue of trade imbalance with China. Although the overall volume of bilateral trade remained satisfactory, Indian imports from China exceeded its export to China. Hu Jintao promised that he would look into the matter.

General Liang Guanglie, Chinese defence minister and member of the Central Military Commission, visited India from 2–6 September 2012. It was the first visit of a Chinese military general to India in eight years. General Liang Guanglie called on the Indian prime minister and defence minister. The Indian and Chinese defence ministers had an extensive exchange of views on defence and military exchanges and cooperation between the two countries. They also discussed the regional security situation and international issues of common interest and concern. The two defence ministers agreed to work together to enhance mutual trust in the field of security and continue to maintain peace and tranquillity in the India–China border areas.[14] Other important high-level visits that took place from India to China in the year 2012 were the ones by Vice Admiral Anil Chopra, Flag Officer Commanding in Chief Eastern Naval Command, during the port call by the naval ships *INS Shivalik*, *INS Rana*, *INS Shakti* and *INS Karmuk* to Shanghai in June 2012, visit by the National Defence College (NDC) delegation led by Air Marshal P. K. Roy in September 2012, visit by an Indian multicommand delegation led by Major General A. L. Chavan to Beijing and Chengdu military region in July 2012 and visits by Defence Staff Services College delegation and Indian Air Force (IAF) delegation in September 2012. The important visits from China to India included port call by PLAN Ship Zhenghe to Kochi in June 2012, visits by NDU delegation under Major General Hong Xiaodong and Nanjing Army Command College delegation led by Major General Geng Weidong and visit by six-member delegation led by Major General Yuan Jichang for DEFEXPO 2012.[15] The Chinese Foreign Minister, Wang Yi visited New Delhi between 8 and 9 June 2014 in the capacity of Special Envoy to the president of China. The visit was intended to establish contact with the new Government of India (GoI) and to provide further momentum to the India–China Strategic and Cooperative Partnership. Xi Jinping, President of the People's Republic of China, paid a state visit to India from 17–19 September 2014. During the visit, President Xi Jinping met the Indian President, Pranab Mukherjee and held talks with Prime Minister Narendra Modi. During the visit of the Chinese president, a total of 16 agreements were signed between the two nations.[16] All these visits manifested the fact that India and China were eager to maintain

[14] Embassy of India, Beijing, 'India–China Bilateral Defence Cooperation in 2012'; available at http://www.indianembassy.org.cn/DynamicContent.aspx?MenuId=5&SubMenuId=0, accessed on 5 May 2013.

[15] Ibid.

[16] Ministry of External Affairs, Government of India, *Annual Report: 2014–15* (New Delhi: Government of India), 2015, p. 9.

close contacts at the political level, and wanted to engage each other in different areas of bilateral cooperation. India–China political relations got enhanced and strengthened by various mechanisms. Close and regular interactions between strategic and foreign policy think-tanks have been taking place in the recent past. However, several unresolved issues between the two nations persisted.

Indian Prime Minister Narendra Modi paid a three-day official visit to China from 14 to 16 May 2015. The visit was undertaken at a time when India–China relationship assumed a 'complex' character with the two Asian giants looking at each other with suspicion. A few key irritants affecting ties were a decades-old unresolved border problem and a mounting trade deficit that threatened to cross US $40 billion in 2015. Added to this was the cordial friendship between China and Pakistan and China's recent announcement of US $46 billion in investments in an economic corridor through Pakistan and a section of disputed Kashmir areas, which enhanced Indian suspicion. In the backdrop of these issues, Modi's visit aroused considerable diplomatic and academic interests. During the visit, the two sides have come up with some non-controversial, yet important pacts to boost bilateral relations. These agreements covered areas from business to security, to the issue of trade deficit and e-visa. The visit helped in reducing trust deficit through inking these important pacts concerning mutual interests and concerns.

On the third and final day of Indian prime minister's visit, Chinese and Indian firms signed 21 agreements worth more than US $22 billion in deals in areas ranging from telecom, steel, solar energy and films. The two countries also decided to set up a hotline between the military headquarters of the two countries. To build trust between the two militaries, China's vice chairman of the Central Military Commission will visit India and India's defence minister will visit China regularly. There will also be an increase in the number of meetings between border personnel and commanders at all sectors of the India–China border areas. Exchange of naval visits as well as joint counterterrorism training has also been suggested.

Further, a Task Force will look at ways to reduce the trade deficit that was US $38 billion in 2013–14 and expected to be in the range of US $40 billion–US $45 billion in 2015–16 financial year (FY). The task force will also examine India's complaints regarding problems faced by Indian information technology (IT) and pharmaceutical companies to enter the Chinese market. It will also look into Chinese complaints about problems faced by the Chinese firms to invest in India. In addition to creating this task force, two dozens of other agreements were signed during Modi's visit to China. Cooperation in areas like mining and minerals, tourism, ocean studies, railways and broadcasting was emphasised in these agreements. Further, Chennai in India and Chengdu in China were declared sister cities. Indian Prime Minister Narendra Modi announced during the visit that India had decided to provide electronic visa on arrival facility to Chinese nationals visiting India. Modi's gesture was aimed at increasing the traffic flow between the two countries. It should be noted in this context that years 2015 and 2016 have been marked as 'Visit India' and 'Visit China' respectively, and nationals of both countries would be willing to visit the other land.

The Brookings Institution, a leading global think-tank, hailed Modi for his frank and candid talks on bilateral issues during the May 2015 visit to China. According to a report of the Institution, the Indian prime minister '... was definitely more candid in his remarks about Indian concerns than is normal for Indian leaders during China–India summits. While senior Indian policymakers often downplay the bilateral differences during visits (incoming and outgoing) and focus more on cooperative elements, in two speeches and in the joint statement released, Modi mentioned them repeatedly. He talked about the relationship being "complex", as well as about issues that "trouble smooth development of our relations" and held back the relationship. He urged China to think strategically (and long-term) and "reconsider its approach" on various issues. First and foremost: its approach toward the border, but also visas and trans-border rivers, as well as the region (read China's relations with Pakistan among others).'[17] Further, China's approach on economic issues was also raised by the Indian prime minister when he pointed out that the partnership was not sustainable if Indian industry did not get better access to the Chinese market. The JS issued during the visit acknowledged that the 'level of the trade imbalance (in China's favor) was not sustainable either. Modi also made clear that India wants China's support for a greater role in international institutions. He specifically highlighted that China's support for a permanent seat for India at the U.N. Security Council (UNSC) and Indian membership of export control regimes would be helpful to the relationship.'[18]

The Indian President, Pranab Mukherjee embarked on a four-day visit to China on 27 May 2016. The visit in effect was divided into two parts: the first, in Guangzhou, highlighting the significance of business and cultural linkages, and the second at Beijing to meet top Chinese leaders, and to boost people-to-people interaction. During the visit, discussions on regional as well as global issues ranging from economic ties to terrorism and global security, took place between leaders of two nations. The Indian president was accompanied by an academic delegation with a view to establish closer contacts between universities and research institutions of both the nations. Regarding the economic ties between the two nations, Mukherjee explicitly spoke about the trade imbalance between China and India. However, the Indian president also opined that there was great potential for economic and commercial cooperation between the two nations. The Chinese President, Xi Jinping promised 'practical cooperation' in the development of new energy, railways and industrial zones, and also offered space assistance to India. These visits by top statesmen of the two countries helped India and China to engage in more meaningful ways.

ECONOMIC RELATIONS

An important and somewhat controversial area in India–China relations is the increasing trade volume between the two countries. India–China bilateral trade, which was as low as US $2.92 billion

---

[17] Tanvi Madan, 'Modi's Trip to China: 6 Quick Takeaways', Brookings Institution, available at https://www.brookings.edu/opinions/modis-trip-to-china-6-quick-takeaways, accessed on 29 September 2016.

[18] Ibid.

in 2000 reached US $72.34 billion till March 2015, making China India's largest goods trading partner. China has emerged as a leading trade partner of India in the recent times. The two countries signed the Most Favoured Nation (MFN) Agreement in 1984. The MFN has helped in enhancing trade between the two nations. However, a large trade deficit exists between the two nations. In this connection, it would be fruitful to look at the volume of India–China trade in the recent years. Table 9.1 highlights bilateral trade since 2007–08 financial year:

Table 9.1: India–China Trade in Recent Years (in US$ billion)

Year	*India's Export*	*India's Import*	*Total Trade*
2007–08	10.87	27.14	38.01
2008–09	9.35	32.50	41.85
2009–10	11.61	30.82	42.43
2010–11	15.48	43.48	58.96
2011–12	18.08	55.31	73.39
2012–13	13.54	52.24	65.78
2013–14	14.82	51.03	65.85
2014–15	11.93	60.41	72.34
2015–16	9.01	61.70	70.71

Source: Department of Commerce, Government of India, Export-Import Data Bank, available at http://commerce.nic.in/eidb/iecnt.asp, accessed on 5 September 2016.

Table 9.1 reveals that bilateral trade volume has gone up significantly since 2007–08, although during the last fiscal (2015–16), total trade has dropped a bit. But the issue of more concern refers to the fact that two-way trade has been suffering from negative trade balance for India. In all seven financial years shown in Table 9.1, India's imports from China remained almost three to seven times more than India's exports to China. This gap must be reduced to achieve a balanced trade between the two countries, because the current trade pattern remains favourable to China. As noted earlier, in the 'Political Relations' section, dialogues are on at the diplomatic level to reduce this gap in bilateral trade. However, growing trade volume indicates that the two Asian giants have engaged each other more in the recent times.

There are several institutional mechanisms for India's economic and commercial engagement with China. India–China Joint Economic Group (JEG) on Economic Relations and Trade, Science and Technology is a ministerial-level dialogue mechanism established in 1988 during the visit of former Indian Prime Minister Rajiv Gandhi to China. A Joint Study Group (JSG) was set up after former Indian Prime Minister Vajpayee's visit to China in June 2003 to examine the potential complementarities between the two countries in expanded trade and economic cooperation. As per its recommendation, a Joint Task Force (JTF) was set up to study the feasibility of an India–China Regional Trading Arrangement. The JTF Report was completed in October 2007. There are also JWGs on Trade, Agriculture and Energy. During Chinese Prime

Minister Wen Jiabao's visit to India in December 2010, India and China agreed to set up the Strategic Economic Dialogue (SED) mechanism. The SED is a forum for both sides to discuss strategic macro-economic issues impacting both nations as a result of the changing international economic and financial scenario. The first India–China SED took place in Beijing from 26–27 September 2011.[19]

Indian and Chinese investments in each other's country have also been growing over the years. From the year 2000, till 2007, Chinese investment in India was US $16 million. Till October 2011, Chinese investments to India rose to US $298.75 million. On the other hand, Indian investment in China till 2007 was US $34 million. This amount increased to US $432.98 million till October 2011. Several Indian companies and banks are operating in the Chinese soil. These include, among others, Dr Reddy's Laboratories, Aurobindo Pharma, Matrix Pharma, NIIT, Bharat Forge, Infosys, TCS, APTECH, Wipro, Mahindra Satyam, Essel Packaging, Suzlon Energy, Reliance Industries, SUNDARAM Fasteners, Mahindra & Mahindra, TATA Sons, Binani Cements, etc. In the field of banking, 10 Indian banks have set up operations in China.[20] On the other hand, '... close to 100 Chinese companies have established offices or operations in India. Many large Chinese state-owned companies in the field of machinery and infrastructure construction have won projects in India and have opened project offices in India. These include Sinosteel, Shougang International, Baoshan Iron & Steel Ltd, Sany Heavy Industry Ltd, Chongqing Lifan Industry Ltd, China Dongfang International, Sino Hydro Corporation, etc. Many Chinese electronic, IT and hardware manufacturing companies also have operations in India. These include Huawei Technologies, ZTE, TCL, Haier, etc. A large number of Chinese companies are involved in EPC projects in the Power Sector. These include Shanghai Electric, Harbin Electric, Dongfang Electric, Shenyang Electric, etc. Chinese automobile major Beijing Automotive Industry Corporation (BAIC) has recently announced plans to invest US$ 250 million in an auto plant in Pune.'[21]

At present, India and China are engaged in Financial Dialogue in accordance with the Memorandum of Understanding (MoU) signed during Chinese Prime Minister Wen Jiabao's visit to India in April 2005. The financial dialogue began in the year 2006 and continued since then. So far, the five financial dialogues have been held between the two countries in April 2006, December 2007, January 2009, September 2010 and November 2011 respectively. The Fifth India–China Financial Dialogue took place in New Delhi on 8 November 2011. A JS was signed and released at the end of the dialogue. During the dialogue, '... both sides exchanged views on the global macro economic situation and policy responses, with specific reference to current risks to the global economy and the role of India and China in the post crisis recovery phase. Discussions also took place on G20 issues including reforms in the International Monetary

[19] Ministry of External Affairs, *India–China Bilateral Relations*, n. 10.

[20] Ibid.

[21] Ibid.

System and the Framework for Strong, Sustainable and Balanced Growth.'[22] The Seventh India–China Financial Dialogue was held on 19 December 2014 in New Delhi. A high-level Chinese delegation, led by Mr Yu Weiping, interacted with the Indian delegation led by Mr Dinesh Sharma, on wide-ranging bilateral issues of mutual concern and interest.

Although India–China financial relations constitute a brighter side of the overall bilateral relations, there is ample scope for improvement in this area. Currently, the total volume of China–India trade constitute less than 2 per cent of total Chinese trade, and less than 6 per cent of total Indian trade. This grey area in bilateral trade requires attention, because these two Asian neighbours are the most developing economies in the world today. India's exports to China constitute 6.6 per cent of its total exports, whereas they make up only 1.4 per cent of China's imports. China's exports to India account for 1 per cent of its total exports, but constitute 6.2 per cent of India's imports. This is simply a reflection of each country's share of world trade, with India's being about 1 per cent and China's about 6.4 per cent. The bilateral trade potential is very high, given the size and economic dynamism of the two countries. China and India are among the 10 largest economies in terms of current exchange rates and among the five largest in terms of purchasing-power parity (PPP). They are also neighbours sharing a long border. To realise the full potential of India–China trade, remaining barriers and constraints have to be relaxed. These include customs rules and procedures, non-tariff barriers, standards, certification and regulatory practices, and rules of origin. Removal of these constraints and barriers in a spirit of mutual understanding will spruce up economic cooperation between the two countries. It is heartening to note that both the countries are signatories to the Bangkok Agreement and participate in the Asian currency union mechanisms. The pace of growth in bilateral trade during the last few years since 2004 may be viewed with optimism.

SECURITY AND CULTURAL RELATIONS

Since 1962 when the two neighbours went to war over border problems, among others, security relations between India and China had been very weak. As noted earlier, Indian Prime Minister Rajiv Gandhi's visit to China in 1988 restored normalcy in relations, including security relations. During Rajiv Gandhi's visit to China in December 1988, the JWG to study boundary issues was set up. Subsequently, the JWG met regularly and these meetings helped ease tension in the long border areas between the two countries. Both the countries put significant effort in reducing tensions in border areas during the period 1988 to 1993 through CBMs, troop reduction, military exercises and regular meetings. Seven rounds of JWG dialogues took place during this period. During the visit of Indian Defence Minister Sharad Pawar to Beijing in July 1992, the first ever by an Indian defence minister since 1962, it was agreed to develop academic, military, scientific and technological exchanges. A senior-level Chinese military delegation made a six-day

[22] Ibid.

goodwill visit to India in December 1993. The visit was aimed at fostering CBMs between the defence forces of the two countries. This visit was reciprocated by the Indian Army Chief General, B. C. Joshi's visit to China in July 1994. Since then, regular exchanges have been taking place at various levels.

Bilateral defence interaction has been growing. A Ministry of External Affairs (MEA) Report observes, 'Peace and tranquillity along the Line of Actual Control (LAC) in the border areas is being largely maintained by both sides in accordance with the agreements of 1993 and 1996.'[23] The MEA Report also contains recent highlights in defence relations between the two nations. Among important bilateral defence visits, the one by the then Defence Minister of India, George Fernandes's visit to China in April 2003 was noteworthy. The visit came after a gap of more than one decade and also helped ease the post-Pokhran II tensions. This was followed, according to the report, '. . . by a return visit by Chinese Defence Minister, General Cao Gangchuan in March 2004. In December 2004, General N. C. Vij visited China, the first by an Indian COAS (Chief of the Army Staff) in a decade, and both the countries agreed to deepen defence cooperation. In May 2005, the Chinese CGS (Chief of General Staff) visited India, a further sign of warming relations between the two countries. The Indian defence minister visited China in May 2006 and signed the first ever MoU on Defence Exchanges between the Armed Forces of India and China. In May 2007, General J. J. Singh, Chairman COSC (Chief of Staff Committee) and COAS visited China. This was the first time that the Chairman COSC visited China and was hosted by the CGS of the PLA. In November 2008, the Chief of Air Staff of the IAF paid an official visit to China. . . . Simultaneously, the Commander of PLA navy paid a visit to India from 2 to 5 November 2008. The Chairman COSC and CNS (Chief of Naval Staff), Admiral Sureesh Mehta visited China and participated in the International Fleet Review to mark the 60th Anniversary Celebrations of PLA navy from 19–25 Apr 2009.'[24]

Interactions at the grassroots level also took place through training institutions like National Defence College (NDC) and Army War College (AWC). With the formalisation of MoU on Exchanges in the Field of Defence Cooperation between India and China, the effort to strengthen and institutionalise defence cooperation between the armed forces of India and China is continuing. According to the MEA Report noted above, 'Important high level visits that took place from India to China in the year 2011 were by an Indian Multi Command delegation led by Maj Gen Gurmit Singh from 19–23 June and a 15-member Staff Officers Delegation led by Air Vice Marshal P. S. Mann from 09–14 January 2012. An eight-member PLA delegation led by Lt. Gen. Lang Youliang, Political Commissar of Tibet Provincial Military Command visited India from 04–09 Nov 2011. Another 26 member PLA Staff Officers Delegation visited Delhi, Agra and Mumbai from 25–30 December 2011. It was headed by Maj. Gen. Jin Lecheng, Deputy Commander, Shanxi Provincial Military Command.'[25]

---

[23] Ibid.

[24] Ibid.

[25] Ibid.

An important indicator of growing defence relations between India and China is the mechanism of Annual Defence Dialogue between the two countries. The First Annual Defence Dialogue between India and China was held in Beijing in November 2007. The second round of the Annual Defence Dialogue was held in India on 15 December 2008. The Chinese side was led by Lt. Gen. Ma Xiaotian, Deputy Chief of General Staff (DCGS), PLA, while the Indian side was led by Vijay Singh, the defence secretary. The third round of Annual Defence Dialogue was held in Beijing on 6 January 2010. The Indian side was led by Pradeep Kumar, defence secretary and the Chinese side was led by General Ma Xiaotian. The fourth Annual Defence Dialogue was held in New Delhi on 9 December 2011. Shashikant Sharma, Defence Secretary and General Ma Xiaotian, DCGS co-chaired the talks. At the fourth Annual Defence Dialogue, both the sides agreed to increase defence exchanges between the two countries.

Joint Training Exercises between the military of the two countries are also indications of increasing security relations. The First Joint Training Exercise (JTE) between the Indian army and the People's Liberation Army (PLA), 'HAND IN HAND 2007' was conducted at Kunming, China. One company each from the Indian army and PLA participated in the exercise which was based on the theme of 'Counter Terrorism'. While Lt. Gen. Susheel Gupta was the senior-most observer from the Indian side, Lt. Gen. Ma Xiaotian was the senior-most from the Chinese side. The Second India-China JTE was held in Belgaum, India, in December 2008, and was based on the same theme. The Annual Defence Dialogue and the JTE, conducted almost regularly now, have helped in enhancing confidence in security areas between China and India.

China and India are not only neighbours, these are the two most ancient civilisations on earth. Civilisational and cultural links between the two date back to 1500–1000 BC. In all ages, close cultural links between India and China continued in the form of religious, travel-related and scholarly visits. Chinese and Indian travellers and pilgrims visited each other's lands from ancient times. Many Chinese students flocked to Nalanda University for higher learning. Many of them were reported to be fascinated by the cultural milieu of the other land. Tagore visited China twice, in 1924 and in 1929. According to the MEA Report cited above, 'Since 1911, Chinese scholars and intellectuals have been visiting and revisiting Tagore's life, works and philosophy.'[26] Apart from Tagore, Bollywood movies have become popular in China.

During the last three decades (1988–2017), China–India cultural relations have been growing. According to the MEA Report that the broad contours of the India–China cultural cooperation was laid down in the Agreement on Cultural Cooperation signed in May 1988, which provides for an executive Cultural Exchange Programme (CEP) for implementation. The latest CEP signed in December 2010 during the visit of Chinese Premier Wen Jiabao to India provides for cooperation in a gamut of cultural fields including exchanges of visits of performing artists, officials, writers, archivists and archaeologists, organising cultural festivals, film festivals and exchanges in the

[26] Ibid.

field of mass media, youth affairs and sports.[27] Under the broad parameters of the CEP, various cultural troops from the two countries have been performing in China and India. More and more academic exchanges have been taking place. For instance, a centre for Indian studies has been set up in Peking University in 2003. Chairs of Indian studies have also been established in Shenzhen University, Jinan University and Fudan University. Similarly, centres for Chinese studies have been set up in many Indian universities. All these efforts have enhanced people-to-people contact between the two neighbours.

During his visit to China in June 2003, Indian Prime Minister Vajpayee had promised to build an Indian style Buddhist temple in Luoyang, Henan province and later, the then Indian President Pratibha Patil inaugurated the temple during her visit to China in May 2010. 'In February 2007, the Xuanzhang memorial hall has been inaugurated at Nalanda. In June 2008, joint stamps have been released, one stamp depicting the Mahabodhi temple at Bodhgaya and the other depicting the White Horse temple at Luoyang. The 60th anniversary of the establishment of India–China diplomatic relations was celebrated with much fan fare in both the countries in 2010.'[28] China and India have announced 2011 as the 'Year of Exchanges' and both countries have resolved to further strengthen cultural exchanges. A 500-member Indian youth delegation, led by the Minister of State for Sports and Youth Affairs, Ajay Maken, visited China in September 2011. A 20-member Indian Council for Cultural Relations (ICCR) troupe comprising people from Bollywood toured China in September 2011. The Indian mission collaborated with the Beijing Film Academy to organise a Film Festival entitled 'You Don't Belong' across several Chinese cities like Beijing, Shanghai, Guangzhou and Kunming in November–December 2011. The MEA Report states, 'In order to connect better with the Chinese youth, the Mission has also opened an account at the popular micro blogging site, Sina Weibo, which has over 5000 followers. The Mission's Flagship Chinese language publication—Jinri Yindu has a readership base of over 20,000 and is still going strong.'[29] During President Pranab Mukherjee's visit to China in May 2016, a large delegation of Indian academics accompanied him with a view to foster educational and cultural relations between the two nations.

India is also making efforts to popularise Chinese language at the school level in India and is planning to build a modern Nalanda University for which the Chinese government has expressed its desire to contribute. According to the MEA Report, 'The new Culture and Information Wing of the Mission began functioning from January 2011 from the New Chancery Premises. A Kathak dance teacher and a Hindustani classical music teacher joined the Mission on ICCR deputation in 2010, in order to expose the Chinese people to various facets of India's rich cultural tradition. This Wing conducts several events every month, including lectures, film/documentary shows, performances, book talks, etc. dealing with Indian culture and heritage. Increasingly, a number of Indian artists have been performing on private visits or participating directly on

[27] Ibid.

[28] Ibid.

[29] Ibid.

invitations of esteemed institutions like the Central Conservatory of Music, National Centre for Performing Arts (NCPA), and Beijing Dance Academy. The Wing also has an open library with around 3,000 reference books on India.'[30] Cultural relations between China and India are not frequently highlighted in analyses on bilateral relations, but it is no exaggeration to say that it has contributed immensely in reorienting China–India relations during the past 25 years.

However, a lot more needs to be done to strengthen further security and cultural relations between the two nations. For instance, a CNA between the two should not be a distant dream. Both China and India are *de facto* nuclear states. A nuclear agreement between the two would not only usher in the possibilities of peace in the region, it would also open up the door for cooperation in nuclear-related trade. China was not very happy with Indo–US nuclear agreement. India may think of a similar agreement with China, and the latter needs to respond positively. The two need to look at the border issues more seriously and avoid intrusion of any kind. In April 2013, Chinese forces violated the borders in the Ladakh region of Jammu and Kashmir, and set up military camps 20 miles deep into the Indian territory. India also retaliated and set up camps within the Chinese territory in the said border region. Such actions escalated tension in the region, and caused some hiccups in bilateral relations. However, good senses prevailed and both countries withdrew and dismantled their respective camps after a few weeks of continuous tension. These kind of activities need to be avoided for the restoration of mutual trust.

China's bid to scuttle India's entry into the Nuclear Suppliers Group (NSG) during the NSG Plenary Meeting in Seoul in June 2016 did not augur well for bilateral relations either. India's bid to secure membership to the 48-nation NSG hit a dead end with objections from a group of countries, led by China. They raked up procedural issues as well as India not signing Non-Proliferation Treaty (NPT) to thwart India's chances to the elite nuclear club. The NSG works through consensus, and halts any decision when a single country raises any objection. India did not take Chinese objections lightly. A spokesperson of India's MEA commented without naming China, 'We understand that despite procedural hurdles persistently raised by one country, a three-hour long discussion took place on the issue of future participation in the NSG.... It has been suggested that India's participation in the NSG requires it to join the NPT. Our stand on the NPT is well known. There is no contradiction between the NPT and India's closer engagement with the NSG.'[31] Although India showed restrained emotions, China's actions on India's membership of the NSG did manifest China's lack of trust in India.

Another sector not given due attention in bilateral relations was tourism. The potential of tourism has not been fully utilised by China and India over the years. Tourist outflow to China and India from the other land is not very high at this moment. Only about 0.21 per cent of China's outbound travellers toured India in 2015. This amounted to around 121,300 Chinese

---

[30] Ibid.

[31] Ministry of External Affairs, Government. of India, 'Spokesperson's Comments on NSG Plenary Meeting in Seoul', available at http://mea.gov.in/press-releases.htm?dtl/26949/Spokespersons_comments_on_NSG_Plenary_meeting_in_Seoul, accessed on 29 September 2016.

tourists to India in 2015. Outbound tourists from India to China totalled 730,500 in 2015. This amounted to 0.16 per cent of total foreign tourists to China in 2015.[32] These data reveal that tourism continues to remain a vastly untapped area in bilateral relations. However, it was heartening to note that during his visit to China in May 2015, Prime Minister Modi hinted at providing on-line visa application facilities for Chinese tourists to India. This measure will help in enhancing Chinese tourist outflow to India. The two countries must work sincerely together to boost tourism further. Student and faculty exchange, and research cooperation between Chinese and Indian universities are also not very encouraging. The two neighbours need to work more closely in this area. Although both China and India are keen to consolidate cultural relations, and they have been working hard to promote tourism, educational and cultural factors, these areas require more attention and priorities than the ongoing endeavours.

CONCLUSION: PERCEPTION PROBLEMS

There is no denying the fact that China–India relations have improved over the years since 1988. The relationship has not only become normal, it has grown substantially during the past 29 years. But at this period of time, in the second decade of the twenty-first century, can the relationship be described as strong? Despite noteworthy improvement in China–India relations during the post Cold War period as noted earlier, it would not be wrong to mention here that the relationship suffers from lack of trust. Border problems are persistent irritants in bilateral relations, with occasional claims on each other's territories. The NSG issue is another stark reminder of mistrust prevailing in bilateral relations. Further, the Tibet issue often comes back to affect relationship. For instance, the visit of the Dalai Lama to India in November 2009 drew Chinese criticisms about India's 'designs'. Moreover, India fears that a militarily and economically strong China might prove to be a security threat for India. India cited the presence of a nuclear neighbour (China) as a security threat to India as justification for Pokhran II in May 1998. Chinese security-related supplies to Pakistan further exacerbate Indian schism. Overall, the element of mistrust prevails in China–India relations at this point of time.

Mistrust breeds schism, and China and India both view each other with suspicion. From the Indian point of view, China's rise as an economic and military power and its increasing (economic and military) presence in South Asia may lead to a new balance of power in the region. China had been traditionally close to Pakistan, India's bête noir in South Asia, and supplying huge quantity of arms and nuclear technology to Pakistan since the mid-1960s. China–Pakistan proximity has always been an intriguing factor in strengthening India–China relations. China also woos Bangladesh often and on with a view to keep India on tenterhooks. Of late China's economic, cultural and security engagements in Afghanistan, Myanmar, Nepal, Sri Lanka and the Maldives are growing significantly. Such engagements provide a fillip to India's schism about

[32] Travel China Guide, available at http://www.travelchinaguide.com/tourism/2015statistics/inbound.htm, accessed on 18 May 2016.

Chinese designs to encircle India. These also instil a sense of insecurity in Indian political circles, and an urge for competition in Indian diplomacy. China is seen by India as a potential rival to its dominance in South Asia.

Although China is way ahead of India as an economic and military power in today's world at this point of time, yet China views India as a potential challenge to its power ambitions in Asia, if not in the world. India's growing economic and military capabilities are watched with caution in China's political establishment. There are speculations within China and outside about an American-Indian-Japanese collaboration to thwart China's power ambitions in Asia and other parts of the world. Russia is also projected as a possible ally of this triad. China also views India as a competitor for its economic designs, and possibly an adversary for its military ambitions. This proposition could be substantiated from recent developments in the South China Sea controversy. Chinese and Indian positions were different, and somewhat opposing with regard to the recent South China Sea (SCS) dispute. Conflicting claims over islands and maritime zones in the SCS have remained long-standing security issues between China, Taiwan, Vietnam and the four Southeast Asian countries. China's hardline on the SCS has affected India too. 'New Delhi was a bit taken aback after Beijing denounced plans by an Indian Company to develop oil fields in the region. The Chinese objection was to ONGC Videsh's (OVL) venture for off-shore oil exploration in water's belonging to Vietnam (not recognized by China). Beijing urged India to refrain from entering into deals with Vietnamese firms exploring oil and gas in the disputed SCS over which China enjoys "indisputable" sovereignty.'[33] During Foreign Minister S. M. Krishna's visit to Hanoi in September 2011, the Minister underlined that OVL would go ahead with oil and gas exploration in the two offshore blocks (127 and 128) claimed by Vietnam. 'China, however, appeared unconvinced and announced plans to expand maritime exploration of 10,000 sq km of seabed in Southwest Indian Ocean.... The Indian position on the security situation in the SCS was made clear by the Indian Foreign Secretary, Nirupama Rao in her address at the National Maritime Foundation, New Delhi on July 28, 2011, where she reiterated the region's importance as an important shipping route and India's support for freedom of navigation in sea-lanes.'[34] The SCS instance is one among many such differences (Chinese strategic projects in Pakistan Occupied Kashmir (PoK) may be cited as another) between the two neighbours over security and economic issues. China's objections to India's entry into the NSG in June 2016 reflected China's concern about India's power ambitions and its rise as a potential competitor. India's concerns for 'one belt one road' (OBOR) plan put forward by China also point towards lack of trust between the two nations. Therefore, perceptions of these two nations about each other do not continuously refer to friendship, rather these manifest attitudes of competitors, if not outright adversaries.

It would certainly require more time to alter such problems in perception, stemming out of mistrust and insecurity. However, intense economic and cultural cooperation may gradually

---

[33] Amit Singh, 'South China Sea Dispute and India', *National Maritime Foundation*, available at http://maritimeindia.org/article/south-china-sea-dispute-and-india, accessed on 18 May 2013.

[34] Ibid.

change elements of mistrust and animosity in China–India relations. Sincere political will from the leaders of the two Asian neighbours can only help accelerate the process of forging strong relations. It was heartening to note that during the visits of the Chinese President, Xi Jinping to India in September 2014, and Prime Minister Modi to China in May 2015, both sides had an open discussion regarding troubled areas in bilateral relations. The discussion sent signals that both China and India were willing to cooperate and rebuild their relationship in the new century. Cooperation between these two big nations is necessary for lasting peace in South Asia in particular and Asia in general.

10

INDIA AND RUSSIA
Rebuilding Older Ties

HIGHLIGHTS

- Introduction: Fresh Beginning on a Rich Heritage
- Political Relations in the New Century
- Economic Relations
- Security Relations
- Recommentations for the Future

INTRODUCTION: FRESH BEGINNING ON A RICH HERITAGE

India had friendly and strong bilateral relations with the former Soviet Union. For over six decades, India and Russia shared a long-standing friendship based on mutual trust and confidence.[1] The Russian Federation created out of the former Soviet Union in 1991, also tried to develop cordial relations with India. After the end of the Cold War, the two countries took fresh initiatives to forge friendly relationship in a new world order. During the first Yeltsin Presidency in the Russian Federation (henceforth Russia), relationship started to take new shape. It took some time to consolidate bilateral relations as both Russia and India were trying to adjust to the post Cold War international order. However, the two sides began working sincerely on bilateral relations since 1992–93. During the January 1993 visit of Russian President Boris Yeltsin to India, the two countries signed agreements that promised to open up roads to new economic and defence cooperation between the two nations.

A new Treaty of Friendship and Cooperation, which replaced the 1971 Indo-Soviet Treaty of Friendship, was signed during Yeltsin's visit. The new treaty dropped security clauses present in the 1971 Treaty because both India and Russia felt that they were not necessary in the altered scenario.

[1] Ministry of External Affairs, Government of India, *Annual Report: 2014–15* (New Delhi: Government of India), p. 42.

Yeltsin announced that Russia would provide cryogenic engines for India's space programme under a US $350 million deal between the Indian Space Research Organisation (ISRO) and the Russian space agency, Glavkosmos. The Russian president expressed his country's support for India's position on Kashmir. A defense cooperation agreement for the continued supply of Russian arms and spare parts for India's military, and for promoting the joint production of defense equipment was also signed during Yeltsin's visit.[2] Indian Prime Minister Narasimha Rao and the Russian president agreed that bilateral trade, which had fallen drastically during the 1991–92 period, would get a boost following the resolution of the dispute over India's debt to Russia. Earlier in May 1992, the two countries decided to abandon the 1978 rupee–rouble trade agreement in favour of the use of hard currency. Although the cryogenic engine deal did not materialise, the Yeltsin visit helped to set the ball rolling for a new era of cooperation.[3] However, Yeltsin's Russia was struggling to get its identity in international politics, and also, manage a transition from the earlier one-party rule to a new democratic internal politics. It was not a smooth passage for Yeltsin in domestic as well as in international politics. His foreign policy was a bit uncertain. But his visit to India within two years of assuming Russian presidency signalled his inclination to establish close contacts with India.

Narasimha Rao, the first prime minister of India (1991–96) to assume office after the Cold War, visited Russia in July 1994. Rao and Yeltsin signed declarations, which promised to continue close bilateral cooperation, and supply of Russian arms and military equipment exports to India. Rao's visit yielded positive results for India. Apart from ensuring the continuation of Russian defence-related exports to India, Rao was able to restore the sale of cryogenic engines to India, which was seen in Indian foreign policy circles as a diplomatic victory. In December 1994, Russian Prime Minister Viktor Chernomyrdin visited New Delhi to discuss bilateral issues with Indian leaders. Eight agreements were signed between the two countries during Chernomyrdin's visit. These agreements covered military and technical cooperation from 1995 to 2000, trade, merchant shipping, promotion and mutual protection of investments and cooperation in outer space. The success of Chernomyrdin's India visit was hailed by the Indian and Russian Media as a return to the warmer ties shared between Soviet Union and India.[4] Regular top-level visits and close cooperation in different areas of bilateral interest have been continuing since the Chernomyrdin visit.

POLITICAL RELATIONS IN THE NEW CENTURY

Russia and India got closer and enhanced their cooperation at the turn of the new century. In October 2000, President Valdimir Putin of Russia visited India. Russia and India signed

---

[2] Aneek Chatterjee, *International Relations Today: Concepts and Applications* (New Delhi: Pearson), 2010, p. 252.

[3] Ibid.

[4] Ibid.

10 agreements in all during Putin's visit. The most important agreement signed personally by Indian Prime Minister Vajpayee and the Russian president was the declaration on strategic partnership between India and Russia. This declaration was very significant for the two countries as Russia and India instituted an inter-governmental commission for military-technical cooperation under the co-chair of the two defence ministers. Both the sides have committed themselves to not participating in any military, political or other arrangements or armed conflicts threatening either side. Under the strategic partnership, long-term and diversified Indo-Russian cooperation would be organised in the sphere of metallurgy, fuel and energy, information technology (IT) and communications. Defence and military technical cooperation arrangements would be put in place in a long-term perspective with special emphasis on cooperation between the defence forces of the two countries. India and Russia would cooperate in the peaceful usage of nuclear energy and outer space.[5] The annual summit meetings between the heads of government of both nations were also planned as part of the strategic partnership. Putin assured the Indian leaders that Russia was willing to share cutting-edge defence technologies to India—an unprecedented commitment that went a long way to consolidate security partnership between the two nations. The other agreements related to increased cooperation across the spectrum of political, economic, defence, technological and cultural areas.

Vajpayee paid an official visit to Russia in November 2003. A Joint Declaration (JD) was issued during the visit and the Indian prime minister signed several agreements on bilateral cooperation with the Russian president in Moscow on 12 November. The agreements covered the spheres of bilateral trade, defence supplies, science and technology, space and earthquake research. The JD referred to an agreement between the two countries on the war against terrorism. Vajpayee and Putin affirmed a consistent and uncompromising approach on tackling the terrorist threat. Russia endorsed the Indian position on resuming a dialogue with Pakistan, agreeing that an end to cross-border terrorism was necessary to initiate a purposeful dialogue. The JD recommended a concrete and time-bound action plan under the aegis of the United Nations (UN) for the restoration of democracy and sovereignty in Iraq as early as possible. Both the leaders also agreed that the role of the UN should be restored in dealing with problems of peace and security in the world. They also agreed, as per the JD, that all support should be given to the transitional government in Afghanistan to enable it to emerge as a stable country free from external interference. India and Russia also shared the view that the future international order should be based on multipolarity, and must be determined by collective and multilateral decisions rather than unilateral initiatives. The JD also reiterated that closer India–Russia cooperation in all areas of mutual interest would be expanded in the near future.

With the Congress party assuming power in New Delhi in 2004, it was hoped that India–Russia relations would get further boost considering the Congress party's traditional preference for Moscow. Regular top-level visits continued after 2004 along with closer bilateral cooperation

---

[5] Ibid., p. 253.

in different areas. The new Indian Prime Minister, Manmohan Singh visited Russia in the first week of December 2005 for the annual summit meeting with the Russian President, Vladimir Putin. During Singh's visit, India and Russia signed some important agreements. These were:

(i) Space exploration cooperation agreement
(ii) Agreement on reciprocal protection of intellectual property rights in military technical cooperation
(iii) Agreement on cooperation in the field of solar physics and solar terrestrial relationships
(iv) Agreement on implementation of programme for military and technical cooperation up to 2010.

However, contrary to expectations, the visit was low-key and yielded little significant results. Compared to Manmohan Singh's highly successful visit to the US in July 2005 when India and the US decided to achieve the civil nuclear agreement, his December 2005 visit to Russia appeared to be an exercise of routine diplomacy.[6]

However, the visit of the new Russian President, Dmitry Medvedev to India in December 2008 yielded positive results. He was the first world leader to visit India after the 26/11 terrorist attack on Mumbai. Obviously, terrorism was placed on the top of the agenda. The JD, signed by the Russian President and Prime Minister Manmohan Singh, urged the international community to provide all assistance to India to bring to justice the terrorists who executed attacks on Mumbai. One of the major achievements of the visit was the new thrust on the proposed Indo–Russian peaceful nuclear cooperation. Apart from signing an agreement for construction of four more reactors at the Kudankulam plant in Tamil Nadu where Russia was in the final stages of building two reactors, both sides expressed the desire to build additional reactors there, as well as to go for new nuclear plants elsewhere in India. During Medvedev's visit, India and Russia also signed a deal totalling US $700 million for Russian nuclear fuel supply to India. The JD further appealed to the international community to resolve the Iran issue through peaceful means, dialogue and negotiations. While requesting all sides for demonstrating flexibility and restraint, Russia and India upheld Iran's right to conduct research, production and use of nuclear energy for peaceful purposes in accordance with the terms of the Non-Proliferation Treaty (NPT) and other international obligations. The Medvedev visit (of December 2008) would be remembered for preparing the groundwork for the Indo-Russian Civil Nuclear Cooperation Agreement, signed next year, and also for strengthening defence and trade ties between the two nations.[7]

Prime Minister Manmohan Singh of India paid an official visit to Russia in December 2009 for the annual summit meeting with the Russian president. The landmark civil nuclear cooperation agreement between India and Russia was signed on 7 December 2009 after talks

---

[6] Ibid.

[7] Ibid., p. 254.

between Prime Minister Manmohan Singh and President Dmitry Medvedev in Moscow. The two leaders, in their Joint Statement, described the agreement as 'pathbreaking' and expressed hope that the agreement would strengthen the already existing nuclear cooperation between the two countries. By the terms of the agreement, the Russians would build 12 to 14 nuclear reactors in India. The agreement with Russia was believed to be much more advantageous to India than the 123 agreement India signed with the US, especially because the new agreement contained assurances on uninterrupted supplies of uranium to India for the atomic reactors and on transfer of nuclear technology. The two sides also signed agreements on extending their long-term military cooperation programme for another 10 years till 2020. Singh and Medvedev also discussed regional issues, including the situation in Afghanistan, in which both the countries have a stake and favoured a 'stable and prosperous' Afghanistan. This visit of the Indian prime minister was considered highly successful in view of the positive outcomes it yielded for New Delhi.[8]

During the visit of President Dmitry Medvedev to India in December 2010, it was decided to further elevate the strategic partnership to the level of a 'special and privileged strategic partnership'. The visit of President Medvedev encouraged India and Russia to sign 30 agreements covering a wide range of areas ranging from defence, space, nuclear energy, pharmaceuticals, relaxation of visa norms among others. The signing of all these agreements demonstrated a matured and strong relationship envisaged by the two nations since the bilateral trade by 2015. The highlight of Medvedev's visit was the signing of US $295 million deal to jointly design and develop the Fifth Generation Fighter Aircraft (FGFA) between Russia's Sukhoi Design Bureau and Rosoboron export and India's Hindustan Aeronautics Limited.

Prime Minister Manmohan Singh's visit to Russia in December 2011, to participate in the 12th Annual bilateral summit, yielded five agreements. These agreements included two protocols, two memoranda of understanding and one pact related to exchange in education. The first deal clinched between the two countries during the annual meeting was an inter-governmental agreement on the production of 42 more Sukhoi-MKI 30 jets by Hindustan Aeronautics Limited (HAL). A Memorandum of Understanding (MoU) between the Competition Commission of India and the Federal Antimonopoly Service (Russian Federation) was the second agreement signed between India and Russia. The primary objective of the MoU is promoting cooperation and exchanges between the two anti-monopoly agencies. The Department of Science and Technology, Government of India (GoI), and the Interregional Association 'Siberian Accord', Siberian Federal District, Russian Federation, signed a Protocol of Intentions aimed at facilitating development and application of technologies for the utilisation and safe management of fly-ash in the Siberian Federal District; experience sharing; investment projects and mutual exchange of scientific personnel. An MoU on cooperation in the pharmaceutical field overseeing the safety and quality issues between the Central Drug Standard Control

---

[8] Ibid.

Organisation, India, and the Federal Service for Surveillance in the Sphere of Public Health and Social Development, Russia.[9] The fifth agreement inked between India and Russia was an educational exchange programme between the Ministry of Education and Science of the Russian Federation and the Ministry of Human Resource Development (MoRD) of India on cooperation in the field of education. The purpose of the agreement is to boost cooperation in the field of education via inter-institutional arrangements, and experience sharing in the sphere of pedagogy. Russia also supported India's bid for a permanent seat in an expanded United Nations Security Council (UNSC) as well as its intentions to join the Shanghai Cooperation Organization (SCO), while India welcomed Moscow's entry to the World Trade Organization (WTO).

Russian President Vladimir Putin visited India on 24 December 2012 for the 13th Annual India–Russia summit. He held discussions with the Prime Minister Manmohan Singh and President Pranab Mukherjee. Sushma Swaraj, the leader of the Opposition, and Sonia Gandhi, Chairperson of United Progressive Alliance (UPA), called on the Russian president. The year 2012 also marked 65 years of the establishment of diplomatic relations between India and Russia (earlier Soviet Union). To commemorate the occasion, 10 bilateral documents were signed during Putin's visit. An MoU to establish an Indo–Russia Joint Investment Fund, worth US $2 billion, to encourage direct investment and acquisition of assets in critical infrastructural, manufacturing and hydrocarbon extraction sectors was one of the most important documents signed.[10] Other notable documents included the Joint Venture (JV) to set up a modern industrial facility for the manufacture of Russian helicopters in India to promote the development of a high technology based domestic aerospace industry; the joint collaboration to manufacture pharmaceuticals in Russia along with the IT agreement for developing software, systems integration and emergency response systems to help in producing niche products. The two nations also entered into contracts for the supply of 71 Mi-17 helicopters and 42 Sukhoi-30 MKI fighter jets worth US $3.5 to 4 billion to give a boost to India–Russia defence cooperation.

The annual summit between the prime minister of India and the president of the Russian Federation is the highest institutionalised dialogue mechanism. Since the Declaration of Strategic Partnership, 16 summit meetings have taken place alternatively, either in India or in Russia.[11] The Indian Prime Minister, Narendra Modi visited Moscow between 23 and 24 December 2015 for the sixteenth annual summit. During Modi's visit, 17 new documents covering a wide range of cooperation in civil nuclear energy, defence, hydrocarbons, satellite navigation, railways, solar energy, heavy engineering, supercomputing, visa simplification, Ayurveda and media were

---

[9] Source: Press Information Bureau, India; http:www//pib.nic.in/newsite/printrelease.aspx?rehid=78856; accessed on 15 May 2017.

[10] For further details, see www.idsa.in › Publications › IDSA, accessed on 15 May 2017.

[11] Source: https://www.mea.gov.in/Portal/ForeignRelation/India_Russia_Relation_DEC2016.pdf, accessed on 15 May 2017.

signed by the two countries.[12] Prime Minister Modi and President Putin also adopted a JS entitled 'Shared Trust, New Horizons' during this visit. Besides the annual summit meeting in December 2015, the Indian prime minister met the Russian president on the sidelines of the SCO Summit in Tashkent (Uzbekistan) on 24 June 2016. During the Russian presidency of BRICS (Brazil, Russia, India, China and South Africa) from April 2015–February 2016, India actively participated in a number of ministerial and high-officials meetings. The prime minister of India visited Ufa (Russia) to participate in the 7th BRICS Summit there on 8–9 July 2015. On 15 February 2016, India assumed the next presidency of BRICS and hosted the next summit in Goa on 15–16 October 2016. BRICS also provides a forum for regular interaction between the heads of governments (HoGs) of India and Russia.

The two governments have also established two Inter-Governmental Commissions (IGCs), known as IRIGC or the Indio-Russia Inter-Governmental Commission. One of the two IRIGC is on trade, economic, scientific, technological and cultural cooperation, co-chaired by the Indian external affairs minister and the Russian deputy prime minister; while the other is on Military Technical Cooperation co-chaired by the two defence ministers, both of whom meet annually. In addition to the IRIGC, there are other bodies that conduct economic relations between the two countries. These include, the Indo–Russian Forum on Trade and Investment, the India–Russia Business Council, the India–Russia Trade, Investment and Technology Promotion Council and the India–Russia Chamber of Commerce. In this context, it would be pertinent to look at the economic relations between India and Russia in the recent times.

ECONOMIC RELATIONS

Economic engagements between India and Russia are growing through institutional mechanisms; but at this point of time, actual trade figures are below expectations. Russia does not figure among the top 10 trading partners of India, nor does India rank among the notable trading partners of Russia. A decline in bilateral trade in recent times (see Table 10.1) is also an area of concern. The principal institutional mechanism for supervising economic relations between the two is the 'India–Russia Inter-Governmental Commission on Trade, Economic, Scientific, Technological and Cultural Cooperation (IRIGC–TEC)', co-chaired by the external affairs minister of India and the deputy prime minister of Russia. The IRIGC–TEC integrates six working groups on economic and trade cooperation, modernisation and industrial cooperation, energy, tourism and culture, science and technology and Information Technology (IT). It meets regularly in New Delhi and Moscow.

An analysis of the trade and investment areas between India and Russia would bring to light the need to further strengthen cooperation in these significant segments of bilateral relations. Table 10.1 below highlights India–Russia two-way trade during the financial years 2011–12 to 2015–16:

---

[12] Indian Embassy in Moscow, *India–Russia Relations*, available at http://indianembassy.ru/index.php/en/economic-cooperation/overview, accessed on 10 August 2016.

Table 10.1: India–Russia Two-way Trade during the Last Five Fiscals (in US $ million)

Year	*India's Imports from Russia (A)*	*Indi's Exports to Russia (B)*	*Total Trade (A + B)*	*Trade Balance (A – B)*
2011–12	4,764.31	1,778.27	6,542.58	2,986.04
2012–13	4,231.56	2,295.68	6,527.24	1,935.88
2013–14	3,894.40	2,121.26	6,015.66	1,773.14
2014–15	4,249.22	2,097.01	6,346.23	2,152.21
2015–16	4,596.07	1,587.81	6,183.88	3,008.26

Source: Department of Commerce, Government of India, Export-Import Data Bank, available at http://www.commerce.nic.in/eidb/iecnt.asp, accessed on 10 August 2016.

A look at Table 10.1 shows a decline in total trade from 2011–12 to 2015–16. In the fiscal year 2011–12, total trade between India and Russia was US $6,542.58 million. It came down to US $6,183.88 in 2015–16. This is not a healthy trend in the light of the fact that the two nations enjoyed strong ties in the past. In December 2014, the leaders of the two countries set a target of US $30 billion bilateral trade by 2025.[13] Recent indications, however, suggest that the two nations will have to work very hard to reach that target. Moreover, trade balance is also growing steadily in favour of Russia. Although trade balance has not assumed dangerous proportions, this issue requires careful handling by both the countries.

Major items of Russian export to India include fertilisers; electrical machinery and equipment parts; TV and audio-recording equipment; iron and steel; automobiles and parts, etc.; nuclear reactors, boilers, machinery and mechanical appliances, etc.; important items of Indian export to Russia include pharmaceutical products; electrical machinery and equipment; coffee, tea and spices; tobacco and its industrial substitutes; boliers' machinery and mechanical appliances.[14] Of late (2013–16), several areas have been identified for intense cooperation in trade between the two nations. These include: hydrocarbons, IT, pharmaceuticals and biotechnology, metals and minerals, fertilisers, food processing, construction and engineering services, financial services, tele-medicine, and machine building. Trade in rough diamonds has also been identified as a key sector, because Russia is a major producer of rough diamonds and India is one of the leading processing centres. During Vladimir Putin's visit to India in March 2010, Russian company Alrosa concluded a medium-term contract with three Indian companies for trade in rough diamonds. Moreover, there are significant opportunities for Russian companies to do business in India, particularly in the area of construction and engineering services. According to recent estimates, India may absorb about US $1.7 trillion for infrastructure development over the next 10 years.[15]

Indian investment in Russia is estimated to be about US $8 billion, which include Imperial Energy Tomsk; Sakhalin I; Volzhsky Abrasive Works Volgograd; and Commercial Indo Bank.

---

[13] Ibid.

[14] Ibid.

[15] Ibid.

Russian investments in India total about US $3 billion, including Kamaz Vectra in Hosur; Shyam Sistema Telecom Ltd, Sberbank and VTB.[16] A major part of these investments have utilised the Rupee-debt fund. Both the governments have undertaken initiatives to promote bilateral investments, primarily through facilitating high-level government to business and business-to-business contacts apart from the on-going investment process in the strategic sectors in both the countries. Investment cooperation has been envisaged within the framework of the 17th IRIGIC 2011 in various sectors such as hydrocarbons, power, coal, nuclear power, fertilisers, IT, pharmaceuticals, mineral and metallurgy amongst others. The fifth India–Russia Forum on Trade and Investment 2011 emphasised on facilitation of cross-flows on investment and explore the possibility of investment cooperation through mutually identified projects. Major investments by Indian companies in Russia are ONGC Videsh Ltd in Sakhalin-I Project; Commercial Bank of India Ltd (a JV of SBI and Canara Bank); ICICI Bank for opening subsidiary ICICI Bank Eurasia; TATA Motors–for assembly of small capacity lorries and buses; Imperial Energy; SUN Group for energy and real estate; Carbonandum Universal for production of abrasives; TATA Tea; De Core; Choron Diamonds; L&T; Universal Food Technologies; harma companies such as Torrent Pharmaceuticals; Dr. Reddy's Laboratories Ltd; Cadila Pharmaceuticals Ltd; Pharmasyntez; Unique Pharmaceutical Laboratories; and Sun Pharmaceuticals. Major Russian investments in India are: JV between Russian Kamaz Inc. and India's Vectra Group; India–Russia JV for production of titanium products; by AFK Sistema in Sistema Shyam Telelink Services; branches by VTB and Siber bank; a Memorandum of Understanding (MoU) was also signed between Severstal, Russia and NMDC in establishing two MTPA (expandable to five MTPA) Integrated Steel Plant in Karnataka, using Indian iron ore and Russian coking coal.[17]

Apart from the IRIGC–TEC, many other institutional mechanisms are contributing towards strengthening bilateral economic relations. An India–Russia Joint Task Force (JTF) has been constituted to monitor the implementation of the recommendations of India–Russia Joint Study Group (JSG). The JSG was set up to work out a programme for enhancing bilateral trade and to explore the possibility of a Comprehensive Economic Cooperation Agreement (CECA) between the two countries. Efforts are also being made by both India and Russia to promote the establishment of new contacts and wider cooperation between commercial and industrial circles and business associations of the two countries. For these, the main institutional mechanisms are: (i) India–Russia Forum on Trade and Investment (IRFTI). Established since 2007, the forum has met five times with wide business participation from both the sides; (ii) India and Russia have agreed to have enhanced Indian participation in the prestigious St. Petersburg International Economic Forum (SPIEF). The Confederation of Indian Industry (CII) and SPIEF Foundation have entered into an MoU for regular institutionalised business-to-business interactions and exchanges; (iii) Engineering Export Promotion Council (EEPC) of India organises business fairs

---

16 Ibid.

17 Ibid.

and other promotional events in Russia to attract investment.[18] India also participates regularly at the Annual International Industrial Fair, also known as 'Innoprom', organised by the Russian industry. Through these efforts, both the countries are trying to consolidate economic ties.

SECURITY RELATIONS

Like the former Soviet Union, post-Soviet Russia has remained an important security partner of India. Today, a major share of India's arms supply is met by Russia. The two countries have also entered into cooperative ventures for the production of arms. Although security relations between the new Russian Federation and India began in 1991 after the emergence of Russia, significant cooperative ventures between the two countries commenced in 1998 with an agreement to jointly develop the BrahMos cruise missile. The BrahMos became operational in the Indian military in 2006. A new variant, the BrahMos II, with increased capacity and speed, was inducted in the Indian military in 2014. The other major joint venture has been the development of a Fifth-Generation Fighter Aircraft (FGFA). This US $35 billion project between HAL and the Sukhoi company of Russia, is designed to produce an aircraft analogous to the American F-22 Raptor. India was invited to become a partner in the development of the FGFA by Moscow in 2007. HAL and Sukhoi had also worked together on the licence production of the Su-30MKI. The Indian investment of some US $6 billion in the project had contributed towards enhanced research and development (R&D). In December 2010, a further joint venture was announced between HAL and the Russian firm Ilyushin, to design and build a new medium-lift transport aircraft. Known as the Multirole Transport Aircraft (MTA), this will be based on the existing design of the Ilyushin 214.[19] Indians are familiar with the Ilyushin company also, having for some time operated the heavy-lift transport aircraft, the Il-76.

The India–Russia Inter-Governmental Commission on Military Technical Cooperation (IRIGC-MTC) is the apex institutional structure to oversee defence cooperation. Under the IRIGC-MTC, the defence ministers of the two nations meet annually, alternately in Russia and India, to review the ongoing projects and other issues of military technical cooperation. There are two working groups and seven sub-groups under the IRIGC-MTC, which review and discuss military technical issues. In 2008, a high-level committee called the High Level Monitoring Committee (HLMC) was set up with Defence Secretary of India and Director of Federal Service for Military Technical Cooperation (FSMTC) from the Russian Federation as its co-chairs.

An Indian embassy report outlines the on-going projects and other areas of bilateral cooperation in the defence sector. According to this report, '... bilateral projects currently underway include

[18] Ibid.

[19] Rod Thornton, 'India–Russia Military Cooperation: Which Way Forward?', *Journal of Defence Studies* 6 (3): 105, 2012.

indigenous production of T-90 tanks and Su-30-MKI aircraft, supply of MiG-29-K aircraft and Kamov-31 and Mi-17 helicopters, upgrade of MiG-29 aircraft repair and refit of the aircraft carrier *INS Vikramaditya* and the supply of the Multi-Barrel Rocket Launcher Smerch'.[20] Over the years, Indo–Russian cooperation in the military technical sphere has evolved from a purely buyer-seller relationship to joint research, design development and production of state-of-the-art military platforms. The production of the BrahMos cruise missile is an example of this trend. 'Joint army and navy exercises between the two armed forces are held under the title INDRA. The last joint exercise INDRA-2012 between the two armies was held in Russia in August 2012. Indian and Russian navy ships conducted a joint advanced passage exercise called INDRA-2012 off the coast of Mumbai in December 2012.'[21] An Indian contingent participated in the military parade in Moscow on 9 May 2015 during the 70th anniversary of the victory in the Second World War.

Unlike the Soviet era, Russia now faces competition from other nations for supplying arms to India. With the onset of globalisation, and India's economic growth, India does not solely depend on Russia now for arms supply, although Russia provides a sizeable quantity of total arms import by India. Enhanced economic potentials have enabled India to ask for quality and price as far as arms supply from Russia, or from any other country is concerned. With economic progress, India's bargaining power has also increased. However, more than a buyer-seller relationship as observed earlier, India's close cooperation with Russia in R&D of defence resources has emerged as one of the unique features of bilateral relations in the recent times.

Russia has emerged as an important partner of India in peaceful uses of nuclear energy. In December 2014, India's Department of Atomic Energy (DAE) and Russia's Rosatom signed the Strategic Vision for strengthening cooperation in peaceful uses of atomic energy between India and Russia. The Kudankulam Nuclear Power Plant (KKNPP) is being built in India with Russian cooperation. KKNPP Unit 1 became operational in July 2013, and attained full generation capacity on 7 June 2014. India and Russia have signed a General Framework Agreement on KKNPP Units 3 and 4 and subsequent contracts are under preparation at the moment. The secretary of the DAE visited Moscow on 9 June 2015 to review the wider cooperation in the field of peaceful uses of nuclear energy.[22] India–Russia cooperation in the area of peaceful uses of outer space dates back to about four decades. This cooperation has been strengthened in the recent years. In 2007, India and Russia signed a framework agreement on cooperation in the peaceful uses of outer space, including satellite launches, GLONASS navigation, remote-sensing and other societal applications of outer space. In June 2015, the space agencies of both nations have signed an MoU on expansion of cooperation in the field of outer space for peaceful purposes.

---

[20] Embassy of India in Moscow, *India–Russia Defence Cooperation*, available at http://www.indianembassy.ru/index.php/en/bilateral-relations/india-russia-defence-cooperation, accessed on 19 October 2013.

[21] Ibid.

[22] Ibid.

An agreement was signed between C-DAC and GLONASS for cooperation in technologies based on satellite navigation.[23]

RECOMMENDATIONS FOR THE FUTURE

Both Russia and India are emerging economies, and these two nations have immense potentials to make their opinions count in global politics. Traditionally, their relationship has been time-tested and close. In a new international order after the Cold War, both nations took a little time to adjust to the new scenario, and to refresh their relationship. New roads to bilateralism with India opened up during the Yeltsin Presidency in Russia, although bilateralism got hugely strengthened during the Putin presidency. Russia and India are close partners now, and the trust factor between the two has consolidated over the past decade. Both India and Russia require each other in a new world order, not only for economic prosperity and security gains, but to ensure a multi-polar world order where they can emerge as important actors. For this purpose, they need to cooperate intensely.

India needs Russia for many reasons. Russia is a potent military power. It has retained nearly 75 per cent of total armaments, conventional and non-conventional, of the former Soviet Union. It is a permanent member of the Security Council, and in that capacity, a big actor in international politics. Its mineral and energy resources are adequate, and its industrial-technical bases are strong. In the event of the world going uni-polar (with the US as the centre of power), or bipolar (US and China), Russia can provide the option of an alternate platform. Russia being a trusted and time-tested friend, India must keep that option open. Moreover, India–Russia economic relations have enormous potentialities. The two countries must adopt proper measures to make bilateral trade volume reach US $50 billion by 2025. This projection is achievable with the inclusion of additional items in the export and import lists. Russian investment in India stood at US $3 billion in 2015, a meagre amount, considering India's large market and economic potentials. India must try to attract more Russian investment in the near future. The target should be around US $10 billion by 2020. For this purpose, India must project more areas for Russian investments beyond telecommunications. Indian investment in Russia amounted to US $8 billion in 2015, mostly in the energy sector. Indian companies must also look to other areas for investment. Russian President Vladimir Putin rounded optimistic about trade relations when he observed, 'one of the priorities is to boost the trade turnover and improve its structure, as well as stimulate economic activity of our business communities'.[24]

Russia also needs India for realising Russian national interests. India constitutes one of Russia's large export markets for defence equipments. Russian interest would be to keep this export market going steady and strong. As observed earlier, in an age of globalisation, Russia faces competition

---

[23] Ibid.

[24] Vladimir Putin, 'Seventy Years Together: Russia and India', *The Times of India*, May 31, 2017.

from other countries for arms exports, including nuclear-related exports, to India; and India has also emerged as a strong bargaining power in this field, unlike earlier (Soviet era) times. In this scenario, Russia's objectives would be to retain the arms export market in India, and keep good political relations with India. There is little doubt that defence cooperation between Russia and India is the stronger area of bilateral relations, and Russia would be interested to make it strongest for economic benefits. India has started to look for level-playing field in this area, and must play the role of an equal partner in defence and strategic cooperation with Russia. Russia also needs India for political reasons. As a trusted friend, India may serve Russian interests more than any other actor in global politics. Russia had supported India's bid for full membership of the SCO. Both countries want a multi-polar world based on equal opportunities for all nations. In their quest for a multi-polar world, Russian and Indian interests are likely to converge more in the future. It is true that the post Cold War political calculations have changed, and that Russia is also inching closer to Pakistan and China, yet the level of confidence and trust it shares with India is high; and Russia's goal would be to maintain this trust and confidence. India's economic potentials would be an added attraction for Russia at a time when Russian economy is trying to regain its place in the world.

Russia–India relations are close at this point of time. The 'Special and Privileged Strategic Partnership', launched in 2010 is a case in point. However, India must come forward to clear any Russian misperception about genuine cooperation. Now that the nuclear plant at Kudankulam in Tamil Nadu (built with Russian assistance) has gone critical (in July 2013), India must ensure that it starts commercial production safely. It has the potential to meet acute power shortages in Tamil Nadu, and revive Russian confidence about India's commitment to international treaties. India has the responsibility, like Russia, to manifest its desire to consolidate strategic partnership. Till date, both India and Russia have committed themselves well to strengthen strategic partnership. As Putin correctly observed, 'the enormous potential of cooperation between the two great powers will be further explored for the benefit of the peoples of India and Russia and the international community in general. We have everything necessary to achieve this—political will of the sides, economic viability and shared global priorities. All this is based on the glorious history of the Indian Russian friendship'.[25] For their interests, both nations must carry forward close cooperation to new heights in the future.

---

[25] Ibid.

11

INDIA AND JAPAN
Partners in Peace

HIGHLIGHTS

- Introduction
- Political Relations in the New Century
- Economic Relations
- Security and Cultural Relations
- Recommendations for the Future

INTRODUCTION

Japan and India shared a close relationship since ancient times. With the introduction of Buddhism in Japan in the early sixth century AD, exchanges started between the two nations. Buddhism brought with it shades of Indian culture to Japan and the process of cultural interactions began. After the Second World War, Japan and India signed a peace treaty and established diplomatic relations in April 1952. This treaty was one of the first peace treaties Japan signed after the Second World War. For some time, in the post Second World War period, raw materials from India, particularly, coal and iron ore helped in Japan's industrialisation programme, and its recovery from the devastation of war.[1] After Japanese Prime Minister Nobusuke Kishi's visit to India in 1957, Japan decided to provide aid loans to India. In 1958, India received the first Yen aid provided by the Japanese government. Since 1986, Japan has remained as India's largest aid donor.

The Japanese Constitution of 1947, also known as the 'pacifist constitution', did not allow Japan to play an interventionist role in global politics. Japan played a politically passive role during the Cold War period. As a consequence, it was possible for Japan to develop friendly relations with many countries including India. During the Cold War period, Japan–India relations were cordial

[1] Aneek Chatterjee, *International Relations Today: Concepts and Applications* (New Delhi: Pearson), 2010, p. 258.

as both avoided being parties to the Cold War. With Japan's thrust on economic diplomacy, one of the few nations in the world to initiate economic diplomacy as a potential tool in international relations, Japan–India ties continued to be warm after the Cold War. However, Indian nuclear tests in 1998 elicited strong reactions from Japan leading it to cancel economic and technological assistance to India for some time. Japan's harrowing experience with nuclear bombs during the Second World War made it an ardent protagonist of non-proliferation of nuclear weapons. In this background, India's nuclear tests in 1998 did not go well with the Japanese political elite, as Japan imposed economic sanctions on India in May 1998. However, with continuing dialogues and diplomatic negotiations between the two countries, economic sanctions were waived and normalcy restored in Japan–India relations since the year 2000. Barring this nuclear-related hiatus, Japan–India relations remained warm since the end of the Cold War.[2]

POLITICAL RELATIONS IN THE NEW CENTURY

Japanese Prime Minister Yoshiro Mori's visit to India in August 2000 laid the foundation for closer Japan–India relations in the new century. The two nations signed an important agreement entitled 'Global Partnership between Japan and India in the 21st Century' during Mori's visit. This agreement called for enlargement of exchange and cooperation in economic fields, including information technology (IT) between the two nations. New Delhi and Tokyo agreed to facilitate comprehensive dialogue and wider cooperation by way of expanding regular bilateral exchanges of important ministers and leaders of the two nations. Since Mori's visit, annual meetings of the top leaders of the two countries have been taking place regularly. India's Prime Minister Atal Behari Vajpayee visited Japan in December 2001. Vajpayee's visit was the first visit to Japan by an Indian prime minister after nine years. During Vajpayee's visit, both countries agreed to cooperate on a variety of issues such as terrorism, Afghanistan, and disarmament and non-proliferation, from both regional and global perspectives. After the Summit Meeting between the two prime ministers, the 'Japan–India Joint Declaration' was announced as a guideline for future cooperation. In July 2002, Indian Defence Minister George Fernandes visited Japan. The year 2002 also marked 50 years of political relations between India and Japan. Strengthening of military and political ties, improving cooperation on bilateral issues and border problems between India and Pakistan were discussed during Fernandes' visit to Japan. The Indian defence minister held discussions with his Japanese counterpart Nakatani, Foreign Minister Yoriko Kawaguchi, and Japanese Prime Minister Junichiro Koizumi on issues related to bilateral cooperation.

High-level visits reflecting new spirits in bilateralism continued between India and Japan. In April 2005, Japanese Prime Minister Junichiro Koizumi visited India, while the Indian Prime Minister, Manmohan Singh paid a reciprocal visit to Japan in December 2006. During Manmohan Singh's visit, Japan agreed to engage in discussions with India on civilian nuclear cooperation

---

[2] Ibid.

under proper and appropriate international safeguards. Although Japan stopped short of any direct support to the landmark Indo–US nuclear deal, however the Japanese leadership opined that international civilian nuclear energy cooperation should be enhanced through 'constructive approaches' under appropriate International Atomic Energy Agency (IAEA) safeguards. Prime Minister of Japan Shinzo Abe visited India in August 2007. During his visit, Abe and Manmohan Singh agreed to take forward the growing relationship between the two Asian states. They agreed that Japan and India shared universal values of democracy, open society, human rights, rule of law and market economy, and the two nations also shared common interest in promoting peace, stability and prosperity in Asia and the world. Based on this recognition, the two leaders reaffirmed that the Japan–India partnership is a bilateral relationship with the largest potential for growth.[3] Following Indian Prime Minister Singh's visit to Japan in October 2008, Japan and India signed the 'Joint Statement on the Advancement of the Strategic and Global Partnership between Japan and India'.[4] The Joint Statement (JS) aimed to promote cooperation in a wide range of fields such as political, economic, environmental protection, energy security and climate change. Moreover, the 'Joint Declaration on Security Cooperation between Japan and India' was also signed during the visit to consolidate security relations between the two countries.

The Prime Minister of Japan, Yukio Hatoyama visited India in December 2009 as part of the annual bilateral summit meetings. The JS issued after the summit between Hatoyama and the Indian Prime Minister, Manmohan Singh focused on different areas of bilateral cooperation. According to the JS, the two prime ministers took note of the status of the Economic Partnership Agreement (EPA)/Comprehensive Economic Partnership Agreement (CEPA) negotiations with a view to conclude a mutually beneficial agreement at the earliest.[5] The two prime ministers hoped that economic relations between India and Japan would develop further after the conclusion of the EPA/CEPA. Hatoyama and Singh shared the view that Japanese Official Development Assistance (ODA) would continue to play an important role in India's poverty alleviation, economic and social infrastructure development and human resource development.[6] The two prime ministers reaffirmed their commitment to realise a comprehensive reform of the United Nations Security Council (UNSC), and vowed to continue their cooperation with the G-4 and other like-minded states in this regard. The two prime ministers re-affirmed their resolve to work together in the framework of regional cooperation, and Manmohan Singh lauded the sincere initiative taken by the Japanese prime minister for an East Asian community.[7]

Manmohan Singh paid an official visit to Tokyo from 24 to 26 October 2010 for the Annual Bilateral Summit. According to Indian Ministry of External Affairs (MEA), 'This landmark visit has imparted a further momentum and continuity to the India–Japan Strategic and

[3] Ibid., p. 259.

[4] Ibid.

[5] Ibid.

[6] Ibid.

[7] Ibid.

Global Partnership.'[8] The Indian prime minister and his wife had an audience with the Emperor and the Empress of Japan. He also held extensive talks with the Japanese Prime Minister, Naoto Kan. Minister for foreign affairs and minister for economy, trade and industry of Japan also met the Indian prime minister. The opposition leaders from Liberal Democratic Party, New Komeito Party and Your Party also called on Manmohan Singh.

In December 2011, Japanese Prime Minister Yoshihiko Noda paid an official visit to India from 27 to 29. During the visit, Yoshihiko Noda delivered an address at the Indian Council for World Affairs (ICWA) and attended a luncheon meeting hosted by the Chambers of Commerce and Industry. He also called on the vice president of India and held a summit meeting with the Indian prime minister. The two prime ministers signed a JS entitled 'Vision for the Enhancement of Japan–India Strategic and Global Partnership upon Entering the Year of the 60th Anniversary of the Establishment of Diplomatic Relations' between the two nations. The JS declared, 'In the context of the two countries commemorating the 60th anniversary of the establishment of diplomatic relations in 2012, the two prime ministers reaffirmed that Japan and India enjoy deep mutual understanding and vibrant people-to-people contact as the relationship is based on universal values such as democracy, human rights and rule of law, as well as wide-ranging strategic and economic interests. They stressed the need to enhance the Strategic and Global Partnership for peace and prosperity.'[9] Prime Minister Noda expressed his profound gratitude for the heartfelt sympathy and support extended to Japan by the government and the people of India after the Great East Japan earthquake. The two prime ministers reaffirmed the significance of annual summits between them. They also expressed satisfaction at ministerial-level and other policy dialogues such as those between foreign ministers and defense ministers of Japan and India. The two prime ministers welcomed the entry into force of Japan–India CEPA on 1 August 2011. Asserting that CEPA is an important milestone in the trade and economic relations between the two countries, they expressed hope that CEPA will further strengthen their economic engagement in terms of trade in goods, services, investment, and contribute immensely to mutual prosperity.[10] The two prime ministers expressed their resolve to continue to maintain and strengthen multilateral trading system, based on the outcome of the 8th WTO Ministerial Conference held in Geneva in December 2011.

Manmohan Singh visited Japan again in May 2013 for the Annual Bilateral Summit. This visit was scheduled to take place in November 2012, but New Delhi had to postpone the visit due to announcements of election dates in Japan, and dissolution of the Japanese Parliament. During the visit from 27 to 30 May, a JS signed by Manmohan Singh and the

---

[8] Ministry of External Affairs, India, 'India–Japan Relations', available at http://www.mea.gov.in/Portal/ForeignRelation/India-Japan_Relations.pdf, accessed on 2 November 2013.

[9] MOFA, Japan, 'Vision for the Enhancement of Japan–India Strategic and Global Partnership upon Entering the Year of the 60th Anniversary of the Establishment of Diplomatic Relations', available at http://www.mofa.go.jp/region/asia-paci/india/pmv1112/joint_statement_en.html, accessed on 2 November 2013.

[10] Ibid.

Japanese Prime Minister Shinzo Abe was issued in Tokyo. The JS entitled 'Strengthening the Strategic and Global Partnership between India and Japan Beyond the 60th Anniversary of Diplomatic Relations' expressed satisfaction at the steady growth of political exchanges, dialogue and policy coordination between the two countries. Observing that the CEPA has given a boost to economic and trade relations, Prime Ministers Singh and Abe stressed the importance of continued efforts to further enhance trade in goods and services as well as investments. The two prime ministers also welcomed the signing of the Agreement between India and Japan on Social Security in November 2012 and directed their relevant authorities in the governments to work towards its early entry into force. They expressed hope that this agreement would contribute to further accelerating bilateral activities of the private sectors.[11] The JS reaffirmed the importance of civil nuclear cooperation between the two authorities in the governments to work towards its early entry into force. They expressed hope that this agreement would contribute to further accelerating bilateral activities of private sectors.[12] The JS reaffirmed the importance of civil nuclear cooperation between the two countries, while recognising that nuclear safety is a priority for both the governments. In this context, they vowed to accelerate the negotiations of an Agreement for Cooperation in the Peaceful Uses of Nuclear Energy towards an early conclusion.[13] The two prime ministers welcomed the signing of the Memorandum between the Department of Atomic Energy (DAE) of India and the Ministry of Economy, Trade and Industry (METI) of Japan on cooperation in rare earths industry in India. They shared the view that the commencement of commercial production of rare earths by Indian and Japanese enterprises should take place at the earliest.[14]

The Prime Minister of India, Narendra Modi visited Japan from 30 August to 3 September 2014 for the 9th Annual Summit Meeting with the Prime Minster of Japan, Shinzo Abe. During the visit, the two sides decided to upgrade the relationship to a 'Special Strategic and Global Partnership' and launched an India–Japan Investment Promotion Partnership under which Japan announced its intention to invest in India approximately US $35 billion over the next 5 years. Prime Minister Shinzo Abe paid an official visit to India earlier for the 8th Annual Summit with Prime Minister Manmohan Singh from 25–27 January 2014 and was the Chief Guest at the Republic Day parade in New Delhi. During the visit, both the prime ministers signed a JS sharing their vision on intensifying the India–Japan Strategic and

[11] MEA, India, 'Joint Statement on Prime Minister's visit to Japan: Strengthening the Strategic and Global Partnership between India and Japan beyond the 60th Anniversary of Diplomatic Relations', available at http://www.mea.gov.in/bilateraldocuments.htm?dtl/21755/Joint+Statement+on+Prime+Ministers+visit+to+Japan+Strengthening+the+Strategic+and+Global+Partnership+between+India+and+Japan+beyond+the+60th+Anniversary+of+Diplomatic+Relations, accessed on 2 November 2013.

[12] Ibid.

[13] Ibid.

[14] Embassy of India, Tokyo, 'India–Japan Economic Relations', available at http://indembassy-tokyo.gov.in/india_japan_economic_relations.html, accessed on 3 November 2013.

Global Partnership. The following agreements were signed during the visit of Narendra Modi to Japan: (i) Memorandum on Defence Co-operation and Exchanges between Ministry of Defence of the Republic of India and the Ministry of Defence of Japan; (ii) Memorandum of Cooperation between the Ministry of Health and Family Welfare of the Republic of India and the Ministry of Health, Labour and Welfare of Japan in the Field of Healthcare, (iii) Memorandum of Cooperation in the Field of Women and Child Development between the Ministry of Women and Child Development of the Republic of India and the Ministry of Foreign Affairs of Japan; (iv) Framework of Cooperation between Ministry of Road Transport and Highways Government of India and Ministry of Land, Infrastructure, Transport, and Tourism of Japan in the Roads and Road Transportation Sector; (v) Memorandum of Understanding between Ministry of New and Renewable Energy, Government of India, and Japan Bank of International Cooperation; and (vi) Confirmation of the intention regarding the Partner City Affiliation between City of Varanasi and City of Kyoto.[15]

The foreign minister level 8th Strategic Dialogue was held in New Delhi on 17 January 2015. The two foreign ministers reviewed all aspects of the bilateral Strategic and Global Partnership and discussed regional and international issues of mutual interest. Bilateral Foreign Office Consolation was also held between Japan's Deputy Foreign Minister Shinsuke Sugiyama and Indian Foreign Secretary, S. Jaishankar in New Delhi on 6 April 2015 alongside the 'two plus two' bilateral dialogue at the level of foreign and defence secretaries.[16]

The Annual Bilateral Summits between the prime ministers of Japan and India, and other institutional mechanisms for dialogues and cooperation like the Annual Strategic Dialogues, Annual Defence Dialogues, Two Plus Two Dialogues. Exchange visits by parliamentarians and leaders indicate towards healthy and satisfactory political relations between the two significant Asian countries in the new century. After the initiation of these institutional mechanisms at the beginning of the new century, Japan and India have engaged each other more in recent times. As observed, both the nations try continuously to explore new areas of cooperation through these dialogue mechanisms. The Annual Bilateral Summits and other top-level engagements between the two nations have contributed towards strengthening confidence and mutual trust in Indo–Japan political relations in recent times.

ECONOMIC RELATIONS

Japan–India bilateral economic relations showed improvement in the recent past. For instance, bilateral trade reached US $18.32 billion in the financial year (FY) 2011–12, an increase of

[15] Ministry of External Affairs, Government of India, *Annual Report: 2014–15* (New Delhi: Government of India), 2015, p. 37.

[16] Ministry of External Affairs, Government of India, 'India–Japan Relations', available at http://www.mea.gov.in/Portal/ForeignRelation/Japan_2015_07_23.pdf, accessed on 21 August 2016.

33.52 per cent over FY 2010–11.[17] However, there was a decrease in total volume of bilateral trade during the last three FYs as Table 11.1 below indicated. India has been the largest recipient of Japanese Official Development Assistance (ODA) since 2003–04. Cumulative commitment of ODA till March 2013 reached Yen 3807.763 billion on commitment basis.[18] The CEPA between Japan and India became effective in August 2011 after 14 rounds of negotiation. The agreement is most comprehensive of all such agreements concluded by India in the recent times and covers not only trade in goods but also Services, Movement of Natural Persons, Investments, Intellectual Property Rights, Custom Procedures and other trade related issues. CEPA aims to strengthen all areas of bilateral economic relations in the foreseeable future.

A look into Japan–India bilateral trade since 2010–11 brings out a picture of ups and downs in this area. Table 11.1 below shows bilateral trade in recent years:

Table 11.1: India–Japan Bilateral Trade in Recent Years (in US $ billion)

Financial Year	*India's Export*	*India's Import*	*Total Trade*
2010–11	5.09	8.63	13.72
2011–12	6.32	12.00	18.32
2012–13	6.10	12.41	18.51
2013–14	6.81	9.48	16.29
2014–15	5.38	10.13	15.51
2015–16	4.67	9.84	14.51

Source: Embassy of India, Tokyo, 'India, India–Japan Economic Relations', available at http://indembassy-tokyo.gov.in/india_japan_economic_relations.html, accessed on 13 August 2016.

Table 11.1 above shows steady progress in bilateral trade in the three fiscals since 2010–11. The total volume of bilateral trade went up from US $13.72 billion in FY 2010–11 to US $18.51 billion in FY 2012–13. These three fiscals marked steady progress in bilateral trade volume. However, from FY 2013–14, the total volume of bilateral trade went down continuously. In 2013–14, the total volume of India–Japan trade was US $16.29 billion. In the next financial year (2014–15), it went down to US $15.51 billion. In the last financial year of 2015–16, India–Japan trade volume further went down to US $14.51 billion. This is not a healthy trend considering the fact that India and Japan shared good economic relations in the past. India's primary exports to Japan have been petroleum products, iron ore, gems and jewellery, marine products, oil meals, ferro alloys, inorganic and organic chemicals. India's primary imports from Japan are machinery, transport equipment, iron and steel, electronic goods, organic chemicals and machine tools.

[17] Ibid.

[18] Ibid.

As far as Foreign Direct Investment (FDI) is concerned, India is emerging as a favoured destination for Japanese FDI. Japanese companies have made actual investments of US $12.66 billion to India between April 2000 and June 2012. This accounted for 7 per cent of total FDI inflow into India and made Japan the fourth largest investor in India.[19] In 2012, Japan's FDI into India increased by 19.8 per cent over 2011 to reach US $2,786 million, although it accounted for only 2.3 per cent of Japan's overall FDI outflow in 2012. In 2013, the FDI declined by 22.64 per cent which is 1.6 per cent of the total FDI outflow from Japan. FDI from Japan to India was US $01.7 billion during January–December 2014.[20] The number of Japanese affiliated companies in India has grown significantly over the years. As on December 2014, 1,209 Japanese companies were registered in India which constituted a 13 per cent increase over 2013 figures. There were also a total of 3,961 establishments of Japanese businesses operating in India, a rise of 56 per cent compared to the year before.[21] During Indian Prime Minister Modi's visit to Japan in August–September 2014, both countries launched an India–Japan Investment Promotion Partnership under which Japan announced its intention to invest in India approximately US $35 billion over the next 5 years. The Japanese FDI into India has mainly been in automobile industry, electrical equipments, pharmaceuticals, trading and telecommunications sector.[22] India's growing economy and stable investment climate offer large opportunities for Japanese companies. India continued to rank as the top promising country over long term in both FY 2012 and FY 2011 as per surveys conducted by the Japan Bank of International Cooperation (JBIC). India was also ranked top as promising country for overseas operations over medium term with regard to automobile industry in the 2012 JBIC survey. India, however, ranked overall second following China as the promising countries for overseas business over the medium term. India also positioned second after China as a promising country for overseas operations with regard to major industries, including chemicals, general machinery, electrical equipment and electronics.[23] Some of the areas which provide significant opportunity for Japanese investment include infrastructure, manufacturing, automobiles and auto parts, power, metals, renewable energy, food processing and electronic hardware.[24]

A Japan–India Business Leaders' Forum (BLF) was envisioned during Prime Minister Manmohan Singh's visit to Japan in December 2006. The first meeting of the BLF took place in August 2007 in New Delhi. The Joint Proposal of the Forum stressed the importance of early conclusion of the CEPA, cooperation in hardware and software development, environmental and energy fields and high technology trade. The second meeting of the BLF was held in

---

[19] Ibid.

[20] Ibid.

[21] Ibid.

[22] Ministry of External Affairs, 'India–Japan Relations', available at http://www.mea.gov.in/Portal/ForeignRelation/Japan_2015_07_23.pdf.

[23] Ibid.

[24] For further details, see www.unitedasia.in/indo-japan-business.php, accessed on 19 May 2017.

October 2008. In this meeting, the Japanese delegate stressed the importance of increased assistance to infrastructure projects in India through effective public-private partnerships (PPP) between ODA and private investment. The two sides emphasised EPA as a necessary institutional infrastructure to further accelerate and consolidate expansion of bilateral investment and trade. The third meeting of the BLF was organised in Tokyo in October 2010. The business leaders of both the sides recognised that India–Japan CEPA is the cornerstone to further evolve and establish strategic economic partnerships. However, more frequent meetings between the business leaders are necessary to remove institutional hurdles and bring about greater liberalisation of trade and investment.

India is building a Dedicated Freight Corridor (DFC) and the Delhi Mumbai Industrial Corridor (DMIC) with the help of Japan. The DFC is intended to meet the transport requirements of the two busy trunk routes—Eastern and Western Corridors,—of the Indian Railways for the next 15 to 20 years. The DMIC project is proposed to be implemented on either side of the 1,483 km-long Western Dedicated Rail Freight Corridor between Dadri (in Uttar Pradesh), and Jawaharlal Nehru Port (in Navi Mumbai). The project intends to create a strong economic base with a globally competitive environment and state-of-the-art infrastructure to activate local commerce, enhance investments and attain sustainable development. The DMIC will cover the six states of Uttar Pradesh, Haryana, Madhya Pradesh, Rajasthan, Gujarat and Maharashtra and a majority of projects in DMIC are proposed to be implemented through the PPP mode.[25]

In addition to these economic engagements, the CEPA between Japan and India has created a strong mechanism for close cooperation in the future. As observed earlier, the CEPA became operative in August 2011, and worked as a cornerstone in bilateral economic relations. Article 1 of the CEPA (it has 147 Articles and 10 Annexes) brings out the objectives of this agreement. These are to:

(i) Liberalise and facilitate trade in goods and services between the parties;
(ii) Increase investment opportunities and strengthen protection for investments and investment activities in the parties;
(iii) Ensure protection of intellectual property and promote cooperation in the field thereof;
(iv) Promote cooperation for the effective enforcement of competition laws in each party;
(v) Improve business environment in each party;
(vi) Establish a framework to enhance closer cooperation in the fields agreed in this agreement; and

[25] MEA, India, 'Joint Declaration on Security Cooperation between India and Japan', available at http://www.mea.gov.in/bilateral-documents.htm?dtl/5408/Joint+Declaration+on+Security+Cooperation+between+India+and+Japan, accessed on 5 November 2013.

(vii) Create effective procedures for the implementation and application of this agreement and for the resolution of disputes. These objectives, if realised properly, would go a long way in consolidating Japan–India economic relations in future.

SECURITY AND CULTURAL RELATIONS

Security relations between India and Japan accelerated at the turn of the new century, leaving behind the strains of Pokhran II. Now, there are various frameworks of security dialogue between Japan and India. The Comprehensive Security Dialogue at the level of Joint Secretary/Director General was set up in 2001 and 10 rounds of dialogue have been conducted since then. Between the coast guards of the two countries, combined exercises on anti-piracy, search and rescue work have been conducted regularly since 2000. The heads of the coast guards of both the countries visit each other almost every year. The two coast guards exchanged a Memorandum of Cooperation on the occasion of Commandant Ishikawa's visit to India in November 2006. But the crowning glory in security relations was achieved in 2008 when both the nations entered into a landmark Security Cooperation Pact on 22 October 2008 during Prime Minister Manmohan Singh's official visit to Japan. With the conclusion of this Security Pact, India became only the third country after USA and Australia to have signed a comprehensive security document with Japan since the Second World War. Prime Minister Singh of India and Prime Minister Taro Aso of Japan concluded the agreement in Tokyo. The security pact identified the following 'Elements' of cooperation:

(i) Information exchange and policy coordination on regional affairs in the Asia Pacific region and on long-term strategic and global issues.
(ii) Bilateral cooperation within multilateral frameworks in Asia, in particular the East Asia Summit, ASEAN Regional Forum and ReCAAP processes.
(iii) Defence dialogue and cooperation within the framework of the JS signed in May 2006 between the two defence ministries.
(iv) Cooperation between the coast guards.
(v) Safety of transport.
(vi) Fight against terrorism and transnational crimes.
(vii) Sharing of experiences in peace-keeping and peace-building.
(viii) Disaster management.
(ix) Disarmament and non-proliferation.[26]

The security pact also provides for the following 'mechanisms' of cooperation:

1. Consultations will be conducted between the two foreign offices by way of;

[26] Ibid. (for full text).

I. Strategic dialogue at foreign minister-level,

II. Meeting between the foreign secretary of India and the vice-minister for foreign affairs of Japan,

III. Dialogue on disarmament and non-proliferation at director general/joint secretary level,

IV. Track 1.5 Strategic Dialogue,

2. Cooperation will be conducted between the two defence authorities by way of various ways such as;

   I. Meetings between the defence ministers,

   II. Meetings between the defence secretary of India and the vice-minister of defence of Japan including defence policy dialogue,

   III. Military-to-Military Talks at director general/joint-secretary level,

   IV. Exchange of service chiefs,

   V. Navy-to-Navy Staff Talks,

   VI. Service-to-service exchanges including bilateral and multilateral exercises,

   VII. Exchange of students and researchers for respective defence institutions (for example, Indian National Defence College, Japanese National Institute for Defense Studies).

3. Consultation will be conducted between the National Security Advisor (NSA) of India and the Japanese counterpart.

4. The two coast guards will continue to promote cooperation to ensure maritime safety, maritime security and to protect marine environment through joint exercise and meeting between the two coast guards, according to the Memorandum on Cooperation between the Indian Coast Guard and the Japan Coast Guard.

5. In relation to the safety of transport, shipping policy forum will be conducted between maritime authorities and private sectors, and consultation will be conducted between the railway authorities.

6. Comprehensive Security Dialogue will be conducted at Director General/Joint Secretary level.

7. Bilateral consultation will be conducted to promote counter-terrorism cooperation through such means as Joint Working Group (JWG) on counter-terrorism between the relevant government offices, including the Ministries of Foreign Affairs.

8. Mechanism of sharing of information will be sought with regard to suspicious transaction on money laundering and terrorist financing between the two financial intelligence units (FIUs).

9. Cooperation will be conducted to develop a tsunami disaster map in India.

10. The two sides will promote capacity-building in disaster prevention, preparedness, sharing knowledge and experience of both countries.
11. Cooperation will be conducted between the Indian Space Research Organisation (ISRO) and the Japan Aerospace Exploration Agency (JAXA) in the field of disaster management.[27]

Regarding 'Implementation' provisions, the Pact said, 'India and Japan will develop an action plan with specific measures to advance security cooperation in the above areas and report to the Prime Ministers at an early date.'[28] The Security Cooperation Pact of 2008 was also a laudable achievement in bilateral relations in the sense that it was signed after only 10 years of Japanese military and economic sanctions on India after India's nuclear tests in 1998 (Pokhran II). Many perceived this pact as a counterweight to China's growing economic and military might in Asia, although both India and Japan denied this factor.[29]

The action plan to implement the security pact was issued during Japanese Prime Minister Hatoyama's visit to India in December 2009. The Annual Senior Officials 'two plus two' dialogue, which was agreed to be established in 2009, was held continuously. Maritime Self Defense Force (SDF) joined in the 'Malabar 09' which was co-hosted by the US and India in April 2009. The Defense Minister of India, A. K. Antony visited Japan in November 2011 to hold the Japan–India Defense Ministerial meeting with Yasuo Ichikawa, the Japanese defense minister. During the meeting, the two ministers decided to carry out bilateral exercise between the Japan SDF and the Indian navy. At the annual summit in December 2011, Prime Minister Noda and Prime Minister Singh affirmed that they would expand cooperation in the area of maritime security, including safety and freedom of navigation. The coast guards of both the nations conducted a joint exercise at Chennai in January 2012.

The civil nuclear cooperation is an important element of Japan–India friendship and is expected to play a significant role for strengthening relations in the future. Both the countries have been searching for ways to conclude a Civil Nuclear Agreement (CNA) early. Several rounds of negotiation have been conducted for achieving a CNA, but the talks got stalled after the Fukushima radiation disaster in Japan in March 2011. However, talks were resumed in late 2011 for civil nuclear cooperation. During his talks with Prime Minister Noda in December 2011, Prime Minister Manmohan Singh expressed hope for sharing Japanese nuclear technology and

---

[27] Ibid.

[28] Rajaram Panda, 'India and Japan: Exploring Strategic Potentials', *Journal of Defence Studies*, 4 (4): 94, 2010. Also, Ministry of Defense, Japan, 'Summary of National Defense Program Guidelines for FY 2011 and Beyond', available at http://www.mod.go.jp/e/d_act/d_policy/pdf/summaryFY2011.pdf, accessed on 5 November 2013.

[29] Ministry of Defense, Japan, 'Summary of National Defense Program Guidelines for FY 2011 and Beyond', available at http://www.mod.go.jp/e/d_act/d_policy/pdf/summaryFY2011.pdf, accessed on 5 November 2013.

experience, especially in the nuclear safety field. In response, Mr Noda stated that Japan wished to negotiate with India in a productive and cooperative manner so that both sides may reach a mutually satisfactory agreement. In early 2012, the foreign ministers of the two countries met in New Delhi and instructed their negotiators to carry forward the nuclear negotiations. In view of the multi-faceted cooperation and dialogue between India and Japan in the area of renewable and energy conservation, it was expected that an India–Japan CNA would be concluded soon. During Japanese Prime Minister Shinzô Abe's visit to India in December 2015, Japan and India reportedly made progress on a nuclear deal that they have been discussing for more than seven years. According to a leading Indian newspaper, the governments did not actually conclude the deal: the Joint Statement released by the Prime Ministers only includes a droll phrase welcoming the 'agreement reached . . . for Cooperation in the Peaceful Uses of Nuclear Energy' and expresses the hope that '. . . this Agreement will be signed after the technical details are finalized'.[30] However, Japan is placing increasing importance to India in security matters. This could be substantiated from the fact that Japan's 'National Defense Program Guidelines for FY 2011 and Beyond' put emphasis on security cooperation with India along with a few other countries of Asia. The document stated that Japan will enhance security cooperation with countries such as the Republic of Korea, Australia, ASEAN countries and India.[31]

Both India and Japan decided to further enhance security cooperation in the recent times. They agreed to regularise and increase the frequency of maritime defence exercises, while India agreed to purchase the US-2 amphibious aircraft for reconnaissance along its maritime frontier. Moreover, to enhance science and technology cooperation, the two countries agreed to step up cooperation in cyber security. With these measures, bilateral security cooperation has widened and deepened.[32] Given other growing areas of cooperation such as bilateral coast guard and naval exercises and the rapid institutionalisation of the US–Japan–India Trilateral Dialogue, Japan–India channels of communication have expanded, triggering bilateral political and security confidence. During the visit of Indian Prime Minister Narendra Modi to Japan in August–September 2014, an important Memorandum on Defence Co-operation and Exchanges between Ministry of Defence of the Republic of India and the Ministry of Defence of Japan was signed. This will further facilitate security cooperation between the two nations.

The much awaited India–Japan Civil Nuclear Cooperation Agreement was finally signed in Tokyo on 11 November 2016 during Prime Minister Narendra Modi's visit to Japan. Modi and his Japanese counterpart Shinzô Abe signed the landmark agreement in Tokyo, after several years of sustained and sometimes difficult negotiations between the two countries. According to Indian MEA sources, 'The Agreement provides for bilateral cooperation in the

[30] *The Hindu*, New Delhi, 17 December 2015.

[31] Ministry of External Affairs, India, 'India–Japan Relations', available at http://www.mea.gov.in/Portal/ForeignRelation/India-Japan_Relations.pdf, accessed on 10 November 2013.

[32] For further details, see www.belfercenter.org/publication/japan-india-security-cooperation, accessed on 19 May 2017.

field of Nuclear Energy. This would provide for the development of nuclear power projects in India and thus strengthening of energy security of the country. The present agreement would open up the door for collaboration between Indian and Japanese industries in our Civil Nuclear programme.'[33]

After signing the agreement, Prime Minister Narendra Modi said, 'Today's signing of the Agreement for Cooperation in Peaceful Uses of Nuclear Energy marks a historic step in our engagement to build a clean energy partnership'.[34] India was the first non-NPT signatory country with which Japan entered into a civil nuclear agreement. This manifested Japan's growing trust on India, and a strong bilateral relationship. The civil nuclear agreement marked a significant achievement for Modi's foreign policy also. Nine other agreements were also signed between the two countries during Modi's visit. These agreements covered areas of cooperation in agriculture, textile, defence, space research, investment, education and culture.

India–Japan cultural engagement dates back to early sixth century when Buddhism was introduced in Japan. Since then, close cultural contacts between the two Asian territories continued. In more recent times, cultural relations were institutionalised when the cultural agreement between India and Japan was signed in 1956, and took effect the following year. In 1951, India established a scholarship system for overseas students. This system provided an opportunity to young Japanese scholars engaged in Indian studies to study in India.[35] According to Ministry of External Affairs (MEA) sources, cultural contacts picked up in the 1980s with Japanese local governments becoming involved in exchange activities with their Indian counterparts. Traditional Indian performing arts are regularly shown in Japan. Festivals to promote Indian and Japanese cultures are organised in both the countries regularly. During the visit of the prime minister of India to Japan, a year-long Festival of India in Japan 2014–15 was announced. The dance festival organised in October included more than 20 performances in 20 cities across Japan by Bharatanataym, Manipuri, Kudiyattam and Mohiniyattam dance groups from India. As a part of the festival, Indian Home Minister Rajnath Singh, along with Japan's State Minister for Internal Affairs and Communication Kosaburo Nishime inaugurated the Exhibition of Buddhist Art at the Tokyo National Museum on 16 March 2015. Other programmes under the festival included a Symposium on Buddhist manuscripts, food festival and India–Japan literary festival.[36] Japan has also been extending cultural grant-in-aid to research institutes, universities, and cultural faculties to encourage their activities. In addition, through the United Nations Educational, Scientific, and Cultural Organization (UNESCO) and the Japan Trust Fund for the Preservation

---

[33] Ministry of External Affairs, 'List of Agreements/MoUs Exchanged During the Visit of Prime Minister to Japan', http://mea.gov.in/bilateral-documents.htm?dtl/27597/List_of_AgreementsMOUs_exchanged_during_the_visit_of_Prime_Minister_to_Japan; accessed on 18 May 2017.

[34] *The Times of India*, New Delhi, 12 November 2016.

[35] Source: MOFA, Japan; see, www.mofa.go.jp › Regional Affairs › Asia › India, accessed on 19 May 2017.

[36] Ministry of External Affairs, 'India–Japan Relations', available at http://www.mea.gov.in/Portal/ForeignRelation/Japan_2015_07_23.pdf.

of the World Cultural Heritage, Japan is helping with the preservation and restoration of the Buddhist monuments of Sanchi and Satdhara.[37]

Cultural bonds have contributed positively in enhancing friendship and trust between the two countries. In an 'opinion survey' conducted by the Ministry of Foreign Affairs of Japan in India on the image of Japan during February–March 2013, it was revealed that 80 per cent of respondents perceived the current state of Japan–India relations either as being 'very friendly' or 'friendly'.[38] More than 70 per cent of respondents expressed interest in learning the Japanese language and more than 60 per cent responded affirmatively to the suggestion that more young people should study in Japan in order to gain a higher education. Seventy-six per cent of respondents said that they followed Japan-related media reports regularly or occasionally.[39] Overall, these figures indicate strong interest in Japan and the Japanese language and culture among the Indians.

RECOMMENDATIONS FOR THE FUTURE

Japan–India relations have vast potential for significant growth. But this potential has not been realised to its full till date. Japan is one of the strongest economies and India is one of the fastest growing economies in the world. But bilateral trade volume has not grown in the recent years. Japan–India economic relations require more steam. India accounts for less than 2 per cent of the total trade of Japan. Japan–India trade constitutes less than 2.5 per cent of total global trade of India. According to MEA sources, '... the share of the India–Japan bilateral trade has hovered in the range of 2.21 to 2.46 of India's total trade during the last five fiscal years. This is quite small considering the size of the two economies.'[40] India is not a major export or import destination of Japan. Indian exports to Japan in the financial year (FY) 2015–16 constituted only 2.01 per cent of India's total export, and fell from 2.41 per cent in FY 2005–06. Likewise India's imports from Japan made only 2.47 per cent of India's total imports in FY 2015–16, and fell from 2.73 per cent in FY 2005–06.[41]

Japanese FDI to India is insignificant compared to total Japanese FDI outflow abroad. Although FDI from Japan to India is increasing, it has not yet reached a substantial volume. In its report, the MEA has observed that '... the current level of FDI from Japan reflects neither the potential of Japan to invest nor the capacity of India to absorb'.[42] Japan also holds reservations about India's nuclear programme, and supports the view that India should sign the NPT. This view of

---

[37] See in this context, MOFA, Japan, 'Opinion Survey on the Image of Japan in India', available at http://www.mofa.go.jp/press/release/press6e_000122.html, accessed on 10 November 2013.

[38] Ibid.

[39] Ibid.

[40] Ministry of External Affairs, 'India–Japan Relations', n. 16.

[41] Ibid.

[42] Ibid.

Japan added to delaying the conclusion of the civil nuclear agreement between the two countries. However, much ice has been broken in this area in the recent times and the agreement was finally signed. In view of the presence of these grey areas in bilateral relations, some recommendations are provided below for further development in India–Japan relations:

- Both countries should try to ensure that bilateral trade volume reach US $50 billion by 2025.
- Full and speedy implementation of CEPA is necessary to boost economic relations.
- Necessary infrastructure must be created by India to absorb more FDI from Japan.
- Full and effective implementation of the 'security pact' is required to strengthen bilateral security relations, including counter-terror programmes.
- The conclusion of the much awaited CNA is laudable—not only to boost peaceful uses of nuclear energy, but also to enhance the trust factor in bilateral relations. However, half-hearted measures in this area should be avoided by both the countries.
- Indian studies in Japan and Japanese studies in India must be promoted through regular university-level cooperation, and research collaboration. Such 'studies' should aim to cover different areas like art and culture, history, language and literature, society and politics, and science and technology.
- Increasing collaboration in the fields of environment, energy, and science and technology is necessary.
- Both nations must cooperate closely, as they have done in the past, for restructuring the United Nations Security Council (UNSC), at the East Asian Summit, and other multilateral fora.

India and Japan are partners in peace and prosperity. The relationship between these two Asian countries is free from any dispute—territorial, ideological, cultural and political. Both share sound commitment for democracy and rule of law. The people of both the nations have respect and liking for one another, as revealed by the 'opinion survey' conducted by the Ministry of Foreign Affairs (MOFA). These two nations have been friends since the ancient times. But in the twenty-first century, this cultural bonding must also be backed by strong economic and security relationship. It is heartening to note that India and Japan have already accorded economic and security relations top priorities in bilateral engagement. This is evident from the CEPA, the security pact and the CNA concluded by the two nations in the recent times. With full realisation of these mechanisms, India–Japan relations would reach new heights in the coming years.

12

INDIA AND THE EUROPEAN UNION

Growing Relations

HIGHLIGHTS

- Introduction: A New Phase in Relationship
- EU–India ties in the 1990s
- Cooperation in the New Century
- India–EU Economic Relations
- India–EU Strategic Partnership
- Conclusion: Action Plan for the Future

INTRODUCTION: A NEW PHASE IN RELATIONSHIP

Britain's decision to move out of the European Union (EU) may have posed a challenge to the organisation, but it has not affected the India–EU relations in the recent times. The European Union (EU) is a very important economic and political block in today's world. India is also an emerging economic power. Therefore, the two can hardly ignore each other at this point of time. In a strict technical sense, the EU came into existence in 1993 after the Masstricht Treaty, signed by 12 European states in 1991, and ratified in 1993 by the parliaments of the signing countries. But the history of the EU dates back to the late 1940s when preparations for a united European Economic Community (EEC) started. The European Coal and Steel Community (ECSC) formed in 1950 was an early manifestation of such efforts. The EEC, which came into existence in 1957, consolidated the concept of a united Europe. The EU is a continuation of that process. From 12 in 1993, the membership of the EU had risen to 28 with five more countries waiting for its membership (as of May 2017). These five countries are: Macedonia, Montenegro, Serbia, Albania and Turkey. If these five nations are accorded membership of the EU, only 16 other European states would remain outside the EU. These figures indicate the growing importance of the EU among the European nations. Nearly 75 per cent of the European nations have already become members of the EU. At nearly 500 million, the population of the EU is the third largest in the world after China and India. It accounts for the greatest share of world trade and generates one-quarter of global wealth. The EU is the world's biggest trader, accounting for nearly 20 per cent of global exports and imports.[1] As one of the top emerging economies of the world, India has also made its mark in global economy and politics in the recent years. It is natural therefore that both EU and India would want to establish closer links. In fact, since the beginning of the new century, EU and India have strengthened their relationship, although India's engagement with the EEC could be traced back to the early 1960s. However, since the year 2000, a new and brighter phase in relations began with the initiation of EU–India summits. This chapter aims to analyse this growing relationship between India and the EU since the official launch of the latter.

EU–INDIA TIES IN THE 1990S

The emergence of the EU from the earlier EEC saw the rise of a potent economic and political bloc in the world. With India liberalising its economy in 1991, both EU and India looked at each other with renewed interest. In the 1990s, EU and India had established closer relations in several important areas covering trade and economic ties, political negotiations, cultural exchanges and partnership in development. In December 1993, India and the EU signed the Cooperation Agreement on Partnership and Development (CAPD), a landmark agreement which opened up possibilities for partnership and cooperation in several areas. The CAPD, which came into force in August 1994, provided for a Joint Commission (JC) comprising personnel from both India and the EU to monitor and develop areas of cooperation between the two. Three important sub-commissions were formed to speed up cooperation in trade, other economic partnerships and development. The sub-commissions would report directly to the JC.

In July 1996, the European Commission released a document entitled, 'EU–India Enhanced Partnership', which outlined a plethora of activities to strengthen relationship in line with the recommendations of the earlier CAPD. The document outlined areas of mutual interest, and suggested enhanced partnership in these areas. The identified areas of mutual interests covered trade and economic issues, sustainable development, opportunity creation, supporting social development and basic services, removing barriers for increased trade, reinforcing democracy and international political issues. The document put special emphasis on information exchange and regular visits by leaders and officials. It suggested intensifying the political dialogue between EU and India, trade and investment facilitation, and helping India face structural adjustment. To achieve enhanced partnership, the document placed additional emphasis on building institutional framework, increasing cultural understanding and working through priorities. Elaborating on building the 'institutional framework', the document identified the following measures:

(i) Respect for human rights and democratic principles as an essential clement

---

[1] *'The EU in the World: The Foreign Policy of the European Union'*, available at http://ec.europa.eu/publications/booklets/move/67/en.pdf, accessed on 18 March 2016.

(ii) Development and diversification of trade and investment in mutual interest
(iii) Encouragement of understanding and strengthening of ties between the two regions in respect of technical, economic and cultural matters
(iv) Building up India's economic capability to interact more effectively with the EU
(v) Promotion of exchanges and communication between business communities
(vi) Acceleration of India's development in particular to support new Indian policies in key areas fostering sustainable social progress and poverty alleviation; and
(vii) Support for environmental protection and sustainable use of natural resources.[2]

In the political realm, such institutional framework would relate to (a) defending democracy, human rights, peace and a stable, just, international order in line with the UN Charter; (b) reinforced co-operation to promote prosperity, economic reform, liberalisation, free trade and economic stability as well as social progress and cultural links; (c) allowing each others' interests to be taken into account in decision-making procedures; and (d) a better mutual understanding to increase co-operation on international questions such as non-proliferation, the fight against terrorism, drug trafficking, money laundering and issues linked to international peace and stability.[3] It should be noted in this context that the EU had always assisted India in its development activities. In 1996, when the document was released, the EU was the second largest bilateral aid donor to India providing 16 per cent of total aid the country received, and the largest grant donor, accounting for 60 per cent of all grants to India. Such close cooperation between India and EU continues, not only in economic sphere, but in all areas of socio-political segments.

COOPERATION IN THE NEW CENTURY

India's relations with the EU got a tremendous fillip with the Inaugural India–EU Summit held in Lisbon on 28 June 2000. In this summit, both the sides signed the Civil Aviation Cooperation Agreement, which was the beginning of a series of agreements in many other areas in the following years. An important decision, to hold regular summit meetings in the future, was taken in this summit. Both EU and India pledged to cooperate closely to promote peace in their respective regions through dialogues and confidence-building measures with the countries concerned. The first summit in Lisbon heralded the beginning of regular Annual Summits between the two sides, which manifested the urge to establish closer ties through mutual friendship. In keeping with the promise generated at the Lisbon Summit, the Second India–EU Summit took place in New Delhi in November 2001. Besides a joint communiqué which emphasised on the need for enhanced cooperation in areas like trade, environment and science and technology, the Second Summit also

---

[2] See in this context, Commission of the European Communities, *EU–India Enhanced Partnership* (Brussels: EU Commission), 26 June 1996, p. 16.

[3] Ibid.

produced an agenda for action, a declaration against terrorism, the India–EU vision statement on information technology (IT), and the India–EU agreement on science and technology. These bilateral agreements paved ways for stronger partnership in the future.

In the Third Bilateral Summit held in Copenhagen in October 2002, a five-year strategy for cooperation and an agenda for action were adopted. The European Commission released its country strategy paper for 2002–06 for India, which promised increased cooperation in economic activities and development efforts. The Fourth Summit held in New Delhi in November 2003, initiated a Euro 14.1 million trade and investment development programme and a bilateral maritime shipping agreement. This agreement helped to launch the India–EU Maritime Transport Project aimed at improving infrastructure and efficiency in the major Indian ports. For instance, Electronic Data Interchange (EDI) in Indian ports was introduced under this project. Infrastructural development and the EDI in Indian ports would help facilitate trade between the two sides. In the Fifth Bilateral Summit held in November 2004 at the Hague, India and the EU resolved to upgrade their relationship to the level of a 'strategic partnership'. Both sides agreed to take their relations beyond trade and commerce, and decided to forge closer ties in other areas, like defence, health, education, culture, science and technology and counter-terrorism. After the introduction of 'strategic partnership' in 2004, India and EU have remained engaged in increased cooperation in all these areas.

The Sixth Summit held in New Delhi in September 2005, issued a Joint Action Plan (JAP). The JAP addressed several issues like political and cultural cooperation, trade and investment, combating terrorism and organised crime, academic exchanges and civil society contacts. The JAP also proposed the establishment of a high-level trade group to explore the scope for a future investment agreement, and to suggest avenues for increased economic flow between the two sides. The JAP, revised in 2008, aimed at realising the full potential of strategic partnership in key areas of interest to India and the EU. The two sides now have in place an institutional framework, cascading down from the annual EU–India Summit, to a senior-official level Joint Committee, to the Sub-Commission on Trade and to the working groups on technical issues such as technical barriers to trade (TBT), sanitary and phytosanitary measures (SPS), agricultural policy or industrial policy. These are the mechanisms where a number of day-to-day issues, such as EU market access problems, are discussed.

The Seventh India–EU Summit was held in Helsinki in October 2006. The areas of primary focus in this summit included India–EU relationship, cooperation in counter-terrorism, and energy. A Joint Statement (JS) and the Joint Action Plan Implementation Report were issued at the summit. The highlight of the Seventh Summit was the acceptance by the leadership of both the sides of the recommendations of the High Level Trade Group (HLTG) to launch negotiations on a broad based trade and investment agreement with the maximum coverage possible, and to work towards conclusion of this agreement. Both the sides also expressed satisfaction over the establishment of a fourth new working group on petroleum and natural gas.

The Eighth Summit meeting between India and the EU was held in New Delhi on 30 November 2007. A JS and a Joint Action Plan Implementation Report were issued at the summit.

Both sides expressed their determination to further strengthen the Strategic Partnership and to cooperate at a global level for the cause of peace, security and sustainable development for all. The two sides also took note of the work of the HLTG since the last summit, when it was decided to work towards concluding a broad-based trade and investment agreement. At the summit, the importance of EU–India cooperation in science and technology was also highlighted.[4]

The Ninth India–EU Summit was held in Marseilles, France in September 2008. The leaders put emphasis on strong India–EU relations in the future. They also deliberated on global and regional issues. A speedy implementation of the trade and investment agreement, and closer economic ties between India and EU were also discussed at Marseilles. While welcoming the signing of a horizontal civil aviation agreement, they encouraged the conclusion of a mutually beneficial maritime transport agreement. The two sides also noted that joint cooperation within the framework of the International Thermonuclear Experimental Reactor (ITER) Agreement remains a priority, which will be further enhanced through the conclusion of a bilateral agreement between Euratom and India in the field of fusion energy research, for which negotiations are being finalised. India and the EU also announced their intention to promote dialogue and cooperation in education and culture. The summit approved the following:

- A revised JAP extending the strategic partnership of 2005 to new areas;
- A joint work programme on energy, clean development and climate change;
- A horizontal civil aviation agreement;
- The launch of a European Business and Technology Centre in India, to support business-to-business and research cooperation between the EU and India.[5]

The Tenth India–EU Summit was held in New Delhi on 6 November 2009. The summit reviewed India–EU relations and exchanged views on developments in India and EU. It also recognised the need to pursue the reform of the main bodies of the United Nations (UN); and resolved to jointly fight terrorism in all its forms and manifestations. The leaders took note of the signing of the India–EU agreement in the field of nuclear fusion energy research, underlining the importance of energy security and clean energy; agreed to work towards early conclusion of the broad-based trade and investment agreement and the Maritime Transport Agreement. The leaders also identified trade and investment, energy, counter-terrorism, science and technology, climate change and the movement of people as priority areas of cooperation.[6]

The Eleventh India–EU Summit was held in Brussels on 10 December 2010. This was the first summit after the entry into force of the Lisbon Treaty. The summit reviewed India–EU relations; stressed the importance of an ambitious and balanced conclusion of the India–EU Broad-based

---

[4] Source: Indian Embassy to the EU, see www.indembassy.be/pages.php?id=55, accessed on 17 May 2017.

[5] Embassy of India to Belgium and the European Union, 'Overview of India–EU Relations', available at http://www.indembassy.be/political_dialogue.html, accessed on 25 January 2013.

[6] Ibid.

Trade and Investment Agreement (BTIA) in the spring of 2011. It welcomed the increasing cooperation in the field of security and defence; and issued a Joint Declaration on International Terrorism. An India–EU Joint Declaration on Culture was also signed during the summit.[7] In the Joint Statement issued by the leaders, it was agreed to present the results of the 2008 Joint Work Programme on Energy, Clean Development and Climate Change at the next India–EU summit in 2011. The JS also called for an early conclusion of the India–EU Agreement for Research and Development Cooperation in the Peaceful Uses of Nuclear Energy; a swift finalisation of the agreement on satellite navigation initialled in 2005; and an early implementation of the civil aviation agreement. The summit also witnessed exchange of views on regional and global issues covering Afghanistan, Pakistan, G-20, climate change and disarmament. An India–EU Business Summit was held on the sidelines of the summit.[8]

The Twelfth India–EU Summit was held in New Delhi on 10 February 2012. The leaders expressed satisfaction about gradual maturing of bilateral relationship. An MEA Report observed that India and EU, as long-standing strategic partners, are committed to working together with a balanced and result-oriented approach, bearing in mind each sides' respective development priorities, based on common shared values, relating to democracy, rule of law, civil liberties, fundamental freedoms and respect for human rights.[9] Both the sides discussed bilateral, regional and multilateral issues of mutual concern with a view to, inter alia, strengthen their multifaceted bilateral cooperation, coordinate responses to regional issues and tackle international challenges, including the current financial crisis.[10]

The Thirteenth EU–India Summit was held in Brussels on 30 March 2016. At this summit, the two sides reaffirmed their commitment to strengthen the EU–India Strategic Partnership based on shared values and principles. They confirmed their strong interest in building global peace, security and prosperity, and fostering non-proliferation and disarmament. The two sides also expressed their commitment in creating jobs and inclusive economic growth, promoting sustainable development, and tackling global challenges such as terrorism and climate change in addition to other challenges such as migration and refugee crisis. To achieve a stronger, result-oriented and mutually beneficial strategic partnership, the leaders endorsed the 'EU–India Agenda for Action-2020' setting out a concrete road-map for the EU–India Strategic Partnership for the next five years.[11]

---

[7] Source: MEA, GoI, see www.mea.gov.in/Portal/ForeignRelation/india-eu-relations-january-2012.pdf, accessed on 17 May 2017.

[8] Ibid.

[9] Source: MEA, GoI, mea.gov.in/in-focus-article.htm?18352/Joint...by+India...European...IndiaEU..., accessed on 17 May 2017.

[10] Ibid.

[11] Ministry of External Affairs, Government of India, 'India–EU Joint Statement on the 13th India–EU Summit, Brussels', available at http://http://www.mea.gov.in/bilateral-documents.htm?dtl/26576/IndiaEU+Joint+Statement+on+the+13th+IndiaEU+Summit+Brussels, accessed on 7 September 2016.

An analysis of India–EU summits since the year 2000 highlights that the two sides had been very eager to forge close ties in almost all areas, economic, strategic, political, science and technology, counter terrorism, environment and educational. The two sides placed greater emphasis on multifaceted bilateralism, keeping in view the importance of both the EU and India in the emerging global economic and political order. Bilateral relations have been strengthened in the new century due to the annual bilateral summits between the two sides. This could be ascertained from the growing economic and strategic relations between India and the EU. In the following section, economic relations between the two would be focused to highlight how the EU and India have forged strong connections in the recent times.

INDIA–EU ECONOMIC RELATIONS

India and the EU are now engaged in relatively strong economic cooperation. India has become an important trade partner of the EU in the recent years. The total value of EU–India trade grew from €28.6 billion in 2003 to €77.58 billion in 2015. EU investment in India grew nearly six times between 2003 and 2013: going up from €759 million in 2003 to €4.3 billion in 2013. Trade in commercial services tripled during the same time-period, going up from €5.2billion in 2002 to €23.7 billion in 2013.[12] In 2015, India became the ninth largest trading partner of the EU with a share of 2.2 per cent of the total EU trade. However, in the year 2011, India was the eighth largest trading partner of the EU accounting for 2.5 per cent of the total EU trade. Therefore, India's share of the total EU trade has fallen marginally in recent years. EU remains the largest trading partner of India with nearly 15 per cent share of India's global trade in 2015.[13] Table 12.1 highlights EU–India trade in recent years:

Table 12.1: EU–India Trade in Recent Years (in Euro billion)

Year	*Import*	*Export*	*Balance*	*Total Trade*
2005	19.114	21.250	2.136	40.364
2006	22.637	24.241	1.604	46.878
2007	26.668	29.181	2.515	55.847
2008	29.632	31.356	1.724	60.988
2009	25.503	27.499	1.996	53.003
2010	33.464	34.891	1.427	68.354
2011	39.927	40.582	0.665	80.509
2012	37.528	38.541	1.014	76.069
2013	36.843	35.959	–0.884	72.801
2014	37.146	35.625	–1.521	72.771
2015	39.448	38.141	–1.307	77.589

Source: European Commission, *Trade: India,* available at http://trade.ec.europa.eu/doclib/docs/2006/september/tradoc_113390.pdf, accessed on 21 May 2016.

It could be observed from Table 12.1 that EU–India trade has grown

[12] European Commission, *Trade: India*, available at http://ec.europa.eu/trade/creating-opportunities/bilateral-relations/countries/india, accessed on 25 January 2013.

[13] Ibid.

significantly during the year 2015. From a total trade volume of Euro 72.77 billion in 2014, bilateral trade registered a growth of Euro 77.58 billion in 2015. This accounts for a 6.60 per cent growth in trade in 2015. However, this volume is lower than the total trade volume achieved in 2011 between EU and India. The total trade volume between EU and India was Euro 80.50 billion in 2011, the highest in recent times. EU–India trade registered nearly 30 per cent growth in 2010 over the previous year. In 2011, it registered nearly 20 per cent growth over the preceding year. This substantial growth rate in trade has pushed India to the eighth position among the largest EU trade partners in the year 2011. In this connection, it would not be irrelevant to identify largest trade partners of the EU. Table 12.2 focuses on the largest trade partners of EU in 2015:

Table 12.2: Largest Trade Partners of the EU in 2015

Rank	*Name of the Country*	*Total Trade in 2015 (in Euro Million)*	*Per cent Share of Total EU Trade in 2015*
1.	USA	619,660	17.6
2.	China	520,909	14.8
3.	Switzerland	253,199	7.2
4.	Russia	209,672	6.0
5.	Turkey	140,714	4.0
6.	Norway	123,128	3.5
7.	Japan	116, 318	3.3
8.	South Korea	90,248	2.6
9.	India	77, 589	2.2

Source: European Commission, *Trade: India,* available at http://trade.ec.europa.eu/doclib/docs/2006/september/tradoc_113390.pdf, accessed on 21 May 2016.

Table 12.2 above shows that India is the ninth largest trade partner of the EU with 2.2 per cent share of the total EU trade in 2015. India is just behind South Korea in terms of total trade with the EU in 2015. The EU is also one of the largest sources of FDI for India. As observed already, investment from EU countries in India grew six times from 2003 to 2013. The most important countries in the EU for FDI in India are Germany, the UK, Italy, Sweden and Belgium.

India and the EU have held several rounds of negotiations for a bilateral BTIA (Broadbased Trade and Investment Agreement). Negotiations commenced in 2007 and covered the following areas: trade in goods, sanitary and phyto-sanitary measures and technical barriers to trade, trade in services, investment, Intellectual Property Rights (IPRs) and Geographical Indications, Competition Policy, Customs and Trade Facilitation, Trade Defence, and Dispute Settlement. The India–EU Joint Commission with its three sub-commissions on trade, economic cooperation and development cooperation meets annually. India and EU have Joint Working Groups (JWGs) on counter-terrorism, consular issues, agriculture and marine products, energy, environment, technical barriers to trade and sanitary and phyto-sanitary issues, textiles, steel, information technology and communications, pharmaceuticals and biotechnology, food processing industries and customs cooperation. Both sides also have regular dialogues on security, human rights, macro-economy and science and technology.

India and the EU have also signed bilateral agreements which includes cooperation in the field of science and technology in 2001, which was renewed in 2007; Joint Vision Statement (JVS) for promoting cooperation in the field of information and communications technology in 2001; customs cooperation agreement in 2004; Memorandum of Understanding on Cooperation on Employment and Social Affairs in November 2006; Horizontal Civil Aviation Agreement in 2008; Joint Declaration in the field of education in 2008; Joint Declaration on Multilingualism in March 2009 and Agreement in the field of nuclear fusion energy research in November 2009 and Joint Declaration on Culture in December 2010.[14] The India–EU Joint Commission dealing with economic and commercial issues meets annually, as do its three sub-commissions on trade, economic cooperation and development cooperation. The last joint commission meeting at the level of secretaries was held in New Delhi on 26 June 2014 and the last meetings of the sub-commissions on economic cooperation and trade were held in Brussels on 6–7 March 2014, while the sub-commission on development cooperation met on 3 June 2014 in New Delhi.[15]

INDIA–EU STRATEGIC PARTNERSHIP

As mentioned earlier, India and the EU signed in June 2004, a Strategic Partnership Agreement (SPA), which defined five priority areas of cooperation: (1) multilateral cooperation in the international sphere with an emphasis on conflict prevention, anti-terrorism, non-proliferation, the promotion of democracy and the defence of human rights; (2) strengthened economic cooperation involving sectorial dialogues with jointly drafted regulatory policies; (3) cooperation in development so as to enable India to achieve the Millennium Goals as framed by the UN; (4) intensifying intellectual and cultural exchange; and (5) improving the institutional framework of Indo–European relations. Both India and the EU have decided to give greater emphasis to counter-terrorism cooperation, as outlined in the framework of the strategic partnership. A tie between Europol and the Indian agency concerned may also come up in the future. Establishing a distinct intelligence capability under the new European External Action Service (EEAS) is a possibility.

Although the strategic partnership has produced some tangible results in improving cooperation, a lot more need to be achieved in India–EU relations. However, some concrete achievements deserve mentioning. For example, India has become a participant in the ITER and GALILEO programmes, thus significantly improving the potential for much enhanced cooperation between

---

[14] Ministry of External Affairs, Government of India, *India–EU Relations* (New Delhi: Government of India), 2011.

[15] Ministry of External Affairs, Government of India, *India–EU Relations*, available at http://http://www.mea.gov.in/Portal/ForeignRelation/India-EU_Relations_Website_Brief_-July_16__2015.pdf, accessed on 7 September 2016.

the European Space Agency and its Indian counterpart, the Indian Space Agency.[16] Furthermore, a 33 million euro scholarship scheme, within the Erasmus Mundus framework, has been established in order to encourage student exchange between India and the EU. The creation of a Jean Monnet Chair in European Studies at the University of Delhi should also contribute to achieving these objectives. The BTIA and other bilateral agreements cited earlier also contribute towards realising the strategic partnership.

Observers of the EU–India strategic partnership are unanimous that even after many annual summits the EU–India strategic partnership remains under-explored. For instance, the plan to achieve a Free Trade Agreement (FTA) has not yet materialised, despite several rounds of negotiation on this issue. It is true that the complex structures, intertwines of various European institutions, stands of member-states on various issues and participation in different systems (like Euro, Schengen) are difficult to overcome, yet both India and the EU must pay more attention to improving their relations. Given the Indian foreign policy establishment's preoccupation with its immediate neighbourhood and the USA, the energy and concentration required to study the unique evolution of the EU seem to be missing. The EU was equally slow to recognise India's potential as an important international actor. As both India and EU are committed to a multi-polar world order and determined to address the current challenges, re-energising the EU–India strategic partnership is an urgent necessity.

CONCLUSION: ACTION PLAN FOR THE FUTURE

India accounted for only 2.2 per cent of total EU trade in 2015. Although India was among the 10 largest trading partners of the EU in 2015, India lagged behind other potential economies like China and Russia in forging strong economic partnership with the EU. While China and Russia accounted for 14.8 per cent and 6.0 per cent respectively of total EU trade in 2015 (see Table 12.2), India's records in this respect was hardly encouraging. Therefore, the first and most important action plan for India would be to augment India's trade with the EU in the near future. The full realisation of the BTIA within a specific time-frame of 4–5 years should be aimed at by the two sides. An early FTA may help in boosting economic relationship between the two sides.

According to a leading expert, the EU also needs to follow certain policies to boost relations with India in the future.[17] The first of these is to strengthen a sense of European unity and to prevent the overriding trend of each member-state to go it alone in its relations with India. 'Given India's size, its burgeoning economy and its increasing political and military power, the only possible European partner for India is the European Union as a whole. The sooner this reality is

---

[16] https://spire.sciencespo.fr/hdl:/2441/f5vtl5h9a73d5ls974os14q2h/resources/art-cj.pdf, accessed on 17 May 2017.

[17] Christopher Jaffrelot, *India and the European Union* (Paris: CERI, Sciences Po), 2006.

accepted the better for all of Europe', thinks the expert.[18] Second, EU's policies in relation to India vis-à-vis China need to be rebalanced. In India, the pro-Chinese bias of the EU is not received well. 'For Indians the Sino-centrism of Europeans is paradoxical, given Europeans' purported concern with promoting democracy and the Rule of Law, two areas in which China's record leaves a great deal to be desired. A more balanced European policy would be well received in India if it also involved actively supporting India's campaign for a permanent seat on the UNSC, an objective opposed by China and one on which the US is very reticent. Supporting India's permanent membership on the UNSC would have the added advantage of bringing India back to the multi-lateralist fold', writes the expert.[19]

Third, EU needs to focus on its industrial strengths to rejuvenate its cooperation with India. There are two vital areas here, namely infrastructure and environmental protection because they are both areas of crucial importance for India. India requires cooperation in the areas of energy, conventional and modern, climate change, and problems of drinkable water, besides infrastructural development. The EU may establish long-term cooperative projects with India in these areas. Finally, '... to turn to initiatives that would help revive EU–Indian cooperation in areas that are both symbolic and substantive, like those of higher education and work experience. By being far more flexible in providing visas to Indian students and professionals, considerable progress could be made in removing one of the continual thorns in the side of EU–Indian relations', believes the expert.[20] A flexible visa system for students, businessmen and tourists would certainly help in the process of trust and confidence building. With a burgeoning economy, more and more Indians are wishing closer contact with the Europeans. A rigid visa regime, as effective now, would only enhance distance between India and a unified Europe. This would not help in the projected strengthening of India–EU relations in the future. The EU needs to look at India with new vision and new strategies in the twenty-first century. In this context, it is heartening to note that the two sides have endorsed at the 13th EU–India Summit in March 2016, the 'EU–India Agenda for Action-2020' setting out a concrete road-map for the EU–India Strategic Partnership for the next five years. Now they require commitment for effective implementation of this agenda.

---

[18] Ibid.

[19] Ibid.

[20] Ibid.

13

INDIA AND BRITAIN

Strategic Partners?

HIGHLIGHTS

- Introduction
- Political Relations
- Economic Relations
- Security and Cultural Relations
- Recommendations for the Future

INTRODUCTION

For seven decades since India's independence in 1947, India–Britain relations have remained reasonably steady. History, democracy and shared values have contributed to the uniqueness of Indo–British relations. Much of Indian public life has been structured around British laws, ideas and values. Indian political and legal institutions, constitutional government, free press, civil service, modern universities and research laboratories have all been fashioned through British influence. Britain contributed at various levels in India's developmental projects after India's independence. However, it was only in the late 1980s that India and Britain began to view each other as genuine partners, free from the hangover of the colonial experience. After the Cold War, the relationship moved beyond culture, curry and cricket, as Britain became India's foremost trading partner. The strong Indian diaspora living in Britain acts as a catalyst for close bilateral ties. The population of Indians living in Britain is estimated to be 1.6 million, mostly engaged in 'white collar' jobs and business. Further, a large number of Indian students pursue higher studies in British universities.

India's commitment to continue good relations with Britain was reflected immediately after independence when India decided to remain a member of the British Commonwealth, later renamed as the Commonwealth of Nations. India always supported the Commonwealth movement and played an engaged role in matters of the organisation, including hosting the Commonwealth Games in 2010. Moreover, the large Indian community living in England is now very active in British politics, and is capable of having an impact on the courses of bilateral relations. The present British government attaches importance to developing a special relationship with India in the field of education. Approximately 34 British universities have opened offices in India and are approaching students even from small towns in India, besides the four metropolitan cities.[1] Trade and security relations have been on the rise in the recent times. Britain also supported India's bid for a permanent membership of the United Nations (UN). All these factors indicate that Britain and India are engaged in a meaningful bilateral relationship mutually beneficial for both nations at the middle of the second decade of the twenty-first century.

POLITICAL RELATIONS

The new century began with close cooperation between the two countries, as top-level bilateral visits continued facilitating a multi-faceted relationship. Prime Minister Atal Behari Vajpayee visited Britain in November 2001. In a joint press meet with the British Prime Minister, Tony Blair, Vajpayee praised bilateral cooperation in the area of counter-terrorism. He observed that Britain was the first country to ban six terrorist groups operating in the Indian sub-continent and thanked the British prime minister for this positive action. The Indian prime minister noted at the press meet, 'I also welcome the additional measures, which have been taken, and those that are being contemplated. They will strengthen the regime against international terrorism. The ongoing fight against terrorism provided an important context for our discussion today. Both our countries have been familiar with the ugly face of terrorism for long before 11 September. We have to go beyond Al-Qaeda in our global war against terrorism and target all its sponsors, who finance, train, equip and harbour terrorists.'[2] Blair paid a return official visit to India in January 2002. He was the first British prime minister in 12 years to visit India, although many important leaders from Britain came to India during this period. In New Delhi, Blair focused on the importance of the resumption of a 'comprehensive' dialogue between India and Pakistan. He opined that for talks to be meaningful, all terrorist activities should stop. Talks between the British and Indian prime ministers in New Delhi on 6 January resulted in a joint declaration condemning all supporters and sponsors of terrorism. Clearly, the agenda for counter-terrorism got preference as an issue in bilateral relations in the aftermath of the 9/11 terrorist attacks on the US.

The Prime Minister of India, Manmohan Singh paid an official visit to Britain in September 2004 and met his British counterpart and other leaders. During the visit, the two prime ministers signed a Joint Declaration (JD) titled 'India–UK: Towards a New and Dynamic Partnership', which paved ways for annual summit meetings between prime ministers and meetings between

---

[1] Ministry of External Affairs, Government of India, *Annual Report: 2014–15* (New Delhi: Government of India), 2015, p. 106.

[2] Press Information Bureau (PIB), Government of India, PIB releases, available at http://pib.nic.in/archieve/lreleng/lyr2001/rnov2001/12112001/r1211200114.html, accessed on 20 June 2012.

foreign ministers of the two nations. This JD created new and positive chapters in India–England relations at the beginning of the new century. Since 2004, the prime ministers of Britain and India, as well as their foreign ministers have been meeting regularly, initiating greater confidence and engagement in bilateral relationship. The JD also outlined areas for future cooperation in civil nuclear energy, space, defence, counter-terrorism, economic ties, science and technology, education and culture. The British prime minister mooted the idea of India joining the G-8 discussions. At his invitation, Singh visited England again in July 2005 for the 'G-8 plus 5' Gleneagles Summit featuring heads of government of five emerging economies (India, China, South Africa, Brazil and Mexico) with the G-8 leaders. This was a good opportunity for India to get an entry into the 'rich industrial club' of the world.

In his capacity as the President of the EU, British Prime Minister Tony Blair visited India in September 2005, for the EU–India Summit on 7 September, and also for the second UK–India bilateral Summit held on 8 September in Udaipur, Rajasthan. At the summit, the two prime ministers put emphasis on measures to significantly enhance trade and investment exchanges, including in the new and promising area of healthcare, and in promoting exchanges in the area of services. They also agreed to intensify cooperation in areas of science and technology and the knowledge sector, in which both the countries have special strengths. Several Memoranda of Understanding (MoUs) and agreements were finalised during the summit. These related to:

(i) Cooperation in the area of hydrocarbons, important for overall energy policy of the two nations
(ii) An MoU on sustainable development
(iii) An agreement on Intellectual Property Rights (IPR)
(iv) An agreement on co-production of films; and
(v) A new Air Services Agreement. The British prime minister reaffirmed his commitment to India's candidature for the permanent membership of the expanded United Nations Security Council (UNSC). The Indian prime minister conveyed to his British counterpart that the Government of India (GoI) had decided to create a Chair named after Jawaharlal Nehru at Cambridge University. Manmohan Singh also welcomed Prime Minister Blair's Education Initiative, which would enhance student exchanges and academic relationships between the two nations at the university level. Prime Minister Singh visited Britain again in October 2006 for the third Annual UK–India Summit.

British Prime Minister Gordon Brown visited India in January 2008. During his visit, the fourth UK–India Annual Summit was held in New Delhi. After the summit, the two sides issued a JS on India–UK Strategic Partnership. The two sides also agreed to cooperate in developing collaboration between small and medium enterprises, entrepreneurs and venture capitalists. It was agreed to establish an education forum to work towards an early conclusion of an education partnership agreement and to enter into an MoU on an Indo–UK Higher Education Leadership

Development Programme to develop leadership skills in higher education.[3] The two prime ministers also agreed to promote cooperation in civil nuclear energy and promised to work towards a bilateral agreement for this purpose. Gordon Brown informed Prime Minister Manmohan Singh that Britain supported the India–US civil nuclear cooperation initiative.

In January 2009, British Foreign Minister David Miliband paid a three-day official visit to India. His visit was marked by some amount of controversy as he linked terrorism to the 'unresolved' problem of Jammu and Kashmir. The Indian foreign ministry expressed its reservations over Miliband's views and said that India did not want unsolicited advice on India's internal issues such as Jammu and Kashmir. The opposition Bharatiya Janata Party (BJP) in India termed the visit as a 'disaster', while the opposition Conservative Party in Britain called it as 'damaging' for good UK–India relations. However, Miliband's views, expressed in the *Guardian* newspaper, were termed as 'personal and unintended' to hurt Indian sentiments by the British government. Apart from this hiccup, which did not go ways to affect bilateral ties, Britain–India relations remained cordial after the Cold War.[4]

British Prime Minister David Cameron's visit to India in July 2010 laid the foundations for 'Enhanced Partnership for the Future', which was defined by a high-level economic and technological cooperation and close coordination on many regional and global issues. The British prime minister was accompanied by the largest ever delegation to India since 1947 that included Foreign Secretary William Hague, Chancellor George Osborne and 67 other members from the fields of business, culture, sports, parliament, media, local government, science and education and technology. The mission, as Cameron himself observed, was '... to take the relationship between India and Britain to the next level, to make it stronger, wider and deeper.'[5] During the visit, the two governments announced a deal between BAE Systems, Rolls-Royce and India's leading aerospace company Hindustan Aeronautics Limited (HAL) to supply 57 Hawk trainer aircraft to India. It followed a previous agreement to supply 66 Hawk aircraft to India. The deal was worth about £700 million, of which more than £500 million is for BAE Systems and up to £200 million for Rolls-Royce. The deal will support 200 jobs in Britain. The British prime minister declared that the deal was an evidence of Britain's new commercial foreign policy in action, and he identified India as a leading partner in this policy.[6]

High-level bilateral visits from India and Britain continued after 2010. The two countries also devised several bilateral mechanisms for closer cooperation. These mechanisms are:

(i) Foreign Office Consultations (FOC), which are held annually between the foreign officials of the two nations

---

[3] Source: Press Information Bureau, GoI; see pib.nic.in/newsite/erelcontent.aspx?relid=34816, accessed on 17 May 2017.

[4] Aneek Chatterjee, *International Relations Today: Concepts and Applications* (New Delhi: Pearson), 2010, p. 265.

[5] See, *The Hindu*, 28 July 2010.

[6] BBC News, *David Cameron Launches Indian Trade Drive*, available at http://www.bbc.com/news/uk-politics-10784317, accessed on 16 August 2015.

(ii) Joint Working Group (JWG) on counter-terrorism and strategic dialogue
(iii) India–UK Round Table where multi-faceted bilateral issues are discussed every year
(iv) India–UK Joint Trade and Economic Committee (JETCO)
(iv) India–UK financial dialogue
(v) India–UK investment summit
(vi) India–UK education forum for forging closer partnership in the field of education; and
(vii) UK–India Education and Research Initiative (UKIERI).

These useful mechanisms have helped strengthen bilateral relations in the new century.

Engagements between India and England intensified after the new government took office in India in May 2014. British Foreign Secretary, William Hague and Chancellor of the Exchequer, George Osborne jointly visited India during 7–8 July 2014. They held meetings with the new Indian Prime Minister Narendra Modi and External Affairs Minister Sushma Swaraj to discuss political, strategic and economic issues as also matters relating to Indian students in the UK, and skill development.[7] The two sides have had a number of high-level bilateral visits and interactions in the recent past. The Indian prime minister met his counterpart, David Cameron on the sidelines of the G-20 Summit in November 2014 in Australia, and discussed issues of mutual interests. Indian external affairs minister visited Britain during 16–17 October 2014 to inaugurate the Regional 'Pravasiya Bharatiya Diwas', where she had bilateral meetings with the British deputy prime minister and foreign secretary. The Indian Minister of State for External Affairs, V. K. Singh visited London from 3–4 December 2014 to attend the London Conference on Afghanistan.

The Indian Minister for Commerce and Industry, Nirmala Sitharaman visited London from 18–20 January 2015 for the 10th JETCO. Arun Jaitley, the Finance Minister, visited London from 13–14 March 2015 to unveil the statue of Mahatma Gandhi in British Parliament Square. The Indian Minister of State for Power, Coal and New and Renewable Energy visited the UK from 22–23 May 2015 and held meetings with the Parliamentary Under Secretary, Department of Energy and Climate Change (DECC) and Parliament Under Secretary, Department for International Development. From the British side, many high-level visits took place in 2014–15. Nick Clegg, the Deputy Prime Minister of Britain, visited India from 25–27 August 2014; former British Foreign Secretary William Hague, accompanied by Chancellor of the Exchequer George Osborne, Minister for Government Policy in Cabinet Office, Oliver Letwin and the then Head of Downing Street Policy Unit, Jo Johnson visited India in July 2014.[8] British Business

[7] Ministry of External Affairs, Government of India, *Annual Report: 2014–15* (New Delhi: Government of India), 2015, p. 104.

[8] Source: MEA, GoI; see www.mea.gov.in/Portal/ForeignRelation/United_Kingdom_2015-07_27.pdf, accessed on 17 May 2017.

Secretary, Vince Cable visited India in October 2014 and Minister for University, Science and Cities, visited India in November 2014. British Foreign Secretary Philip Hammond visited India from 12–13 March 2015 for bilateral consultations.

The Prime Minister of India, Narendra Modi visited Britain from 12–14 November 2015. During the visit, the Indian prime minister and his counterpart endorsed a 'Vision Statement' setting out the fundamental principles on which UK–India partnership would be built and outlined a road-map for deepening cooperation.[9] 'Both Prime Ministers resolved to hold biennial PM-level Summits to advance the partnership and agreed on a new Defence and International Security Partnership aimed to intensify cooperation on defence and security, including cyber security, counter-terrorism and maritime security. They also endorsed a Joint Statement on Energy and Climate Change and issued a Statement of Intent to scale up bilateral cooperation to a global partnership for development cooperation in third countries.'[10] The Indian Finance Minister, Arun Jaitley visited the UK in January 2016 to attend the 8th India–UK Economic and Financial Dialogue. These bilateral visits in the recent times indicate a strong relationship between the world's largest and one of the oldest democracies.

ECONOMIC RELATIONS

Britain's decision to leave the European Union (EU) generated some tension about Indo–British trade in the future. However, as things turned out, the decision did not affect bilateral economic relations between the two countries. As statistics reveal, economic relations between India and Britain have got strengthened over the years through increased trade and investment flows. The policy planners in both the countries showed manifest interest to strengthen economic and commercial cooperation between India and Britain. Important and result-oriented bilateral mechanisms have been set up to augment economic cooperation. Other useful mechanisms like India–Britain Economic and Financial Dialogue (EFD), India–Britain JETCO, and India–UK Financial Partnership (IUFP) form the basis of institutional engagements between the two countries. According to Indian MEA sources, 'The India–UK Economic and Financial Dialogue (EFD) was officially established in February 2005 through signing of an agreement between former finance ministers of the two countries to strengthen the financial and economic relationship between India and the UK, in the light of each country's economic policy agenda and within a global economic perspective.'[11] The Eighth India–UK EFD, held on 19 January 2016 in London explored new areas of cooperation in the financial services sector. The dialogue, led by Finance Minister of India, Arun Jaitley and British Chancellor of the Exchequer, George Osborne covered, 'discussions

---

[9] Source: PIB, GoI; see pib.nic.in/newsite/PrintRelease.aspx?relid=130408, accessed on 17 May 2017.

[10] High Commission of India in the UK, *India–UK Relations*, available at https://www.hcilondon.in/pages.php?id=19, accessed on 23 March 2016.

[11] Ministry of External Affairs, Government of India, *India–United Kingdom Relations*, available at http://www.mea.gov.in/Portal/ForeignRelation/UK-Jan_2016_en.pdf, accessed on 11 May 2016.

on Global Economic Challenges, Macroeconomic Risks and Policy Responses, Infrastructure Finance and Financial Services. The UK government agreed to support the delivery of major infrastructure projects in India across key sectors including smart cities, renewable energy and railways, all of which are vital for India's future economic growth.'[12] The Tenth JETCO meeting was held on 19 January 2015 in London. At this meeting, both government and industry leaders came together for discussions at the JWGs on 'Education', 'Technological Collaborations' and 'Smart Cities'. The latest IUFP meeting was held in London on 2 November 2015. The meeting decided that the partnership would focus on the following work-streams: development of corporate bond market, mutual sharing of expertise on the financial sectors and market regulations (with an initial focus on India's Insolvency Regulation), pensions, infrastructure funding, financial inclusion, internationalisation of the rupee, cross-border provision of financial and insurance services (with an initial focus on re-insurance), enhancing financial training and qualification and divestments.[13]

Elaborate institutional mechanisms established over the years helped India and Britain to strengthen bilateral trade and investment. The volume of two-way bilateral trade was US $14.33 billion in the financial year (FY) 2014–15, up from US $12.67 billion in FY 2010–11. India's merchandise export to Britain went up to US $9.32 billion in 2014–15 from US $7.32 billion in 2010–11, although Indian imports dipped a little and stood at US $5.01 billion in 2014–15 from US $5.39 billion in 2010–11. India's main exports to Britain are garments and textiles, machinery and instruments, petroleum products, footwear and leather, manufactures of metals, gems and jewellery, engineering goods, transport equipment and parts, spices, drugs and pharmaceuticals and marine products. The main imports from the UK to India are machinery and equipment, ores and metal scraps, precious and semiprecious stones, silver, metallic ferrous, aircrafts and parts, beverages and spirits, machinery, engineering goods, and other professional instruments other than electronics, non-ferrous metals and chemicals. Britain is currently ranked 18th among 25 leading trade partners of India.[14] Table 13.1 reveals India–Britain trade during the last five fiscals:

Table 13.1: India–England Trade in Recent Years (in US $ billion)

Year	*Exports*	*Imports*	*Total Trade*
2010–11	7.28	5.39	12.67
2011–12	8.58	7.13	15.71
2012–13	8.61	6.29	14.90
2013–14	9.77	6.04	15.81
2014–15	9.32	5.01	14.33

Source: Compiled by the author from Export-Import Data Bank, Ministry of Commerce, Government of India.

Britain is the third largest inward investor in India after Mauritius and Singapore with a cumulative equity investment

[12] Ibid.

[13] Ibid.

[14] Ibid.

of US $21.60 billion (April 2000–September 2014). It also ranks first among the G-20 countries and accounts for around 9 per cent of all investment into India for the period April 2000–September 2014.[15] In 2013–14, the UK invested US $3.2 billion in India, more than any other G-20 country and more than Japan (US $1.7 billion) and the USA (just under US $1 billion), who are ranked second and third respectively. Although FDI from Britain to India dropped in the FY 2014–15 compared to earlier years, it remained one of the top inward investors to India among the EU countries. Table 13.2 presents FDI from England to India during the last five financial years:

Table 13.2: Foreign Direct Investment from England to India in Recent Years (in US $ billion)

Year	*Amount of FDI*
2010–11	2.7
2011–12	7.8
2012–13	1.0
2013–14	3.2
2014–15	1.1

Source: Ministry of External Affairs, Government of India, *Annual Report* (2010–11 to 2014–15).

India has also emerged as the third largest source of FDI for Britain after the US and France in terms of number of projects. According to a report released by the UK Trade and Investment (UKTI), the US remained the largest source of inward investment, with a total of 564 projects in 2014–15, followed by France (124 projects) and India (122 projects). During the year, investment from India increased by 65 per cent. This resulted in the creation of 7,730 jobs as well as protection of 1,620 jobs. The key sectors where Indian companies invested include healthcare, agri-tech, food and drink.[16]

SECURITY AND CULTURAL RELATIONS

India and Britain have strengthened their defence relationship by establishing capability partnerships in strategic areas, through which they work together for military effectiveness. These partnerships enable transfer of strategic capability between the two nations, including defence technologies and manufacturing in areas of mutual interest. India and Britain stand united against terrorism in all its forms and manifestations and support the early finalisation of a Comprehensive Convention on International Terrorism.[17] They work together to prevent terrorist attacks and counter violent extremism, including exchange of best practices and technologies. Both the countries also work together to drive forward international efforts to counter extremism and the ideology that encourages it.[18]

---

[15] Ministry of External Affairs, Government of India, *Annual Report: 2014–15* (New Delhi: Government of India), 2015, p. 105.

[16] *The Hindu*, 23 June 2015.

[17] For further details, see https://www.gov.uk/.../news/uk-india-defence-and-international-security-partnership, accessed on 17 May 2017.

[18] Ibid.

India and Britain are key partners on cyber and digital technology. The two countries have agreed, during Indian Prime Minister Modi's visit to Britain in November 2015, to expand the British Chevening Cyber Scholarships programme for India and to establish a Cyber Security Training Centre of Excellence. The two countries have decided to improve their ability to tackle cross-border cyber crime and online child sexual exploitation. Britain will provide advice on the setting up of the new Indian Cyber Crime Coordination Centre, and expert-level links will be developed between practitioners and policymakers in this field.[19] During Modi's visit, India and England also signed an Agreement on Civil Nuclear Cooperation between the two countries. Moreover, they planned to work together to enhance their cooperation against serious and organised crime through information sharing, operational cooperation and exchange of best practice to disrupt and dismantle criminal networks, bring the perpetrators to justice, and protect their citizens. Further, they have pledged to join hands to promote a secure international maritime domain. The two countries will strengthen their naval cooperation in the Indian Ocean, and exchange of information to enhance Maritime Domain Awareness (MDA). England and India come together to tackle the scourge of piracy, coordinating closely in the UN Contact Group on Piracy off the Coast of Somalia and work together to build the capacity of littoral states to respond to piracy and maritime crime.

The two countries have created important mechanisms to augment cooperation in security areas. They have decided to hold annual strategic dialogues between the defence ministers, and between the joint/integrated and single service chiefs. The two countries will hold annual Defence Consultative Group and Executive Steering Group Talks, and will introduce a sixth steering group to coordinate joint forces and integrated defence staff cooperation. India and Britain will intensify their biennial military exercise programme, starting with the naval, army and air force exercises. The two countries aim to strengthen the training and lecture exchange programmes across their Defence and Staff Colleges and training establishments. The two countries will develop their annual JWGs on counter-terrorism and cyber, including encouraging close contacts between respective agencies of both nations. Further, India and Britain have decided to continue their regular consultations on disarmament and non-proliferation issues. The two nations plan to deepen their cooperation in the region by holding a new annual senior official dialogue on South Asia, which also includes maritime issues.

India and Britain enjoy centuries-old cultural linkages. As observed earlier, much of Indian public life and education in modern times have been structured around British idea, law, values and education. This strong link continues to flourish in recent times. British universities continue to draw a large number of Indian students. In fact, in recent years, Indian students make the second largest student community in the UK after Chinese students. As per the statistics released by the UK Council for International Student Affairs (UKCISA), the total number of Indian students in the UK in 2014–15 was 18,320. However, changes in law introduced by the British government for study in universities in the UK have reduced the number of Indian students to the UK. For instance, in 2011–12, number of Indian students in

[19] Ibid.

the UK was 29,900. It came down to 22,385 in 2012–13. The number was further reduced to 19,750 in 2013–14.[20] However, Indian students still composed the second largest foreign student community in Britain in the year 2014–15 after Chinese students.

Britain and India have set up the UKIERI in 2005. Long-term objectives of UKIERI are as follows: (i) Bringing India and the UK together through academic engagement; (ii) Developing long-term sustainable partnerships; (iii) Developing new institutions and centres of excellence as global knowledge hubs; (iv) Successfully integrating research, education and business needs; (v) Enhancing capacities of institutions through development of sustainable initiatives in leadership, skills development and innovation; (vi) Providing opportunities for joint learning through adapting models, standards and practices prevalent in both India and the UK across sectors; and (vii) Contributing to the mutual recognition of learning.[21] After successful completion of Phase I and Phase II of the programme, UKIERI has initiated Phase III in April 2016 to enhance further cooperation in education and research between Britain and India. The UKIERI-III, with higher budgetary allocation of 3 million GBP per year (from 2.5 million GBP in earlier phases) from each side, will provide a basic framework for bilateral cooperation between India and the UK over the next 5 years. It will focus on leadership and faculty development, integration of skills in the education system, e-partnership and research incubation and enhancing mobility. Further, India and Britain have declared the year 2016 as 'UK–INDIA Year of Education, Research and Innovation'.

The High Commission of India in the UK acts as a cultural outreach to people living in the UK. The Nehru Centre of the High Commission 'organises a wide range of cultural evenings at its premises, showcasing Indian music, dance and theatre, besides a range of activities aimed at strengthening and deepening the intellectual dialogue between the two countries, such as exhibitions, lectures, illustrated talks, book launches, film screenings, seminars and round tables'.[22] The Indian and British cultural institutions signed an MoU in 2010 on collaboration in areas related to museology. The MoU stressed on management and administration, research and development of skills, loans and exhibitions, digitisation of collections, etc.—all related to museology. According to an MEA Report, 'The respective cultural institutions are taking this initiative forward and proactively pursuing specific projects in order to enhance cooperation between the two countries.'[23] The British Council is currently working on a five-year arts and cultural initiative named 'Reimagine to Build New Creative Linkages between the Peoples of India and Britain'. Under the initiative, 'several bilaterally relevant projects are being financed and supported by the British Council'.[24]

---

[20] All figures from statistics released by the UKCISA in its website, http://institutions.ukcisa.org.uk// info-for-universities-colleges--schools/policy-research--statistics/research--statistics/international-students-in-uk-he/#International-(non-UK)-students-in-UK-HE-in-2014-15, accessed on 20 May 2016.

[21] Source: UKIERI, see www.ukieri.org/objectives.html, accessed on 17 May 2017.

[22] Ministry of External Affairs, 'India–UK Relations', available at http://mea.gov.in/Portal/ForeignRelation/United_Kingdom_Feb2015.pdf, accessed on 20 May 2016.

[23] Ibid.

[24] Ibid.

The role of the Indian diaspora needs special mention in strengthening India–Britain relations. In 2016, 1.6 million people of Indian origin live in the UK. They comprise nearly 2 per cent of the total population, and make one of the largest ethnic communities in Britain. The Indian diaspora acts as a bridge, political, cultural, and economic, between the two nations. The MEA Report observes, 'There is deep appreciation in India for the contribution of the Indian diaspora in the UK, including in the Parliament, government, business, healthcare and education and in furthering bilateral relationship.'[25] Not only in India, the diaspora has also earned special appreciation in British political and public life as well. Many Indians remain in the top bracket of rich individuals in Britain; and companies owned by them provide jobs to people in Britain. The diaspora is now capable of having an impact on British politics and economics, and India–Britain relations.

RECOMMENDATIONS FOR THE FUTURE

India–Britain relations, although deep, have never attained its full potentials. As discussed earlier, the two countries have resorted to encouraging developments to strengthen bilateral relations, but ties between the two needed more fillip. Bilateral trade could be cited as a case in point. Among all the major powers discussed in this volume, India's trade with Britain remained one of the lowest during the last five fiscals. Table 13.3 reveals India's bilateral trade with the major powers during the last five fiscals:

Table 13.3: India's Bilateral Trade with Major Powers during the Last Five Fiscals (in US $ billion)

Country/ Organisation	*2010–11*	*2011–12*	*2012–13*	*2013–14*	*2014–15*
USA	45.34	58.19	61.35	61.64	64.26
China	57.64	73.39	65.78	65.85	72.34
Japan	13.72	18.32	18.51	16.29	15.51
Britain	12.68	15.72	14.90	15.82	14.33
Russia	5.28	6.54	6.52	6.01	6.34
EU	75.95	89.45	84.52	80.90	80.86
ASEAN	67.35	68.16	75.87	74.41	76.53

Source: Compiled by the author from Export-Import Data Bank, Department of Commerce, Government of India.

As Table 13.3 reveals, except Russia, India's bilateral trade with all the major powers/blocks remained higher than Britain during the FY 2010–11 to 2014–15. It must be remembered in this context that Russian–India trade relations started afresh in 1991, after the disintegration of former

[25] Ibid.

Soviet Union; but India's trade relation with Britain is nearly four-decades old. However, the two countries were not able to augment bilateral trade to a substantial level. While India's trade with China and USA reached reasonable heights, trade with Britain witnessed sluggish progress. Therefore, it is recommended that India and Britain must try to achieve a bilateral trade volume of US $20 billion by the year 2020. This is a modest target, not difficult to achieve. In an era of economic diplomacy, bilateral trade is surely an indicator of a strong relationship.

Another segment that requires intense attention is bilateral security relations. Although this area witnessed encouraging developments since the end of the Cold War due to lessening of divergent interests, this segment required more close cooperation. For instance, India's defence-related imports, particularly arms imports, from Britain have dropped significantly over the years. According to one source, 'UK's share of the value of India's total arms imports has declined even further since the end of the Cold War. During the 1990s, its decadal share of the value of India's total arms imports came down to 6.95 per cent and dropped even further to 4.6 per cent in the 2000s.'[26] India's defence exports to Britain are also negligible. India exported only transmitting tubes to Britain in 2014–15. India's total defence exports to different countries were to the tune of only Rs 1,397 crore from April to December 2015.[27] However, it must be remembered in this context that India's defence instruments and technology is mostly import-oriented. Despite the projection of a 'Strategic Partnership' between India and Britain, defence relations have not moved beyond institutional mechanisms and joint exercises. Admittedly, these factors are also important; but the two countries have not made substantial progress in defence trade over the years. This area requires significant attention with a view to achieve 'Strategic Partnership' in the real sense of the term.

Intense scientific and technological collaboration in all areas ranging from agriculture to climate to health and sanitation to defence must be taken up by the two countries, both at the government and private levels. Such endeavours would further fulfil the desire of a 'strategic partnership'. While UKIERI is a welcome development in this respect, the allocation of money under UKIERI and other such projects should be much more than the current allocated amount. The two countries need to collaborate more on climate change, health and counter-terrorism areas which are vital to their mutual interests. Intense technological collaboration in these areas through more funds for research and equipments is the order of the day. It is high time that these two mature democracies take up such issues as major agenda for bilateral cooperation to emerge as natural partners in the twenty-first century.

---

[26] S. Kalyanaraman, 'The Limits of the India–United Kingdom Defence Relationship', *Journal of Defence Studies*, 7 (1): 232, 2013.

[27] *Hindustan Times*, 28 March 2016.

14

INDIA AND THE ASEAN

Emerging Partnership

HIGHLIGHTS

- Introduction
- The 1990s and Beyond: Growing Relations
- From Fifth to Commemorative to 14th Summit (2007–16): Relations Mature
- ASEAN–India Economic Relations
- Conclusion: The Future of ASEAN–India Relations

INTRODUCTION

The Association of South East Asian Nations (ASEAN), formed in 1967 in Bangkok with five member-states, has matured into a leading economic bloc in today's world with strong trade and political relations with almost all nations and regional organisations. Currently, ASEAN has 10 member-states (henceforth only members), but has developed a very elaborate partnership mechanism—like ASEAN-10, ASEAN-3, ARF (ASEAN Regional Forum), EAS (East Asian Summit), etc.—to maintain closer links with the rest of the world. The 10 members of ASEAN are: Thailand, Malaysia, Indonesia, Philippines, Singapore (the five founding states in 1967), Brunei Darussalam (joined in 1984; henceforth only joining years), Vietnam (1995), Laos, Myanmar (1997) and Cambodia (1999). It is to be observed here that China, Japan or South Korea, the stronger economies of the region, are not members of the ASEAN; but these nations comprise an integral part of the ASEAN-3 mechanism. The ASEAN Secretariat is located in Jakarta, Indonesia.

Historically, India had closer relations with the nations of the South-East Asian region. After independence, India started reaching out to the South-East Asian countries during the 1950s by supporting the Indonesian struggle for independence and involving itself in the Indo-China crisis in the 1960s. It also signed bilateral friendship treaties with Indonesia, Philippines and Myanmar and consolidated its bilateral and diplomatic relations with these nations.

However, India's relations with ASEAN as a bloc did not take off well. In 1971, four years after the formation of the ASEAN, India signed a strong Friendship Treaty with the Soviet Union. This treaty, considered by many nations as a security treaty, cemented the Indo-Soviet relations, and gradually proximity between the two countries increased. Many ASEAN members did not hold high opinion about Soviet Union, and its proximity with India made the later an object of suspicion for the ASEAN.[1] India's recognition of the Kampuchean regime in 1980, purportedly under the influence of the Soviets, did not go well with the ASEAN either.[2] As a consequence, relations between India and the ASEAN suffered in the 1980s. During the 1970s and the 1980s, India and the ASEAN were not keen to develop close ties. Relations between these two were adversely affected by Cold War political calculations.

THE 1990S AND BEYOND: GROWING RELATIONS

India's economic liberalisation in 1991 and India's 'Look East Policy', introduced in the same year, heralded a new beginning in India–ASEAN relations. While the 'Look East Policy' (LEP), initiated by the Narasimha Rao Government, and pursued vigorously by the successive Indian governments, tried to obliterate Cold War estrangements, India's economic reforms attracted the attention of the ASEAN towards an earlier ignored country. India became a sectoral dialogue partner of ASEAN in 1992. The sectors of partnership were trade, investment, tourism and science and technology. Mutual interests in wider partnership led ASEAN to accord India a full dialogue partner status during the Fifth ASEAN Summit in Bangkok in December 1995 (effective since early 1996), and a member of the ASEAN Regional Forum (ARF) in July 1996.

In the new century, relations took an upward turn with the hosting of the First ASEAN–India summit in Phnom Penh, Cambodia in November 2002. As some scholars noted, '... this came about through a confluence of factors. One, there were strong signals from Indian leaders of the desire to fortify relations with ASEAN via a series of bilateral visits by Indian leaders to many ASEAN members. Two, ASEAN leaders have recognized the need to actively engage India so as to develop a more balanced relationship with all of the major Asian economies, particularly as China is also pursuing an FDI-led, labour intensive manufacturing exports strategy. Three, there is a growing body of literature suggesting that India's economic structure is largely complementary (service-oriented) to ASEAN economies (light manufacturing) with significant areas of mutual gain.'[3] The hosting of the first summit was conceived as a positive outcome of the LEP. As a

---

1 Mohammad Ayoob, *India and Southeast Asia: Indian Perceptions and Policies* (London: Routledge), 1990.

2 Zhao Hong, 'India's Changing Relations with ASEAN: From China's Perspective', *East Asian Institute Working Paper* no. 133, October 2006.

3 Rahul Sen, Mukul G. Asher and Ramkishen S. Rajan, 'Asean–India Economic Relations: Current Status and Future Prospects', *Research and Information Systems for the Non-Aligned and Other Developing Countries RIS Discussion Paper*, no.73, 2004.

consequence, regular bilateral summits have been taking place since 2002. These summits were instrumental in strengthening India–ASEAN relations in the recent years. Before analysing the impact of bilateral summits, it would be worthwhile to look at the following table which gives an idea of regular summits between ASEAN and India:

Table 14.1: ASEAN–India Bilateral Summits

Summit	*Year*	*Place (Country)*
First	2002	Phnom Penh (Cambodia)
Second	2003	Bali (Indonesia)
Third	2004	Vientiane (Lao PDR)
Fourth	2005	Kuala Lumpur (Malaysia)
Fifth	2007 (January)	Cebu (Philippines)
Sixth	2007 (Nov.)	Singapore
Seventh	2009	Chaam Hua Hin (Thailand)
Eighth	2010	Hanoi (Vietnam)
Ninth	2011	Bali
Tenth	2012 (Nov.)	Phnom Penh
Commemorative	2012 (Dec.)	New Delhi (India)
Eleventh	2013 (Oct.)	Bandar Seri Begawan (Brunei Darussalam)
Twelfth	2014 (Nov.)	Nay Pyi Taw (Myanmar)
Thirteenth	2015 (Nov.)	Kuala Lumpur
Fourteenth	2016 (Sept.)	Vientiane

As evident from Table 14.1, regular bilateral summits between India and ASEAN have been taking place since 2002. These summits have been instrumental in strengthening relations between ASEAN and India. The JS issued after the First Summit in 2002 stated, 'Given new developments and challenges arising in the 21st Century, the Leaders of ASEAN and India resolved to further advance their cooperation to a new height to address common challenges confronting the region and the world. Based on the foundation of their close cooperative relationship and recognising the importance of concerted efforts, they had convened the First ASEAN–India Summit in Cambodia. . . .'[4] Clearly, leaders emphasised upon the need to cooperate closely in the new century. This was evident from the language framed in the JS which stated, '. . . ASEAN and India committed themselves to jointly contribute to the promotion of peace, stability and development in the Asia-Pacific region and the world, and respond positively to the challenges of a dynamic regional and international environment.'[5] The need for closer economic

[4] ASEAN Secretariat, *Joint Statement of the First ASEAN–India Summit*, Phnom Penh, 5 November 2002, available at http://www. asean.org/resources/document-arc, accessed on 20 April 2013.

[5] Ibid.

and development cooperation between ASEAN and India constituted major parts of the JS. It observed, 'Acknowledging that economic progress would also enhance regional peace, security and stability, they (the leaders of ASEAN and India) shared the view that continued economic cooperation between the two sides would promote dynamism and prosperity of the Asia-Pacific region. In this regard, they agreed on the importance of enhancing their close economic cooperation and to work towards India–AFTA Linkages. They welcomed the adoption of an India–ASEAN Regional Trade and Investment Area as a long-term objective at the First ASEAN–India Economic Ministers' Consultations, held at Brunei Darussalam, on 15 September 2002. They also noted the decision to set up an ASEAN–India Task Force on Economic Linkages, which is to prepare a draft Framework Agreement to enhance ASEAN–India Economic Cooperation. . . .'[6] The thrust of the two sides on economic and development cooperation was amply highlighted during the First Summit at Phnom Penh in 2002. This emphasis continued to attract priority in the following ASEAN–India summits.

At the Second ASEAN–India Summit in Bali (Indonesia) in 2003, the ASEAN–India Framework Agreement on Comprehensive Economic Cooperation was signed by the leaders of ASEAN and India. 'The Framework Agreement laid a sound basis for the eventual establishment of an ASEAN–India Regional Trade and Investment Area (RTIA), which included FTA (Free Trade Area) in goods, services and investment.'[7] The agreement wished to 'minimise barriers and deepen economic linkages between the Parties; lower costs; increase intra-regional trade and investment; increase economic efficiency; create a larger market with greater opportunities and larger economies of scale for the businesses of the Parties; and enhance the attractiveness of the Parties to capital and talent'.[8] A press statement released by the ASEAN Secretariat after the Bali Summit noted an enhancing relationship between the two sides. The statement said, 'We were pleased to witness the signing of the Framework Agreement on Comprehensive Economic Cooperation between the Association of South East Asian Nations and the Republic of India. The agreement would strengthen and enhance economic, trade and investment cooperation between the two sides. We affirmed that the agreement would facilitate the effective economic integration of the new ASEAN member states and bridge the development gaps among ASEAN members.'[9] At the Bali Summit, India came forward with various proposals of cooperation in the following areas: agriculture, biotechnology, human resources development and agro-processing. The establishment of a joint working group (JWG) on agriculture was also discussed by the leaders of the two sides at the summit.

---

[6] Ibid., parenthesis by the author.

[7] Source: www.trungtamwto.vn/sites/default/files/overview_asean-india.pdf, accessed on 19 May 2017.

[8] ASEAN Secretariat, *Framework Agreement on Comprehensive Economic Cooperation between the Republic of India and the Association of Southeast Asian Nations*, available at http://www.aseansec.org/15278.htm, accessed on 20 April 2013.

[9] Website of the ASEAN Secretariat, available at http://www.asean.org/resources/document-arc, accessed on 20 April 2013.

At the Third ASEAN–India Summit held in Vientiane on 30 November 2004, leaders of the two sides reiterated their commitment towards further cooperation and development. In the JS issued after the summit, leaders pledged to 'Foster friendship, good neighbourliness, peaceful co-existence and prosperity in the region; promote a long-term co-operative partnership based on equality, shared ownership and mutual respect which will enable us to impart synergies to our respective strengths and complementarities to achieve our respective long-term national and regional development goals; cooperate in a coordinated manner to accelerate and mutually reinforce sustainable growth and development of our economies towards shared prosperity, poverty alleviation and reduction of social disparities, to enable our people to enjoy unhindered access to opportunities for development. . . .'[10] At this summit, cooperation in a vast range of areas like science and technology, in particular information technology (IT) and biotechnology; combating terrorism; development of regional infrastructure and road, rail, sea and air transportation links; human resource development; joint research and development and commercialisation of new technologies; facilitating travel and tourism between ASEAN and India by developing links of tourist centres to enhance synergies of tourism destinations; were proposed.[11] This summit also clearly chalked out the time-frame for achieving FTAs among ASEAN, India and members of the ASEAN. The JS pledged to 'Work through both conventional and innovative trade and economic arrangements, and full implementation of the ASEAN–India free trade area by 2011 for ASEAN-5 and India, 2016 for the Philippines and India and by 2011 by India and 2016 by the 4 new ASEAN Members Countries, including the early implementation of the Early Harvest Programme, to achieve freer movement of goods, services, investment, and cooperation in other economic areas. . . .'[12] At this summit, the two sides not only continued to work on plans formulated in the preceding summits, but also devised newer areas of cooperation.

The Fourth ASEAN–India Summit was held in Kuala Lumpur in 2005. Both the sides reviewed the progress of cooperation in different areas as envisaged in the earlier summits. The 'Chairman's Statement' (CS), issued after the summit was very candid in evaluating the status of the relationship. The statement observed, 'We noted the Progress Report of Implementation of the Plan of Action to Implement the ASEAN–India Partnership for Peace, Progress and Shared Prosperity signed at the Third ASEAN–India Summit on 30 November 2004 in Vientiane. Progress was made in the areas of cooperation, including agriculture, health and pharmaceuticals, science and technology, human resource development (HRD), transport and infrastructure, ICT and people-to-people interaction. We expressed appreciation to India for the US $2.5 million replenishment to the ASEAN–India Cooperation Fund. We tasked our Ministers and Senior Officials to accelerate the implementation of the ASEAN–India Plan of Action through concrete activities, programmes

[10] ASEAN Secretariat, *ASEAN–India Partnership for Peace, Progress and Shared Prosperity*, available at http://www.asean.org/news/item/asean-india, accessed on 20 April 2013.

[11] Source: Prabhas Chandra Sinha, ed. 'Handbook of ASEAN and Regional Cooperation: 12th Summit and Beyond (New Delhi: Pentagon Press), available at https://books.google.co.in/books?isbn=8182742765, accessed on 19 May 2017.

[12] Ibid.

and projects.'[13] However, the CS noted the dissatisfaction of the ASEAN with the slow rate of progress in implementing the ASEAN–India FTA. It observed, 'We noted that negotiations to establish the ASEAN–India Free Trade Area (AIFTA) have not progressed as expeditiously as originally envisaged despite sincere efforts from both sides. The ASEAN Leaders requested India to positively consider the ASEAN's position to move the negotiations on the AIFTA forward and take into account the broader strategic consideration of an enhanced ASEAN–India relations. We agreed to work closely to enhance our trade and investment ties through the ASEAN–India Free Trade Area (AIFTA) and acknowledged that our two economic regions could serve as engines of growth for each other. In this regard, we resolved to expedite and conclude the ongoing negotiations on the AIFTA through a pragmatic and flexible approach.'[14] At the same time, the ASEAN commended India's efforts to help the organisation and its members in different areas. The CS noted, 'We appreciated the assistance provided by India in the context of ASEAN–India development cooperation, especially the capacity building programmes for Cambodia, Lao PDR, Myanmar and Viet Nam (CLMV). We also welcomed the announcement of India to set up permanent Centres for English Language Training (CELT) in Cambodia, Lao PDR, Myanmar and Viet Nam, which would equip students, civil servants, professional and businessmen with adequate English language proficiency and communication skills imparted in small classrooms equipped with modern teaching aid.'[15] The CS also welcomed India's announcement to contribute US $1 million to the ASEAN Development Fund (ADF).

FROM FIFTH TO COMMEMORATIVE TO 14TH SUMMIT (2007–16): RELATIONS MATURE

The Fifth ASEAN–India Summit, held in January 2007, worked further to achieve the FTA. The Fifth Summit generated hopes for a quick negotiation for the FTA because both sides showed some flexibility. The proposed FTA would create a large market of 1.5 billon people with a combined gross domestic product (GDP) of US $1.8 trillion. At the Fifth Summit, ASEAN was willing to accept India's offer of a negative list of 490 items and India also responded by agreeing to cut the tariff on four sensitive commodities by 50 per cent by 2022. In contrast to its previous stand, India also agreed to consider the removal of the five-year moratorium on duty cuts over these commodities after the establishment of the FTA. Both sides agreed to reduce their tariff on the 700 items from 0–5 per cent till 2018 with the remaining items being finalised through further negotiations so that an FTA could be achieved early. The Sixth Summit, held in Singapore in November 2007, promised a healthy future in ASEAN–India relations. The 'Chairman's Statement' issued after the summit bore testimony to such promise. It said, 'We were

[13] ASEAN Secretariat, *Chairman's Statement of the Fourth ASEAN–India Summit, Kuala Lumpur*, 13 December, 2005, available at http://www.asean.org/news/item/external-relati, accessed on 20 April 2013.

[14] Ibid.

[15] Ibid.

pleased to note that ASEAN–India bilateral trade had already reached US $30 billion, and looked forward to achieve the target of US $50 billion in 2010. We recognised that the establishment of an AIFTA would anchor the strategic engagement between both the sides and sustain the momentum of the relationship. We agreed that the AIFTA, when realised, would act as an important building block for a regional FTA in Asia. We were heartened by the latest progress made in the negotiations of the ASEAN–India Trade in Goods Agreement. We recognised that decisions on the Agreement must be made on a strategic basis, and urged that the remaining matters be handled with flexibility and resolved quickly. We agreed that ASEAN and India are committed to the speedy completion of negotiations, and look forward to the conclusion of the Agreement by March next year. Acknowledging the immense potential in ASEAN–India trade and investment relations, we re-affirmed our continuous work on the FTA, which when implemented, would further strengthen our economic partnership towards the shared goal of regional economic integration.'[16] The promise of a bright future in relationship emanated also from India's proposal to establish an ASEAN–India Network on climate change that would pool and share expertise and exchange best practices. India also offered to set up an 'ASEAN–India Green Fund' with an initial contribution from India of US $5 million.

The Seventh ASEAN–India Summit in 2009 in Thailand witnessed stronger cooperation in more areas. The 'Çhairman's Statement' issued after the summit referred to these areas of cooperation and mechanisms to implement these. The CS observed, 'We noted with satisfaction the steady progress of implementation of the ASEAN–India Partnership for Peace, Progress and Shared Prosperity, and agreed that a new and more enhanced phase of the Plan of Action to implement the said Partnership be launched before the next ASEAN–India Summit, in order to seize the opportunities and overcome the challenges arising from the global financial crisis and evolving political and economic landscape. We welcomed the signing of ASEAN–India Trade in Goods Agreement at the 41st ASEAN Economic Ministers Meeting on 13 August this year and encourage its early implementation by January 2010. We are confident that the Agreement will allow our producers and exporters to derive full benefits from the potential of our combined markets. For our people to further reap the benefits of free trade, we entrusted our Ministers and officials to work towards the early conclusion of services and investment agreements. In view of the Trade in Goods Agreement (TGA), we agreed to revise our bilateral trade target to 70 billion USD to be achieved in the next two years, noting that the initial target of 50 billion USD set in 2007 may soon be surpassed.'[17] The TGA proved to be a useful mechanism in strengthening ASEAN–India trade and commercial relations in later years. At the Seventh Summit, both the sides encouraged the re-activation of the ASEAN–India Business Council and the ASEAN–India Business Summits in order to strengthen business networks and opportunities. The ASEAN leaders

---

[16] ASEAN, *Chairman's Statement of the 6th ASEAN–INDIA Summit, Singapore, 21 November, 2007*, available at http://www.asean.org/news/item/external-relati, accessed on 20 April 2013.

[17] Ministry of External Affairs, Government Of India, *Chairman's Statement at the 7th ASEAN–India Summit*, available at http://mea.gov.in/Speeches-Statements.htm?dtl/1, accessed on 21 April 2013.

suggested that India as a member of the G-20 can play an important role in coordinating efforts between the developed and emerging economies to mitigate the negative impact of the current global economic and financial crisis. India can also work with ASEAN to complement the global efforts in the reform of the international financial architecture and accelerate the early recovery of the global economy.[18]

In the Eighth Summit in Hanoi in 2010, India extended the visa-on-arrival-facility to the citizens of Cambodia, Vietnam, Lao PDR and Philippines with effect from 1 January 2011. This gesture manifested India's willingness to follow more 'open door' policies to promote business and tourism. Speaking at the Summit, the Indian Prime Minister, Manmohan Singh said, 'India believes that ASEAN is the core around which the process of economic integration of the Asia-Pacific region should be built.... In recent years, there has been a substantial increase in people to people exchanges as a result of better air connectivity between India and ASEAN. More than 3 million Indian tourists visit ASEAN every year and about 380 flights connect Indian and ASEAN cities every week. This is well below the potential. We invite many more tourists from the ASEAN countries to visit India to see the splendour of its rich cultural heritage. I am happy that the text of the ASEAN–India MoU for cooperation in Tourism has been finalized. I am also pleased to note that ASEAN will soon establish an ASEAN Promotional Chapter for tourism in Mumbai.'[19] The summit pledged to further cooperate in science and technology, economy, environment, tourism and human resource development.

The Ninth Summit was held in Bali in 2011. At the Ninth Summit, according to an MEA Press Release, '... the Leaders took stock of the progress made in the India–ASEAN relationship and agreed to enhance co-operation on a range of issues, including trade, maritime security, food and energy security, and physical and people-to-people connectivity. They reaffirmed their commitment to further strengthen India–ASEAN cooperation, through the implementation of the Plan of Action 2010–15, in the run-up to the Commemorative Summit.'[20] The Tenth Summit took place in Phnom Penh in November 2012. This summit preceded the Commemorative Summit, marking the 20 years of ASEAN–India relationship (1992–2012), in New Delhi in December 2012. The Prime Minister of India, Manmohan Singh in his opening remarks at the Tenth Summit observed, 'India's relationship with ASEAN members and with ASEAN institutionally continues to grow in all dimensions. Commerce and connectivity are vital areas of this relationship and we have made good progress in both. The India–ASEAN Agreement on Trade in Goods has served us well. Our trade was nearly 80 billion US dollars in the Indian financial year ending March 2012, exceeding our target of 70 billion US dollars.... India is

---

[18] Ibid.

[19] Ministry of External Affairs, Government of India, Investment and Technology Promotion (ITP) Division, 'PM's Statement at the 8th India-ASEAN Summit', available at http:// www.indiainbusiness.nic.in/business-news/speeches_statements/pm_oct30_10.htm, accessed on 21 April 2013.

[20] Ministry of External Affairs, Government of India, 'India–ASEAN Relations', available at http://mea.gov.in/foriegn-relation.htm?ForeignRelation_212, accessed on 21 April 2013.

prepared to conclude the Agreement on Trade in Services and Investment Promotion before the Commemorative Summit in Delhi in December. This will be a strong signal of our deepening economic engagement, and will allow for rapid expansion in trade and investment flows in both directions. Connectivity with ASEAN in all its dimensions—physical, institutional and people-to-people—continues to be a strategic priority for India. Two major commemorative events this year—the India–ASEAN Car Rally and the ASEAN sailing expedition of the Indian Naval Ship Sudarshini—highlight the importance and the potential for connecting India and ASEAN by sea, surface and air links.'[21] This lengthy reference to the Indian prime minister's remarks helps bring out the strength in ASEAN–India relations that have developed over the years.

With a view to mark the twentieth anniversary of the ASEAN–India dialogue partnership and the tenth anniversary of ASEAN–India Summit-level partnership, India hosted the ASEAN–India Commemorative Summit in New Delhi on 20–21 December 2012. The theme of the Summit was 'ASEAN–India Partnership for Peace and Shared Prosperity'. The summit produced a 'Vision Statement', which would chart the future direction of ASEAN–India relations. The ASEAN–India Eminent Persons' Group (AIEPG) submitted their recommendations to the leaders on the future relations between ASEAN and India at the 10th ASEAN–India Summit in Phnom Penh.[22] The ASEAN–India Commemorative Summit was the culmination of several events organised in celebration of the partnership. These included a number of ministerial-level meetings, people-to-people initiatives, business-to-business activities and cultural programmes both in India and the ASEAN countries.[23]

The Prime Minister of India, Narendra Modi attended the 12th ASEAN–India Summit held at Nay Pyi Taw on 12 November 2014 along with the heads of governments of the ASEAN countries. At the summit, leaders reiterated their commitment to the implementation of the ASEAN–India Vision Statement 2012, which elevated the ASEAN–India Partnership to a strategic level.[24] The customary 'Chairman's Statement' released after the Summit detailed progress of cooperation between ASEAN and India in economic, security, cultural, ecological, scientific and technological areas. The 'Chairman's Statement' noted in Section 4, 'We expressed satisfaction with the progress in the implementation of the ASEAN–India Plan of Action (PoA) to implement the ASEAN–India Partnership for Peace, Progress and Shared Prosperity (2010–15).[25] We looked forward to the third ASEAN–India PoA (2016–21) to serve as an action-oriented document to further deepen the ASEAN–India Strategic Partnership, as well as ASEAN community-building and integration. We agreed that it should build on and

[21] Press Information Bureau, Government of India, 'Opening Remarks by Prime Minister at 10th India-ASEAN Summit', available at http:// http://pib.nic.in/newsite/erelease.aspx?relid=89110, accessed on 21 April 2013.

[22] For further details, see www.mea.gov.in/aseanindia/c-summit.htm, accessed on 19 May 2017.

[23] Ibid.

[24] Ibid.

[25] Ibid.

strengthen the strong sense of community between the peoples of ASEAN Member States and India.'[26]

At the Thirteenth ASEAN–India Summit held in Kuala Lumpur in November 2015, India commended the ASEAN member-states on the establishment of the 'ASEAN Community' and reiterated its support for ASEAN's efforts in building a region that would be politically cohesive, economically integrated and socially responsible. The CS released after the summit observed, 'The ASEAN Leaders welcomed India's initiatives, namely the "Act East Policy" and "Make in India" and noted that the initiatives could complement ASEAN's community-building efforts. In that regard, the ASEAN Leaders encouraged India to work with ASEAN to realise the vision and goals outlined in the *ASEAN 2025: Forging Ahead Together*.'[27] Section 5 of the CS noted, '... the significant progress of ASEAN–India dialogue relations, with the implementation of various programmes and activities across the three pillars as outlined in the Plan of Action of the ASEAN–India Partnership for Peace, Progress and Shared Prosperity (2010–15). We looked forward to further enhancing ASEAN–India relations through the new Plan of Action 2016–20 adopted at the ASEAN–India Ministerial Meeting in Kuala Lumpur in August 2015, which includes cooperation in such areas as science and technology, renewable energy, food security, tourism, climate change and connectivity.'[28] Clearly, ASEAN and India wanted to continue with their engaged relations, and forge a strong partnership in the future. At the Fourteenth Summit in Vientiane held in September 2016, the same commitment was reiterated again by both ASEAN and India.

ASEAN–INDIA ECONOMIC RELATIONS

From a Sectoral Dialogue Partner in 1992, to a Full Dialogue Partner in 1996, to the First ASEAN–India Summit in 2002, to the Commemorative Summit in 2012, to the latest Fourteenth Summit in 2016, ASEAN–India relations have come a long way and gradually got strengthened. In this evolutionary path, the contribution of the economic factors behind a strong relationship could never be ignored. From negligible trade volumes at the beginning of the century, to US $76.53 billion trade in FY 2014–15, ASEAN–India economic relations are on a high. In FY 2001–02, the total volume of ASEAN–India trade was US $7.84 billion. In FY 20014–15, it went up to US $76.53 billion. It showed that there was more than ten-fold increase in ASEAN–India trade

---

[26] Ministry of External Affairs, Government of India, 'Chairman's Statement of the 12th ASEAN–India Summit in Nay Pyi Taw, Myanmar, November 12, 2014', available at http://www.mea.gov.in/outoging-visit-detail.htm?24243/Chairmans+statement+of+the+12th+ASEANIndia+Summit+in+Nay+Pyi+Taw+Myanmar, accessed on 2 June 2016.

[27] ASEAN Secretariat, 'Chairman's Statement of the 13th ASEAN–India Summit', Kuala Lumpur, 21 November 2015, *Our People, Our Community, Our Vision*, available at http://asean.org/wp-content/uploads/images/2015/November/27th-summit/statement/Final-Chairmans%20Statement%20of%2013th%20ASEAN%20INDIA%20Summit.pdf, accessed on 22 June 2016.

[28] Ibid.

in 13 years. The AIFTA has also added dynamism in economic relations. In this context, it would be worthwhile to look at the trade volume over the years. Table 14.2 highlights bilateral trade since FY 2001–02:

Table 14.2: ASEAN–India Bilateral Trade (in US $ billion)

Year	*India's Import*	*India's Export*	*Total Trade*
2001–02	4.39	3.46	7.84
2002–03	5.15	4.62	9.77
2003–04	7.43	5.82	13.25
2004–05	9.11	8.43	17.54
2005–06	10.88	10.41	21.29
2006–07	18.11	12.61	30.72
2007–08	22.67	16.41	39.09
2008–09	26.20	19.14	45.34
2009–10	25.80	18.11	43.91
2010–11	30.61	36.74	67.35
2011–12	42.53	25.63	68.16
2012–13	42.87	33.00	75.87
2013–14	41.28	33.13	74.41
2014–15	44.71	31.82	76.53

Source: Compiled by the author from sources of Export-Import Data Bank, Ministry of Commerce, Government of India.

Table 14.2 above shows that ASEAN–India trade volume has been on the rise in most of the financial years, except FY 2009–10 and 2013–14 when the total volume of trade dropped marginally than the preceding fiscals. However, only once in the last 13 years, in 2010–11, Indian exports exceeded Indian imports to ASEAN. The potential sectors for trade and investment between ASEAN and India are: agriculture and food processing, textiles, garments and accessories, drugs and pharmaceutical, mining, infrastructure, gems and jewellery, palm oil, rubber and rubber products, IT, education, tourism, financial services and banking, biotechnology auto motive sector, wood paper and pulp. Major commodities of export from India to ASEAN are oil meals, gems and jewellery, electronic goods, cotton yarn, RMG cotton, machinery and instruments, primary and semi-finished iron and steel, transport equipments, marine products, drugs and pharmaceuticals, inorganic and organic agro-chemicals, dyes and intermediates. Major commodities of import from ASEAN to India are: coal, coke, briquettes, vegetable oils, petroleum oils, electronic goods, organic chemicals, machinery except electrical machinery, professional instruments, wood and wood products, non-ferrous metals, metalli-ferrous ores and metal scrap.

As far as Foreign Direct Investment (FDI) inflow to India from the ASEAN countries is concerned, significant growth has also taken place in the recent years. For instance during 2008–10, net FDI inflow into India from the ASEAN countries was US $3.94 billion, and cumulative FDI equity inflows from the ASEAN countries to India from 2000 to 2014 was US $21.17 billion. The ASEAN countries accounted for 12.5 per cent of total shares of FDI inflow into India in 2014.[29] Among the different segments, the service sector accounts for 28.20 per cent of FDI inflow into India till 2014. This sector includes financial, banking, insurance, non-financial business, outsourcing, research and development (R&D), testing and analysis. Telecommunications (8.12 per cent); construction development (7.68 per cent); petroleum and natural gas (7.12 per cent); computer software and hardware (6.31 per cent) and 'other sectors' (42.57 per cent) account for the total FDI inflow into India.

The AIFTA was signed on 13 August 2009 in Bangkok. The AIFTA came into force from 1 January 2010. As noted earlier, at the Second ASEAN–India Summit in Bali in 2003, the ASEAN–India Framework Agreement on Comprehensive Economic Cooperation was signed. The Framework Agreement laid a solid foundation for the eventual establishment of an ASEAN–India RTIA, which includes FTA in goods, services and investment. ASEAN and India signed the ASEAN–India Trade in Goods (TIG) Agreement in 2009 which in effect paved ways for the AIFTA. Initially, the AIFTA became operative with Malaysia, Singapore and Thailand.[30] With the remaining ASEAN members, it would come into force after these members completed their internal requirements. As per the provisions, the AIFTA has to be fully operational by 2016. The AIFTA is significant because it is the first multilateral FTA that India has negotiated till date.

The FTA would liberalise tariffs on about 4,000 items accounting for nearly 80 per cent of trade between India and ASEAN. Electronic goods, chemicals, certain capital goods and some categories of textiles are among the items covered. Tariffs on the products covered would sink to zero between 2013 and 2016. With the signing of AIFTA, India has made commitments to reduce or eliminate tariffs for over 89 per cent of all of its agriculture, marine and manufactured goods by 2016. A bilateral safeguard mechanism would address any sudden surge in imports with 'safeguard tariffs' to protect domestic industries for a period of four years. India's trade with ASEAN is mainly concentrated in Indonesia, Malaysia, Singapore and Thailand. These four countries remain the largest markets for Indian exports in the ASEAN region as well as the largest sources for India's imports from the ASEAN region. Among them, Singapore is the largest destination for Indian goods and the largest source of imports for India followed by Malaysia, Indonesia and Thailand.

While it is beyond doubt that there would be many benefits of the ASEAN–India FTA like increasing trade volume, there are concerns also, especially in India, that the agreement would have negative impact on the Indian economy. ASEAN economies are largely export-driven, as member-nations depend mostly on exports. This factor, along with the global financial crisis and India's expansive domestic market, would only encourage the ASEAN countries to view

---

[29] ASEAN Secretariat, available at http://www.india-aseanbusinessfair.com/cf4dec/ASEAN.pdf, accessed on 27 November 2015.

[30] Source: see https://en.wikipedia.org/wiki/ASEAN–India_Free_Trade_Area, accessed on 19 May 2017.

India as a home for exports. Since the early 2000s, India has had an increasing trade deficit with ASEAN with imports exceeding exports, as Table 14.2 has highlighted. It is feared that a gradual liberalisation of tariffs and a rise in imported goods into India would threaten several sectors of the economy, especially the plantation sector, some manufacturing industries, and the marine products industry. As a dominant exporter of light manufacturing products, ASEAN has competitive tariff rates that make it difficult for India to gain access to the industry market in the ASEAN countries. Further, Indian states like Kerala is an important exporter of plantation products. Kerala fears that cheap imports of rubber, coffee and fish would lower domestic production, adversely affecting farmers and ultimately its economy.[31] To alleviate such fears, the Government of India (GoI) must be able to effectively redistribute some of the wealth to those industries who suffer from the increased competition with the ASEAN markets. This way, the total welfare gains in India would increase and India might ultimately benefit from trade with ASEAN.

An India–ASEAN Business Summit and Exhibition was held from 2–6 March 2011 at New Delhi. Delhi Dialogue-III, a 'Regional Security and Cooperation Dialogue', was also held back-to-back with the business summit. The Secretary-General of ASEAN visited India to grace this occasion. Delhi Dialogue IV on the theme 'India and ASEAN: Partners for Peace, Progress and Stability' was held from 13–14 February 2012 in New Delhi. The visit of the ASEAN Committee of Representatives (CPRs) to India from 12–17 February 2012 coincided with Delhi-Dialogue IV.[32] An MoU on Strengthening Tourism Co-operation between India and ASEAN was signed at the India–ASEAN Ministerial Meeting on Tourism on 12 January 2012 in Manado, Indonesia.[33] Currently, there are 25 mechanisms coordinating the ASEAN–India cooperation in the areas of political-security cooperation, economic and socio-cultural cooperation. Since India became a Dialogue Partner of ASEAN, the collaboration has transcended the realm of functional cooperation to cover political and security dimensions. India acceded to the Treaty of Amity (TAC) and Cooperation in South-East Asia in 2003. India also participates in a series of consultative meetings with ASEAN under the ASEAN–India Dialogue Relations. These include summit, ministerial meetings, senior officials meetings and meetings at experts level, as well as through dialogue and cooperation frameworks initiated by ASEAN, such as the ARF, the Post Ministerial Conference (PMC) 10+1, ASEAN Economic Ministers+1 Consultations, the EAS, ASEAN Defence Ministers Meeting Plus (ADMM Plus), Mekong-Ganga Cooperation and Bay of Bengal Initiative for Multisectoral Technical and Economic Cooperation

---

[31] Before the agreement was signed, the then Chief Minister of Kerala, V. S. Achuthanandan led a delegation to the Indian prime minister protesting against the FTA. See in this context, *Business Standard*, New Delhi, 31 July 2009.

[32] Source: www.iasmind.com/general-study/international-relations/asean-india/, accessed on 19 May 2017.

[33] MEA, Government of India, *India–ASEAN Relations*, available at https://www.mea.gov.in/Portal/ForeignRelation/India_2016.pdf; accessed on 25 November, 2015.

(BIMSTEC), which help contribute to enhancing regional dialogue and accelerating regional integration.[34]

CONCLUSION: THE FUTURE OF ASEAN–INDIA RELATIONS

At the ASEAN–India Commemorative Summit in New Delhi, 20 December 2012, organised to mark the 20th year of ASEAN–India Dialogue Relations, a 'Vision Statement' was released to chart the future courses of activity and partnership. The 'Vision Statement' (VS) highlighted three major areas—political and security cooperation, economic cooperation and socio-cultural and development cooperation, in chalking out the future of Indo-ASEAN relations. The VS recognised the successful implementation of the First Plan of Action for the period 2005–10, and announced the introduction of a New Plan of Action for 2010–15 to implement the ASEAN–India Partnership for Peace, Progress and Shared Prosperity.[35] Besides adopting the future programmes for the three major areas noted above, the VS also declared '... the ASEAN–India Partnership stands elevated to a strategic partnership'.[36] With a view to realise the full potential of this Strategic Partnership, the VS provided for a detailed plan of action. It declared, 'We will strive towards the full, effective and timely implementation of the ASEAN–India Dialogue Relations across the whole spectrum of political and security, economic, socio-cultural and development cooperation, through further strengthening of relevant institutional mechanisms and broadening of the network between government institutions, parliamentarians, business circles, scientists, think-tanks, media, youth and other stakeholders, for the building of a peaceful, harmonious, caring and sharing community in our regions. In this context, we will continue to support and encourage active participation of relevant stakeholders in the Delhi Dialogue.'[37] Under the 'Political and Security Cooperation' section of the VS, sub-sections 8 and 9 are important. These proclaim, 'We are committed to fostering greater security cooperation and information sharing in the form of regular and high-level security dialogues to further address traditional and non-traditional security challenges, including transnational crimes, and strengthening the effective implementation of the ASEAN–India Joint Declaration for Cooperation to Combat International Terrorism.... We are committed to strengthening cooperation to ensure maritime security and freedom of navigation, and safety of sea lanes of communication for unfettered movement of trade in accordance with international law, including UNCLOS.'[38]

---

[34] '*ASEAN–India Eminent Persons' Report to the Leaders*', available at http://www.mea.gov.in/Uploads/PublicationDocs/20831_ASEAN-India_Eminent_Persons__Report_to_the_Leaders.pdf, accessed on 28 April 2013.

[35] See in this connection, ASEAN Secretariat, 'Vision Statement: ASEAN–India Commemorative Summit', 21 December 2012, available at http://www.asean.org/news/asean-statement-communiques/item/vision-statement-asean-india-commemorative-summit, accessed on 1 May 2013.

[36] Ibid.

[37] Ibid.

[38] Ibid.

In the area of economic cooperation, the VS announced, 'We are committed to reaching greater trade volume through our FTA and realising our trade and economic potential under our strategic partnership by expanding trade facilitation initiatives. We are, therefore, committed to achieving a target of USD 100 billion for ASEAN-India trade by 2015, and also expect tariff-free lines to increase beyond the existing level in subsequent years.... We are committed to realising the ASEAN–India Free Trade Area (FTA) with a combined market of almost 1.8 billion people and a combined GDP of USD 3.8 trillion. In this regard, we welcome the successful conclusion of the negotiation on ASEAN–India Trade in Services and Investment Agreements. The signing of these Agreements will facilitate further economic integration between ASEAN and India, and also contribute to the overall East Asian economic integration.'[39] In order to strengthen socio-cultural and development cooperation, the VS declared, 'We will strengthen socio-cultural cooperation and promote greater people-to-people interaction through increasing exchanges in culture, education, youth, sports, creative industries, science and technology, information and communication technology and software, human resource development and scholarly exchanges. We will also enhance contacts between parliamentarians, media personnel, academics and Track II institutions such as the network of think-tanks.'[40]

Official rhetoric notwithstanding, there is little doubt that ASEAN–India relations have matured in the last two decades. But a lot more needs to be done to strengthen relations further. For instance, bilateral trade volume is not expected to reach the targeted amount of US $100 billion by the middle of 2017. The AIFTA is still in its infancy and requires more efforts on the part of the ASEAN members, and India to realise its full potential. Both sides must engage continuously in widening the base of the FTA to include services and investments. ASEAN–India trade should reach US $200 billion by 2020. But both the sides need to put extra efforts to reach the target. Tourism, educational and cultural exchange programmes have a huge potential for development cooperation. Currently, both the sides are engaged in these areas, but a lot more could be achieved. Policies like the open sky, land connectivity, travel through luxury cruise in the seas of the region, more student exchange, restoring historical sites for tourist attractions, are some of the areas, which require further closer cooperation.

There are many reasons for intense cooperation, because both India and ASEAN need the other. However, they also need to show their commitment more for stronger relations. As two prominent authors have correctly noted that from the ASEAN perspective, the key consideration is whether India has the interest and the commitment to engage ASEAN on a sustained and long-term basis. This would depend to a large extent on how both India and ASEAN perceive their shared interests in the region. India saw the need to engage ASEAN in order to increase trade and investment flows, to forestall a perceived threat of an Islamic arc spreading from its western front to the east, and to check the rising influence of China in ASEAN, particularly Myanmar which shares a land border with India. On the ASEAN side, India's growing economic

---

[39] Ibid.

[40] Ibid.

strength, its status as a *de facto* nuclear weapon state, and its readiness to engage all players in the Asia-Pacific would offer not only new economic opportunities for ASEAN but India's active involvement in the region would provide additional driving space for ASEAN in dealing with the other major powers.[41] Encouragingly, both sides have shown ample willingness to engage with the other and carry forward the relationship. With its emerging economic status, India must learn to live in multi-lateral engagements. The future of India's relations with ASEAN would be a crucial testing ground for India in this respect.

---

[41] S. D. Muni and See Chuk Mun, *ASEAN–India Relations: Future Directions*, paper submitted to the ASEAN–India Eminent Persons Group Meeting, Kuala Lumpur, 10 March 2012, available at http://ISAS_Special_Report_05_Asean-India_Relations-_Future_Directions_New_25052012172612.pdf_Adobe, accessed on 1 May 2013.

BIBLIOGRAPHY

Abdali, Shaida Mohammad, *Afghanistan Pakistan India: A Paradigm Shift*, New Delhi: Pentagon Press, 2016.

Abel, Denzil, 'Myanmar's Perception of India', in Vishal Chandra, ed., *India and South Asia: Exploring Regional Perceptions*, New Delhi: Pentagon Press, 2015.

Arndt, Michael, *India's Foreign Policy and Regional Multilateralism*, New York: Palgrave Macmillan, 2013.

Athwal, Amardeep, *China–India Relations: Contemporary Dynamics*, New York: Routledge, 2008.

Bajpai, Kanti, Huang Jing, and Kishore Mahbubani, eds, *China–India Cooperation: Relations Between the Giants of Asia*, New York: Routledge, 2015.

Bammi, Y. M., *India–Bangladesh Relations: The Way Ahead*, Delhi: Vij Books, 2010.

Banerjee, Dipankar, *EU–India Relations: Beginning a New Era*, New Delhi: KAS Publications, 2005.

Barfield, Thomas, *Afghanistan: A Cultural and Political History*, Princeton: Princeton University Press, 2012.

Basu, Shrabani, *Re-Imagine: India–UK Cultural Relations in the 21st Century*, New Delhi: Bloomsbury, 2013.

Bertsch, Gary K., Seema Gahlaut, and Anupam Srivastava, eds, *Engaging India: U.S. Strategic Relations with World's Largest Democracy*, New York: Routledge, 2011.

Bhatia, Rajiv, *India–Myanmar Relations: Changing Contours*, New Delhi: Routledge, 2016.

Chandra, Vishal, ed., *India and South Asia: Exploring Regional Perceptions*, New Delhi: Pentagon Press, 2015.

Chatterjee, Aneek, 'Will Democracy Survive? Afghanistan and the International Community Post 2014', *Journal of South Asian and Middle Eastern Studies* 38 (4), Summer 2015.

———. 'India–Pakistan Relations: A Framework for Peace in Future', in Riaz Shaikh, ed., *Back from the Brink: India–Pakistan Ties Revisited*, Karachi: Ushba Publishing International, 2012.

———, 'India–U.S. Relations: Expectations, Reality and the Future', *Journal of South Asian and Middle Eastern Studies* 34 (3), Spring 2011.

———, 'From Uncertainty to Solidarity? An Anatomy of Post Cold War India–U.S. Relations', *Jadavpur Journal of International Relations* 14 (1), 2010.

———, *International Relations Today: Concepts and Applications*, New Delhi: Pearson Education, 2010.

Chaudhuri, Rudra, *Forged in Crisis: India and the United States since 1947*, London: C. Hurst & Co, 2013.

Chopra, V. D., *New Trends in Indo-Russian Relations*, New Delhi: Kalpaz Publications, 2003.

Cohen, Stephen P., *India: Emerging Power*, New Delhi: Oxford University Press, 2001.

Devi, Sanasam Sandhyarani, *India–Nepal Relations: Historical, Cultural and Political Perspectives*, New Delhi: Vij Books, 2011.

Dhungel, Dwarika N., and Santa B. Pun, eds, *The Nepal–India Water Relationship: Challenges*, New York: Springer, 2009.

Dixit, J. N., *India–Pakistan in War and Peace*, London: Routledge, 2002.

———, *India's Foreign Policy and its Neighbours*, New Delhi: Gyan Publishing, 2010.

Dubey, Muchkund, *India's Foreign Policy: Coping with the Changing World*, New Delhi: Orient BlackSwan, 2015.

Erixon, Fredrik, and Krishnan Srinivasan, eds, *Europe in Emerging Asia, Opportunities and Obstacles in Political and Economic Encounters*, New York: Rowman and Littlefield, 2015.

Fang, Tien-sze, *Asymmetrical Threat Perceptions in India–China Relations*, Oxford: Oxford University Press, 2013.

Frankel, Francine R., and Harry Harding, eds, *The India–China Relationship: Rivalry and Engagement*, Oxford: Oxford University Press, 2004.

Ganguly, Sumit, *Engaging the World: Indian Foreign Policy Since 1947*, New Delhi: Oxford University Press, 2016.

———, *Deadly Impasse: Indo-Pakistani Relations at the Dawn of a New Century*, Cambridge: Cambridge University Press, 2016.

———, *Indian Foreign Policy*, New Delhi: Oxford University Press, 2015.

Ganguly, Sumit, and S. Paul Kapur, *India, Pakistan, and the Bomb: Debating Nuclear Stability in South Asia*, New York: Columbia University Press, 2010.

Ganguly, Sumit, and Manjeet S. Pardesi, 'Explaining Sixty Years of India's Foreign Policy', *India Review* 8 (1), 2009.

Gottschlich, Pierre, 'New Developments in India–Myanmar Bilateral Relations?', *Journal of Current Southeast Asian Affairs* 34 (2), 2015.

Goud, R. Sidda, and Manisha Mookherjee, eds, *India–Sri Lanka Relations: Strengthening SAARC*, New Delhi, Allied Publishers, 2016.

Grover, Verinder, ed., *Great Britain, Commonwealth and India's Foreign Policy*, New Delhi: Deep & Deep, 1992.

Gupta, K. R., *India–Pakistan Relations with Special Reference to Kashmir*, New Delhi: Atlantic, 2003.

Guruswamy, Mohan, and Zorawar Singh Daulet, *India–China Relations: The Border Issues and Beyond*, New Delhi: Viva Books, 2011.

Haqqani, Husain, *Pakistan: Between Mosque and Military*, New Delhi: Viking, 2016.

Harshe, Rajen, and K. M. Seethi, *Engaging with the World: Critical Reflections on India's Foreign Policy*, New Delhi: Orient BlackSwan, 2005.

Horimoto, Takenori, and Lalima Varma, eds, *India–Japan Relations in Emerging Asia*, New Delhi: Manohar, 2013.

Jacques, Kathryn, *Bangladesh, India and Pakistan: International Relations and Regional Tensions in South Asia*, London: Macmillan, 2000.

Jain, B. M., *India–U.S. Relations in the Age of Uncertainty: An Uneasy Courtship*, New York: Routledge, 2016.

Joshi, Nirmala, and Raj Kumar Sharma, 'India–Russia Relations in a Changing Eurasian Perspective', *India Quarterly* 73 (1), January 2017.

Josukutty, C. A., *India–U.S. Relations and Asian Rebuilding*, New Delhi: New Century Publications, 2015.

Kapur, Ashok, Y. K. Malik, H. A. Gould, and A. G. Rubinoff, eds, *India and the United States in a Changing World*, New Delhi: Sage, 2002.

Khan, Shamshad Ahmad, *Changing Dynamics of India–Japan Relations: Buddhism to Special Strategic Partnership*, New Delhi: Pentagon Press, 2017.

Khanna, V. N., *Foreign Policy of India (6th edition)*, New Delhi: Vikas Publishing, 2010.

Kothari, Raj Kumar, *India–Russia Relations in the Post Soviet Years*, Saarbrücken: Lap Lambart Academic Publishing, 2013.

Kumar, Nagesh, Rahul Sen, and Mukul G. Asher, *India–ASEAN Economic Relations: Meeting the Challenges of Globalization,* Singapore: Institute of Southeast Asian Studies and RIS, 2008.

Kumar, Sanjay, Dhirendra Dwivedi, and Mohammad Samir Hussain, *India–Pakistan Relations: Issues and Challenges*, Delhi: G.B. Books, 2016.

Kux, Dennis, *Estranged Democracies—India and the United States: 1941–1991*, New Delhi: Sage, 1994.

Lalit, Gulab Chandra, and Sanjay Kumar, *Indo–Afghan Relation: Shifting Balance of Security in South Asia,* New Delhi: Pragun Publication, 2012.

Leonard, A. G., *India's Trade Relations with Japan: An Economic Analysis*, New Delhi: Indus Publishing, 1993.

Liyanage, S., *Perspectives on India–Sri Lanka Relations*, New Delhi: Manak Publications, 2011.

Malone, David M., *Does the Elephant Dance? Contemporary Indian Foreign Policy*, New Delhi: Oxford University Press, 2012.

Malone, David M., C. Raja Mohan, and Srinath Raghavan. *The Oxford Handbook of Indian Foreign Policy*, New Delhi: Oxford University Press, 2015.

Mandal, Monika, ed., *Indo–Nepal Relations*, New Delhi: K.W. Publishers, 2014.

Mitra, Debamitra, *Indo–Bhutan Relations: Political Process, Conflict and Crisis*, Delhi: Academic Excellence, 2010.

Mohan, C. Raja, *Modi's World: Expanding India's Sphere of Influence*, New Delhi: HarperCollins India, 2015.

———, *Samudra Manthan: Sino–Indian Rivalry in the Indo-Pacific*, Washington D.C.: Carnegie International, 2012.

———, *Impossible Allies: Nuclear India: The United States and the Global Order*, New Delhi: India Research Press, 2006.

———, 'India's Strategic Future', *Foreign Policy*, 4 November 2010.

Mohapatra, Dipti Ranjan, *Trade and Investment Flows between India and the European Union: Issues and Challenges*, Buzau: Bridge Center, 2015.

Mukherjee, Rohan, and Anthony Yazaki, eds, *Poised for Partnership: Deepening India–Japan Relations in the Asian Century*, London: Oxford University Press, 2016.

Muni, S. D., *Pangs of Proximity: India and Sri Lanka's Ethnic Crisis*, New Delhi: Sage, 1993.

———, *India and Nepal: A Changing Relationship*, New Delhi: Konark, 1992.

Observer Research Foundation, *India–Nepal Relations: Challenges Ahead*, New Delhi: Rupa, 2007.

Ogden, Chris, *Indian Foreign Policy*, Cambridge: Polity Press, 2014.

Osman, Nazariah, and Debendra Mahalik, *The Quest for Security in India–ASEAN Relations: The Order of Realignment*, Hershey: IGI Global, 2016.

Panda, Jagannath, *India–China Relations: Politics of Resources, Identity and Authority in a Multipolar World Order*, New Delhi: Routledge, 2016.

Pant, Harsh V., *Indian Foreign Policy: An Overview*, New Delhi: Orient BlackSwan, 2016.

———, *India's Afghan Muddle: A Lost Opportunity*, New Delhi: HarperCollins, 2015.

———, 'Looking Beyond South Asia: India's 'Look East' Policy Gathers Momentum', in Harjeet Singh, ed. *South Asia Defense and Strategic Year Book 2014*, New Delhi: Pentagon Press, 2014.

———, ed., *Indian Foreign Policy in a Unipolar World*, New Delhi: Routledge, 2013.

Pant, Harsh V., 'India–Russia Ties and India's Strategic Culture: Dominance of a Realist Worldview', *India Review* 12 (1), 2013.

———, 'India in Afghanistan: A Trajectory in Motion', *Jadavpur Journal of International Relations* 17 (1), 2013.

Pattanaik, Smruti S., ed., *Four Decades of India–Bangladesh Relations: Historical Imperatives and Future Direction*, New Delhi: Gyan Publishing, 2012.

Paul, T. V., ed., *The India–Pakistan Conflict: An Enduring Rivalry*, Cambridge: Cambridge University Press, 2005.

Rajput, Madhu, *India–Bhutan Relations through Prism of History*, New Delhi: Manak Publications, 2011.

Raju, Adluri Subramanyam, and S. I. Keethaponcalan, *Maritime Cooperation between India and Sri Lanka*, New Delhi: Manohar, 2014.

Rao, P. V., ed., *India and ASEAN: Partners at Summit*, New Delhi: K.W. Publishers, 2011.

Reddy, K. Raja, *Foreign Policy of India and Asia Pacific*, New Delhi: New Century Publications, 2012.

———, *India and ASEAN: Foreign Policy Dimensions for the 21st Century*, New Delhi: New Century Publications, 2005.

Research and Information System for Developing Countries (RIS), *ASEAN India Connectivity Report*, New Delhi: Bookwell, 2012.

Roy, Jayanta Kumar, and Muntassir Mamoon, *India–Bangladesh Relations: Current Perspectives,* New Delhi: K.W. Publishers, 2011

Saha, Rekha, *India–Bangladesh Relations*, Kolkata: Minerva, 2000.

Sarin, Vishal, *India–ASEAN Trade and Economic Relations*, New Delhi: New Century Publications, 2016.

Schaffer, Teresita C., *India and the United States in the 21st Century: Reinventing Partnership*, Washington, D.C.: CSIS Press, 2009.

Scott, David, 'The Rise of India: U.K. Perspectives', *International Affairs* 93 (1), January 2017.

Sikri, Rajiv, *Challenge and Strategy: Rethinking Indian Foreign Policy*, New Delhi: SAGE India, 2013.

Singh, Jasjit, ed., *India–Russia Relations*, New Delhi: K.W. Publishers, 2012.

Singh, Surendra, *The New Dimensions of India–Russia Relations*, Saarbrücken: Lap Lambart Academic Publishing, 2013.

Sisodia, N. S., and G. V. C. Naidu, eds, *India–Japan Relations: Partnership for Peace and Security in Asia*, New Delhi: Bibliophile South Asia & IDSA, 2007.

Small, Andrew, *The China–Pakistan Axis: Asia's New Geopolitics*, London: C. Hurst & Co., 2015.

Stobdan, P., *India and Bhutan: The Strategic Imperative* (IDSA Occasional Paper no. 36), New Delhi: IDSA, 2014.

Upadhyay, S. S., *India and Sri Lanka: Economic & Political Relations*, New Delhi: Abd Publishers, 2007.

Winning, Nicholas, 'U.K., India Seek to Reboot Relationship', *Wall Street Journal*, 12 November 2015.

Winand, Pascaline, Marika Vicziany, and Poonam Datar, *The European Union and India: Rhetoric or Meaningful Partnership?* Camberley: Edward Elgar Publishing, 2015.

Wulbers, Shazia Aziz, *The Paradox of EU–India Relations: Missed Opportunities in Politics, Economics, Development, Cooperation and Culture*, Lanham: Lexington Books, 2011.

INDEX